A4/m

LEAVES FROM THE GARDEN

LEAVES FROM THE GARDEN

Two centuries of garden writing

EDITED BY
CLARE BEST AND CAROLINE BOISSET

JOHN MURRAY

© 1987 Waterstone & Co. Limited
First published 1987
by John Murray (Publishers) Ltd.
50 Albemarle Street, London WIX 4BD

Book design by Peter Ward
Typeset by Rowland Phototypesetting Limited, Bury St Edmunds, Suffolk
Printed and bound in Great Britain
by Blantyre Printing & Binding Co. Limited, Glasgow

British Library CIP data

Leaves from the garden: two centuries of
garden writing.
1. Gardening
I. Best, Clare   II. Boisset, Caroline
635   SB450.97

ISBN 0-7195-4393-2

A garden is a beautiful book, writ by the finger of God: every flower and every leaf is a letter. You have only to learn them – and he is a poor dunce that cannot, if he will, do that – to learn them and join them, and then to go on reading and reading. And you will find yourself carried away from the earth by the beautiful story you are going through.

From the preface to William Robinson's
Alpine Flowers for English Gardens

Contents

PREFACE

I

THE FORMAL GARDEN

Humphry Repton — *Of Pleasure-Grounds and Flower-Gardens*   17
William Gilpin — *Dress Ground*   22
Shirley Hibberd — *The Parterre*   26
Reginald Blomfield — *In Favour of the Formal Garden*   30
John D. Sedding — *The Geometrical Garden*   34
Viscountess Wolseley — *Ornamental Pots*   35
Paul Edwards — *The Topiary Garden*   41
Russell Page — *A Small Excursion into Formality*   45

II

ORNAMENT

John B. Papworth — *Fountains Rediscovered*   51
George Sitwell — *Statues: The Imaginative Ideal*   54
Thomas Mawson — *Statuary and Garden Seats*   57
Christopher Hussey — *The Place of Ornament*   64
George Carter — *Sculpture in the Garden*   76

III

THE TOWN GARDEN

J. C. Loudon — *A Modest Villa Garden*   83

Donald Beaton — *The Society's Garden at Kensington Gore*   88

Thomas Hay — *Gardening in London*   91

Beverley Nichols — *A Note on London Gardens*   100

Lanning Roper — *Problems and Limitations*   104

Xenia Field — *Gardening in Boxes, Baskets and Tubs*   114

John Brookes — *Planting a Very Small Garden*   123

IV

ROCK AND WALL GARDENING

William Cobbett — *Enclosing Kitchen-Gardens*   129

Edward Kemp — *Rock and Fern Gardens*   135

Canon Ellacombe — *Old Walls*   140

Herbert Maxwell — *Some Plants for Walls*   143

Gertrude Jekyll & Christopher Hussey — *Overgrowth*   153

Will Ingwersen — *Building and Planting a Retaining Wall*   160

V

BORDERS

Shirley Hibberd — *Hardy Border Flowers* 165
Gertrude Jekyll — *The Main Hardy Flower Border* 174
Jason Hill — *The Miniature Herbaceous Border* 180
Margery Fish — *That Patch of Silver* 185
Percy Cane — *Special Borders* 193
H. E. Bates — *Planting for Late Summer* 198

VI

ROSES

William Paul — *The Formation of the Rosarium* 205
S. Reynolds Hole — *A Note on Manures* 217
Reverend Joseph Pemberton — *A Guide to Planting* 224
E. A. Bunyard — *Old Roses* 230
Graham Stuart Thomas — *Rose Species in Nature and in the Garden* 244
F. C. Stern — *Growing Roses on Chalk* 253

VII

THE FRAGRANT GARDEN

Frances Jane Hope — *Pleached Alleys*   261

William Robinson — *Sweet-Smelling Flowers*   264

Jason Hill — *The Invisible Garden*   267

E. A. Bowles — *Fragrance: An Appreciation*   276

Arthur Hellyer — *The Search for Summer Fragrance*   286

VIII

WOODLAND AND SHRUBBERY

Jane Loudon — *Trees and Shrubs in Pleasure-Grounds*   289

William Robinson — *The Woodland Garden*   292

Charles Eley — *Hedges*   296

M. Haworth-Booth — *Planting, Feeding and Weeding*   304

A. T. Johnson — *Rhododendrons in Woodland*   312

Patrick M. Synge — *Coloured Bark in the Winter Garden*   320

IX

THE WILD GARDEN

William Robinson — *Notes on the Wild Garden*   325
Walter P. Wright — *Working with Nature*   332
Sir Arthur Hort — *Wild Corners*   336
Christopher Lloyd — *Meadow Gardening*   339
Robin Lane Fox — *The Wild Garden in the Long Grass*   352

X

THE CHALLENGING GARDEN

Osgood Mackenzie — *Gardening in the Western Highlands*   355
Frances Perry — *The Water Garden*   365
Vita Sackville-West — *Starting From Scratch*   371
Valerie Finnis — *Raised Beds for Rock Plants*   386
Anne Scott-James — *Chalk Gardening*   392
Beth Chatto — *Dry Gardening*   400

Acknowledgements   405

Index   411

Preface

Britain has earned an unrivalled reputation for her gardens. For this we have to thank not only our temperate climate and the wide range of native and foreign plants which thrive here, but also the work and influence of gardeners and garden writers whose enthusiasm and expertise have been shared with us through books, journals and lectures.

This book is a lasting tribute to those men and women, from Repton onwards, who have created, and who are sustaining, our great British gardening tradition. It is the only means for today's gardener to benefit from their collective wisdom, through the best and most typical of their writing. *Leaves from the Garden* is also a source book of garden history, the natural partner to Miles Hadfield's *A History of British Gardening* (Hutchinson, 1960, Penguin 1980, London) since it highlights those gardeners who have created our finest gardens. Above all, this is a necessary companion and guide, providing inspiration and reminding us of the historical context within which we design gardens and of the variety of styles available to us.

Selecting the exhibits and exhibitors for this gallery of garden art has been as challenging as it has been delightful. No apology is made for the fact that, having chosen pieces which first fulfilled the criteria of being well-written, reliable and of historical importance, the final arbiter has been personal taste.

The earliest piece included is by Humphry Repton, since he was responsible for the re-introduction of the flower garden at the end of the eighteenth century and set a precedent for the great nineteenth-century surge of interest in the private garden as we still understand it today. There was a move away from the vast landscaped schemes of 'Capability' Brown, and the first part of the nineteenth century witnessed the consolidation of a more intimate and distinctively British style of gardening which, although it drew on elements of foreign gardening styles and relied increasingly on the use of new plants brought here by the plant hunters, has been the envy of the world ever since. During that period gardeners such as William Cobbett, Shirley Hibberd, John Papworth and the Loudons did much to develop and popularise the art of gardening.

The heyday of British gardening came during the latter half of the nineteenth century and the first quarter of our century and it is from this period that much of the writing in this book originates. This was the era of Harold

Peto, George Sitwell, William Robinson and Gertrude Jekyll and a time that saw the planting of Bodnant, Hidcote, Hestercombe, Leonardslee and Great Dixter.

If the First World War dealt a heavy blow to the idea of the grand house and its extensive gardens, the Second World War almost brought about its demise. Happily many of the great historic gardens left in Britain are now administered by the National Trust and by public authorities and have been carefully restored, so that they continue as delightful examples of their period. Gardening on the grand scale is now beyond the reach of all but a very few, but the number and quality of smaller private gardens has never been higher, nor enthusiasm for gardening greater, than in the 1980s.

Recent pieces by modern garden writers have been included, though for obvious reasons it has only been sensible to select pieces which are of outstanding interest or which are not otherwise readily accessible, such as Anne Scott-James's stimulating article on chalk gardening or Robin Lane Fox's plea for a revival of real wild gardening.

It has been impossible to include pieces on fruit and vegetable cultivation or to stray into greenhouse and conservatory; to have done so would have swelled the book to twice its present bulk and turned it, simultaneously, into a strange hybrid. The editors recognise the need for another volume covering those subjects and hope, in due course, to provide one.

Good gardening owes much to sound technique and to a thorough understanding of plants, and gardeners now have access to many excellent modern books which give technical advice and up-to-date information on specific plants. What will be found in this book is the wisdom of more than fifty highly experienced gardeners, in essays of informative length which retain the freshness and vision of their period. The reader can judge for himself how best to re-interpret J. C. Loudon's plan for a small town garden, William Robinson's wild garden, Gertrude Jekyll's colour schemes, the deliciously scented alley of Frances Jane Hope or the formality of Russell Page. There is also an enormous amount to be learned from the pieces by specialists writing on their own subjects – E. A. Bunyard's straightforward account of old roses, for instance, or Christopher Hussey's discussion of the use of garden ornaments, Henry Ellacombe's charming essay on plants for old walls, or Vita Sackville-West's honest description of starting her garden from scratch at Sissinghurst Castle.

Due to a shortage of space, it has not been possible to give details of all the honours conferred on the contributors. The only award shown is the Victoria

Medal of Horticulture (VMH) which is recognised as the highest accolade of its kind. Instituted by Queen Victoria for her jubilee, the total number of VMH's held at one time only ever totals sixty-three, the full number of years of her reign.

The black and white photographs provide a visual record of changing gardening styles from the mid-1800s to the present day. Care has been taken to illustrate the text wherever possible using photographs contemporary with it, showing particular gardens or special features of gardens for which there are direct references. In other instances, the aim has been to capture the atmosphere of a place or an effect which has since changed, disappeared or fallen out of fashion. The use of colour photographs has been reserved mainly for the illustration of unusual plant combinations and foliage effects. Two rare, old, coloured photographs (lumière autochromes) provide a fascinating insight into the fashionable colour schemes of the early years of this century.

County names in the text have been left as in the original piece; only those which appear in captions have been updated to enable the reader to find particular gardens more easily.

In the same way, and in order to retain historical continuity of plant nomenclature, synonyms have been included only as footnotes and this only when plant names have been significantly changed. For example, all *Funkia* species are now called *Hosta* but *Buddleia* is now spelt with a *j* and *Wistaria* correctly spelt *Wisteria*. In addition, after 1954, as recommended by the *International code of nomenclature of cultivated plants*, cultivars are distinguished from genera and species, preferably by single quotes. Where this is not so, in articles prior to this date, the editors have not altered the original text. By suggesting synonyms it is hoped that readers will seek further information on plants, and be able to buy them and grow them in their own gardens.

Among the best reference works available at present are the Royal Horticultural Society's *Dictionary of Gardening* (second edition, Oxford University Press); W. J. Bean's *Trees and Shrubs Hardy in the British Isles* (eighth edition, John Murray, London); and Graham Thomas's *Perennial Garden Plants* (second edition, Dent, London). In order to distinguish between the authors' own footnotes and the editors' subsequent ones, the former are marked with asterisks and the latter with small numerals.

It would be an impossible task to give a full bibliography on all the aspects of gardening covered in this book but those books listed on the acknowledgements page would together form the core of a superb gardening library.

For readers wishing to see for themselves the gardens described, the recent HMSO publication, *Yesterday's Gardens* by Alastair Forsyth, is useful, and the booklet published annually by the National Gardens Scheme *Gardens open to the Public*, essential. Members of the Royal Horticultural Society with specific queries on plants or further reading will find the staff at Vincent Square informed and helpful. *British Gardeners: A Biographical Dictionary* (Zwemmer, London, 1980) is an invaluable reference work for all those interested in historic gardens and their creators.

This book could not have been created without Roderick Brown who recognised the need for it and Celia Van Oss whose inspiration and guidance were indispensable. The editors are also grateful to Marilyn Ward, Miss Morris, Dr. Brent Elliott and Barbara Collecott, without whose assistance the search for raw material would have been a much more difficult task, and to Hélène de Quercize whose patience and optimism helped so much in the rediscovery of many of the black and white photographs.

Clare Best
Caroline Boisset
London 1986

Hatfield House, Hertfordshire

This lumière autochrome of 1910 shows an extravagant period style of
bedding-out using tender plants. The garden was originally laid out by Isaac
de Caus in the early seventeenth-century for Robert Cecil, and John Tradescant
the Elder was head gardener when the formal gardens were designed in
the French manner.

HESTERCOMBE, SOMERSET.
Designed by Edwin Lutyens and Gertrude Jekyll in 1905, this is a
perfect example of Christopher Hussey's theories of careful, integrated
design: 'Regarding a pool as an ever-changing picture, its frame should
be left as plain as possible.'

III   An Ornamental Summer House

A painted and patinated copper sheet representing the night sky makes a
weather-proof alternative to fresco painting in a Norfolk garden. It forms a focal
point to the vista closed by this summer house.

IV   THE HILL, HAMPSTEAD, LONDON.

A lumière autochrome of 1910 showing the ornamental pool and terrace seen
from the pergola. The elaborate garden was designed by Thomas Mawson for
Lord Leverhulme and remains substantially the same today.

V   STRAWBERRY HOUSE, CHISWICK MALL, LONDON.

Laid out in the 1920s by a stage designer, this town garden has been transformed
by its current owner, the Countess of Rothes. Formal outlines and loose planting
combine to give an illusion of space and delicate plants are protected by brick
walls and select mature trees.

A WELL-PLANTED WALL BASKET.

The colours, textures and shapes of the various pelargoniums, ivies, fuchsias, lobelia and house-leeks make an interesting and easily maintained miniature garden which blends with its surroundings.

VII THE DRY WALL AT THE SAVILL GARDEN, WINDSOR, BERKSHIRE.

The main garden was planted by Sir Eric Savill in 1932 and the wall is full of
alpines brought back to England by Reginald Farrer. Pleasing colour patterns are
created by aubrieta, alyssum, iberis and euphorbia.

PITMEDDEN, ABERDEENSHIRE.

The herbaceous border planted by Lady Burnett of Leys (creator of Crathes'
Garden). The plants chosen for their strength of tone and architectural forms are set
against a background of espalier apples and fan-trained plums; they include, salvia,
alchillea, asters and astilbes.

IX   KIFTSGATE COURT, MICKLETON, GLOUCESTERSHIRE.

This garden, which is renowned for its skilled use of colour, was created
from scratch by Mrs. Muir in the 1920s. Graham Thomas described the first crop
of blooms from the large shrub roses as 'almost overwhelming'.

X   ILMINGTON MANOR, SHIPSTON-ON-STOUR, WARWICKSHIRE.
The garden was actually planted in the 1920s, under the influence of nearby
Hidcote, but it has a strong traditional feel which harmonises with the
seventeenth-century house. The Rose Garden has been recently designed to be
low-maintenance: shrub roses and modern long-flowering cluster roses are
edged with lavender.

XI   HYBRID MUSK ROSE, PENELOPE.

This immensely popular fragrant shrub rose was introduced in 1924 by Joseph
Pemberton who bred roses at Havering-atte-Bower, Essex.

XII   Tyninghame, East Lothian.

A heavily scented enclosure was recently created by Lady Haddington from the rough ground of an old tennis court. Mixed lavenders combine with roses, clematis and honeysuckle.

XIII   LEONARDSLEE, WEST SUSSEX.

A woodland of rhododendrons, evergreen azaleas and camellias is reflected in the lake. This famous garden was first planted in the 1860s by Edmund Loder.

BETULA ERMANII: PAPERBARK BIRCH.
The silvery peeling bark contrasts well with the dark conifers behind giving
good autumn and winter display

XV   GREAT DIXTER, EAST SUSSEX.

Nathaniel Lloyd and Lutyens worked together to create this outstanding garden and Christopher Lloyd's plantsman talents have increased its variety. The naturalised planting of, for example, snakeshead fritillaries, wild orchids, primroses and bluebells in the Moat Meadow Gardens however, is really the achievement of Mrs. Lloyd.

XVI   WHITE BARN HOUSE, ESSEX.

The canal bed in Beth Chatto's garden displaying great contrast of foliage and form with sun-loving marginal plants such as *Heuchera, Hosta sieboldiana, Iris laevigata* and *Lysichitum americanum*.

CHAPTER I

The Formal Garden

Humphry Repton

OF PLEASURE-GROUNDS AND FLOWER-GARDENS

In the execution of my profession, I have often experienced great difficulty and opposition in attempting to correct the false and mistaken taste for placing a large house in a naked grass-field, without any apparent line of separation between the ground exposed to cattle and the ground annexed to the house, which I consider as peculiarly under the management of art.

This line of separation being admitted, advantage may be easily taken to ornament the lawn with flowers and shrubs, and to attach to the mansion that scene of 'embellished neatness', usually called a pleasure-ground.

The quantity of this dressed ground was formerly very considerable. The royal gardens of Versailles, or those of Kensington Palace, when filled with company, want no other animation; but a large extent of ground without moving objects, however neatly kept, is but a melancholy scene. If solitude

Humphry Repton (1752–1818) re-introduced the terrace and the flower garden, and his influence on British gardening has been fundamental. His landscaped gardens survive at Ashridge Park, Hertfordshire, Holkham Hall and Sheringham Hall, Norfolk.

17

delight, we seek it rather in the covert of a wood, or the sequestered alcove of a flower-garden, than in the open lawn of an extensive pleasure-ground.

I have therefore frequently been the means of restoring acres of useless garden to the deer or sheep, to which they more properly belong.

This is now carrying on with admirable effect at Bulstrode, where the gardens of every kind are on a great scale, and where, from the choice and variety of the plants, the direction of the walks, the enrichment of art, and the attention to every circumstance of elegance and magnificence, the pleasure-ground is perfect as a whole, while its several parts may furnish models of the following different characters of taste in gardening: the ancient garden, the American garden, the modern terrace-walks, and the flower-garden: the latter is, perhaps, one of the most varied and extensive of its kind, and therefore too large to be otherwise artificial, than in the choice of its flowers, and the embellishments of art in its ornaments.

Flower-gardens on a small scale may, with propriety, be formal and artificial; but in all cases they require neatness and attention. On this subject I shall transcribe the following passage from the *Red Book* of Valley Field:

> . . . although I have never seen Valley Field, myself, yet it flatters me to learn, that, under the direction of my two sons, by taking advantage of the deep romantic glen and wooded banks of the river which flows through the grounds and falls into the Firth of Forth at a short distance from the house, an approach has been made, which, for variety, interest, and picturesque scenery, may vie with any-thing of the kind in England; while it remains a specimen of the powers of landscape gardening, in that part of Scotland where the art had been introduced only by those imitators of Mr. Brown's manner, who had travelled into the north. His own improvements were confined to England.

To common observers, the most obvious difference between Mr. Brown's style and that of ancient gardens, was the change from straight to waving or serpentine lines. Hence, many of his followers had supposed good taste in gardening to consist in avoiding all lines that are straight or parallel, and in adopting forms which they deem more consonant to nature, without consider-ing what objects were natural and what were artificial.

This explanation is necessary to justify the plan which I recommended for the canal in this flower-garden; for, while I should condemn a long straight line of water in an open park, where everything else is natural, I should equally object to a meandering canal or walk, by the side of a long straight wall, where everything else is artificial.

A flower-garden should be an object detached and distinct from the general scenery of the place; and, whether large or small, whether varied or formal, it ought to be protected from hares and smaller animals by an inner fence: within this enclosure rare plants of every description should be encouraged, and a provision made of soil and aspect for every different class. Beds of bog-earth should be prepared for the American plants: the aquatic plants, some of which are peculiarly beautiful, should grow on the surface or near the edges of water. The numerous class of rock-plants should have beds of rugged stone provided for their reception, without the affectation of such stones being the natural production of the soil; but, above all, there should be poles or hoops for those kind of creeping plants which spontaneously form themselves into graceful festoons, when encouraged and supported by art.

Yet, with all these circumstances, the flower-garden, except where it is annexed to the house, should not be visible from the roads or general walks about the place. It may therefore be of a character totally different from the rest of the scenery, and its decorations should be as much those of art as of nature.

The flower-garden at Nuneham, without being formal, is highly enriched, but not too much crowded with seats, temples, statues, vases, or other ornaments, which, being works of art, beautifully harmonize with that profusion of flowers and curious plants which distinguish the flower-garden from natural landscape, although the walks are not in straight lines.

But at Valley Field, where the flower-garden is in front of a long wall, the attempt to make the scene natural would be affected; and, therefore, as two great sources of interest in a place are variety and contrast, the only means by which these can be introduced are in this flower-garden, which, as a separate object, becomes a sort of episode to the general and magnificent scenery.

The river being everywhere else a lively stream, rattling and foaming over a shallow bed of rock or gravel, a greater contrast will arise from a smooth expanse of water in the flower-garden: to produce this must be a work of art, and, therefore, instead of leading an open channel from the river to supply it, or making it appear a natural branch of that river, I recommend that the water should pass underground, with regulating sluices or shuttles to keep it always at the same height. Thus the canal will be totally detached from the river, and become a distinct object, forming the leading feature of the scene to which it belongs; a scene purely artificial, where a serpentine canal would be as incongruous as a serpentine garden wall, or a serpentine bridge; and, strange as it may appear, I have seen such absurdities introduced, to avoid nature's supposed abhorrence of a straight line.

The banks of this canal, or fish-pond, may be enriched with borders of curious flowers, and a light fence of green laths will serve to train such as require support, while it gives to the whole an air of neatness and careful attention.

But, as the ends of this water should also be marked by some building, or covered seat, I have supposed the entrance to the flower-garden to be under a covered passage of hoops, on which may be trained various sorts of creeping plants; and the farther end may be decorated by an architectural building, which I suppose to consist of a covered seat between two aviaries.

It will perhaps be objected, that a long straight walk can have little variety; but the greatest source of variety in a flower-garden is derived from the selection and diversity of its shrubs and flowers.

1 NUNEHAM COURTENAY, OXFORDSHIRE. 1913

The formal terraces, laid out by William Mason in 1772 and improved in the early nineteenth century by William Gilpin, overlook 'Capability' Brown's parkland.

William Gilpin
DRESS GROUND

*William Gilpin
(1762–1843) was entirely
self-taught and very
successful as a garden
designer. Much of his
work has only been
identified recently and
includes Clumber,
Nottinghamshire, Bicton,
Shropshire and Sudbury,
Derbyshire.*

The dress ground immediately connected with the house should be considered as the foreground of the picture, which the whole scene, taken together, presents to the eye, and should be treated as such. The groups, and single trees upon it, should be planted with reference to the scenery beyond, so as to lead the eye into the remote parts of the picture; excluding, as far as may be, whatever might injure the general composition.

In the formation, then, of the dress ground, I should recommend making a slight sketch from the leading points of view, (usually the windows of the library or drawing-room), of the general scene as it exists; and then add to your sketch such groups of trees and shrubs, and such detached trees, as would hide the less interesting parts of the landscape, and, by breaking the uniformity of other parts, produce that connection so essential to composition. In forming such groups, particularly of larger trees, it should be well considered, whether a massive or a lighter group is requisite; whether the most distant scenery is to be caught through the stems of these trees, or to be altogether excluded by them. I would plant all the larger features with this reference to the general scene, before proceeding to the lesser embellishments of the lawn, such as flower-beds, etc. which should be formed with reference to those features.

The groups of larger trees will usually be accompanied by shrubs of various size and character, to connect them with the lawn: rhododendrons, savine, and other of the pendent evergreens, are very useful for such purpose, when the turf, being carried under them, leaves no cutting line of border. Shrubs, in my opinion, should not be accompanied, in the same bed, by such flowers as require digging; the line of border above mentioned destroying that repose and that variety of form which ought to characterise the former. In a lawn of small dimensions, the loosing of the turf under the shrubs is of the utmost importance, as it gives an appearance of extent to its limited proportion. Paeonies, roses, hollyhocks, and other flowers that are of sufficient height or size to mingle with the shrubs, may be fairly united with them, if it can be effected without showing the mould. In the first formation of these plantations of shrubs, the borders must be dug, and, for a time, kept so; but every opportunity should be taken to break the edgy line, till it can be finally obliterated: to help this end, even in the first instance, periwinkle, St. John's wort, and other ground creepers, may be planted with the shrubs; and, by uniting them with the lawn, will tend to diminish the hard line of the border: a thing that cannot be too strongly insisted upon, as essential to continuity and repose.

Having disposed the masses of trees, shrubs, etc. with reference to the general effect of the whole scene, we come now to the finishing touches of decoration – flowers.

From the general love of flowers, and their increasing varieties, we frequently see the breadth and repose of the lawn sacrificed to them. In a flower-garden, properly so called, they hold undivided sway, and are at liberty to cover the whole surface, and to assume every variety of form that fancy may dictate; but, when flower-beds are component parts of the dress ground we have been considering, they must be amenable to the rules of composition, otherwise they injure the scenery they are intended to adorn. Beautiful examples of the former arrangement (the flower-garden) will be found at Cassiobury and at Redleaf; the combination requisite to the latter will be found in equal perfection at Danesfield.

The disposition of flower-beds will vary with the character of the house, and the extent and circumstances of the ground about it. At the manorial building, where the straight walks and the appropriate accompaniments are retained, the flower-beds should, in my opinion, be characterized by the same precision and regularity. I have treated them upon that principle at Somerhill, one of the finest specimens of the Elizabethan mansion with which I am acquainted. As, however, beds of this description, being necessarily filled with flowers of low growth, have rather a flat and tame appearance, their effect will be greatly improved by a border, which will elevate them above the lawn, and, by producing a variety of light and shadow, will give richness and variety to the mass. The border may be made of wood or iron, painted to resemble stone, which will unite them more harmoniously with the masonry of the house, terrace, walls, etc., at the same time that it will relieve them from the lawn better than any other colour. The height of the border will depend upon the size of the beds: for those of moderate size, about six inches will be sufficient. When of larger dimensions, a foot is not too high. The effect of flower-beds so constructed may be seen in the garden of Lambeth Palace.

see colour plate 1

Where the character and decoration of the mansion will warrant it, these borders might be made highly ornamental, and might, I conceive, be cast in iron at a moderate expense. The effect, even in the simple style, will be improved by the introduction of vases, flower-stands, and orange trees, or other shrubs, in handsome tubs: the flower-stands should not be of rustic character, but of regular form and exact finishing. Wood or iron is preferable to stone, as less exposed to injury from the roller.

In what may be termed a free disposition of flower-beds, the first care should be to avoid the spottiness which must result from putting a bed wherever room can be found for it: on the contrary, the beds should be treated upon the same plan of composition that arranged the shrubs they are to accompany. The glades of lawn that have been created by the foregoing operation must not be destroyed by scattered beds of flowers crossing them in all directions; though occasionally a bed will be introduced to break the continuity of the line of shrubs, and relieve, by brilliancy of colour, their more sober tone. As breadth, however, equally with connexion, is essential to composition, the beds, in general, should be brought together in masses, leaving lesser glades among them; and these glades, again, should be broken by a single plant or basket, taking care never to place such interruption midway between the sides of the glade. The masses themselves will be lightened by a detached bed or two of a lesser size. There is no objection to the occasional introduction of a regular form in the flower-beds; though, for the most part, the easy curving lines will unite better with each other. Baskets and picturesque stands are also useful to relieve the flat surface of the masses, if they are not too profusely introduced. It may here be observed, that, though basket-like forms may be applied to beds of a large size, the handle should not be added to any one longer than appears capable of being lifted, as the want of proportion is too glaring: and the handle itself cannot be enriched so as to be well united with the contents of the basket.

Gravel walks being necessary to the enjoyment of the scenery we have been considering, it may be useful to offer a few observations upon this part of our subject. The line of walk should, I conceive, be regulated by the size and circumstances of the place. And, first, of whatever extent the grounds may be, I would never carry the walk round the boundary; nothing, as I have before observed, is, to my feeling, so insipid as a long-continued sweep: and the hanging perpetually on the boundary, by betraying the real dimensions of the place, destroys all idea of extent as effectually as it does that of variety. Whoever has seen the pleasure-ground at Caversham (laid out by Brown), cannot but perceive what an improvement it would be to wind the walk amongst the noble trees and rich masses of shrubs, which now trails its monotonous course by the side of the sunk fence.

2   SHRUBLAND PARK, SUFFOLK. 1953

The great stairway and terraces were designed by Sir Charles Barry in the early 1850s. William Robinson objected that there were no flowers, in this large garden, to cut for the house, but even after he had simplified the garden, forty men were required to work on it.

Shirley Hibberd
THE PARTERRE

James Shirley Hibberd (1825–1890) was an early specialist in urban horticulture. He wrote a number of delightful books on garden decoration and foliage plants as well as editing several periodicals.

Geometric gardens may be designed on paper by selecting some part of the pattern of a carpet or wall paper, or by placing a few bits of coloured paper in the debuscope[1], and then copying the multiple scheme so produced. Numbers of designs have been obtained in that way, and about one in a hundred have actually turned out worthy; the rest were not worth the paper they were drawn on, unless it might be to make burlesque of the bedding system. It is a most rare event for a really complicated plan to prove effective, however skilfully planted; and so I begin by advising the beginner to avoid the schemes which combine a great variety of figures, such as ovals, hearts, diamonds, horns of plenty, and true lovers' knots. Elaborate designs are, of course, not to be condemned, for we find them constituting important features in many great gardens, and employing the highest artistic talent in garden colouring. It is above all things necessary to guard beginners against making costly mistakes, and the formation of the parterre is a business requiring more than ordinary caution to guard against waste of time and money, and all the consequent vexation and disappointment. In what we may call 'a quiet garden' of limited dimensions, a few large beds, far separated by well-kept turf will, in many cases, give far more satisfaction than a distinctive geometric scheme, and necessitate, perhaps, only a twentieth of the time and attention to keep them suitably gay, besides offering the peculiar advantage that each bed may be planted to produce an effect of its own without any special reference to the rest, so long as it is decidedly different. The common repetition of oblongs and circles which we meet with in public gardens, where long walks demand flowery dressings, is one of the most effective and satisfactory, though always open to the accusation of an alliance with commonplace and monotony. On the other hand, the common repetition, on the margins of lawns in private gardens, of circular beds containing standard roses, surrounded by geraniums, verbenas, and other such stuff, is ineffective and puerile. Gardens embellished

---

[1] A type of Victorian kaleidoscope

in this way have no character at all, they are mere confusions. Far better would it be to concentrate the energies which the 'pincushion' beds consume to a poor purpose, on a neat and reasonably circumscribed parterre, which would constitute a feature and afford considerable interest. To be sure, it is easy to plant pincushion beds, because they are scarcely co-related, but a parterre demands talent, and that is not always available.

In a majority of instances, geometric gardens are laid out on grass turf, and the green groundwork adds immensely to the beauty of the flowers. In elaborately furnished gardens, a groundwork of silver sand, with box embroidery to define the outlines and fill in the angles, is employed in an open space set see plate 3 apart for the purpose, and the scheme is enriched with statuary, clipped yews, laurels, cypresses, and vases containing yuccas, agaves, or masses of geraniums. The working out of a great design in coloured earths and flower-beds is the most complicated, and, generally speaking, perhaps the least satisfactory form of the parterre. It has this advantage, that, during winter, it affords 'something to look at', but the corresponding disadvantage is that nobody wants to see it. A favourite idea with artists in this line of business is to draw out, on a gigantic scale, a group of rose, shamrock, and thistle in coloured earths and box embroidery, and while the thing is new it looks tolerably well; but the majority of people do not keep themselves sufficiently under control when tempted to indulge a smile as they admire it. Generally speaking, the design vanishes in summer, that is to say, when the beds are full of flowers, the coloured earths that mark out the design are so completely extinguished that, even with a key plan in one's hand, it would be hard to see where the thistle begins and the shamrock leaves off, and where, amidst the confusion, the rose ought to be. The principal materials employed for the intersecting walks in these designs, are pounded Derbyshire spar (white), pounded brick (red), pounded slate (blue), pounded coal (black), sifted gravel grit (yellowish grey).

In planting the parterre it is as easy to make mistakes as in designing it, and the most frequent errors are the employment of primary colours in excessive quantity and strength, and the neglect of neutral tints to soften it, and of brilliant edgings to define it. The stereotyped repetition of scarlet geraniums and yellow calceolarias is in the last degree vulgar and tasteless, and the common dispositions of red, white, and blue are better adapted to delight savages, than represent the artistic status of a civilized people. The increasing use of leaf colours marks a great advance in taste, and strange to say, the most perfect examples of parterre colouring we have seen of late years, have been accomplished by leaves solely, in scenes from which flowers were utterly excluded. Leaf colours, however, are of immense importance in connection with flowers, as any good example of parterre colouring will prove. They afford material for boundary lines, for relief agents, and for marking the rhythm of combinations. Every scheme that is to be viewed as a whole, must be coloured as a whole, and with the object of producing a complete and harmonious picture. Whatever the nature of the materials employed, certain principles must be followed to insure a satisfactory result. The strong colours must be spread pretty equally over the whole scheme with neutral and intermediate tints to harmonize and combine them. The colours containing most light, such as yellow, white, and pink, should be placed in the outer parts of the design, to draw it out to its full extent; and the heavier colours, such as scarlet, crimson, and purple, should occupy the more central portions of the scheme. The most difficult of all colours to dispose of satisfactorily is pure yellow, and its related tints of buff and orange. A bed of yellow calceolarias in the centre of a group will be pretty sure to spoil it, no matter how skilfully in other respects it may be planted. But a few of the most conspicuously placed of the beds in the boundary of the pattern may be planted with calceolarias to assist in defining the arrangement. Bright and sharp edgings are eminently desirable, and it is a good point if the edgings are the same throughout, forming clear fillets of silvery or golden leafage, or some suitable flowering plant, which carries plenty of light in its colour. Objection may be taken to this rule, on the ground that beds containing plants that nearly approximate in tone to that of the general edging, will be spoiled if edged like the rest. But the objection is superficial. When we cannot bring out the masses by means of the edgings, and it is desirable to have the boundary lines alike all through, we must change our tactics, and bring out the edgings. For example, we are to suppose three beds filled with flowers. No. 1 contains scarlet geraniums, and may be edged with a band of blue lobelia, and an outer defining line of silvery cerastium; No. 2 is filled with blue ageratum, and edged with a band of Purple King verbena, with a finishing line of cerastium. No. 3 consists of Mrs. Pollock geranium and blue lobelia, plant and plant, with a finishing band of lobelia, and a boundary line of cerastium. Thus, in three extremely different cases, the final fillet is the same without violation of harmony or detraction from the pronounced character of the beds. It is a matter equally important and interesting, that a perfect hypothetical balance of colours is neither a good practical balance nor agreeable to the educated eye. A square yard each of red, blue, and yellow, whether in grass or gravel, will not make a telling parterre. But a block of blue, between two blocks of red, and all three banded with a silvery grey line or a sufficient breadth of green grass, might constitute an agreeable, though humble feature of a garden. It is well, indeed, in every scheme to allow one colour with its related shades to predominate, and to employ the others as relief agents rather than as features. Lastly, strong contrasts should not be indulged in often; they are the antitheses of harmony, as you may discover by observation.

3   ASHRIDGE PARK, HERTFORDSHIRE. 1898

Repton's parterre in the Monk's Garden complements the formal rhythm of the architecture.

Reginald Blomfield
IN FAVOUR OF
THE FORMAL GARDEN

Reginald Blomfield (1856–1942), landscape architect, was a champion of formality in gardening, taking an opposing view to William Robinson. He remodelled Apethorpe, Northamptonshire and Chequers, Buckinghamshire.

A garden is so much an individual affair – it should show so distinctly the idiosyncrasy of its owner – that it would be useless to offer any hints as to its details. A brief sketch of the development of the formal garden would indicate the very wide field of design which it includes, and the abuses and extravagance which led to its decay and ultimate extinction. The study of its history will at least show the dangers to be avoided, and they can be summarised in the faults of over-elaboration and affectation. The characteristic of the old formal garden, the garden of Markham and Lawson, was its exceeding simplicity. The primary purpose of a garden as a place of retirement and seclusion, a place for quiet thought and leisurely enjoyment, was kept steadily in view. The grass and the yew-trees were trimmed close to gain their full beauty from the sunlight. Sweet kindly flowers filled the knots and borders. Peacocks and pigeons brightened the terraces and lawns. The paths were straight and ample, the garden-house solidly built and comfortable; everything was reasonable and unaffected. But this simple genuine delight in nature and art became feebler as the seventeenth century grew older. Gardening became the fashionable art, and this was the golden age for professional gardeners; but the real pleasure of it was gone. Rows of statues were introduced from the French, costly architecture superseded the simple terrace, intricate parterres were laid out from gardeners' pattern books, and meanwhile the flowers were forgotten. It was well that all this pomp should be swept away. We do not want this extravagant statuary, these absurdities in clipped work, this aggressive prodigality.

But though one would admit that in its decay the formal garden became unmanageable and absurd, the abuse is no argument against the use. I am in favour of the essential reasonableness of the principles of Formal Gardening, and the sanity of its method when properly handled. The long yew hedge is clipped and shorn because we want its firm boundary lines and the plain mass

see plate 5

30

of its colour; the grass bank is formed into a definite slope to attain the beauty of close-shaven turf at varied angles with the light. The broad grass walk, with its paved footpath in the centre, is cool to walk upon in summer and dry on the pavement in winter; and the flower border on either side is planted with every kind of delightful flower, so that the refinements of its colour may be enjoyed all through the summer. It is not filled with bedded-out plants, because for long months it would be bare and desolate, because there is no pleasure in a solid spot of hard blazing colour, and because there is delight in the associations of the sweet old-fashioned flowers. There is music in their very names: –

> *In the garden, what in the garden?*
> *Jacob's ladder, and Solomon's seal,*
> *And love lies bleeding, with none to heal,*
> *In the garden.*

Gillyflowers and columbines, sweet williams, sweet johns, hollyhocks and marigolds, ladies' slipper, London pride, bergamot and dittany, pease ever-lasting, bachelor's buttons, flower of Bristol, love in a mist, and apple of love – these are a few old names to contrast with the horrors of a nursery gardener's catalogue, and these, too, are the sort of flowers for the garden. The formal garden lends itself readily to designs of smaller gardens within the garden – such as gardens of roses and lilies, or of poppies, or 'coronary gardens', as they used to be called, filled with all flowers for garlands, such as Spenser names: –

> *Bring hither the pinke and purple columbine,*
> *With gillyflowers,*
> *Bring sweet carnations, and sops in wine,*
> *Worne of paramours,*
> *Strew me the ground with daffa-down-dillies*
> *And cowslips, and king-cups, and loved lilies,*
> *The pretty paunce*
> *And the chevisaunce*
> *Shall match with the faire flower de luce.*

These and many another fancy, such as English men and women loved three hundred years ago, might be carried out, not for archaeology, not for ostentation, but because they give real pleasure and delight. This, after all, is the only principle. It is nothing to us that the French did this or the Italians that; the point is, what has been done in England, what has been loved here, by us and by those before us. The best English tradition has always been on the side of refinement and reserve; it has loved beauty – not the obvious beauty of the south, but the charm and tenderness, the inexpressible sweetness of faces that fill the memory like half-remembered music. This is the feeling that one would wish to see realised in the garden again, not the coarse facility that overwhelms with its astonishing cleverness, but the delicate touch of the artist, the finer scholarship which loves the past and holds thereby the key to its meaning.

4   CHASTLETON HOUSE, OXFORDSHIRE. 1902

This topiary garden was replanted in the 1820s but retains some elements of the
original seventeenth-century design which represented the solar system.

33

John D. Sedding
THE GEOMETRICAL GARDEN

*John Dando Sedding
(1838–1891) trained as
an architect with G. E.
Street and later developed
a preoccupation with
garden design.* Garden
Craft Old and New
*published posthumously,
is a classic of garden
writing.*

see plate 3

The geometrical garden is capable of great variety of handling. A fair size for a geometrical garden is 120 feet by 60 feet. This size will allow of a main central walk of 7 feet that shall divide the panel into two equal parts and lead down to the next level. The space may have a balustrade along its length on the two sides, and on the garden side of the balustrade a flower-bed of mixed flowers and choice low-growing shrubs, backed with hollyhocks, tritoma, lilies, golden-rod, etc. The width of the border will correspond with the space required for the steps that descend from the upper terrace. For obtaining pleasant proportions in the design, the walks in the garden will be of two sizes, gravelled like the rest – the wider walk, say, 3 feet, the smaller, 1 foot 9 inches. The centre of the garden device on each side may be a raised bed with a stone kerb and an ornamental shrub in the middle, and the space around with, say, periwinkle or stonecrop, mixed with white harebells, or low creepers. Or, should there be no wide main walk, and the garden-plot be treated as one composition, the central bed will have a statue, sundial, fountain, or other architectural feature. Each bed will be edged with box or chamfered stone, or terra-cotta edging. Or the formal garden may be sunk below the level of the paths, and filled either with flowers or with dwarf coniferae.

Both for practical and artistic reasons, the beds should not be too small; they should not be so small that, when filled with plants, they should appear like spots of colour, nor be so large that any part of them cannot be easily reached by a rake. Nor should the shapes of the beds be too angular to accommodate the plants well. In Sir Gardner Wilkinson's book on *Colour* (London, 1858), he speaks of design and good form as the very soul of a dressed garden; and the very permanence of the forms, which remain though successive series of plants be removed, calls for a good design. The shapes of the beds, as well as the colours of their contents, are taken cognisance of in estimating the general effect of a geometrical garden. This same accomplished author advises that there should always be a less formal garden beyond the geometrical one; the latter is, so to speak, an appurtenance of the house, a feature of the plateau

34

upon which it stands, and no attempt should be made to combine the patterns of the geometrical with the beds or borders of the outer informal garden, such combination being specially ill-judged in the neighbourhood of bushes and winding paths.

Of the proper selection of flowers and the determination of the colours for harmonious combination in the geometrical beds, much that is contradictory has been preached, one gardener leaning to more formality than another. There is, however, a general agreement upon the necessity of having beds that will look fairly well at all seasons of the year, and an agreement as to the use of hardy flowers in these beds.

Viscountess Wolseley
ORNAMENTAL POTS

The love for plants in pots seems alive in all true gardeners. Is it the sense of protection of something small, more helpless than ourselves, that we and children feel in tending them? Maybe it is transmitted from the earliest centuries. We know that flowers were grown in pots and bowls as long ago as Homer's time, because there are representations of them upon cups that were then used at solemn ceremonies. In very early Egyptian pictures we see flower pots standing in a garden, much as they are placed in symmetric patterns by Italian gardeners of to-day.

Unlike the Englishman, who puts all in the frame ground, in long, dull rows, the Italians enjoy making a pattern with them. As we look down from a height upon this nursery ground, where roses and lilies in pots are being prepared to decorate the flower garden proper later on, we see circles and ovals of colour. It seems almost as if they were already planted in a flower bed, so cleverly are the pots graduated in height. The tallest stand in the centre of a half-circle, whilst little short ones are at the ends.

Sometimes the frame yard is so arranged that small evergreen trees are

Frances Garnet Wolseley (1872–1936) founded the Glynde College for Lady Gardeners before she was thirty. She later established herself as a gardener and garden writer with a special interest in women's gardening.

planted at regular intervals in the ground. Thus some shelter is obtained from wind or too much sun for the more delicate plants in pots standing upon the earth between. It also takes away the stiffness which would be the effect if pots alone were there.

What we wish now to consider is how our pleasure gardens can be rendered more decorative by means of ornamental pots. Let us move, therefore, from the gardener's playground, the land of frames and cloches, of precious leaf and peat mould, and search out positions for handsome clipped bay trees or other flowering shrubs when they are planted in the great Italian terracotta orange pots.

In a large garden, a circular hedge of yew or beech gives a good background. The hedge can be made to form, at intervals, small semicircular recesses, large enough to give standing room to a tree in an ornamental pot.

The shaded plots can either be grass, closely mown, or beds of bright flowers. In the central circle, either a statue would look well, or, if shadow be needed, a mulberry tree would answer the purpose. In the latter case, it is advisable to have grass below it, for when the tender fruit falls upon gravel it is badly bruised.

There is no fear of bay trees not surviving English winters in the warm parts of England, provided that, from October to April, their stems are carefully wrapped round with bands of straw. Then, too, if anxiety be felt about the pots themselves being cracked by frost, it is easy to stitch thick Hessian canvas round them. This has saved many a breakage in exposed positions; and it has also another advantage, for the roots of the tree are thus kept warm.

Dressings of manure, repeated every three months, and a good soak of water to the roots in dry weather will preserve the lovely dark foliage of these beautiful trees. Small birds love to build in the dense foliage, and in spring it is a joy to find each little tree inhabited by a numerous family.

The real danger of pottery being injured by frost occurs when pots are left without earth or plants in them. Water collects inside and, if ice forms, the terracotta cracks. Another rash thing is to stand them in a damp conservatory or shed where there is bad ventilation. Especially is there risk near London, where fogs cause a close atmosphere. The surface of the pot then often peels, and the lovely decoration of wreaths and festoons is spoilt.

For a very formal little garden, perhaps a forecourt or approach to an old house, the design can be repeated twice or four times, as suits the garden best, with a graceful statue in the centre of each design, and all the flower beds outlined by low walls. Very small Italian oil jars, or some pottery boxes, are set upon these walls, and if sweet-smelling herbs or flowers are planted in them, they give an old fashioned look.

Carnations grow particularly well in terracotta boxes, and this is helpful if rabbits happen to encroach upon a garden. They much like to nibble a carnation stem, it has a special attraction for them. When the plant is in a box and stands upon a wall, they feel it is within the gardener's province, and consequently sometimes show some respect.

Other plants that look well grown thus are roses, sweet-scented geraniums, verbenas, especially the Miss Willmott variety, fuchsias, funkias[1], and chrysanthemums. It should be remembered that proper drainage has to be secured if they are to do well. Not only must they be properly potted with suitable mould and crocks, but good holes must be bored in the bottom of the pottery vase or box. Also, for preference, it is best to stand them upon stone, where water runs away easily.

The shadow paths of shrubberies in Italy are often outlined with pots of arum lilies, which are in flower there about the end of May. These look very well against bushes of box, and give much light and brightness to a dark wood. In England we can obtain a similar effect by using the tall blue and white *Campanula pyramidalis* to outline our paths. In August they look handsome, planted in terracotta pots, and placed where behind them a dark yew hedge shows off the delicacy of the flower spikes.

For a parterre garden, large pots with clipped Portugal laurels, placed in the circles, give height and remind us of the fine ones at Versailles.

Another design, though less simple, and with a touch of French influence, has the trees in pots to outline the walks and lend height and interest to the garden. It was not only in French and Italian gardens that ornamental pots were used. In an old book which gives pictures of Nuremberg gardens, we find a very charming one that belonged to Johan Christoph Golkainer. His was probably a reserve garden, or, at all events, the long narrow beds, with neat box edging round each, could be utilized for cut flowers. A 4 feet high hedge protects this ground from too much wind; but, to relieve the monotony, at intervals the hedge gives place to a tub or ornamental pot, with a clipped tree growing in it.

We have not yet touched sufficiently upon the true Italian flower pot

---

[1] now known as hostas

garden. By this we mean a garden where flower borders are given more height and grace by having handsome orange pots stood upon pedestals in the midst of the flowers. We seldom see this done in England, but it is so beautiful in effect, and gives such magic and height to a garden that we hope it may soon be introduced as a recognized style. Perhaps garden lovers have been held back hitherto by the difficulty of obtaining suitable orange pots. Or, again, the English gardener, not having been abroad, sees none of the beauty and magnifies the obstacles and extra work.

Some two miles or so from Siena there is a good example of an old fashioned Italian walled-in garden. It stands upon a hill. As both sides of the hill belong to it, warmth is to be had if necessary upon the south side, and in the heat of the day excessive sun-glare can be avoided by seeking the cool ilex woods that bound the northern part. The parterre garden, which is in an exposed position, is pleasant when the sun slowly sinks below the summit of the hill. We can then sit and carefully consider the symmetry with which it has been laid out.

The garden is divided into formal beds, outlined by clipped box edges. Circles play a great part in Italian gardens, and in this one, as will be seen, there are many curves. Fruit trees with irises and bulbs beneath, or fruit trees and vegetables, are in the centre of the large beds. All round them are 5 feet wide flower borders.

When we are there in early April we notice, within the box-edging, at regular intervals in the centre of the flower border, flat slabs of grey stone. They vary slightly in shape and pattern, but each has a cross cut deep into the stone. This is because, later, the lemon and orange trees, when it is warm enough for them to be brought out, will stand upon these stones. All moisture that runs away from the pots can freely escape by means of the grooves cut into the stone slabs. The trees consequently flourish, for no stagnant moisture will remain near their roots.

It is May when the eventful day comes round again. The *padrone* has given the order, warm sunshine has come, and there is no longer danger for the little trees.

With pushes, pulls, and many shouts the lemon and orange trees come rolling out. Some are on trollies, others upon rollers. It takes a long time to place them all, and until each tree is in position upon an appointed grey stone slab, the meaning of the whole garden design is not made clear. Yesterday the only height in the garden came from the pale pink of the apple blossom. This was beginning to wane, and we wondered if it would look dull without it. Now it is suddenly clear to us that height comes with the orange and lemon trees, for we have their green foliage above our heads; and later, as the fruit ripens, it will give us colour too.

It is wonderful, apart from the trees that are in them, how well the handsome pots look, mounted upon pedestals of terracotta, in the very midst of flowers. We now can see the doge's cap, papal arms, true lovers' knots, festoons, wreaths, or the seven familiar Medici balls, whatever loved emblem has been moulded on them. Flowers such as delphiniums, lupins, and irises surround the curved pale pink pedestals. The pots themselves make a pleasant break in a long border of flowers, and the quiet restfulness of dark green foliage above gives dignity to the garden.

Why do not English garden lovers throw aside all scruples and venture upon some such fairy garden? In place of oranges and lemons, let there be clipped bay trees and Portugal laurels, or if topiary be out of place, then have lilacs or hydrangeas growing in the handsome pots. If such shrubs are not in favour, why not have sunflowers and lilies, as we see them in old Renaissance gardens, growing in large marble or pottery vases? Often the retaining wall of a terrace was outlined by these, and from personal observation we know that irises look well used in this way in the sunk garden near Kensington Palace. Many are the fine colour effects that can be attained, and above all is the advantage of gaining height in our gardens. If only we can study this point we shall achieve somewhat of the buoyancy and vivacity of foreign garden design.

5   ELVASTON CASTLE, DERBYSHIRE. 1899

Shallow steps and statuesque topiary were used by William Barron to add height
and interest to a site which 'Capability' Brown thought too dull to landscape.

Paul Edwards
THE TOPIARY GARDEN

Most of the examples of topiary, knot, and parterre gardens that we see today date from the revival of this style of gardening that occurred in the mid-nineteenth century. The architectural or Italianate gardens laid out by Sir Charles Barry (1795–1860), and Eden Nesfield (1835–1888) contained parterre gardens with evergreens planted and trimmed to form scrolls and volutes within a strictly formal layout. Although the Italian garden became far less popular by the end of the nineteenth century, some topiary work continued to form a part of most large garden layouts. The Victorians felt that topiary gave an old-world charm to the otherwise all too new and immature grounds of the many recently built country estates. Two of the famous topiary gardens built in the nineteenth century were at Elvaston Castle[1], Derbyshire, and at Compton Wynyates[2], Warwickshire: surprisingly the latter garden was planted as late as 1895. Even more recently planted topiary, but again looking fully mature, is in the National Trust gardens at Hidcote, Gloucestershire, and Nymans in Sussex.

During the early part of this century a number of nurseries in this country made a speciality of topiary growing. Messrs. Cheal and Sons of Crawley, Sussex, and Messrs. William Cutbush and Son of Highgate, London, were well known topiary suppliers at this time. William Cutbush imported many of his fine specimens from the old masters of topiary, the Dutch, as well as growing and training many thousands of topiary subjects in his nursery.

To create and maintain a topiary garden successfully, an open and sunny site should be selected which also has or can be given protection from severe winds. The soil should preferably be loam, or at least have good-quality loam incorporated into the topsoil. Inorganic manures should be avoided. Well-rotted farmyard manure or compost, coarse bonemeal and liquid manure are the best forms of feeding for evergreen trees such as yew and box, the commonest plants of topiary treatment. Planting is best carried out in early

Paul Edwards (1926–   ) is a horticulturist, landscape architect and town planner. He now specialises in the restoration and renovation of historic gardens including Wroxton Abbey, Oxfordshire, the Painswick Rococo Garden, Gloucestershire and the Victorian Rose Garden at Warwick Castle. He was a major contributor to the recent book Recreating The Period Garden.

---

[1] After many years of neglect, this has recently been restored.
[2] Topiary shapes no longer decorate the parterres at Compton Wynyates.

autumn or in the spring. Tub-grown specimens can, of course, be planted at most times of the year when the ground is free from frost. Evergreen trees and shrubs should be moved with as large a root-ball of soil as is necessary to contain most of the roots. Mulching around the roots should continue for several years after planting, and again in later years if the trees appear to have exhausted the soil of available plant nutrients. This exhaustion of the surrounding soil is most likely to occur on light sandy formations. Clipping should be carried out in August and the early part of September. For the mature specimens it will usually be necessary to clip within 1½ to 2 inches of the previous year's growth in order to keep the trees within reasonable bounds. Heavy falls of snow can be most damaging to some specimens of topiary, when ledges and branches are bent down and misshapen or broken by the weight of snow. Early removal of heavy clinging snow can, of course, avoid this unfortunate destruction of years of patient training.

Mazes or labyrinths are usually associated with topiary, as most of the well-known mazes in this country are garden ones formed from hedges such as yew, box, beech, and privet.

A maze or labyrinth consists of a number of enclosed paths or passages which are laid out in such a way that the visitor to the maze repeatedly loses his way attempting to get to the centre of the maze or in simply trying to get out again.

The labyrinth is a term usually applied to unenclosed paths that eventually lead one to the designed end, whereas the maze is formed from enclosed or partly enclosed walks whose design has a number of blocked ends or culs-de-sac. Early labyrinths were laid out with inlaid marble slabs in the floors of cathedrals and churches on the Continent. It is thought that penitents had to follow the path of the labyrinth on their hands and knees, offering prayers on the slow and laborious route.

The origin of mazes goes back into antiquity and many reasons have been put forward by historians for their early construction. The Greeks attached importance to the medical value of mazes, particularly for helping to improve the patients' mental attitude towards medical treatment. It was reasoned that in the maze the patient would undergo a symbolical break with his set attitude or pattern of thought and could then later be purged of his troubles.

The earliest mazes in Britain were simply cut in the turf, and were made up of a number of paths surrounded on either side by turf banks. A number of these turf mazes still survive, notably the one on St. Catherine's Hill, near

Winchester, at Wing, Rutlandshire, and at Skensby, Yorkshire. It is thought that they were originally constructed for races or games on horseback. The game was called City of Troy. The Romans practised a similar game called Troy Game. The game consisted of intricate movements for the horse and its rider which were designed to improve or exhibit the rider's powers of horsemanship. It is interesting to find that a number of similar turf mazes also survive in Scandinavia and were presumably used for similar purposes as they are called Trojeborg (Troy Town).

Garden mazes as a garden feature obviously have a number of attractions for they offer a certain amount of adventure or fascination in walking into the unknown, as well as providing privacy and amusement in the garden. The maze became a popular feature in gardens in Britain, along with other forms of topiary, in the seventeenth century. The most famous garden maze surviving from this period is the one planted in yew at Hampton Court in the late-seventeenth century, when new gardens were laid out to the designs of Christopher Wren and the gardener Henry Wise.

Hedged garden mazes were planted in several nineteenth-century gardens, such as the one at Woburn Park, Bedfordshire, and occasionally for children with low hedging, as can be seen at Wootton Court, Warwickshire. As play places for children they can be most popular and provide endless amusement.

6   Packwood House, Warwickshire. 1969

This topiary garden, thought to have been laid out in 1655 by John Fetherston, represents the Sermon on the Mount. A large, single yew tree is surrounded by 'Apostles', 'Disciples' and the smaller 'Multitude'. Nearly all the nineteenth-century yews survive and their dark symbolic shapes are dramatically impressive. Every summer it takes a month for three men to clip them.

Russell Page
A SMALL EXCURSION
INTO FORMALITY

I like at least to recall the sentiment of a formal garden close to the house, though not a lavish and symmetrical lay-out that extends so largely that the house looks like the odd man left on the chessboard. I have sometimes thought that the formally patterned garden was evolved at a time when the outside world was mainly wild, unknown and incalculable; a garden pattern was reassuring, for it extended the limits of people's authority out towards the wild. In Europe the informal romantic 'landscape' garden became fashionable as the exploration of the physical world began to be achieved and the encyclopaedists busily set themselves to catalogue the planet's geography as well as its flora and fauna. Large formal arrangements of flowers or roses or clipped parterres demand a maintenance so out of proportion to today's possibilities and so irrelevant to our way of life, that in the rare cases when such extravagances are possible, they will still appear inappropriate. I prefer to look back to an earlier form, the *hortus inclusus*, that small enclosed flower garden of the Middle Ages in Europe, designed wholly for pleasure in a period when all that lay beyond the walls of castle or city was farmland, heath or forest. These restricted closes, perhaps only a few feet square, were made for growing herbs and flowers – roses and pinks and columbines – not perhaps very showy by modern standards, but one can see how much they were cherished and appreciated from a hundred paintings and tapestries of the period. How exactly and lovingly depicted are the flowers of the 'Dame à la Licorne' tapestries in the Cluny museum or the flag iris in Dürer's 'Madonna' in the National Gallery in London. Often enough these small garden plots were sophisticated and luxurious compositions: flower beds were bordered with painted trellis-work and set around carved and gilded fountains which recalled those Byzantine waterworks designed to represent the Tree of Life.

Russell Page (1906–1985), a trained painter, was a self-taught landscape gardener who worked all over the world. His English commissions included Charterhouse School, and the Battersea Festival Gardens.

45

A replica of this late Gothic idiom would suit few houses to-day; but the principle of a small space near the house designed for flowers in a formal way adapts itself well to contemporary restrictions.

I like to keep the pattern of a formal garden very simple and to use squares, circles and rectangles outlined by narrow paved paths and edge them, as often as not, with lavender, box, rosemary or santolina. I see them as gardens compartmented like a Persian rug, a series of simple shapes to fill with flowers in any one of a hundred different ways.

Gardens in decorative patterns, laid out as carpets or panels, have persisted through the whole history of European gardening. Knot gardens reproduced the interlaced strapwork patterns which were the convention for applied decoration in the late-sixteenth century. A hundred years later, the elaborate inlaid scroll work and foliations of buhl and counter-buhl in tortoiseshell, silver and gilt bronze, found its vegetable counterpart in parterres of clipped box, coal or brick dust and white marble chippings. Nor did formal patterns entirely disappear during a century-long vogue for romantic gardens. By the early 1800s, dry-looking bands of neat plants in Empire and Regency patterns carried the formal flavour of the drawing-room into the garden; and, for all his talent and his taste for informal landscape, even Humphry Repton worked out quite elaborate parterres to embellish formal terraces and lawns. Although it degenerated into carpet bedding and mosaiculture, pattern-gardening just survived the nineteenth century. Banished from private gardens by a shortage of cash and labour and the advent of herbaceous gardening, it still survives in public parks and gardens.

see plate 3

Before the First World War Lutyens and Inigo Triggs revived the taste for pattern in gardens in a relatively simplified form; many of Lutyens's designs are masterly exercises in robust patterns made from squares and circles.

This sort of garden still has its place, though perhaps on a reduced scale, since a patch of good pattern and bright flower colour can enhance the simplified stretches of a modern labour-saving garden of grass and trees and shrubs. They should be no larger than can be maintained impeccably, but their various compartments must be big enough to tell as colour without looking spotty, and the pattern should be interesting in itself during the flowerless winter months.

At Port Lympne between the wars Sir Philip Sassoon had just such a garden immediately below the house. It was an ingenious chess board – a yard square of finely clipped turf alternating with a square of tuberous begonias or marigolds. But its effect lay in the fact that the flower squares were set nine inches below the turf squares so that when in full bloom all was at the same level. It was this refinement which gave elegance to a basically simple pattern.

I have copied this principle and interpreted it in various ways. In one garden I wanted to give interest to a stone-paved terrace which had been made particularly wide to accommodate garden furniture. The habits of the household changed, people and furniture migrated to another corner, and I had to find some simple way to enliven this overlarge expanse. I did it by taking out a rectangular panel of paving and dividing this empty panel with a criss-cross of narrow bands of the same stone to make a diamond pattern of small beds. These beds are set 6 inches below ground level and are planted with box, clipped flush with the paving. This makes a lively pattern of green and stone and gives interest to the paved space without breaking it up.

In Piedmont there is an austere modern house with glass walls which disappear into a floor of large terracotta tiles set in a basket-work pattern. This house consists of one big room sparsely decorated with abstract pictures and pieces of modern sculpture. Outside, the brick paving continues to the edge of a hillside thickly set with the dwarf pine, *Pinus montanus mughus*[1], and forty or fifty miles away, beyond the often mist-covered plain, glisten the snowy mountains. Here too, the terrace is stark and needed some decoration to relate it more closely to the great room and its contents. It sufficed to draw a zig-zag shape, using the joints in the brickwork as a guide, and devise a broken maze-like pattern which I hollowed out and again planted with box.

Roses, particularly the polyantha or floribunda kinds, are good plants for these small formal gardens if you are careful to outline your underlying pattern of beds with a dwarf hedge, perhaps in such a case of lavender. The paths that make the design should not be more than 18 inches or 2 feet wide and be of gravel or else be paved in brick or stone. Grass paths, which must be wide to be practical, would be out of scale and out of character. For the same reason the beds should be kept small enough to be easily accessible; 4 to 5 feet would be a maximum width.

see colour plate x

---

[1] *Pinus mugo*

These small excursions into formality may be very brightly coloured. Here is a miniature garden in which to experiment with spring plantings and later with a whole range of annual flowers. Or you might want to use these formal beds for a botanical collection, or for rare plants or bulbs which require special cultivation.

On a small site this deliberately designed and deliberately coloured patch may well be flower garden enough, the rest being simply and soberly planted to suggest space. Almost always I like to set these parterres to one side or other of the house and so to enclose them that they are felt to be separate from the main composition of the garden.

At the Moulin de la Tuilerie at Gif, near Paris there is just such a garden, enclosed by buildings on three sides and lying apart from and above the main garden from which it is separated by a retaining wall. Narrow paths of well-worn square sandstone *pavés* divide the whole space into a series of square lavender-edged beds planted with roses. Close at hand, yet hidden and separate from the rest of the garden, this is a convenient place to grow hybrid tea-roses which I think are better out of sight when not in flower.

A walled or partially walled enclosure near the house suggests a small garden for cutting-flowers. They are apt to look uninteresting planted out in rows in the kitchen garden, but you may well set them in a formal pattern of beds, using one variety in each bed. The beds should be small enough to cut from them without having to walk on them. I have found that this kind of garden is all the more effective if you make no attempt at symmetrical planting; an all-over pattern of squares or rectangles with no strongly marked centre will leave you free to plant a low block of blue cornflowers next to high white marguerites, or delphiniums next to Iceland poppies. Hollyhocks will not be too tall nor dwarf dahlias too small to make good neighbours. All these sharp breaks in height, weight and colour will give brilliance and vivacity to what is usually a very utilitarian and common-place kind of gardening.

I find increasingly, when designing gardens to be looked after by one gardener, or none, that I am obliged to 'sketch' and, as it were, suggest a garden by carefully establishing my proportions, reaffirming them by a simple arrangement of hedges and paths, and then giving body to the whole by planting trees and shrubs which can be left to grow without demanding too much labour. Then, looking at the whole as a question of decoration, I feel the need to make some focus of interest and colour so as to tie the composition together. Any strong colour accent set out too far away from the house will likely be distracting; and so my set-piece, with its firm design and ordered colour, will almost always find its place away to one side but closely tied to the house and its immediate surroundings.

7   HIDCOTE MANOR, GLOUCESTERSHIRE. 1930

The Phlox Garden, enjoying complete enclosure and partial shade, is a fine
example of that small-scale formality favoured in turn by Reginald Blomfield,
Major Lawrence Johnston (the creator of Hidcote), Vita Sackville-West and
Russell Page.

CHAPTER II

Ornament

John B. Papworth
FOUNTAINS REDISCOVERED

Sources of water were respected, or held sacred, from very high antiquity in Eastern nations, as is recorded by historians both sacred and profane. The Greeks, Tuscans, and Romans also, employed them as useful and decorative architecture; and hence they were adopted by the Italians and the French. In the formation of the celebrated gardens of Versailles, they were introduced in profuse magnificence, and became a prime feature in all the varieties of falls, fountains and *jets-d'eau*. Fashion immediately took them up, and water was spouting everywhere; no place was complete without a fountain, and the first recommendation of the tasteful towards the embellishment of a garden, court, walk, or alley, was 'certainly place a fountain there'. But in art, as in matters of less importance, it frequently happens that fashion encroaches upon, or supersedes the more steady patronage of fitness and propriety; and in her vacillating progress adopts or discards equally without reflection; and in her dismissal, the subject, which was hitherto her pride and boast, becomes as

John Papworth (1775–1847) is known better as an architect although his practice as an original landscape gardener was extensive. His garden plans include one for Claremont, Surrey and another for Alton Towers, Staffordshire.

51

obnoxious to her distaste. Thus it was with the fountain in ornamental gardening.

As in other cases where fashion predominates, its fulness produced its fall; – their absurd adoption in most instances, with the incessant repetition of them, occasioned satiety and disgust, consequently they were demolished with as little regard to fine feeling or sound judgement as was bestowed upon them when first erected. Time has now banished the impression that was fatal to such designs, and their beauties are again proper subjects for garden embellishment, when circumstances permit an unforced use of them. Water is rarely otherwise than desirable; and the motion and sound of lightly-falling water gives liveliness to a spot however secluded, that is not readily obtained in its absence.

To execute a simple form of fountain it is necessary to be in possession of a body of water at a sufficient height to produce the jet, and it must be something higher than the altitude proposed, because of the resistance the jet meets with, and amongst others, from the pressure of the air, and in striking against its descending waters: the aperture at which the water escapes must be proportioned to the height of the reservoir, and to the diameter of the conducting pipes. The following table will give the practical results, in feet, of the received theories on this subject.

Height of Reservoir	Diameter of conducting Pipes	Diameter of aperture or ajutage	Height of the Jet
Feet			Feet
5	1¾ inch	¼ inch	4
10	2 ——	½ ——	9
20	2½ ——	½ ——	18
30	3¼ ——	⅝ ——	27
40	4½ ——	¾ ——	35
50	5 ——	¾ ——	43
60	6 ——	1 inch	51
80	7 ——	1¼ ——	65
100	8 ——	1½ ——	79

These proportions of conducting-pipes are suitable to jets removed from reservoirs not exceeding 500 feet; but if the water requires to be brought from a yet greater distance the pipes must be of larger diameters.

Unless the bends in pipes of communication from the reservoir to the aperture or ajutage be easy and bold, the escape will be proportionally impeded; and to produce an even and regular jet it is necessary to apply a suitable air-vessel near to the ajutage, the construction of which is well-known to manufacturers in copper, of which material they are usually constructed.

Simple fountains are now usually manufactured in artificial stone, or sculptured in Portland stone; as they were formerly of lead, the convertibility of which valuable metal undoubtedly assisted in the rapid disappearance of fountains as soon as they fell into disrepute. The present rage for cast iron will probably supersede the use of such leaden works, and as iron would offer no premium for their demolition, they may be expected to enjoy a longer triumph of fashionable importance in our gardens.

Few architectural embellishments have so interesting an effect as fountains, and being capable of an inexhaustible variety of design, situation and magnitude, it is rather a matter of surprise that their beauties have been neglected, ever since the general abandonment of them nearly a century ago. At that time certainly their whimsical and profuse introduction in all places, suitable and otherwise, naturally satiated the taste, and was eventually altogether fatal to their cultivation; but, since they have been excluded so long from our country, the motive which effected it is surely banished also, and they may again very properly meet with encouragement, and succeed to some of the patronage by which far less valuable material is now fostered.

When a supply of water is adequate, fountains may in most cases be introduced with propriety; for it is that part of their artificialness which implies scarcity of water, and manual labour in effecting a display of its powers, that is offensive to true taste; and surely it must be most painful to witness such a display, when it is known that, to produce it, a poor fellow, hid in some nook of the premises, is pumping most lustily, and anxiously wishing you would turn your attention to some other object, that his labour may be over. It was formerly, however, no uncommon thing to witness extensive displays at the expense of proportionately laborious means.

George Sitwell
STATUES: THE IMAGINATIVE IDEAL

*George Sitwell
(1860–1943), politician
and father of Osbert and
Edith, was a dedicated
amateur gardener and his
garden at Renishaw,
Derbyshire is a prime
example of the revival of
formal garden design at
the turn of this century.
He spent much of his life
in Italy; undoubtedly an
influence upon his
gardening style.*

Of statues in the garden, Bacon has written that they are for state and magnificence, but nothing to the true pleasure of it; and Temple could see little in them, or rather in the stone of which they are made, beyond a suggestion of coolness in the summer heat; yet from this faint and damning praise we may appeal to Wagner's great rule that as far as possible all the arts should be used in conjunction, and to Spencer's judgment that the highest aesthetic feeling is roused by the exercise of many powers. Let sculpture add yet another appeal to emotion, and the pleasure stirred by beauty in a garden may rise from massive to acute. It is not only that the statues will set off the garden; we have to consider also that the garden will set off the statues, crowning them with a garland of beauty they could not have elsewhere. Further, there is the opinion already so much insisted upon, that the designer should aim at the ideal, not merely at that low form of ideality which goes beyond nature in the perfection of shape and colour and arrangement, of leaf and blossom, turf and tree, but at the nobler kind that mixes imagination with beauty, taking us into a new world of romance out of all relation to experience and knowledge.

Statuary proclaiming the imaginative ideal may strike in the garden a keynote of wonder and romance. The only rules it is necessary to observe are that there should be a background of mystery and obscurity, such as a forest or a great plain or a chain of distant mountains may give; a well-defined boundary; a shock of delight or surprise to lift us over the threshold of fact; an air of grandeur or distinction in the garden itself and in all its parts; that we should not mix the worlds of romance, but should admit only one supernatural, other circumstances being congruous with it and with each other; that we should leave as much as possible to the mind, because imagination flies from a finished picture and loves to accept a bare suggestion, filling in the details for itself. But even where conditions do not favour the ideal, a pleasure-ground, however small, should have its presiding genius, its Nymph of flower-garden or grove or woodland, or Naiad of the Well, appealing to that other emotion of personality which induces the mind to be ever looking for some being like itself, some face among the rocks or figure in the branching wood, to give a personal interpretation to the forces of nature and to feel in lake or mountain or forest the thrill of a living presence. This emotion, springing perhaps from the primal dread of solitude, forms a fresh bond between man and nature, enlarging the human interest and adding to the appreciation of natural beauty; and for this reason sculpture in a garden is to be regarded not as an ornament but almost as a necessity, as like that last touch of colour in a picture which sets the whole canvas in a flame.

Statues of marble seldom look well in Italy, never in England, and of all discords none can be so jarring as to place among the flowers dreadful forms of disease and suffering, cripples or beggars, or the monstrous dwarfs that look down from the Valmarana garden, Vicenza as if to symbolize the starved and stunted life of the wall-coping. Art, like laughter, should be the language of happiness, and those who suffer should be silent. Time and Care may wait without the gateway, but Time the ungracious guest, who is always late for the wedding feast and early for the funeral – envious Time the spoiler of the roses, who lays his hateful scythe to the root of the fairest flowers, should have no image, no altar, in the garden, for it is by events and not by the measure of them that we grow old, and hours spent in a garden are stolen from Death and from Time. Only health and strength and beauty are at home among the flowers, shepherds and shepherdesses, youths and maidens in the garb of long ago, portly noblemen in periwigs and armour, warriors and Amazons, nymphs and satyrs, virtues and graces. We may personify the particular place in a figure or bust, taught by the gate at Capua and the pulpit at Ravello, or commemorate an historic event by reference as in the cavalier's garden at Norton Conyers, where a leaden warrior speaks discreetly of the Edgehill fight. We may represent the great elemental forces of nature, the higher motives which sway the human drama, the hoped-for triumph of Love over Death. We may build in some secluded nook a Cupid's altar, where many generations of lovers shall carve their names and make their offerings of flowers, or may set in the four quarters of the garden our pageant of the Seasons: Spring, as a winged youth, primrose-crowned, with flute and flower-embroidered robe; proud Summer as a weary king; spendthrift Autumn with open purse and lifted cup and gathered fruit; hoary Winter having a sealed casket under his foot, his beard hung with icicles and his mantle broidered with double-faced jests. No statue, however bad, should be condemned to a desolate old age. In a decorative landscape the figures are never happy unless they are enjoying themselves, and in a portrait even ugliness is rendered charming by the presence of a child, a dog or bird. Diana in a garden should not be without her hound, nor Neptune without his sea-monster; Mars may be mated with Venus, Flora with Vertumnus, Cupid with Psyche; every Amazon should have her warrior and every nymph her satyr.

see plate 8

8   RENISHAW HALL, DERBYSHIRE. 1938

The path through the Hanging Wood watched over by a Roman warrior and an Amazon guard.

Thomas Mawson
STATUARY AND GARDEN SEATS

Statuary, when well-chosen and happily placed with due regard to scale, supplies that touch of the exquisite needed to transport the mind from the hard materialistic common literal facts of daily life, which it is our object to escape from in the garden, to the ideal. The function of statuary of the right kind is to give versimilitude to the imaginative. Everyone knows how the children gaze upon the statue of Peter Pan in Kensington Gardens, and inspired by J. M. Barrie's book, it leads them to the jumping-off place from the tangible and real to enter into imaginative companionship with Peter amidst the trees and along by the ponds peopled by fairies and gnomes. This is garden statuary when it fulfils its highest function. Take another instance: ensnared with the peace and the delightful seclusion we wander down an umbrageous grass glade. The springy turf under our feet, the sunshine, the birds, the flowers, all join in the transcendent harmony of the soul and lead it into the region where, peering out from under a leafy canopy, we discern a statue of Pan with his reed pipes. The spell is complete. At any moment we expect the god to stamp his cloven foot and the glade to swarm with satyrs and nymphs dancing to the strains of his music. It may be used purely as design because of its beauty of line and form to grace some choice position, and in this case, if well chosen, it is appropriate.

Poor plaster casts from the antique or conventional figures in glaring white marble are totally unsuited for garden decoration, for, apart from questions of subject and treatment, their insistent white silhouettes cause over-emphasis of the point they are supposed to adorn. This does not mean that statuary in other materials, such as lead or bronze, which tones and harmonizes with the foliage, rightly placed and in keeping with their setting both as to scale and sentiment, may not be used with happy results.

Severe restraint is, however, more necessary in the introduction of statuary, because it represents the last and culminating point in the composition beyond which there is no further emphasis. In music, the sudden crash of sound, in pictorial art, the most vivid contrasts of tone and colour, in rhetoric, the highly figurative hyperbole, must be used but rarely and with caution,

Thomas Mawson (1861–1933) worked at various nurseries before setting up his own nursery and landscape design business near Windermere. His commissions included public parks at Hanley, Burslem and Newport as well as many private gardens. The garden he designed at Dyffryn, near Cardiff, is now open to the public.

because they represent the exhaustion of the full range of the powers of expression, and so, in the employment of statuary which takes much the same position in our own art, restraint and reserve are equally necessary, and the highest point must be touched but seldom with the consummate skill of a master.

It is evident that the subject matter of a statue goes far to determining its suitability or otherwise for a place in the garden, but this does not mean that we must fill our pleasaunces with representations of Ceres, or our woodland glades with Dianas. Quaint shepherds and shepherdesses will strike a rural note more acceptable to modern minds, while, if a more classical subject is desired, cupids, dryads, satyrs and fauns allow of almost endless scope for taste and discrimination in their posing, placing and application.

There is another way in which this form of garden ornament may be used. This is in what may be called 'applied sculpture'. Fountains invite this type of decoration probably more than any other form of garden equipment, but observation of existing examples shows the necessity for caution in its choice and arrangement, so that none but the best obtainable is used.

This strong insistence on the assertion that no statuary but that which is really good be included in the garden, does not mean that it must be excluded from the domain of the man of moderate means. Old lead figures of real merit may occasionally be picked up at moderate prices. Where the choice has to be made, I strongly advise the acquisition of a good copy of a well-known subject, even though it lack the quality of uniqueness, in preference to an original conception of second-rate merit. The boy and dolphin from the Uffizi, Mercier's David and Goliath, the well-known Greek Slave, and the half-dozen specially good Cupids which it is possible to obtain, can never pall, and though often repeated, are to be preferred to the uninspiring original creations of the monumental mason.

Subjects from Greek and Roman mythology need some adaptation to their surroundings if they are to be successful, but there is one feature of classical ornament which seems to adapt itself perfectly without the slightest rearrangement. This is the acrolith, which from its nature is only suitable for use in gardens laid out on formal lines, and usually in conjunction with clipped hedges where it can be used to divide the hedge into bays, or mark the position of an opening. It may also be used, however, to emphasize the termination of an avenue or glade, while a pair of these features may be placed so as to break up a plain wall surface and give character and finish to an architectural composition.

Detached columns of traditional classic design often, but not always, surmounted with statuettes or graceful lead urns may be used for the same purpose, as in an instance I came across in a garden at Seville, or one may be placed in the centre of a formal garden to be smothered in rampant roses or clematis. Readers familiar with the Parc Monceau, Paris, will also remember what a charming effect may be obtained with a classic colonnade in conjunction with free foliage and water. Sometimes, too, a single column may support a cubical block of stone, three faces of which might have vertical sundials.

The sundial is a feature which allows variety, and there are examples of quaintly conceived pedestals supporting a polyhedrical block of stone bearing literally dozens of dials on its various facets, each one having its own particular markings carefully calculated in accordance with its placing in relation to the path of the sun. Such arrangements, however, and also the huge topiary sundial at Broughton Castle, partake of the nature of curiosities or freaks, which, however quaint the original examples may be, cannot be repeated indefinitely. The aim should be in this as in every other garden feature, to combine use with beauty and grace of form, and clothe the whole with that sentiment which belongs naturally to the subject, and which has come down to us with an unbroken record of usefulness from the dark ages.

Unlike some other antiques, the sundial will not usually bear removal from its original surroundings without losing the whole of its old-world charm and becoming more or less commonplace, and it is usually therefore much better to design one to fit its surroundings than to purchase one of the old examples. Again, as every position requires a specially designed dial, and every degree of latitude a differently shaped gnomon, once a sundial is removed, it cannot be relied upon to register correct time.

In passing it may be explained that the time told by the sundial is *Solar time*, which varies slightly according to the seasons, and not the *mean* time to which we are accustomed. There is also this difference, that whereas we use Greenwich time throughout Great Britain, and eastern Europe, each place east or west of Greenwich has, of course, its own meridian and its own time, which is registered by the dial. This difference is easily found by reckoning four minutes for every degree of longitude separating the site of the sundial from Greenwich. This gives us Greenwich solar time, and, to discover Greenwich mean time, which is what our watches show, it is necessary to consult a special calendar which shows the difference for each day in the year between the two systems, or the calendar may be so arranged as to translate local solar time directly into that shown by ordinary clocks and watches. In most of the better dials, this calendar is engraved on the plate itself, and, in vertical dials placed on the sides of a block of stone. The dial which faces north may be omitted, substituting for it a plate engraved with the calendar or other information such as the latitude and longitude, the family escutcheon, the date, or a quaint sundial motto.

The ordinary horizontal dial plate may also be given additional interest by the application of chaste and restrained ornament. The centre being occupied with the dial markings, there remain the margins and corners, which may be treated with chased ornament or bas-reliefs.

A mechanical sundial has recently been introduced, which, by projecting a spot of light on to a mark, shows Greenwich mean time most accurately to at least half a minute, but, like many other modern improvements, it has none of the charm and aesthetic interest which clings around the old form of dial. It may be used with advantage on the principal terrace opposite and close to the garden entrance to the house for practical purposes, but, in parts of the pleasaunce, the older form, with its graceful gnomon and quaint motto is preferable.

*   *   *

Garden seats may be of wood, stone or iron. For eleven months of the year, iron and stone are too cold and comfortless, and even dangerous to the health, therefore wood is the only satisfactory material. Stone seats can be fitted with a removable wooden grating, as is often done in the case of seats on classic terraces.

For woodland walks and outlying parts of the grounds, very simple designs are usually best. A very good form is that in which the back is made of solid boards and is hinged so as to close over the seat and keep it clean when not in use. Such a contrivance may, with care, be made quite neat and in keeping with its sylvan surroundings. Of iron seats, it may be said that most of the existing patterns are ugly, and not very comfortably proportioned. There is no reason why this should be so, and I have seen early examples in cast iron which were pleasing. It is the modern productions with their ridiculous filigree ornament which offend the canons of taste.

Curved seats are often required, and are particularly suitable for placing at see plate 10 the end of a garden vista, when additional interest may be given to the arrangement by marking the centre by a sundial or a choice piece of statuary on a tall pedestal. A sense of size and massivity is desirable in stone seats, otherwise the expense is not justified.

9   IFORD MANOR, WILTSHIRE. 1907

The Fountain Court filled with ornaments collected in France and Italy. Harold Peto (1854–1933) used ornament extensively both in his own garden and in other architectural garden designs.

10   IFORD MANOR, WILTSHIRE. 1907

At the North end of the Great Terrace, Harold Peto (probably the figure
in the photograph) built a semicircular seat of Ham Hill stone between the
old gateposts.

Christopher Hussey
THE PLACE OF ORNAMENT

Christopher Hussey (1899–1970), architect and landscape historian, was closely involved with Country Life *and with the National Trust's preservation work. His home was Scotney Castle, Kent.*

There is no doubt that to-day architecture is the most potent extraneous influence on the design of gardens. A century or so ago landscape painting occupied this position, and two hundred years ago the lay-out of grounds was almost a branch of the art of the theatre, so pre-eminent was the desire for a dramatic setting for the ceremonies of life. In neither of these phases was much use made of flowers, owing partly to the comparative paucity of species then available, partly to the origin of the fashionable styles; in one case Italy, with its extreme climate, in the other the landscape paintings of Claude and Salvator Rosa.

Landscape is still the most important element in the English garden. But our attitude to it was modified in the nineteenth century by the picturesque revival of Italian formal design, and by the botanical discoveries of travellers and nurserymen, which showered upon us a previously undreamt-of wealth of natural forms and colours. We thus have to-day three elements at our disposal: landscape, the flora, and architecture.

At this point I must make clear my view of the part to be played by ornament in uniting these three elements. We might define ornament's proper purpose, at any rate in England, as the provision of forms appropriate in idea to the spirit of their surroundings, and in form to the habits of plants; and the fashioning of those forms with materials and suitable texture. Our equable climate makes of flowers and shrubs our chief interest in gardens, so that to aim too exclusively at architectural effect is to waste both money and opportunities. Similarly, to shut our eyes to the picturesque possibilities of our meadowland and woodland is to neglect England's chief beauty. The claims of architecture, therefore, are subservient on the one hand to the picturesque, and on the other to the flora. It should be a foreground for the one and a frame for the other. Architecture can form the skeleton of a design, but flowers should almost hide that skeleton, and it should melt picturesquely into the surrounding landscape.

This triple mode is the result of the warfare waged round about the close of last century, when the doctrine of the wild was preached by Mr. William Robinson and the merits of formality were championed by Sir Reginald Blomfield and Mr. Inigo Trigg. Both schools of thought are as alive as ever. Mr. Robinson himself, Miss Jekyll and Miss Willmott have as many followers as the architects. But as their doctrines were assimilated, a group of designers arose who aimed at uniting the methods of both parties, to use architecture picturesquely as a frame for the house, but to let formality melt into wildness farther off. I need only mention Sir Edwin Lutyens, Mr. Harold Peto and Mr. Avray Tipping as foremost developers of this picturesque-formal method, though each holds a different opinion on the desirable ratio between landscape, flowers, and ornament.

It is acknowledged by all parties that the immediate surroundings of the house need to be predominantly formal. The problem in every case is, how far and how much formality should radiate from the house? A formal house naturally needs a more formal setting than a farm-house. The more distinctively modern types of architecture in particular require severely stylized surroundings, defined by lines related to those of the buildings. But in all branches of garden ornament and design the modern desire for simplification is noticeable; a preference for clean lines, simple masses, definite forms.

As an instance of modern buildings needing a stylized setting, I may contrast the treatment of gardens at the Wembley Exhibition (1924), and at the Press Exhibition recently held in Germany, at Cologne. At Wembley a tenuous water-garden, picturesquely treated, occupied one of the central vistas among the vast buildings. On the banks of the water were grouped large quantities of ornaments, such as lead storks and stone objects. Though tasteful in its way, the effect was exceedingly weak against the severe and ponderous buildings. At the German exhibition I was struck by the close relation of the layout to the rather harsh architecture.

One species of flower was used in enormous quantities to form sheets of colour defined into somewhat angular shapes by box edging, accentuated by miniature escarpments in the adjoining lawn. I saw a red Polyantha rose used in this way below a low circular terrace, round a fountain basin some 80 yards in diameter, and in harmony with a vast semicircular loggia of rosy brick. The effect of this modernist parterre of red and green, patterned into planes related to those of the architecture, seemed to me an example of contemporary garden design as impressive as the Wembley example was weak. Both these examples are of public urban gardens, so that the lesson does not apply literally to the normal problems with which we are confronted here, where even modern houses are generally in the gentle Queen Anne tradition. But it throws light on the relative values of the stylized and the quaint, and the time may not be far distant when increased attention may be turned to the provision of public gardens and their suitable ornament. We would see then whether our national love of rural simplicity will still make us imitate a field, complete with sheep, in the middle of a city, or whether more artificial stylization will be required.

In some respect garden ornament plays a more subordinate part in England than in any other part of the world, owing to the ideal nature of our climate for providing flowers all the year round, which obviates the need for architectural decoration. In Renaissance Italy, in baroque Spain and Germany, and the Versailles period, the formation of pleasure grounds largely without flowers developed the arts of design and decoration to their highest refinements. A modern example of this type of ornamental garden is to be found near Stockholm in Herr Milles's highly personal pleasaunce.

It is essentially a sculptor's garden. In a small space, high on a rock above the sea opposite Stockholm, he has arranged a paved court with a terrace below it, wherein are set some of his most effective works – fountains in black marble and statues in bronze. The lay-out is compact and simple, and for obvious reasons few flowers are used. It is referred to here as an extreme form of the modern stylized garden. Ornament here plays the predominant part. But if it were in England we should, I think, feel acutely the absence of vegetation and the hard effect of the linear design. We should want atmosphere, softer lights and shades, and the many hues of flowers. But in England such an artist as Herr Milles would have availed himself of our climate, and have laced his forms with flowers, banking up his terrace with herbaceous masses, and filling in the design with shrubs. His most important sculptures would stand out, but the lesser ornaments would be used as points in a floral design.

Having now suggested the part that ornament plays in the formation of gardens, I will take some of the principal features one by one, beginning, in imagination, from the house itself.

At the base of the house as seen from a little way off, the eye likes to find a cleanly defined line for the house to stand on, such as is provided by a terrace of mortared paving reflecting the light. There is no need to enlarge on its practical advantages. From the point of view of design, however, full use is not often made of the reflecting surface of the house-terrace and its steps. The terrace itself and the base of the house are often allowed to be obscured by vegetation, or by balustrades, the effect on the house being to upset its proportion and to blur its junction with the ground. In the case of a large proportion of houses this does not much matter. But if a house has any pretensions to refinement of design a clean base-line contributes greatly to its beauty. The demand for vegetation beneath the windows – it is pleasant to have sweet-smelling plants there – can be met without suffering them to obscure more than a small proportion of the base-line. In instances where a clean terrace at the base of the house is impossible, the prominent horizontal line that the eye requires can be provided by a lower terrace as at Ednaston in Derbyshire, by Sir Edwin Lutyens, where the steps and terrace form a perfect base for the house.

As to the surface and use of this flat area, there are many possibilities. As its function of providing a base for the house arises only when it is seen in sharp perspective from some distance away, there is room for considerable variety of surface treatment. Only fine classic façades need an uninterrupted base of mortared paving. On such a terrace knots of stone crops, small lead ornaments, and pots are much better away, though in front of a more picturesque house uneven paving and vegetation are very charming. Brick and stone paving, with the stone forming a simple pattern of light lines, harmonizes very well with buildings of the same materials. A device that might be used more is that of small sunk parterres, clipped level with the surface of the paving and patterned with two or three kinds of dwarf perennials with different coloured foliage, as at Port Lympne, Sir Philip Sassoon's house. see plate 11

The subject of paving may lead us on to consider paths. So long as the garden is formal in character, paved paths are desirable both for appearance and permanence. But the extreme formality of cemented paving can be dispensed with when the terrace is left, the stones being instead bedded in sand. The aim should be gradually to deformalize the paths the further they are from the house. There are many alternative sorts of paving. There are slabs set like stepping-stones in lawn; there is brick paving, better mortared than bedded in sand when grass soon establishes itself in the interstices and makes the path look untidy. Or a grass walk can be paved down the middle or along the edges. In some of Sir Edwin Lutyens' lay-outs a central strip of paving has a deep water channel in it, in which grow irises. At Hestercombe, Somerset, Lutyens has used rough slabs to form a patterned frame for turf in a great plat on which you look down from the house. Besides forming a bold pattern, the stone provides dry walking in winter, and in summer prevents the overhanging plants in the adjoining beds being bruised by passing mowing machines. The sundial has been made taller than is usual to form a bold centre to the plan, and is provided with steps to stand on.

In Italian gardens great play was made with patterned marble paving. We can do nothing so sumptuous, and indeed, have no need to. White paving stones and mown grass sunk to the level of the stones provide a beautiful substitute. Mr. Basil Ionides has made fine use of this combination at Encombe, Hythe. There is a marble well-head surrounded by alternate circles of stone and grass, with here and there a terracotta pot containing Madonna lilies. The design in green and white, with a white pergola and dark Ilexes beyond, is enchanting.

In simpler taste, millstones, tiles, and uneven pieces of stone arranged in patterns in a regular path provide those soft harmonies of tint that our grey skies beautify, but the danger always is that the effect will be spotty or fussy. The popularity of 'random' paving seems fortunately to be waning, partly no doubt owing to the ease with which anybody can now make his own paving stones with sand, gravel, and cement. Excessive overgrowth on stone paths or terraces, like crazy paving, is to be deprecated for its artful rusticity and unintelligibility. Stones *naturally* irregular, being more rounded, can be used with more success, but it is well to pass over their irregularity with mortar rather than to accentuate it. On the other hand, the crazy paths one sometimes sees laboriously pointed with mortar like a wall are surely the worst of all.

see plate 2

Steps possess decorative and suggestive capacities as important as their practical function. In the baroque age the hilly gardens of Italian villas provided scope for veritable dream stairs, dividing, circling, reuniting, twisting, perhaps among waterfalls, or even made of water only. The empirical decorative quality of steps is primarily in their alternation of horizontal bands of light and shade – shining treads and dark risers. If this is always borne in mind their actual design, and proportion of rise to tread, will follow naturally. Thus steps are much more effective when the tread distinctly overhangs the riser, throwing a band of shade. If the rise is too steep in proportion to the tread, not only will the ascent be tedious but the surfaces of the treads will be too narrow to reflect sufficient light to contrast adequately with the dark risers. Conversely, if the ascent is too gradual the feet have a tendency to trip if they go up one step at a time and to slip if they essay two or more, while the light surfaces approach equality with the dark. The dark should exceed the light area by 2 or 3 to 1. Naturally lighting and point of view are variable, but there is generally a point where the spectator tends to halt and survey the view – where the house or scene fits into his angle of vision – and from here the design should be directed.

The *slope* of steps is an important consideration. Just as equality of light and shade is to be avoided, so is an angle of ascent verging on 45°. The eye hates not seeing in a flash if a form is high or broad, a slope steep or easy. This criticism seems to me to apply to the steps at St. Catherine's Court, near Bath. This generalization affects the proportion of width to length in a flight of steps. Thus, a long flight, with great vertical height, can be narrow, accentuating the loftiness of its summit, and a short flight like that at Wilton is more impressive when broad. But when circumstances would approximately equalize width, height, and depth, threatening an architectural platitude, recourse should be had to diplomacy. Instead of the steps breasting the obstacle at right angles, they can, if it is very steep or vertical, be carried up its face sideways as was frequently done in the great Renaissance gardens and as we see at Powis Castle. There are few more satisfying forms of stairway, its disposition enabling it to be ample and dignified, ascending in a series of flights, and the tiers of steps to be seen in perspective. For the view straight up a steep stairway is as unpleasant by association as in itself, and from any other standpoint the steps are scarcely seen at all.

Another way of evading equality of height to width is to adopt for the steps a semicircular or rectangular plan, so that, seen in elevation, the flight has the beauty of a triangle or cone. Any projecting flight is made more effective if it narrows as it ascends, thus exaggerating the perspective. The old steps at Newton Ferrers in Devonshire are a delightful illustration of this point.

As to materials, so far as they affect the eye, excessive perfection of workmanship produces a hard effect, whilst excessive craziness looks affected. There is no better mean to aim at than the slightly broken, rounded regularity of old worn steps with a distinct overhang. Where slate or large rough slabs of a local stone are available, steps are ready-made. Those by Sir Edwin Lutyens at Hestercombe are an example. When brick is used, the play of light is beautiful if the bricks are laid on their edges. Bricks are particularly effective in rounded flights, for then the end of each brick is at a slightly different angle from its neighbour and a series of innumerable facets is provided for the play of light and shade as the sun moves round. Grass steps are scarcely worth the trouble that their maintenance and mowing involves.

The use of balustrades is not frequent nowadays, anyhow on a scale such as exists at Stoneleigh Abbey, Warwickshire, owing to their expense; and in any case the intervals for balusters to be set at – the secret of successful balustrading – is an architectural formula. One or two alternatives to the piers that give the appearance of strength to a balustrade may, however, be noted. At Newton Ferrers, in Devonshire, the granite balustrade has no piers, but an amusing effect is produced by setting a ball on every fourth baluster. At Nashdom, Taplow, Sir Edwin Lutyens has broken a balustrade for the insertion of square tabs. Nowadays solid parapets are in more general use than balustrades, as they are cheaper and generally as satisfactory. Open-work parapets, constructed of tiles or bricks, are on a par with sham half-timbering.

One of the charms of a parapet is the way in which it asks to have things stood on it: urns, pots, statues, or what not; as at Powis Castle, which brings us to the most obvious department of our subject.

There is no better setting for a statue than in a garden where the sculptor is freed from the necessity of being monumental, a quality that few now living embody in their work with success. It must be owned, however, that too many English sculptors have abused this opportunity for informality, with the result that there are few statues of any formal beauty at all to be obtained for garden decoration. If you walk down King's Road, the vendors of lead figures will show you scarcely anything that Cheere or Van Nost, the famous statuaries of Hyde Park Corner, would have admitted to their yards for an instant. The ornamental masons have been scarcely more successful with stone pedestals and pots in spite of the range of models available. A statue can embody in its form the most delicate associations that a garden arouses in our thoughts. A statuary, then, has surely a large enough store of association to draw upon in order to imagine sculpture suitable for garden display. Fat children are all very well, but so few of them are able nowadays to do anything besides hold festoons of flowers. There was a time when they fought together, or acted the four seasons, or played with a swan, as in the eighteenth-century lead examples. But surely we think no more instinctively, in a garden, of babies than of all those other charming creatures who once peopled the groves: centaurs and lapiths, nymphs and fauns, shepherds and shepherdesses, Diana, the Muses, or simply beautiful mortals – athletes, wrestlers, virgins – who rarely inspire our sculptors. Yet beauty of body, athletics, and grace of movement are studied more enthusiastically to-day than they have been at any time since Ancient Greece, and in America already athletics are stimulating sculptors to a renewed study of the nude in graceful poise and rapid motion.

The taste for urns has unfortunately gone out of fashion with the taste for sensibility. Yet in a gloomy walk or beneath a laurel what is more charming than a svelte stone urn? The nineteenth-century cement 'vawse' has perhaps prejudiced us against this intrinsically beautiful form.

However, terracotta oil jars and pots are perhaps more suitable to the horticulturist. The material harmonizes well with brick, and the shape is a noble one. At Folly Farm, Berkshire, Sir Edwin Lutyens has raised an oil jar on a stone plinth and allowed its pure form to be the centre of interest of a small paved garden. A less successful importation is the white marble well-head from Italy. In order not to stand out whitely from its setting it needs to be very carefully placed amid light stone surroundings and with plenty of green about it and pale flowers such as lilies, wistaria, or irises.

The formal function of sculpture is to stress a point in a design, though even in England it has sometimes been used *à l'Italienne* to form an avenue, with a background of dark evergreens. But it is most effective when used most sparingly. A sundial at the meeting of four ways, the silhouette of a graceful lead figure seen through an arch against the sky, or Cupid fluttering on a pedestal above a rose plant – thus placed, sculpture adds both point to a design and an *idea* to a picture as nothing else will do so well.

Topiary is the natural and most fertile substitute for sculptural and architectural ornament. I am inclined to think that it still has a great future before it. If architecture and with it garden design become harsher and more stylized as they are doing in Germany, Holland and France, topiary can best provide the desirable abstract forms. Long ago a kind of abstract sculpture was evolved out of topiary. We see purely geometrical forms shaped in yew in see plate 6 many an old-world setting: there are yews like giant chessmen, or like the conventional trees in a modern stylized painting. And there are yew walls, as broad as they are high, shaped into bold cubes, obelisks, pyramids, and overgrown yews like giant toadstools. They look specially well above a terrace, as at Powis Castle. An imaginative hand could shape yews into a hundred forms more interesting than the familiar peacock and more expressive of our geometrical modern art.

But as a rule topiary should be used with restraint; it provides the ideal formal background to flowers, and, if treated broadly, an admirable foreground to views of landscape or of the house. But a regiment of clipped yews dotted all over a garden produce an undesirably spotty effect, distracting the eye from the main design or the quiet beauty of the house. The famous gardens at Levens Hall, Westmorland, like a fancy-dress ball in the palace of the Sugar

Plum Fairy, are more of an historical curiosity than a model for imitation. Topiary's best use is in dividing up a lay-out into a series of secret enclosures and related parts, with broad simple masses that are always plastic with light and deep shade.

If topiary provides admirably the great dark lines in a lay-out, water will bring the sky itself into a design. Though leaping fountains are fascinating before a palace, the most moving aspect of water is in its still reflections. A large lake either does or does not exist in a place. But it is open to most people to introduce a formal pool to reflect the changing picture of the sky or the deep shadow of neighbouring trees, as do the pools at Bicton, Devonshire. Regarding a pool as an ever-changing picture, its frame should be left as plain as possible. Where there are plenty of high things for it to reflect, the basin should be brim full. In the middle of a flat space, on the other hand, where the eye is perforce at much the same level, it needs more architectural or horticultural treatment, either with sculpture, balustrades, or water-loving plants. The mixture of plants and architectural forms in a pool needs careful thought. When the pool is wild, vegetation can ramp as much as it will. But if it is architectural there is a danger that water-lilies, irises, and too many pots on the brim will produce a busy or straggly effect. The brim should in such instances be left clean and decisive, and where vegetation is to predominate, it should be made to do so in a mass of bloom.

see colour plate II

Though we have become unjustifiably estranged from dolphins and dryads, preferring to unite water with flowers rather than with architecture, there is no denying that a fine active fountain, well maintained, and not so infrequently played that its antics are viewed with the solemnity due to a rare ceremony, is a source of delight. The brilliant contrast of dancing refracting jets against trees or shaded buildings gives the eye that stimulus which is at the root of impressionist painting. A single solitary jet in some suitable setting, for choice where there is a dark background, has the beauty of some miraculous flower; or seen against a soft far-spreading landscape, as at Port Lympne, designed by Mr. Philip Tilden, a fountain dancing like a sylph upon a floor of glass. The home of fountains is in the old Italian gardens. On the slopes of the Alban and Sabine hills water is in abundance, pressure to be had for the tapping, and the hanging hillsides form a perfect, because explanatory, background for fountains. Whatever be the shape, a fountain is most satisfactory, because least far-fetched, when the source of pressure is apparent. Both for this

see plate 11

reason and for the impressionist value of the contrast a fountain *below* a terrace or hill is more beautiful, though less amazing, than a fanfare of water spurting in a plain.

But most people are satisfied with the murmur and lazy splash of a quite small fountain or dripping well – 'one that spouteth rather than sprinkleth into a fair receptacle', to use Bacon's words. If a babbling fountain is near the house its sound is all the more grateful; and more so if it can be seen from within, when, with the variations of light and shade through the day, it provides a lively and changing ornament. A very popular form of fount is that derived from the natural dripping well, consisting of a circular pool half vaulted over; and a spouting mask. On the vault the reflections play like luminous airy fish, and against its shade the jet of water falls in a diamond bow. There is plenty of scope for sculpture in the invention of spouting masks, and our sculptors have taken advantage of it. If a statue is placed in the centre of a pool it is important that it should be sufficiently dominant, not so much of the pool as of its surroundings. The new Mercury in Tom Quad at Christ Church, Oxford, is large enough for the pool but not for the Quad. In so large and imposing a space something like the great Jacobean fountain at Trinity, Cambridge, is needed.

The last form of ornament that I allude to is pergolas and treillage. It is at first sight strange that the pergola, for long in use in Italy, has been adopted here only so recently. The reason was partly, no doubt, the comparative lack of suitable flowering climbers. Wistaria, for instance, was not introduced till 1818 and rambler roses did not become popular till the middle of last century. A permanent structure, especially as to the piers, is highly desirable. Whether they are to be marble pillars, or of brick or stone, or, as so often in Italy, of roughly plastered rubble, must be decided by the nature of the garden. In association with a paved path and green plants, marble is, of course, the most beautiful material. But rough stone is generally more suitable to England. At Hestercombe, Sir Edwin Lutyens has used the local stone which is obtained in small thin slabs, and alternated round and square piers to obtain variety of light and shade. The pairs of piers should be tied across the path with a stout beam slightly arched. The upward curve, however slight, has a satisfying appearance and is, in fact, a source of strength. If the pergola is for roses, it is better not to have it continuous, but as a succession of piers and transverse beams only, so that the roses have the benefit of light and air all round.

If pergolas are a recent introduction, treillaged walks are one of the oldest forms of ornament. A reproduction of the Jacobean form is to be seen at Easton Lodge, Essex. But trellis work has not often been used to the extent it was during the Versailles period abroad. There its chief function was, in the shape of walls, arches, and arcades, to conceal the 'unsightly' trunks of the trees that composed the groves and bosquets. To these it gave the necessary formality.

see plate 13

Nowadays it is perfectly adapted to the formation of out-of-door dining and sitting rooms, and for the adornment of unsightly walls in town plots. A word may perhaps be said for the iron or wood trellises so often found supporting the curved sheet-iron roofs of early eighteenth-century verandahs. Not only are these verandahs charming in themselves, but a little trellis suits them well. Many modern houses approximate to the simplicity of those 'villas' and could be suitably adorned in the same way.

11   PORT LYMPNE, KENT. 1925

Philip Sassoon's extraordinary bathing pool overlooking Romney Marsh is
flanked by pleached alleys of clipped Cornish elm and hedges.

George Carter
SCULPTURE IN THE GARDEN

George Carter (1948–) who trained as a sculptor, is a practising landscape architect and art historian. His achievements include an exhibition: 'Humphry Repton: Landscape Gardener' and a formal garden design exhibited at the Chelsea Flower Show in 1985.

The range of sculptural ornament suitable for the small garden is at present limited. Cast stone or fake bronze and lead reproductions after mainly eighteenth- and nineteenth-century models are commonly available and of middling price, but are often poorly cast after inferior originals in unsympathetic materials. At the cheap end of the spectrum are unpretentious, almost 'folk art' productions; perhaps very crude travesties of classical urns or the ubiquitous gnome. These are bound before long to acquire the charm that Staffordshire fairings now have, but are at present largely unacceptable. At the other extreme antique statuary and ornament or unique works of art by living artists often, unfortunately, cost more than garden owners are willing to spend.

Stimulated partly by Sir Roy Strong's interest in the subject, several moves have recently been made to improve the range of reasonably priced, mass-produced garden sculpture and ornament. In a competition organised by the Merseyside Development Corporation and *The Sunday Times*, artists and designers were asked for proposals, some of which have gone into production and were on show at the Liverpool Garden Festival (1984). One or two manufacturers of cast stone, who have hitherto specialised in reproductions, have commissioned artists to augment their range with new work. A recent exhibition organised by the Oxford Gallery, *A New View in the Garden* showed forty-two new pieces of garden sculpture and furniture.

It is not primarily the purpose of this article, however, to make selections from what is currently available, but to suggest ways in which sculpture and ornament might be used in gardens of differing types.

Formal gardens are presently enjoying a revival in favour, and I shall start with a few remarks relevant to them. It is a common misconception that the formal architectural garden typified by Le Nôtre in France and Bridgeman in England is only suited to the grand scale. Small formal gardens can, in fact, be highly successful and are particularly appropriate in towns or where low maintenance is desired. Sculpture here can take on a prime role. The first prerequisite is an efficient method of enclosure to exclude incompatible surroundings. Walls, hedges and treillage covered fences, with or without climbing plants, form the sort of plain background that makes an excellent foil for elaborate sculpture. Here one may indulge in flight of fancy that might be excessive in the luxuriant vegetation of a plantsman's garden.

A grotto framing a stone and mirror glass sculpture by Raf Fulcher actually terminates the main axis of a sunny country garden, but could work equally well in a shady town one where it would make a virtue out of shadow. An important function of sculpture is to set the mood of a part, or indeed the whole garden. Gloom and dankness, for instance, take on their own charm when associated with a grotto, though the mood can be lightened by the animating glitter of spas, mirror glass or running water.

Shiny or glittery materials are not nowadays much favoured for gardens, though Francis Bacon in 1625 recommended 'broad plates of round, coloured glass gilt' for hanging in arbour hedges. In the 1930s there was a brief revival of the use of mirror glass in the garden: Charles Moreux, for instance, used a silver sphere as a finial to a column forming the focal point of a garden. Robust interior silvered glass spheres were used in two schemes at the Liverpool Festival, and in fact look very well in a variety of garden settings. I imagine a pair about a foot in diameter used to great advantage at ground level flanking an opening in a yew hedge giving onto a plain square lawn.

There are essentially two categories of material suitable for garden sculpture. One group, marble, glass, gilded and painted surfaces, resists weathering and patination but has the virtue of reflecting light and always forms a lively contrast against plant material. More conventionally chosen are stone, concrete, bronze, copper, lead, terracotta and unpainted wood. These are tough materials that can weather well, tone down and take on a new and changing interest with patination.

It is important to consider colour and to exploit the effect of patination. Various beautiful shades of green can be chemically and permanently induced on copper and bronze, an effect which bronze filled resins cannot copy. Patinated copper in its various hues looks well against dark foliage or the bright green of grass. Surprisingly vivid shades of apple green and turquoise can have a fine effect in a shady situation. The mottled surface of a patina considerably increases the interest of plain surfaces. At the Oxford Gallery exhibition, William Pye showed a copper foundation small enough to be moved about, which rested on the terraced balustrade of a Harold Peto garden near Oxford where it made an effective screen through which to view the garden.

Garden sculpture need not be thought of solely in terms of the single object in the round. A pierced screen perhaps linking visually two separate parts of the garden offers delightful possibilities. Similarly an extended structure, perhaps physically linked by rails in a similar vein to the decorative Tudor post and rails shown in the famous painting of the Hampton Court garden, could be used to articulate the space of the garden, forming its underlying bone structure in place of hedges or edgings.

Plaques and bas-reliefs too are a useful element, particularly in small gardens where no great distances render them indistinct. They can emphasise axes or create focal points in informal layouts. They need not necessarily be fixed to walls or associated with architecture. For example a lead plate engraved with a simple grid can be attached to a wooden post or stela; though very simple, it forms a compelling termination to a gravel walk. Lead, of course, patinates well to the familiar whitish grey which looks well in a strongly lit position. It harmonises well with grey and silver foliage. Bas-reliefs in all materials should be placed in a sunny position to maximise their effect.

A painted and patinated copper sheet depicting the night sky, though not at all in relief fulfils a similar function in my own garden. In the British climate it makes a weatherproof alternative to fresco painting.

see colour plate III

How might one go about choosing a theme or subject for sculpture? Today we lack any system of selection or code which could help in this respect. In the eighteenth century and earlier, garden makers were aided by a constant reference to classical mythology and its method of personifying the various elements of nature. Thus Batty Langley in his *New Principles of Gardening* (London, 1728) was able to suggest statuary suitable for various situations in the garden: Neptune for ponds, Pomona for orchards, etc. These references gave an added dimension to the garden which generally we now lack.

This brings one to the idea of the garden forming a kind of narrative composed of various incidents; buildings, statuary, inscriptions, linked by paths and a specific route or tour. Such a scheme need not be confined to places on the scale of Stourhead or Rousham. Nor need architecture and figurative statuary necessarily be used, or an elaborate and recondite passage from classical mythology attempted, though this might still have its charm.

I can visualise delightful schemes based on the eighteenth-century idea of consulting 'the genius of the place'; that is determining the essential or underlying character of the site one is dealing with, and adopting a scheme whose whole point is to intensify it. Here again we return to the idea of mood in the garden. Even the smallest town plot has a character peculiar to itself; one has only to decide what it is.

A simple method to carry out this sort of scheme might be to devise a series of inscriptions on stone blocks placed at various strategic points in the garden. Short texts in a simple serif typeface engraved on vertical blocks, or slabs placed horizontally on the ground could, at moderate expense, be executed by a monumental mason. The poet and artist Ian Hamilton Finlay has arranged several such tablets in his garden at Stonypath, in Lanarkshire and else-where. Often both witty and lyrical they are always pertinent to their situation.

One way to stimulate the imagination might be to research the history of a few of one's favourite plants in the garden, and to formulate texts relevant to them which would be placed near the plant.

I have in mind another range of subject matter not culled from the classical repertoire, but similarly conjuring up charmingly bucolic scenes. It is sug-gested again by Batty Langley who used tokens redolent of the British country-side and farming within the elaborate formal framework of his gardens. It represents an interesting transitional stage in the change from the formal to landscape styles. He incorporated actual tiny 'Inclosures of Corn, Grass, Clover etc.', miniature 'Paddocks of Sheep, Deer, Cows', and those rural objects, 'Haystacks and Wood Piles', all within a rigid complex of circular, polygonal and square hedged areas. My idea is to have such objects treated sculpturally in a simplified and straightforward manner, perhaps in cast stone, disposed about the garden in a rather formal manner, possibly in pairs and on simple block plinths. Sheaves of corn, haystacks, symmetrical wood piles, baskets of fruit, trophies of garden tools, sheep, pigs and bee skeps, are the sorts of object that might be treated in this way with good effect.

A wooden cut-out of a sheaf of corn on a plinth, cheap and easy to construct, was a variation on this theme, and effective at a distance against a simple background. Wooden cutouts, sham bridges, figures or urns – though despised by some, were popular in the eighteenth century, when instant if ephemeral effects were more common in gardens than is often supposed. Charmingly gimcrack structures in painted plaster, timber and canvas occur in contemporary accounts and in the rococo landscapes painted by Thomas Robins. Such objects have, of course, long since disappeared. Wooden cut-outs can provide a useful way of testing out ideas destined for more durable materials, as well as forming cheap if short-lived objects in their own right.

These sorts of object might need a certain amount of clear space adjacent to them though they need not be entirely isolated on an open lawn. They could look well placed, for instance, at the front of a border, surrounded on three sides by planting which should not be too diverse in tone or of very mixed habit.

The kind of garden that is very unstructured with luxuriant foliage and chance effects can benefit greatly from a particular sort of minimal geometric sculpture. The often quoted reason for the success of the Sissinghurst Garden or the Lutyens/Jekyll partnership is a product of the same sort of interplay between rampant, flamboyant growth against the geometric structure of walls, paths and hedges.

see plate 39

Hard edged, sharply defined forms represent the antithesis of wild nature and therefore give the eye and the intellect a point of reference. Without this polarity a free-form type of garden can seem formless and meaningless.

A single white concrete block of slim vertical form perhaps 4 or 5 feet high placed in a prominent position rising out of foliage might provide the required contrast in a small garden. It need not be placed axially but should be positioned to balance the forms of foliage or ground contour.

If a pristine white marble-like surface is desired, a mix using a white cement, white marble chippings and silver sand is used, cast from a mould lined with a shiny plastic laminate. If a weathered appearance, which might look equally well, is desired, a cast stone with a more pitted surface can be encouraged to patinate more quickly. Moss and mould grow best if the object is placed under the drip of trees or at least in shade. A spray of liquid manure speeds up the process. If one lives in an unpolluted atmosphere, lichens, though very slow, can be encouraged by gluing pieces from a similar substrate onto the object.

A more ambitious variant on the same theme of simple geometric shapes was shown at the Liverpool Garden Festival. Cast stone cubes, spheres, cones and pyramids can be assembled to form composite units or used individually. They are inspired by the precisely clipped topiary of late-seventeenth- and early eighteenth-century formal gardens. Trees and shrubs so clipped represented an ideal of perfectly formed nature. The gardens they inhabited seem pure sculpture, perhaps pure architecture. The plants, walls, grass, gravel and water articulate and compose outdoor space into a series of volumes and voids in harmonious relationship to one another. The notion that they also represent an ideal state of nature is not, to today's eye, apparent.

I visualise these geometric shapes used in a variety of ways. In a simple formal layout of grass, gravel, wall, fence or hedge they might be used as points of emphasis in the design. Four pyramids might mark the corners of a lawn or two composite units flank a gateway or mark the start and finish of paths. Even in the most informal setting paths and routes round the garden need an object or goal; an important role for sculpture. It need not be fully visible from every viewpoint, and in fact considerable interest can be generated from the notion of expectation and surprise. From various points it may be now hidden, now glimpsed, now fully seen. This can be devised in the smallest garden by judicious planting.

In a less formal plantsman's garden Stone Topiary might fulfil the 'contrast' role previously described, or in symmetrical groups of two or four, provide an underlying framework round which the planting is organised. Alternatively, two tall units might form a foreground frame through which an informal garden is viewed from the house; an idea propounded by the landscape gardener Humphry Repton who conceived of the view of the garden from the house in pictorial terms, requiring a foreground, middle ground and distance.

I have not so far dwelt on figurative sculpture, partly for the reason that, despite a recent resurgence of figuration in art, not much that appeals has come to my notice. The stone carver Simon Verity has, however, made a series of garden figures some of which can be seen at Barnsley House in Gloucester-shire. Inventive figures for a grotto were shown by him at the recent Oxford Gallery exhibition, along with a grotesque fountain mask incorporating plant-ing in the fissures of the face which heighten its effect.

Elizabeth Tate had a pair of chastely Neo-classical stone term figures, inspired by antique prototypes, on show at Liverpool. The boldly simplified heads have bronze and lead detail. They are of a scale suitable for a small garden, and though at Liverpool were dramatically silhouetted against the sky, they might be placed to equal advantage in niches cut out of a hedge or against an ivy-clad wall.

I have not attempted so far to highlight the distinction, which I have only hinted at, between a self-contained piece of sculpture which stands on its own as an entity regardless of its setting, and the idea of the garden space itself as a sculptural concept, made up of a variety of elements, hard and soft, which might be individually bland, but which grouped together can contain the same spatial excitement and harmonious relationship of volumes as an individual piece. Indeed I would argue that the latter process, though it offers the greater challenge, offers more scope and interest to the plantsman. It is however, a complicated manoeuvre to orchestrate all the various elements in the garden to a controlled whole. We have been urged by various writers to consider garden composition in painterly terms, but ought not to neglect the sculptural approach.

CHAPTER III

The Town Garden

J. C. Loudon
A MODEST VILLA GARDEN

When planting the front garden the boundary fences may be planted with gold and silver-leaved ivy, intermixed with a little common ivy; and the boundary fences of the back garden may be wholly planted with either the common or the giant ivy, or with a mixture of both. In the centre of the lawn, in the front garden, may be planted a laurestinus, an arbutus, a phillyrea, an aucuba, a double-blossomed furze, *Cotoneaster Uva ursi*[1], a common or variegated box, an evergreen rhododendron, or some other compact growing hardy evergreen shrub; or a deciduous flowering shrub may be substituted for an evergreen tree, if there should be chiefly evergreens in the adjoining gardens. Among the beautiful deciduous shrubs of moderate growth which require little or no pruning and management, may be mentioned the *Cydonia japonica*[2] (either the pale or the deep red-flowered variety, or a plant of each put into one hole), the

John Claudius Loudon (1783–1843) did much to encourage amateur gardening and to advocate the imaginative planting of London squares and parks. He launched The Gardener's Magazine, the first popular journal, in 1826.

[1] *Cotoneaster distichus*   [2] *Chaenomeles japonica*

Persian lilac, and the *Ribes sanguíneum*. Of all these plants the two most suitable are the laurestinus and the *Cydonia japonica*[1], because neither require any pruning, and both flower in the winter season. As these plants, however, from their beauty, cheapness, and easy culture, may possibly be common in the adjoining gardens, if expense should not be an object, one of the evergreen berberries or mahonias, such as *Berberis dealbata* or *Mahonia Aquifolium*, or *Garrya elliptica* (a valuable winter shrub), may be selected as the evergreen; or, if a deciduous shrub be preferred, *Spiraea ariaefolia*[2], or *S. bella*, or some other species of that genus, or a yellow azalea, may be substituted. These comparatively rare evergreen and deciduous shrubs are as hardy as the others; and, like them, require no pruning whatever, further than cutting off dead wood or dead flowers. But if all the adjoining front gardens are planted with the more rare and beautiful foreign trees and shrubs, and the occupier should have the laudable desire of increasing the general variety in the street, he may step from the garden into the fields, and place in the centre of his grass plot, for an evergreen, the common spurge laurel, or the double-blossomed furze; and for a deciduous shrub (if he should prefer one), the spindle tree, or any dwarf British willow, may be made choice of. Should even these be already introduced, he may have recourse to the pine and fir tribe, and take one of the dwarf varieties of the common spruce, such as *Abies excelsa Clanbrasiliana*[3], or a dwarf pine, such as *Pinus sylvestris pumilio*, or *P. s. Mughus*[4].

In the back garden, we would merely introduce a few standard low flowering trees, or fruit trees, placing them along the centre of the lawn, that they may not interfere with the walks, along the lawn side of which clotheslines will probably occasionally be placed. The tree nearest the house should be a double-blossomed hawthorn, because it comes sooner into leaf than any other low tree, and the flowers being double, are not succeeded by fruit, so that the tree is in no year so exhausted but that it can flower abundantly the year following; whereas a single-blossomed thorn, or tree of any kind in which the flowers are succeeded by a large crop of fruit, seldom blossoms well two years in succession. Such trees, therefore, should never be chosen for points of view where it is wished to have a fine show of blossoms every year; but rather trees which, like the above-mentioned variety of thorn, bear double blossoms. The next tree may either be a *Pyrus spectabilis*, or transparent or Siberian crab, or

---

[1] *Chaenomeles japonica*   [2] *Holodiscus discolor*
[3] *Picea abies* 'Clanbrassiliana'   [4] *Pinus nigra* 'Pygmaea' and *Pinus mugo*

some description of apple which has showy blossoms and bears abundantly, such as the Hawthornden. The third tree may be a perfumed cherry, standard all-saints' cherry, double-blossomed cherry, an almond, or a *Cotoneaster frigida*, *C. affinis*, or some similar tree. The next tree may be a mulberry, which thrives and bears abundantly in the very heart of London, and which should always be planted on grass; because, as the fruit drops the moment it is ripe, it can be picked up clean for use, which it cannot if it falls on dug ground or gravel. The two succeeding trees may be a laburnum and a scarlet thorn; or, if the occupier prefers fruit trees, they may be two pears, say a glout morceau, and a Marie Louise, or a beurré de Capiaumont; or they may be two plums, or cherries: or, if he prefers evergreen trees, they may be two variegated hollies. We recommend the variegated holly, because it is one of the most cheerful of evergreens, and is in no danger of growing out of bounds, so as to require pruning. Next to it, for the climate of London, the cedar of Goa may be planted; but, as the cedar of Goa is somewhat tender, perhaps a preferable plant for a smoky situation would be the *Quercus Ilex*, of which the willow-leaved and beech-leaved varieties may be selected; or, for colder climates, the common red cedar. We have here recommended only one line of trees down the centre of the lawn, because they will there have abundance of room: they will not require pruning for many years, and their leaves will drop on the grass, and not litter the walks. When low-growing trees are planted near the walks, their branches hang over them; and every year those which inconvenience persons passing along the walks require to be cut off, or tied up, and this would occasion expense in keeping, which it is one of the desiderata in this mode of laying out and planting to avoid as much as possible. For this reason no tree or shrub is directed to be planted against the house, because that would be to incur the expense of training and pruning. The trees should be procured of 6 feet or 8 feet in height, so that their tops may be, when planted, out of the reach of injury from children; and the grass may either be sown, or turf may be procured and laid down. The latter produces the more immediate effect, though it is by much the more expensive, and, in the end, the turf is inferior, from its usually containing a mixture of unsuitable grasses and broad leaved plants. The grass seeds will produce a close verdant surface in about three months, and, in a year, a much finer lawn than turf brought from common pasture, or meadow, or an old grass field. The flagstones or slates should be laid on brick piers, built on a solid foundation; so that their surface may be at all times level and even at the joints, for walking on. The surface of paved walks, like that of all others, as far as it is practicable, should be rather higher than the adjoining surface: otherwise, in heavy rains, they become receptacles for water which, being often muddy, disfigures the stones, the pavement, or the gravel. If the shrub planted in the centre of the front garden be one of the more rare kinds, the natural loam, which we have supposed to be the soil in both gardens, may require to be mixed with a little sand, peat earth, or vegetable mould, to lighten and enrich it.

In planting a garden of this kind in a situation exposed to the smoke, care should be taken to use only those kinds of trees and shrubs which will thrive in close situations, as there are some kinds of shrubs and trees which experience proves will thrive even in the midst of smoke. Thus, for the plot in front, we should recommend *Aucuba japonica* as an evergreen, because this remarkable plant, though a native of Japan, endures the smoke of London better than any indigenous evergreen shrub whatever; and, as a deciduous shrub, the common purple lilac, which is both hardy and beautiful, and comes early into leaf. The trees in the back garden might be the double-blossomed and scarlet thorns, both of which will grow and look well for at least eight or ten years; the laburnum, the almond, the mulberry (which thrives admirably in the most smoky places), and the weeping or allsaints' cherry (which is one of the few flowering trees that prosper in the gardens of Lambeth Palace, though enveloped in the smoke of numerous houses and manufactories). Ivy, whether common, giant, or variegated, will thrive in the very heart of London. Grass will not live, and look well, in smoky situations, for any length of time; but, if the *Poa annua* be used, it will ripen its seeds and sow itself every year; and it has this advantage, that during winter it is greener than any other grass that will grow in a town. Should it fail in any part, and leave bare patches, seeds may be procured from the seed shops, and, being sown at any season, will come up in a few days.

To lay out and plant a larger garden of the same kind, and for the attainment of the same objects, all the difference would be that, instead of one shrub in the front garden, there should be several; and, instead of one row of trees in the back garden, there should be two, or perhaps three; or, what would be much better, that the trees should be planted in quincunx, so as to give the appearance of breadth to the centre of the lawn, and to make the garden seem much larger than it really is. The walks would still be laid with flagstones, or some description of pavement; the walls would be planted with ivy; and the house would still be left without a vine, a fig, or a rose, trained against it. For a suburban street residence, the house and front and back gardens of which

86

occupy a space 60 feet in width, by 200 feet in length, the entrance walk passes through the centre of the front garden, on each side of which there is a grass plot, with a large shrub in the centre, and smaller ones at each angle. There is a servants' entrance at one side, and a sunk area, both before and behind; that in front being narrow, and serving merely to keep the walls dry, while that behind is broad, and contains a larder, bottle-rack, and similar conveniences required for a house of the second rate. The back garden is planted with four rows of low trees, two near each walk, in quincunx, leaving a broad space in the middle, about 100 feet in length, well adapted for a party walking backwards and forwards on in the summer season, for a dance, or for placing a tent on, for sitting under, at the farther end. A garden of this kind might be laid out and planted for £30 or £40; and kept perfectly neat for 30s. or 40s. a year.

12   CAMERA SQUARE, CHELSEA, LONDON. 1910

In the front gardens of these modest town houses, shrubs and cutting flowers have been planted in rows or have been evenly distributed over the whole area, much in the style recommended by the influential J. C. Loudon.

Donald Beaton

THE SOCIETY'S GARDEN
AT KENSINGTON GORE

*Donald Beaton
(1802–1863) was an
outstanding gardener and
frequent contributor to
the gardening press. He
spent many years
developing his garden at
Haffield House,
Herefordshire, and later
moved to Kingsbury
where he concentrated his
interests on
hybridization.*

Out in the garden the works have progressed much more rapidly than any one accustomed to such things could expect, seeing the torrents and the pourings of last summer, and the Greenland of this winter. The large coloured engraving of the plan of the garden, which was distributed to the Fellows of the Society, gives but a very faint idea of the beauty of the place. But it is so entirely a terrace garden, and so jealously excludes the faintest idea of any other style, that hundreds had been led by the engraving to doubt of the telling effect of the beauty of the garden on the public mind. But when you come to see the idea of the artist realised, and put into shape and order before you, flight by flight as you go up from the side entrance, or come down from the conservatory, which is on the highest part of the slope, you must have a queer notion of terrace gardens if you will not be highly delighted with the whole thing. I never went near it from our anniversary of last May, when the first turf was only just lifted, to this day (Shrove Tuesday), and the first thing I did was to step over every foot of the paths without any one with me; so that I could judge for myself, without any influence for or against all or any part of the whole; that was before the sun was on the meridian of its course, which is very near the meridian of this terrace garden; I went over it again in the afternoon with a good light from the sun coming sideways, and I think I am not deceived in the opinion that the new garden at Kensington Gore[1] will be the nearest step to the perfection of that style that we have in England; but it is a fleabite as compared with the grounds of the Crystal Palace and those of Kew. It is just a town garden in the first style of the art; and so it ought, seeing the mere finishings and furnishing will cost over £5000 the acre. There cannot be 20 acres in, or within, the arcades, which is strictly the terrace garden, but say 20 acres over which the ground

---

[1] The Royal Horticultural Society moved here in 1861. All that remains of the garden, which covered the area between the Albert Hall and the Natural History Museum, is a statue of Prince Albert.

landlords are to spend £50,000 and the tenant just as much, and if the thing, or any part of it should turn out otherwise than as it ought, it could not be excused on the plea of want of money. I never strove to temperate my feelings when I saw things in my own way going awry; and I think that is the only reason I can lean to for the enjoyment – the real downright pleasure I can feel in a thing with which I have no earthly concern, when it comes up to what I have been taught to call the 'real thing'.

Now, although our town garden is yet in the rough, I felt a good deal of the pleasure of hope when viewing it by myself, and more so on seeing this hope is not likely to be long deferred. They are pushing on vigorously, the heavy planting is all but finished – I mean all the large trees for the dark groups on the plan. The slopes and flats for the different flights of the terrace are set out, and could soon be finished for turfing. All the main walks are as far forward as the rough gravelling of them; and all the Box compartments are finished, planted, and partly set off. This setting off was the only thing in the plan on which I had my own doubts. It consists of small spaces as for flower-beds, coming in between the lines of a free-flowing tracery in Box, and they (these spaces) are to be filled with a diversity of coloured gravels, so to speak. A few of these compartments are already filled, or covered in with the, or rather with only two, colours – a grey slaty blue, as the colour of ice at a distance, and a pure white. Well, hitherto – for it is of no use to disguise facts – my eye has only been tutored to pure white, and to two or three shades of red, in Box-work decoration, on the fly-fancy style of composition – that is, pure white Reigate sand, or sand like it in colour, such as that which Mr. Taylor, at Shrubland Park, uses to plunge his pots in, and the different colours of the gravel used in our walks – say four shades of red and pure white; and I had my doubts about the effect of introducing tints of colours in gravels along with tints of colours in real flowers.

The lines of dwarf Box in these Box tracings are most beautifully designed, and will be perfectly new to a great number of the Fellows of the Royal Horticultural Society, and cannot fail to become the sampler patterns for imitations in this style of terrace gardens; and the coloured grit or gravel that will be employed to fill in the designs cannot fail to lay a more sure foundation for the better arrangements of the tints of flowers than we have yet had access to; and thus the very thing which I at first dreaded would lead to namby pambyism in flower gardening, will be a sure and certain source for the more extension of the natural tints of flowers, and a more extended use of different sized beds in the designers of flower-bed's compositions, in order to embrace a larger assortment of different shades of colours from flowers. A new field will be thus opened for the cross-breeders of popular flowers for decoration, and any tint, and every shade of colour will find a patch or bed, and the proper place for it in composition planting.

The mauve and light lilac tints which were so fashionable in 1859 have given way already, and all the shades of the newer magenta colour are fast taking their places. New shades of Verbenas, and of the Nosegay breed of Geraniums will soon make this magenta colour as fashionable in the flower gardens as it is already in the tops and bottoms of Parisian fashion; and he who can best keep pace with the magazines of fashion with his new seedlings, may least fear the schedules of the income tax. Every seedling that will tell on the fashion of the day will be sure to pay, and anything that will pay its cost is as sure to tell; and were it not on such terms alone, let alone the call for high artistic designing, I should hail the flowing lines of Mr. Nesfield, at Kensington Gore, as the best auxiliaries to what I have myself been aiming at in my doings and sayings for the last twenty years; and I congratulate the Fellows of the Royal Horticultural Society on the charms and excellencies of their town garden as they are already manifested in the rough, and look forward with great interest to the day on which Her Gracious Majesty will open it in person for us and ours, and the like of us, or all who like to see a first-class town garden kept in first-rate order by first-class gardeners, for I should like all to see it; and if the public could see it, on certain days, by paying a small sum for a great sight, as was once in contemplation, what with the Queen herself and the Royal Family at the head of it, and the novelty of the thing so near to the richest and most fashionable parts of London, there could be little fear about those thousands of pounds having been cast in a sinking fund. The thing must surely pay and be a credit to all concerned.

Thomas Hay
GARDENING IN LONDON

'What can I grow in my London garden?' is a question familiar to every London park official, and the easiest of all answers is to 'Keep an eye on the parks'; and when this advice is tendered you are at once informed that the parks have great facilities, unlimited finances, and resources far beyond the ordinary garden owner, which is only partly true.

In trying to answer the question it seems advisable to lay down some general rules before we descend to particulars. Your ambitions may lead you into a desire for trees few or many, and here many London garden owners go astray in that they plant species of trees that may be termed of the forest variety, which in time get too large for the ordinary garden; this mistake was so common in the past that it provides a great deal of work annually for tree loppers and pruners, the result being that all over our city we see trees in the wrong place, or rather the wrong tree in what might be a fine station for a suitable tree, one that might be a joy to the owner instead of a worry, and an asset to the city instead of an eyesore.

Far more use ought to be made of flowering trees, particularly where the space for development is limited. What is there in nature to excel in beauty a Cherry tree in full flower? This vision has captivated a whole nation, who look on the time of Cherry blossom as a sacred festival. It may interest you to know that London is at last going to have a Cherry avenue of its own; this gift, of which more will be heard later, is to be made immediately in one of the Royal Parks.

In addition to the Cherries there are the *Prunus* and *Pyrus* in many species and varieties, all of which are good Londoners. Then there are Laburnums, Magnolias, Thorns, Robinias, and many others, all much more suitable for a garden than the giant Plane, Elm, or Beech.

Dealing with shrubs that can be grown in London, your greatest trouble will be in making a selection. I have a preference for all those that are deciduous – that is, those that shed all their leaves in autumn and break forth in spring fresh, green, and joyous to look upon. Unless you wish to screen or hide some

Thomas Hay VMH (1874–1953), whose own garden was near Haslemere, was superintendent of the Royal Central Parks and thus had considerable first-hand experience of gardening in towns.

91

ugly object, I am tempted to advocate the avoidance of evergreen shrubs of all sorts. Many of them under city conditions are in a continual state of dirt and filth, and unless they can be frequently treated to a heavy watering and washing with the hose-pipe they have little attraction to offer at any period of the year[1].

There are now very many deciduous species to select from, many of them providing you with fine foliage, highly coloured fruits, and lovely flowers. Many of the deciduous Barberries make fine town plants, and there is a wealth of variety and charm among such genera as *Philadelphus*, *Syringa*, *Spiraea*, *Diervilla*, *Dipelta*, and *Viburnum*.

I ought also to say that many flowering trees such as the Cherries, Prunus, and Laburnums can be pruned and kept small in size and yet retain their free-flowering character, and are most suitable for small gardens.

A visit, or rather series of visits, to the London parks (it matters not what area of London you choose) will show you that park superintendents have not been unmindful of the wealth of material now available, and you will find everywhere much to interest you and guide you in the choice of shrubs.

We have discussed trees and shrubs, and now we have arrived at the flower garden, which is perhaps the department that will interest you most. We will generalize first, and it is quite safe to say that when we content ourselves with hardy plants that go completely underground during the winter, our success is most certain.

Under this heading may be grouped nearly all that is best and most decorative in hardy plants. I mention only a few – Delphiniums, Lupins, Pyrethrums, Paeonies, Helianthus, Anchusas, Asters, Rudbeckias, many species of *Campanula*, and a host of other strictly herbaceous plants. Given fair attention, rich loam and plenty of water, all those mentioned, and many more, do well in London. You find them in most gardens and in all our parks.

Our troubles begin with those that retain their foliage through the winter, and among them there are always heavy losses. Plants such as Agrostemmas, many species of *Salvia*, Oenotheras, Kniphofias, Penstemons, are all very difficult, and it is almost impossible to winter these in the heart of the city. That is why we never see such treasures as groups of the Meconopsis that retain their foliage during the winter.

---

[1] The problems of atmospheric pollution in towns, if not solved, have been much improved by The Clean Air Act 1956, which has made London a 'smokeless zone'.

The London gardener who wishes to excel in such things can only hope for success by having his plants brought to his garden in spring, and content himself with the more moderate success that always attends such plants when moved in spring.

Broadly speaking, the alpine enthusiast also will do well to comply with these rules. He has a host of plants to select from that go underground during the winter, and which will give him good results, but if his ambitions soar to encrusted Saxifrages, Ramondias, Haberleas, choice Sedums and Sempervivums, his troubles will be many.

An enthusiastic rock gardener with a garden near Regent's Park purchased one of the rock gardens at a Chelsea flower show and had it reconstructed and planted with all that is best in alpine plants; the first winter played such havoc that he described the losses in a sentence to the effect "I have nothing left but a basketful of Acme labels." A little advice might have saved a great deal of disappointment.

There is nothing to stop the city alpine plant enthusiast from indulging in his favourite hobby, if he will select his plants carefully and, as far as his enthusiastic spirit will permit, content himself with the wide variety available that will do well in London.

London is still, however, without a really fine rock garden until Kew is reached, and there the conditions, imperfect as they may be, are much better than in the city. I am still looking for a philanthropist who will gift and endow London with a fine rock garden. He can, I feel sure, have the choice of many sites, and such a garden, if skilfully planted and properly maintained, would not only be a great attraction to the town dweller but would be of great educational value.

The bulb grower – and he is numbered in London by the thousand – is perhaps the most successful of all those who garden in London. Bulbous plants of many sorts thrive in our city. Safely tucked away underground in late autumn, they know not the odour of fog, smoke, petrol, or soot; safe from all these, they appear above ground into a world from which winter has disappeared, and respond to our care just as well as if they had been planted in the most beautiful of country gardens.

London-grown Daffodils, Tulips, Crocuses, and Hyacinths leave nothing to grumble about, and give unbounded pleasure in every borough of the capital. It is true that all bulbs do not succeed equally well. Daffodils naturalized in grass succeed only for a few years. Snowdrops make no increase, neither do Scillas, Chionodoxa, nor Aconites, while the Crocus flourishes. There are patches of Crocus in Hyde Park planted fifty years ago, and still growing vigorously and multiplying annually.

The vast majority of London gardeners, however, do not specialize; what they want is a gay garden from spring to autumn, and bulbous plants open the year as nothing else can do. In our parks all over London they come to remind us that the winter is past, spring has come, and the time of the singing of birds.

There are also many spring flowers that can be associated with bulbs. You have all seen the fine effect of the association of bulbous plants with Wallflowers, Myosotis, Polyanthus, Aubrietas, Silene, and other simple spring flowers.

Fortunate is the London park superintendent or garden owner who can bring his spring-flowering plants for his London park or garden from a nursery or garden out of London; he is able to produce the very best results, but the superintendent or garden owner who has to grow these plants in London will have many losses and disappointments, and my advice is to plant nothing in the way of evergreen flowering plants until early spring.

For your summer display it can be said that you have the whole realm of plants to choose from, and whatever the position, aspect, or soil of your garden there is no excuse for it to be dull or without flowers. It is almost a waste of your time for me to tell you what you can accomplish. Every plant in the catalogue from A to Z that can be used for the summer embellishment of a garden will grow and flourish in London.

For several years I have had the pleasure and hard work of being one of the judges of the Garden Competition organized by one of the great daily newspapers. The task occupies about twenty judges for five days, and as each judge has to visit about forty to fifty gardens a day, and these gardens are scattered all over London, one can get a very good idea of what can be grown in London, and the variety of plants that find a home and are happy in London gardens is very great indeed.

Roses in many parts are cultivated with great success, and the same may be said of many herbaceous plants. There are small gardens devoted to alpines, others depend for their display on annuals, in fact, there are few plants in the trade lists that are not to be found in one or other of the many thousands of little gardens that give so much joy and pleasure to their owners.

The Antirrhinum, among annual plants, is quite at home in London, and leads in popularity. Superb Gladioli can be grown in the very heart of the city.

All the Californian and South African annuals thrive and flourish. Most of our common garden annuals such as Eschscholzias, Godetias, Clarkias, Lupins, etc., are natives of California, and revel in hot, dry conditions; they are in thousands of instances the only type of plant that is used by the small garden owner. I have seen a lovely little garden entirely composed of these Californian annuals, the proud owner of which told me had only cost 1s. 6d. for seeds. The annuals are, if sown carefully and well thinned so that each plant has space to develop, most successful in a hot, dry summer, and not quite a failure in a wet one.

The Carnation family do well in city gardens, and are often seen. In the days of the old type of florist it was recognized that, in such towns as Sheffield, Birmingham, and Manchester, fine Carnations and Pinks were grown, so that there seems to be something in the atmosphere or soil of city gardens that meet the needs of the Dianthus family.

The same may be said of Hollyhocks. When judging the Railway Station Gardens in and around London, it was noticed how clean and luxuriant the Hollyhocks were, no trace of the dread disfiguring rust: the plant had become naturalized on waste places and embankments, and all in perfect health. At all these stations it was only the single-flowered varieties that were grown. They seem to be more suitable for London than the doubles, but Hollyhocks of all sorts are happier and more free from disease in towns than in the country, and the reason is unknown to me.

Other popular plants are the hardy Asters and Chrysanthemums. In spite of all the criticism and sarcasm that has been poured on the bedding Geraniums and Calceolarias, they both have still untold admirers, and the Geranium, or more correctly *Pelargonium*, is planted out in our city in tens of thousands, and long may this go on; for neatness, brilliancy, and modesty in its demands for care and attention it is unbeatable, and in a small, formal front garden it looks perfectly in place.

Pansies and Violas are both beloved by Londoners, and for the late spring and early summer months are quite happy, but as the hot weather approaches they get less vigorous and unhappy.

Then there is the Dahlia; as a London plant it stands apart from everything else, no other flowering plant has added so much colour to our somewhat drab city, no other plant has given more joy and pleasure to its citizens, and there is no other plant on the horticultural horizon that promises to supersede it. It ranks with the Plane tree in its acceptance of city life and conditions; it is healthier and happier in London than in its native Mexico; its wonderful variety of height, habit, and colour enables us to use it for every possible purpose in the garden and the park.

It has conquered all classes, its popularity is world-wide, for diversity and usefulness, for freedom and long-flowering qualities it has no equal. Enthroned in front of Buckingham Palace, grown in thousands in all our parks, it is just as happy in south-east London as in the more open and favoured suburbs, and particularly successful at Greenwich, while at Bermondsey it is made a great feature, for there it was a popular park plant long before it occupied so much prominence in Central London. In all the Council parks it takes almost pride of place. The finest Dahlias grown in London are to be found on the rich clay loam of Regent's Park.

As a town plant I have only one more to mention, and that is the June-flowering Iris; next to the Dahlia it claims your attention, and will repay you well for any care you bestow on it. In St. James's Park you have seen a great collection, where they vie with the ducks for public favour. It is a plant that has long been used in town gardens, and yearly increases in favour.

The modern Iris is a truly delightful creation; its only fault is the shortness of its flowering period, but this is fast being lengthened. It has been said against the Iris that when the flowering period is past the Iris bed is most unattractive, but this can be remedied to some extent by planting the bulbous Spanish and English Iris in company with the June-flowering types; these extend the flowering period, and it can be further extended if Gladioli be planted among the Iris – this will keep the beds and borders gay throughout the summer.

But you must not condemn the Iris because its flowering is over in a few weeks, as many of our most prized plants last no longer. The Iris is an ideal plant for the small garden, its requirements are few: these are a sunny position, good loam to which lime has been added, and a regular plan of breaking up and dividing the clumps.

As a park plant the Iris deserves far more attention.

When one considers the vast amount of fences and wall space in London, it cannot be said that the London gardener has excelled in the cultivation of climbing plants. He has a liking for Roses, but these are rarely happy on a hot fence or wall. After Roses, Ivy, and Ampelopsis, good climbers are not much in evidence.

It is true that there is much mystery about the Clematis, one of the most lovely of all climbers. I have been given some figures as to the thousands of

Clematis that are sold every year in London, and one wonders what becomes of them all; they are notoriously difficult to get going well, and the London gardener might turn his attention to some of the more recent introductions from China.

Buddleias, Escallonias, the newer species of *Lonicera*, Solanums, Magnolias, and *Ceanothus* are all worthy of more consideration and trial on wall and fences.

For the London gardener then, here are a few hints in tabloid form:

Plant your trees and deciduous shrubs in early autumn, your Rhododendrons and other evergreens in early spring.

If you possess a tree facing the public highway remember it is at the same time a public possession and city ornament. When your tree has to be lopped or pruned call in a skilled workman, and do not give the job to the first person who calls at your front door.

Plant your spring-flowering plants and other evergreen species in spring.

Plant your strictly herbaceous-stemmed plants in autumn.

When you order grass seed tell your seed merchant to put plenty of *Poa nemoralis* in the mixture, it is one of the best grasses for London.

If you have a bare patch on your lawn, due to the heavy shade of a tree or wall, sow *P. annua* and *P. nemoralis* in mixture.

Three or four times between May and July whiten your lawn with sulphate of ammonia and water it in; it is the best and most rapid renovator of a London lawn that can be found, but do not forget the water.

Nothing causes so much dismay among my foremen as to tell them that I want a border of Sweet Peas. Shun Sweet Peas as you would a split infinitive.

If you are a Primula enthusiast your sorrows will be many, but the Candelabra section are not too difficult, and *Primula Florindae* has no objections to a short life in London.

If Gentians fascinate you, *Gentiana frigida*, *G. Lagodechiana*, *G. sino-ornata*, and *G. septemfida* are all easy. *G. acaulis* will grow like a weed, but flowers will be few.

Phloxes are good plants for London, they are often badly grown by being planted too shallow; bury them 8 inches deep and see how they will respond to this treatment.

Of Lilies, *Lilium candidum*, *L. testaceum*, *L. umbellatum*, *L. tigrinum*, are all good Londoners. It is not generally known that many species of Lilies can be grown well in London.

If your next-door neighbour takes no pride or interest in his front garden and allows it go to weeds, keep within the law, but make his life as miserable as you can.

When you purchase bedding plants do not accept those in full bloom in either boxes or pots, many of those are well exhausted and spent, and of little value to you for the garden.

If your right-hand neighbour has Geraniums in his front garden and your left-hand neighbour Dahlias, make that a reason for you to have something different; variety is a great joy to the passer-by.

If you grow Tulips or Daffodils, and find all that you desire among the 160 varieties that you will see in the Royal Parks next spring, remember that they are all British-grown bulbs, and that our bulb-growing industry needs all the encouragement you can give it.

Enough has surely been said to prove that there is a vast variety of plants that can be grown in London, and to show that the city gardener has just as much to interest him as he has any reasonable need for, but I am well aware that there will be a great many who will refuse to be comforted by ordinary fare, and who may bring home from Chelsea, or the Horticultural Hall, or from some great and famous garden visited when on holiday, a desire and longing to see his garden a treasure store of the more rare and difficult plants.

He will dream dreams and see visions – groups of *Meconopis betonicifolia*, towering pillars of *M. Wallichii* mingled with rare Iris, Lilies, Gentians, Primulas, and the like. I hesitate to say a single word to discourage him. If he will be content with a very moderate measure of success nothing is beyond him. Tucked away in many an unexpected little garden I have found rare and choice plants on which a great amount of care and interest is lavished, and every art and device in the way of soil, position and shelter practised. The determined enthusiast gets over many difficulties, and this is as true in plant growing as in anything else.

Speaking as one who has experimented and tried as many plants as most London gardeners, I can but repeat what the lawyer said of his client: "Where there is a will there is a way."

Gardening in London then can be common humdrum, stereotyped, or you can make of it a great adventure.

Now my task is almost finished. I have carefully avoided any asking you to copy park gardening. My idea is that it is poor sport to copy anyone, but when you are in doubt or difficulty you will find no more friendly person than the hundred or more park superintendents who are scattered over our great city, and you will find no one else more qualified to help you out of the troubles that assail all who must garden therein.

13   14, ALEXANDER PLACE, SOUTH KENSINGTON, LONDON. 1930
The wooden trellis work, raised beds, brick paths and central lawn area create a formal 'extra room' which is easy to maintain and which will offer privacy in the garden itself and an interesting outlook from the house.

Beverley Nichols
A NOTE ON LONDON GARDENS

Beverley Nichols (1898–1983), journalist, essayist, novelist and playwright, was a great personality of the Thirties. His witty and sometimes impudent prose conceals a real aesthetic preoccupation with gardening.

The first real London garden I ever had was in Chelsea. It was only about 20 feet by 12, but it produced an astonishing variety of flowers.

During my first year I relied almost entirely upon penny packets, with the happiest results. Some of the packets did not even cost a penny, because of the charming custom which prevails with certain magazines of popular gardening, whose editors present their readers, week by week, with free packets of seeds throughout the spring. There was an extraordinary thrill in receiving these little presents. One read about them for weeks before. In thick black type one learnt that "A Monster Packet of Crimson Flax will be Presented to every Purchaser of our Spring Number." In the next issue, this information was reiterated, together with further particulars of the crimson flax . . . its elegance, its speed in growing, its amiability. In the penultimate issue, one's appetite was whetted almost cruelly, for here, splashed across the page in tints of blood, was the crimson flax's likeness . . . never, one felt, could any flower be lovelier, nor own so sweet a disposition.

Yet, there was still a whole week to wait! The fact that it would have been extremely simple to walk to the seedsman across the street, and buy enough crimson flax to sow a large part of Hyde Park, never occurred to one . . . or, if it did occur, was dismissed as an insulting idea. What was seed which was bought, compared to the packet which was about to be given? Nothing. Worse than nothing.

And then, it arrived at last! The little packet, that rattled when one shook it, glued to the outside cover of the magazine. It had to be peeled off very carefully, because the paper was thin, and it would be tragic if any of the seeds were spilt. How carefully those seeds were sown . . . with what infinite attention to the directions on the packet . . . in soil as sweet and sunny as offered itself.

Yes, they are clever men, the editors of those magazines of popular gardening, for their gifts have a value out of all proportion to their market price. And often, as I have passed the bookstalls, where the newspapers and reviews and other periodicals are heaped high and glistening, I have paused, seen a pile of my favourite magazine, each with its packet of seeds glued to the cover, and have pondered on the miracle which lies there, the unborn beauty which is hidden among the rubbish-heap of trash – have longed for a magic wand that would cause those flowers to break into sudden blossom, and turn the news-stall into a flower-shop of crimson and green.

Besides the annuals, I had several climbing roses, a lilac, and a beautiful syringa. It was an old syringa, and at first we thought it was dead, but it responded to care. However I had even more exciting things than that. For instance, foxgloves!

I have never seen foxgloves in any other London garden, and I cannot think why, because they do extremely well, particularly the white ones. They do not need much sun and they like a coarse soil. The one thing they hate is damp, especially when they are young. In order to avoid damp, I used, quite shamelessly, to put umbrellas over my foxgloves on rainy afternoons and long wet nights. People thought it odd and affected, but I fail to see why it is affected to want to protect a lovely thing like a foxglove, especially when it is so very easy to do. I would always lend an umbrella to any woman who had left hers at home. I like foxgloves more than I like many women. Foxgloves cannot leave their umbrellas at home, because they haven't any umbrellas. Ergo. . . .

If you have a nice clump of foxgloves in your back garden you cannot ever be bored. There is the echo of all the sweet and liquid sounds of the country in their pale bells. In addition, I am told that their roots, if boiled and added to the soup, are guaranteed to make your most disagreeable enemy expire in considerable discomfort within twenty-four hours, but I have not tested this personally.

Pansies, of course, you must have. Only please do behave like a gentleman, or a lady, or whatever you are, with your pansies, i.e. *pick off every dead one*. It is monstrous – the way people neglect their pansies. To leave dead pansies on a plant is as cruel as leaving a cow without anybody to milk it. Also it is not only cruel, but foolish, because if you religiously pick off every flower the instant it is withered, you will be rewarded by flowers almost all the year round.

As soon as you plant a pansy in any town garden, about a thousand slugs will instantly appear from nowhere and begin to devour it. In destroying the slugs you will be able to pass a great many summer evenings very unpleasantly.

Other hardy herbaceous plants which can be recommended for town gardens, from my own experience, are:

Astrantia major　　　　　　*Lilium pardalinum*
Campanula persicifolia　　　　*Pulmonaria angustifolia*
Funkia Sieboldiana[1]　　　　　*Sedum spectabile*

If you do not know what these are, and if you have been lulled into a trance by my easy-flowing style, you can do a little work yourself, for a change, and look them up in a dictionary.

(The somewhat acid tone of that last sentence was due to the fact that as I was making the list, a large and ravishing Persian cat was clearly visible in my back yard, patting my only geranium with a verve which would have been more fittingly reserved for a mouse.)

Therefore we now come to cats. Or rather, cats come to us. These angelic creatures are bound to crop up, sooner or later, in any discussion of city gardens.

I adore cats. I do not mind them at all when they scrape their exquisite claws all down one's best armchair. I have not the heart to reprimand them when they push a cold, purring nose against an ornament and whisk it off my desk . . . because their expression of faint disdain as they regard the ornament, after it has been foolish enough to fall to the floor, is worth any ornament that was ever made. But in a small city garden, their charms, one is bound to admit, are not seen to the best advantage.

In my little Chelsea garden the walls were low and allowed a maximum of sunlight. However, the walls were also broad and supported a maximum of cats. It was soon evident that the boundary wall was the recognized promenade for all the cats of Chelsea . . . it was a sort of feline Piccadilly. Every day, towards the hour of dusk, dark figures would emerge from neighbouring scullery windows, stretch, yawn, and take a sudden bound on to this wall. Having bounded, they would proceed to saunter, with assumed nonchalance, in the direction of my little piece of wall.

As the shadows deepened, more and more of the dark figures emerged. They hopped delicately from the branches of trees. They appeared from sombre doorways, their eyes catching the last glint of the dying sun. Like tiny dots, they were seen in the distance, as though they had fallen from the clouds. And soon the whole wall was crowned with a stealthy procession of arched

[1] *Hosta sieboldiana*

backs and feathery tails, passing to and fro, in a strange and ghostly saraband.

But it was not till they arrived at my particular patch of wall that they deigned to break the silence, to greet one another, to lift their voices in joy or in pain. Why they always chose my little piece, I do not know. Perhaps it was because there were trees in each of the neighbouring gardens, which met and formed a pleasant shelter. Perhaps it was because my part of wall was, for some reason unknown, a little wider than the rest. Whatever the reason, I found that there was only one way to get rid of them. I will tell you it in a moment.

First, however, I tried all the usual methods. I tried opening the window and saying "boo! damn! shish!" followed by a scraping noise in the throat. This appeared to please the cats greatly. A look of dreamy ecstasy came into their eyes, and they gravely seated themselves, waiting for more. "Hosh! Hell! Boo! Blast! Shish!" I yelled. Better and better, thought the cats. Their large green eyes widened, and though they occasionally examined their paws, to see that their nails were properly manicured, they soon resumed their rapt attention. "Yah! Blast! Bang! Hish! Poo!" I shrieked. Then gradually the cats grew a little bored, decided that they had seen enough, yawned, got up and resumed their promenade, absently nibbling a little syringa as they went.

I also tried throwing things. However, since I should never have forgiven myself if I had hit a beautiful black cat (and should have felt even worse if I had hit an ugly one), and since, in addition, I could never have hit one even if I had tried, it cannot be said that this manoeuvre was brilliantly successful.

Then I put wire netting over the seeds. It was instantly agreed, by all the cats in the district, that this was a most thoughtful act on my part. Wire netting, they averred, was the one amenity which hitherto they had lacked. They arrived in hordes to sit on it. Some of them bounced up and down on it as though it were a spring mattress. Others went fast asleep on it. When one went out into the back yard to remonstrate with them, they merely yawned, looked at one with shameless coquetry, and then turned over, with a gesture that said "Leave, oh leave me to repose."

Hell! Cats simply ought not to be allowed to go about, radiating such distracting charm.

But I solved the problem. The remedy sounds even sillier than the umbrellas over the foxgloves, for the remedy was *treacle*. Small pools of treacle, carefully poured on to the top of the wall, and renewed once a week. My original intention had been to scare the cats away altogether. They are the daintiest creatures, and I hoped that when they found themselves stepping

103

into the sticky treacle they would shake their paws, sniff, and go back home. They would think me a common brute, but I could not help that.

However, they did not do what I expected them to do. (No cat ever does.) They approached my wall, stepped in the treacle, paused a moment in astonishment, and then hopped away to a little distance to lick their paws. For one reason or another, they no longer jumped down on to my flower beds.

I am sure that this all sounds very odd, and quite crazy. But it happens to be true.

Lanning Roper
PROBLEMS AND LIMITATIONS

Lanning Roper (1912–1983) studied at The Royal Botanic Gardens at Kew and at Edinburgh and designed gardens in many parts of the world. He was garden correspondent to The Sunday Times *and Assistant Editor of the* Journal of the Royal Horticultural Society.

How many times I have heard a friend say, "We've found the most delightful house and there is a backyard which can be made into a charming garden". How easy it all sounds. The area to be developed is a small one and therefore theoretically requires only a limited number of shrubs and flowers and possibly a tree or two. It will require little upkeep after the initial construction and planting are completed and upkeep will be easy as one can do a little each day or it can all be done on the odd week-end when one stays in town. So the arguments go and a lovely feeling of false security prevails.

I never know who has the more difficult time – the person who has never gardened before or the experienced gardener who has always lived in the country with all the advantages and requisites for a good garden at hand. The former is confronted with the problem of learning everything – what to plant, how to cultivate, how to fertilize, how to design and all the rest. The experienced gardener must probably unlearn a great deal he already knows until he realizes that, when gardening in a city or large town, many established practices must be abandoned, to say nothing of a long list of favourite plants which may not take kindly to existing conditions. It is possible that the novice has the easier time as he feels less mortification at the first or even the second failure; the experienced gardener with the supposed green thumb does not view failure so kindly.

The essential lesson to be learned by both groups is that there are in every city or large town specialized conditions which must be understood if the garden is to be successful. Too often the gardener learns only in retrospect. For that reason I wish to enumerate here some of the conditions and problems which are prevalent so that the gardener may anticipate them and know how to deal with them when and if they arise. Fortunately, many of them may not occur in the reader's own garden and it is to be hoped for his sake that most of them will not.

The morale of the gardener is important. The first signs of spring always awaken resolves and bursts of energy as visions of future glories are stirred up by the patches of crocuses and the green points of daffodils. Then there is a further spurt at the sight of the barrows with their blaze of geraniums and flats of annuals. Window boxes and urns are filled to overflowing with ivy-leafed geraniums and great ruffled petunias; beds are neatly planted and edged with alyssum and lobelias. Alas, then enthusiasm wanes in many cases. The important thing in good gardening is a consistency of interest and effort. There is a daily or weekly routine that cannot be avoided if results are to be satisfactory. It is not enough to buy plants and to water them once. They need attention until they are established and growing happily on their own. For the keen gardener such advice is unnecessary; his garden will always be a major consideration.

The first serious limitation of town gardening is the lack of space. In cities and towns ground represents money, and as ground becomes more valuable up go the rates and taxes. Gardens are by necessity small in area and often restricted further in feeling by the surrounding buildings and walls. As houses are converted into flats in accordance with present day tendencies, the garden, once the sole property of the owner, becomes either communal or the coveted property of the tenant of the ground-floor flat. In building developments each house, whether single, semi-detached or continuous, has its own little sym-metrical property where the layout is to a large extent imposed by the site.

Owing to lack of space, care must be taken with the design of the garden. As it will not be possible to have all the features and all the plants that one would like, simplification is essential. A great deal of thought must go into planning what the function of the garden is to be and eliminating many of the features which one would like to have but for which there is not sufficient room. Not only will there be a lack of space for many of the desired plants, but even perhaps a lack of space to store the necessary tools – the lawn mower, the roller, the bags of peat, the hedge clippers, the empty flower pots, the garden hose and all the rest. Often no proper tool shed is possible and one must make do with a corner of the cellar, an improvised cupboard or part of the garage, if one is lucky enough to have one's own. This problem of storage of tools is a very real one for the city gardener and I can think of more than one friend who gave up the idea of a lawn because there was no place to store the mower, let alone a roller.

Too often there is a tendency for the town gardener to feel that because his garden is small he can get by with the minimum of tools or with none at all. I have planted window boxes for friends with the kitchen spoon and pruned the roses with a paring knife reserved until that time for the vegetables. Always the answer is the same: "I haven't got around to buying tools yet, but I will", or else: "The garden is so small it seems a waste of money to buy tools". The necessity for the right tools cannot be emphasized enough. A handfork or a trowel will not do the work of a spade in turning the soil or digging a trench. It means that trees or shrubs will be planted in improperly prepared soil or in holes that are not large enough to spread the roots properly. In fact, the plants are off to a bad start. It is essential to have the right tools and to keep them in a convenient place and in good order.

Another serious handicap in the small garden is the lack of space for a compost pile or the rubbish heap where fires are possible. As a result all garden refuse, prunings and clippings from hedges must be carted away, and this entails endless clipping of large stems and branches into small pieces so that they can be stuffed into the dustbin in the hope that the dustman will be good natured, for there are those who do not feel inclined to carry off garden refuse unless mellowed with a tip.

An even more disturbing limitation will be the lack of space or of an appropriate place for a cold frame to bring on the young plants and to winter pots of bulbs and cuttings. Anyone who has gardened in the country and is used to the amenities of a frame will miss it even more than the potting shed or the tool house, for the lack of a frame dictates problems which not even great ingenuity can always overcome. In the average city garden the very idea of a frame may have to be ruled out, but in the larger town garden it is a necessity which should be provided for if at all possible.

The country trained gardener will be loath to forgo the compost pile, especially in the city, where endless amounts of organic material are required to put the necessary humus into the hungry soil and more expensive and less satisfactory methods must be resorted to for the equivalent supply of compost. The potential compost that goes into the dustbin will always be a source of grief to the compost enthusiast.

The lack of sun and air are serious limitations. Backyard gardens can be deep traps into which the direct rays of the sun seldom reach because of the height of surrounding buildings. The shaded garden is difficult to maintain if a lot of colour is desired. Most flowering plants which are relied on for bedding like at least half sun and a great many require full sun. Great care should be taken to visit the garden of a proposed house at different hours of the day to see how much sun can be counted on when making garden plans.

Just as plants want sunshine they also need the free circulation of air. Good ventilation in a city garden is essential, for plants do not like dank airless conditions. Nor do most of them like draughts. Sometimes there are narrow openings between buildings which cause detrimental wind passages. These should be blocked by walls or by the planting of very rugged trees or shrubs to act as a wind break.

One of the most serious problems in town gardening is the pollution of the atmosphere. This is an all too familiar problem in a city like London, especially in certain sections, and in the midlands and other industrial areas. Soot collects on the leaves and stems, clogging the pores through which the plants breathe. Many plants succumb at once, others struggle on half heartedly, while a few grow bravely, not seeming to care. It is hard, in fact well nigh impossible, for the individual gardener to combat atmospheric pollution, but he can take certain precautions to ensure the health of his plants and he can learn to select those varieties which have the best chances for survival.

Not only is soot a problem, but so are poisonous fumes. Factories give off fumes containing acids and substances such as sulphur, which are highly injurious both to plant life and human life. Here is one of the places where experience is all-important and the potential gardener should take the trouble to acquaint himself with the local idiosyncrasies of plants from this aspect just as he does with plants which are frost-tender and therefore to be avoided.

For the keen plantsman there is always the challenge and the thrill of making the difficult plant grow, but for the beginner, or the man who wants a decorative garden as a setting for his house, it is better to plant those trees and shrubs which are fundamentally foolproof. It is all right to experiment with herbaceous plants and annuals, which are fillers-in. If they fail they are readily replaced, but one does not want to plant a tree and grow it for a few years, only

107

to lose it in the end and have to start again. This limitation of atmospheric conditions on plant material is a serious one and it is best to seek advice and to learn by observation in neighbouring gardens, both public and private.

Climate is another limiting factor in the selection of plants. Generally the city is slightly warmer than the surrounding countryside. For the beginner, borderline plants should be avoided until the garden is established. Then, if you wish to experiment with tender plants, there is already a background of established plants not only to act as protection but to clothe the garden. In London there are many plants that it is possible to grow. In Paris the number is more limited, partly due to the rigours of the more severe continental winter and to the more intense heat of summer, which take a toll. The best course is to seek advice and to observe and to experiment.

One of the amusing things about city gardens is that because of their sheltered natures and the warmth of walls due to interior heating, it is often found that a quite tender plant will survive although it may not be generally hardy in the area. This is particularly true of wall shrubs and climbers. It is this unpredictability of London gardens that makes them so intriguing and so challenging.

The next major problem is that of soil. First and foremost there is the problem of getting it. The area behind an old house may turn out to be largely rubble or cinders. In newly developed areas all too often the good top soil and the heavy bottom soil have been reversed in the process of excavating, while bombed areas may be full of rubble, broken glass and bits of metal. Sometimes the garden may even have to be made on the site of what was a bit of road or pavement or even the filled-in foundation of an older structure. This may require the removal of the rubble and the substitution of new soils brought in from outside. Notice the use of the word *brought*. Anyone who has done any city gardening knows the value of earth. It is expensive to buy and disconcertingly heavy. A hundred weight of loam is a few bucketsful and a ton is only a relatively small pile. This is discouraging, for the cost of good loam is excessively high and even when given to one, the cost of cartage makes it expensive by the time it reaches the garden.

What can be done? There are various answers. First is to buy the best loam or top soil for surfacing and for actual plant beds, inferior fill being used for unimportant grading and the construction of terraces and foundation work. Secondly, in these days of motor cars a bucket or sack or even a baby's bath tub in the boot of the car can be filled with soil on every country trip or, most precious of all, with manure or sifted leaf mould and carried back and emptied in the waiting space. More than one small backyard garden has been completely created in this way and one's friends join in the game, bringing up the odd bucket when coming to call. I remember my sister-in-law and her husband arriving to see us with a baby's bath full of well-rotted manure for our precious roses before a rather smart wedding, for which they were already dressed. Then I knew that they really understood the difficulties of the London gardener.

Besides the difficulty of obtaining good soil and its expense, there is also the problem of moving it into the garden. Many town gardens have no access save through the house itself, and this entails numerous steps both up and down. The difficulties are not only back-breaking because of the weight of the soil, but hard on the temper of the housewife, who dislikes seeing dirt tracked through her house. But these are all problems that the potential city gardener must face. Not only must the soil come through the house, but also the paving stones, the trees, the garden ornaments and every bit of plant material. For this reason those who buy a new house would be well advised to make sure that the major items for the garden are included before the house is too well settled, and those who build a town house should always consider the convenience of access to the garden so that heavy loads can be easily transferred.

While on the weight of soil, I cannot resist some further words of warning. The weight of soil can hardly be exaggerated. A large tub filled with earth weighs a great deal, and on terraces and roof gardens it is imperative that the structural soundness of the building be determined before any large amount of soil is installed. Blocks of flats can withstand relatively little depth of soil on terraces or roof gardens unless they are specially constructed for it. I am not, of course, talking about window boxes or pots, but about actual flower beds and boxes containing small trees.

Sculpture also can cause no end of grief. I know of one roof which was structurally damaged by the weight of a stone figure and of another where the house, which was very old, did not take kindly to the passage of a marble Buddha of sizeable dimensions up the front stairs and on to a terrace. All appeared to be well until the first storm and then the rains came flooding into the dining room, the entrance hall and the library. In fact, a marriage was almost broken up over that bit of garden statuary.

Drainage is a serious problem in town gardens. All too often there are overflows from internal pipes which empty into the garden or drains which are inadequate or improperly constructed. In some gardens the water from large paved areas drains into surrounding borders, deluging the plants and causing dank unhealthy conditions. Or there may be an inadequate depth of soil and hence no proper drainage away from the roots in the subsoil.

This matter of drainage needs careful consideration. A walled garden may resemble a tank. If there are not sufficient outlets or if what there are become clogged up, the water table rises higher and higher with disastrous results. This same situation occurs on a smaller scale in tanks, tubs and pots and especially in raised beds constructed on paved surfaces on terraces or roof gardens. Drains must be constructed where needed and proper drainage material used at the bottom of containers no matter what their scale. Drainage is one of the major problems of the town garden, and on it success or failure may depend.

The problem of watering is also serious. Where gardens are surrounded by buildings or walls, rain may not fall freely on certain sections because of the angle of the rain due to prevailing winds, or because of over-hanging eaves, balconies or the dense shade of trees. As a result certain plants may never get adequate rain and may require watering even in a wet season. This often explains the failure of newly planted wall plants, both climbers and shrubs. More than one camellia or climbing rose has succumbed for this reason, although planted with the greatest care in a perfectly prepared hole with rich soil.

Still another problem haunts the town gardener, namely the neighbours' cats and dogs, to say nothing of his own. Dogs are easier to contend with as they can be fenced out. Cats are a different matter, for the roof tops and wall copings are their favourite means of access while trees serve as natural ladders and brick walls offer only slight difficulty. In fact, it must be admitted that it is well-nigh impossible to cat-proof a garden, or if one does it becomes such a maze of wire coverings and cages that it loses all semblance of a garden. What is to be done? Careful staking of plants is essential and brush used among plants where cats tend to walk will offer them some discouragement. Constant shooing is not enough, for as soon as your back is turned they are in the garden again. Our own cats act as a lure to others and even our scheme to import tough country cats from an isolated farm to beat up the Chelsea and Kensington cats did not succeed. The city cats were made of tougher fibre than the country boys, who spent much of their early life in the top of the pear tree calling for help.

Small children present problems in a small garden. The answer is to be fair and to recognize them as such. If the garden is to be a playground, then it must be designed with this in mind. A small lawn is soon reduced to a muddy patch if it is constantly used as a play area for running feet and tricycles. The best solution is to pave such a garden, thus providing the children with an area where they can play without doing much harm, while a good way to make a child respect plants is to give him a small section for his own. Both cats and children can be destructive forces like *Polygonum baldschuanicum* and Willow Herb if allowed a free run of the garden.

The question of garden maintenance in towns and cities is critical. The ideal state is to be able to do it all oneself, for not only is it a pleasure for the good gardener to work his garden through the seasons unassisted, but it is the best answer to the difficult question of outside labour. Alas, many town gardeners do not have the time, the strength or the inclination. Secondly, when they may go off on vacations or on business for long periods, the garden work must be carried on. There are various solutions. Firms have grown up in many areas which agree to maintain a garden for a fixed fee throughout the year, providing the plants and bulbs, the labour and even the tools. This may be an expensive service but it is a possible solution. Of course, it removes the personal element and this can be detected all too readily in the personality of the garden, just as it can in the house produced by the decorator.

It is sometimes possible to get a good gardener locally from one of the parks or squares who will come after work or on week-ends and who, in a few hours, can work miracles in the limited space as only a good gardener can. But it is increasingly difficult to get outside help, and apart from the heaviest work such as carrying in the earth, laying paving, preparing holes for tree and shrubs, heavy digging and the like, it is best to do it oneself. The fatal thing is to take on unknown casual labour.

Last summer I came home to find that a great quantity of prunings, weeds and garden refuse had been thrown over the wall into a secluded corner of our garden, onto what was actually the compost pile, which is in its way a nearly sacred thing. My neighbour was full of apologies, but too worried about more serious problems to be concerned about our temporary inconvenience. The jobbing gardener who had rung the bell during my neighbour's breakfast had claimed great ability, willingness and knowledge, promising to work miracles in the course of the day for a large sum. Not being a gardener himself, my neighbour, occupying the house on a sub-let and remembering his promise to maintain the garden, agreed with alacrity. By nightfall the wretched labourer had wrought untold havoc. Not only had he cut down the fine old thorn tree, which was the feature of the garden, but succeeded in breaking the arm off a small statue, in removing some of the better plants and in generally tidying up to such a degree that the charm and character of the shrubs and trees were reduced to a clipped shambles.

I quote this, a drastic case but a true one, to show the dangers. In our own garden at the end of the war the gardener, who claimed to be expert, decapitated all the cherries rather than shortening some of the longer branches as anticipated, and cut off clematis at ground level to strengthen the roots. These dire tales are a warning which perhaps may serve as the needed incentive to continue the struggle alone. If it is not possible to employ trained assistance, the solution is to supervise constantly every operation and to use assistance only to perform an operation that is impossible without help.

Having faced these varied problems and factors, both good and bad, it is possible to do something constructive about them. Annoying features should be corrected or eliminated, if not at once, then as soon as possible. It is well to remember that it is both easier and less expensive to do one major job than a series of minor ones. It is easier to remove an unwanted rock garden at the same time as constructing a pool or laying the foundations for the terrace. Then the stones can be used, while at a later date they will have to be removed with both labour and expense. If the pool is too small now it will always be too small and a source of annoyance, so it is far better to remedy it at once, either by enlarging it or by filling it in while other work is in progress.

14   12, EMBANKMENT GARDENS, CHELSEA, LONDON. C.1919

Flagstones and mixed beds have been combined with ornamental sculpture to
give a sense of space and an air of mild neglect adds to the romantic atmosphere so
refreshing in a town. This was the home of Lady Victoria Manners for the first twenty
years of this century.

Xenia Field

GARDENING IN BOXES, BASKETS AND TUBS

Xenia Field was the gardening correspondent of the Daily Mirror *for many years and, as well as specialising in planting containers for outdoor decoration, she has been honorary Vice-President of the National Rose Society. She is the author of nine books, the most recent being* Xenia Field's Diary Week-by-Week.

Window box gardening is a humble form of the art calling for a humble approach. It is impossible to be erudite about a 3 foot box and foolish to be ambitious about the plants that fill it. The window box garden is a very special one – being so close at hand it can be watched in the early morning, adding pleasure to the first cup of tea, or in the late evening to the nightcap or last cigarette.

TYPES

The present day gardener has a choice of many styles of boxes. My first choice is the fibreglass type, some of which are available as eighteenth-century reproductions. They are light, strong, weather resistant and most decorative, but the reproductions are expensive.

The Florentine pottery box, traditionally Italian and moulded in pink terracotta is pleasant to look at. Different lengths and patterns are imported, but they may sometimes be a little small in capacity. Another drawback is vulnerability to severe frost.

Among other boxes are the stone box from the Somerset quarries and the cement box, which is weather resistant, rot-proof, durable, light and washable. The latter are also easy to paint and reasonable in price.

There are others of plastic; these are obtainable at many garden centres and retail stores. They are claimed to keep the soil at a more uniform temperature than other types, and they require less watering. The yellow-grey stone Spanish boxes, often a composite of granite sandstone and local stones, may have relief carvings and are finished by craftsmen. These can be very expensive. The ammunition box, a war-time left over, lingers on, but these are not to be recommended as the metal overheats, the soil dries out quickly and the plant roots suffer accordingly. Finally there is the home-made window box, of wood.

In order of durability the choice is teak, oak, ash or deal. A teak window box will outlive its owner and can safely be bequeathed as a useful if unusual legacy. A deal box deteriorates quickly and the length of its life is unpredictable but short. The gardener who buys goods to last will go for hardwood; the bargain hunter will content himself with soft timber. Stout packing cases of hardwood 1 to 1½ inches thick can also make useful boxes.

The length of the window sill, naturally, decides the box's length. The average size of box is 36 inches long, 9 inches deep and 10 inches wide. If the ledge is more than 5 feet long, two boxes are more practical than one. Handles are useful if the box is to be lifted in and out, and 2 inches can be left at each end to allow for this.

The wood at the corners should be dovetailed and screws used rather than nails. Always remember that the grain of the wood should run along the length of the box. Sloped wooden ledges fastened to the underside of the box will raise it from the sill, promote ventilation and will also prevent moisture accumulating.

PRESERVATION

Green cuprinol can be used to protect the wood from rotting, but the solvent must be allowed two to four weeks to evaporate completely before filling the box with soil. A wooden box should be painted, with an undercoat and two or three coats of paint every other year.

DRAINAGE

If the windows are high up and the landlord testy, zinc roofing trays are needed to catch the water draining through the window box, and of course you water when the neighbour is out. The drainage holes are better burnt out with a red hot poker and not bored, so that they are more resistant to rot. They should be half an inch in diameter, about 5 inches apart and placed diagonally across the bottom of the box.

Crocks should be clean and placed on the bottom of the box, convex side upwards. On top of these comes a layer of roughage such as peat to prevent the soil from clogging the drainage holes.

BOX LININGS

Lining a box has the advantage that soil and plants can be removed without disturbance, and the contents of the window quickly renewed. The temporarily discarded lining and contents could be taken to the country for a season's refreshment.

SECURITY

Decorative window boxes are an embellishment – safe ones are an obligation. So the window box must be safely attached. Special bracket hooks and eyes are used for this purpose.

SOIL

A good soil mixture is vital with a good layer of damp peat over the roughage at the bottom of a box. As a number of different plants are usually grown in the box it is impossible to please them all. The aim should be to provide a good balanced compost to satisfy most of them. John Innes composts 1, 2 and 3 are carefully proven mixtures. Although these are based on a standard formula, the final product as made up by different merchants is not always the same so buy from a reputable merchant. Approximately 56 pounds of compost will be required to fill a box. Don't buy more than you need for immediate use as the compost deteriorates with age.

In large towns the atmosphere is often polluted and it may be advisable to change the soil every year. In an unpolluted area John Innes can be left in the box for two or three years provided fertilizers are used with discretion.

The countryman should find no difficulty in providing a desirable soil for his box, such as three parts of fibrous loam, one part decayed leafmould or peat, half a part dried cow manure plus bonemeal. Ordinary garden soil seldom gives the best results.

TOOLS

These are a matter of the gardener's preference. A trowel for planting, a pronged implement, usually a large dinner fork, for keeping the soil open, a pair of scissors or secateurs for pruning, a syringe, a potting stick or dibble, a sharp knife, a small pair of tweezers for thinning out seedlings, a watering can fitted with a rose, and a basket for the sake of tidiness.

THE BUDGET

The most expensive window boxes are those maintained by florists or nurserymen. In these the boxes are changed up to eight times in a year to keep them looking fresh.

For those who wish to keep their own boxes going I give some ideas below. There is the choice of gardening in pots, i.e. plants placed inside the box while remaining in their own pots. This is an easy way of doing things, but much of the fun of gardening is lost, although there is the advantage that unsatisfactory plants can be readily replaced by a quick buy from the florist. Geraniums lend themselves well to this method and often flower more freely with their roots restricted.

PLANTING

If the root ball is dry it should be soaked in a pail of water. A pot plant should be given a good soak the night before. Careful handling of seedlings is important and every plant should be spaced so that it has enough light and air. Lastly give the plant a drink.

EVERYDAY MANAGEMENT

I believe in keeping the dinner fork moving, and giving the soil plenty of aeration. The box should be watered liberally because although rain may freshen up the plants the moisture does not always penetrate the soil. The sheltered box under an overhanging roof must be watched for dryness. When you water give a good soak and water early in the morning.

FERTILIZING

As a general rule, the best time to apply fertilizer is before the plant flowers. A plant that is resting or sick should not be fed. Never fertilize a dry plant – water it first and perhaps give a short drink afterwards. A general liquid fertilizer is best in most cases, watered on the soil. Foliar feeding gives quick results, but is effective only at certain times.

Organic manures are excellent, particularly hoof and horn which keeps well and is clean to handle. Fish and meat meal are very helpful, dried blood is excellent in starting a plant off in spring, and bonemeal, although slow acting, has the advantage that it never burns roots.

DEADHEADING

This is a very important job. Plant life is highly concerned with regeneration. The annual has a short life and flowers as soon as conditions are suitable. Once the flower fades the seed will set. As the seed pod swells the plant loses its vigour and all energy turns to reproduction. So remove dead heads to keep the flowers coming.

THE SPRING BOX

Spring flowering bulbs are the obvious choice for this. Go to a reputable nurseryman for bulbs, and on opening the bag make sure that the bulbs are firm.

Dwarf narcissi are ideal for window boxes, such as the sturdy, free-flowering 'Peeping Tom'. Suitable tulips are the early singles and doubles, and the double deep crimson lake 'Electra' with pale margins is a favourite of mine. The water lily tulips (*kaufmanniana*) in yellow, scarlet, red and crimson also look well in window boxes. Crocus will grow well and I recommend 'Joan of Arc' which has bright orange stigmas and 'E. A. Bowles' which is a yellow beauty. Snowdrops are not reliable, but scillas never fail and should not be missed.

An attractive idea for spring is to plant bulbs in three layers. Daffodils are laid on the bottom layer to flower in April; golden double tulips 'Van de Hoef' lightly covered with soil form the second layer; small bulbs such as *Iris reticulata* that do not flower later than mid-April are planted in groups for the third layer. In this way there is nothing to hold up the summer planting.

THE SUMMER BOX

Here there is a wide choice. Nothing is more beautiful than white petunias or more garish than scarlet and purple ones. A box of ivy-leaved geraniums with many different colours and shades of pink, red, mauve and purple with perhaps a few pure white 'Snowdrift' here and there. This is a favourite of mine. 'La France', the lovely lilac-mauve geranium with top petals feathered white and purple is still the best.

Lobelia tightly blocked together makes a vivid splash of Oxford or Cambridge blue whilst a planting of *Phlox drummondii* has a modest charm.

Other window box plants which can be raised from seed are candytuft, morning glory, Bijou sweet peas, *Linaria* (toad flax), Virginia stock, *Phacelia campanularia*, nasturtium, and the Minette, Elfin and Imp *Impatiens*, the modern 'patient Lucys'.

Among the more popular bedding plants are *Ageratum*, *Antirrhinum*, begonias (the little fibrous-rooted begonias are versatile and can be potted up before the frost and brought into the house where they may be treated as a house plant), daisies (*Bellis*), *Celosia* (cockscomb, an acquired taste), dwarf chrysanthemums (these are long lasting), heliotrope ('Cherry Pie Garfield' is not showy but has a heavenly scent), mimulas, pansies and violas, petunias and verbenas.

Or you may choose fuchsias. The dwarf 'Tom Thumb' with light crimson sepals and purple corolla or *F. pumila* which has small scarlet and mauve flowers look most attractive.

The choice is unending. The summer box will carry on into the autumn cheered by a few china asters, or by the delightful Dutch miniature dahlias that are such perfect lilliputs.

THE WINTER BOX

If you haven't a duplicate box for winter, evergreen shrubs such as hebe (alias veronica) or *Pernettya mucronata* with pink or purple berries are easy choices.

If you do have a duplicate box there are several euonymus cultivars which are suitable. 'Emerald 'n' Gold', recently introduced from America, is a gold evergreen shrub that turns a bronze-pink in winter. 'Silver Pillar' with broad white margins and *E. fortunei* with bright silver variegation are two other good plants for the winter box. *Elaeagnus pungens* 'Maculata', another favourite, is handsome but must be controlled. All of these eventually grow to be too big for the window box, in spite of regular pruning. Then there are the less well-known hebes such as *H. darwiniana* which has grey foliage and a compact habit and *H. subalpina* which is very tough with green foliage and of pincushion shape. The alpine conifer, *Juniperus communis* 'Compressa' is a tidy miniature shrub and enhances a box of this kind. There are a number of slow-growing yellow, golden, grey and blue dwarf conifers to choose from for the duplicate box.

THE PERMANENT BOX

This is for the real gardener who has not the heart to disturb his plants and gets a great deal of pleasure of growing a little of this and that. The deep yellow *Iris danfordiae* and *I. histrioides* 'Major' which is blue with a golden crest, are two miniature very early flowering bulbs that are perfect residents for this box where they can stay undisturbed. I have seen them in February poking their noses through the snow in a city box.

There are a host of other suitable perennials among them being pink crimson thrift (*Armeria*), *Campanula isophylla* and *C. carpatica* which are lilac blue and blue respectively, *Heuchera*, *Nepeta*, the neglected *Lysimachia nummularia* (creeping jenny) and *Saxifraga umbrosa* (London pride) that share a box so well, *Polygonum* 'Donald Lowndes', saxifrages and sempervivums.

THE CHEAP, ALL-THE-YEAR-ROUND BOX

First the box should be quite thickly planted with a small amenable ivy such as 'Très Coupé' with deeply cut leaves and bushy growth. This gives a green cover to the soil, which looks attractive all the year.

Three or five places should be left to be filled with pot plants or bulbs at different seasons. For spring, bulbs such as daffodils, hyacinths or tulips, for summer, geraniums, verbenas, or perhaps marguerites. Dwarf chrysanthemums can be used in autumn should the geraniums look tatty.

When winter comes, grey, blue or golden dwarf conifers that have spent the summer in the country should be brought to town. They may remain in their pots or be planted out.

Planting part of the box is cheaper than filling the whole box and the result can be most effective.

THE BOX IN THE SHADE

Everyone can manage the box in the sun but one in the shade is a different matter. Fibrous and tuberous rooted begonias are some of the plants that are happy in the shade. I suggest buying from a specialist, by colour rather than by name. Beware of huge heads that tumble off at the slightest touch.

Meanwhile there are the new strains of *Impatiens*, Imp, Elfin, and Minette that come to our aid – they are the only other bedding plants that keep flowering without the sun!

THE HOT BOX

Here the mesembryanthemum or ice plant fills the bill admirably. It flourishes in the sun and loves the seaside.

WINDOW BOXES FOR SPECIALISTS

Many gardeners like to specialise in groups of plants and here are some suggestions.

Miniature roses are excellent for growing in a duplicate box, with 'Easter Morn', 'Scarlet Gem' and 'Yellow Doll' among the best.

The box of scented plants is quickly increasing in popularity. Ornamental thymes and scented leaf geraniums are very suitable though unfortunately the latter are not frost hardy.

Among plants with ornamental foliage the most useful are the variegated ivies and geraniums. Few plants give as much leaf colour as the geraniums 'Crystal Palace Gem', 'Lady Churchill' or vivid 'Mrs. Henry Cox', the brightest *tricolor* of them all. Then there are also the grey and silver leaved plants and there is a wide choice of these. A couple of plants of *Senecio* 'White Diamond' backing the pink rock-rose 'Wisley' spilling over the front edge is very attractive indeed.

Grasses can also be attractive and here *Briza minor*, the quaking grass, should be given pride of place together with the enchanting green and silver cocksfoot, and to the front blue grey *Festuca glauca* which grows to a height of only 6 inches.

The crested lady fern so delicately designed can play an important part in a window box of ferns. The frost may cut back the fronds but fresh green frills will later take their place. The common hart's tongue fern has been known to survive well in built-up areas.

Some salad vegetables can be grown, but this planting is entertaining rather than profitmaking. Tomatoes are only rewarding in a good summer. 'Dwarf Gem' is a tasty sweet tomato and the lettuce 'Tom Thumb', which is crisp and the smallest grown, both suit the box. Mustard and cress can be useful. Sow cress ten days before mustard.

Chives and spring onion 'White Lisbon' should be found a place and parsley a comfortable corner. Herbs may also be grown and several nurseries offer a six variety box that may include French marjoram, lemon thyme, mint, parsley, sage and rosemary.

BASKETS

The size of the basket is determined by the strength of the owner. Both wire and wooden baskets are heavy to handle, and as they dry out quickly it is an advantage to be able to take them down in hot weather and soak them in a container. The basket can be lined with polythene, but I prefer to use a good layer of moist sphagnum moss taking care that there are no gaps where soil can escape. A mixture of medium loam (not too light), with an addition of leafmould, peat and sand should be used, or John Innes compost, leaving at least an inch between the soil surface and the rim of watering. The basket is then planted and then it should be immersed in water for a good soak and drained. Baskets dry out rapidly and need to be watched much more closely than boxes for watering.

see colour plate VI

In planting a basket it can be built high in the centre with fuchsias, heliotropes or begonias surrounded by trailers and edging plants. *Nepeta* and *Tradescantia* can be used to fill gaps. *Fuchsia procumbens* and *F. pendula* 'Pillar of Gold' and 'Mrs. Marshall' are good additions, and the pendulous begonias are always interesting.

Among other suitable plants are musks, nasturtium cherry-rose, *Saxifraga sarmentosa*, and the strawberry begonia, also known as mother of thousands. Geraniums, lobelias, and *Campanula isophylla* are natural basket residents and there should be at least one or two marguerites to lighten the effect. The window basket has an Edwardian gaiety of its own.

TUBS

Many a city dweller has the space for a tub in a back yard, on a balcony or doorstep. Unless the tub has legs it should be stood on bricks. Tubs are many and various ranging from the beautiful cube Versailles *caisse* to the beer barrel with 6 to 8 inch openings cut into its side in which to grow strawberries. It is important to start with a good rich soil. Top dressing must be carried out once or twice a year – the tired top soil being scraped away and replaced. Tubs should be watered freely throughout summer but kept on the dry side in winter. Wet roots are vulnerable to frost. It is a mistake to overpot, a small shrub seldom does well in a large tub. Camellias, yew, acer, fuchsia, roses and agapanthus all look well in tubs. The rhododendron lover frustrated by a lime soil in his garden could grow a standard rhododendron in a tub adding sequestrene to the compost. The rhododendron is one of the most satisfactory tub plants. Bay trees on either side of the hall door are shapely and give a prosperous look. Hydrangeas are amenable to town life and tolerate shade.

The most attractive tubs I have ever seen were in Copenhagen in springtime. These had small silver birch trees with golden *Trollius* and forget-me-nots at their feet. And were indeed the perfect final touch.

John Brookes
PLANTING A VERY SMALL GARDEN

After you have decided on the type of hard surfacing and the type of enclosure in your area, the third major ingredient will be the planting and part of it might well be synonymous with enclosure.

The new garden owner is usually anxious to make his plot private straight away, and cannot wait for plants to do the trick, although many shrubs grow exceedingly quickly. The type of soil, to an extent, will encourage or inhibit growth, but with good initial cultivation and, possibly more important, mainte-

John Brookes (1933–   ) is a well-known garden and landscape designer. He is the author of Room Outside, *amongst other books, and specialises in imaginative schemes for small gardens.*

nance, particularly in the first year, the majority of plants grow away fast.

To build up a green screen immediately through newly planted shrubs, the use of annuals should not be overlooked – both in beds and as climbers. Helianthus (sunflowers), for instance, grown in masses, instead of the usual row, get up to 8 to 10 feet in a summer; nicotiana (tobacco plants) 3 to 4 feet. Annual climbers like *Ipomoea purpurea* (morning glory), cobaea, and even runner beans, can go up to 20 feet in a good season in the right position.

Before actually choosing your plants, it is well to consider what effect you are trying to achieve, over what period, and more important, what the plants must do – and this includes trees, where there is room.

What a plant must do (because you are really building up a sculptural composition, in the same way as a bowl of flowers is arranged, or pieces set about to furnish a room) presupposes that their ultimate shape is known. Little clue to their potential is given in most garden centres, and one container of twigs looks pretty much like another when you are making a selection from those vast rows at planting time, whether in winter or spring.

Plantsmen's catalogues presuppose too that their reader is more knowledgeable than he often is. The characteristics of a plant, of whatever size – tree, shrub, herbaceous, rock plant – can be summarized as follows:

DIMENSIONS OF TREES, SHRUBS
AND HERBACEOUS PLANTS DESCRIBED IN CATALOGUES

Size

Trees

Forest	Ultimately over 40 ft (12 m)	Not suitable
Medium	20–40 ft (6–12 m), sometimes flowering	Limited use
Small	Under 20 ft (6 m), mostly flowering	Most suitable

Shrubs

Largest	Ultimately up to 20 ft (6 m)
Medium	Ultimately 4–20 ft (1·2–6 m)
Small	Ultimately up to 4 ft (1·2 m)

Size

Herbaceous

Perennials	Sometimes up to 8 ft (2·4 m) – every year
Biennials	Most small, up to 3 ft (90 cm) – plant one year, flowers the next
Annuals	Up to 10 ft (3 m) from sowing to flowering in one year

It will be seen that the most suitable plants are therefore the odd small-to-medium tree, depending on the area size, shrubs of all sorts, probably interplanted with herbaceous subjects and/or annuals.

OVERALL SHAPE

The overall shape of the plant is as important to you as its ultimate height. This is usually appreciated when describing trees as weeping, horizontal, twisted, fastigiate, pyramidal, round or flat topped; but less commonly pointed out is that all the other categories of plant have the same characteristics, although there is an area where many subjects, particularly shrubs, have no great shape, although possibly possessing many other virtues. Those plants having shape within the categories of small shrub and herbaceous material are mysteriously known as architectural plants.

see plate 14

DECIDUOUS/EVERGREEN

Whether a plant retains its foliage or not during winter will obviously be one of the major characteristics to consider when making your plant selection. Unfortunately, most evergreen plants are slower growers than deciduous subjects, although some forms of cotoneaster, viburnum, and privet are the exceptions as is the sweetly scented *Lonicera halliana*. In addition to these must be added the conifers, some of which are fairly fast growing as well, although not entirely suited to an urban situation.

To confuse the issue, between the deciduous plant and the evergreen one are quite a number of plants which, although basically deciduous, retain their dead leaves through the winter, only dropping them in spring; beech and hornbeam, as hedging, are examples; some cotoneasters and buddleias too.

These three characteristics are going to be the ones to consider when making your first selection of plant material in the new garden, as it will be they that create your screen, framing or blocking a view. They then make up the skeleton of the garden, and should be considered in the same light when selecting your hard surfacing materials or building a boundary – suitability in character to site and house; the orientation of the site, and what will grow where; how blocks of such and such will contrast with or complement areas of brick, or concrete slab.

Against and in this basic design for the area, select the showier plants for the garden. In doing this, other small-scale characteristics will be considered.

TEXTURE

see colour plate xiv

The textural variations of leaves, stems, bark, or flower can be used in building up a plant composition. And it is some of these qualities that will give particular plants their winter interest, when flower colour is scarce. The orange, red, or yellow stems of willows and dogwood, the peeling bark of some cherries, the great glossy heart-shaped leaves of *Hedera colchica* (ivy) and the furry grey leaves of *Stachys lanata* (lamb's ear), for instance.

LEAF SHAPE

see plate 14

The craggy, furred stems of sumach (*Rhus typhina*), with its finely cut leaf fronds, the great gleaming oval leaves of elephant's ear (*Bergenia* sp.), fine robinia or birch leaves, catalpa's lime green heart-shaped leaves, are all characteristics to be enjoyed a whole season through, as opposed to a more ephemeral colour. Leaf shape becomes of particular importance in the shadier garden, and far from this type of garden being 'impossible to grow anything in' – the normal cry – it presents the excuse for using some splendid plants which will not grow in full sun. One of the most popular plants in this category is the much-used hosta, but all sorts of gentle plants like digitalis (foxgloves) and *Anemone japonica* (Japanese anemones) are ideal too. One of the least-used types of plant for a town garden is the fern: all have wonderful leaves, in contrasting shapes, they grow to various heights from 6 inches to 5 feet, and some even retain their leaves right through the winter.

COLOUR

It is this aspect of a plant – whether it be in its flower colour, its leaf, or stem – that excites more interest than anything else. But it is a mistake in a limited area to select a nondescript-shaped plant, just because it has a good flower for a fortnight of the year. Where space is precious, each plant ought to earn its keep having one of a few qualities which will ensure it contributes as a member of a group to create a good visual effect the whole time.

The smaller the garden area the more important the amount of evergreen you have in it – not only to keep it looking attractive the whole time but to baffle or muffle the boundary line of the area too. Many evergreen plants have, unfortunately, little flower colour, although they have the best variations of leaf, and a good many have splendid crops of berries. It is in such a situation that pots of bright annuals or spring bulbs can be grouped against a permanent background.

SKELETON PLANTING

A. Fast growing evergreens and conifers suitable for screen planting:
   Bambusa (bamboo, tall varieties), slow to establish but persistent later
   Cotoneaster × 'Cornubia', *C. lacteus*, with an added attraction of winter berries
   Berberis, *B. darwinii* and *B.* × *stenophylla* are among the most popular varieties
   × *Cupressocyparis leylandii*, fast growing, but attaining 60 ft (18 m) in maturity
   Escallonia, especially the cultivar *E.* 'Iveyi', *E. rubra* var. *macrantha*, *E.* 'Apple Blossom', *E.* 'C. F. Ball'
   Ligustrum lucidum, large-leafed member of the privet family
   Prunus laurocerasus (cherry laurel)
   Prunus lusitanica (Portugal laurel), extremely tough when established
   Pyracantha (firethorn), most varieties having red, orange or yellow berries
   Thuja plicata (western red cedar)
B. Slower growing evergreens suitable for long-term planting:
   Arbutus (the strawberry tree)
   Camellia, ideal for the town garden, not standing wind
   Ceanothus × *burkwoodii*, has rich blue flowers through summer and autumn

Choisya ternata (Mexican orange blossom)

Elaeagnus × *ebbingei*, *E. glabra*, good shelter-making evergreens

Euonymus japonicus, succeeds in sun or shade

Ilex (holly)

Mahonia, the cultivar 'Charity' is deservedly popular

Olearia (daisy bush), excellent for maritime exposure

Phillyrea, a handsome little-known shrub or tree much loved by Victorian gardeners

Rhododendron species

Taxus (yew), tolerant of most soils and situations, sun or shade

Viburnum × *burkwoodii*, *V. rhytidophyllum*, *V. tinus* (laurustinus)

C. Some fast growing deciduous shrubs which can be interplanted with slow growing evergreens and later removed as the evergreens mature:

Buddleja davidii, *B. globosa*

Cornus alba (dogwood)

Cytisus scoparius (broom)

Lupinus arboreus (semi-evergreen lupin tree)

Philadelphus (tall-growing varieties)

Prunus cerasifera (myrobalan)

Sambucus (elder)

Sorbaria aitchisonii

Spartium junceum (Spanish broom)

Syringa (lilac)

D. Some fast growing deciduous shrubs having a longer life-span, not therefore suitable for early removal:

Carpinus (hornbeam, semi-evergreen, hedging)

Cotoneaster frigidus, *C. wardii*

Crataegus (ornamental thorn)

Hippophae rhamnoides (sea buckthorn)

Rosa (shrub roses, vigorous forms)

Viburnum opulus sterile (snowball tree), *V. tomentosum* 'Lanarth'

CHAPTER IV

Rock and Wall Gardening

William Cobbett

ENCLOSING KITCHEN-GARDENS

Under this head we are first to speak of the walls, which ought to be 12 feet high, 2 feet thick to the surface of the ground, and 9 inches from the ground to the top, with a jam coming out 6 inches from the wall on the outside; and these jams ought not to be more than 8 or 10 feet apart. This would give a wall quite smooth in the inside of the garden; and, on the outside, there would be space for a good large wall-tree between every two jams. The top, or coping, of the wall, ought to consist of semicircular bricks, which should be put on in the firmest and best manner, and the joints well grouted or cemented. When I come to speak of the manner of preserving the blossoms and young fruit of wall-trees from the effects of frost and other severe weather, I shall have to say something more about the construction of a particular part of the wall: at present it will be sufficient to add, that it ought to be made of good, solid, smoothly-finished and well-burned bricks; that the mortar ought to be of the best; that the joints ought to be uniform in size and well filled with mortar; and

William Cobbett (1762–1835) included horticulture among his diverse interests and talents. He worked for a while at Kew Gardens and published several books on gardening.

129

that the wall ought to be erected, not later than the month of June, in order for it to become thoroughly dry in every part before the arrival of frost. In making the foundation, great care must be taken to go lower down than the depth of the trenching, in order to come at the solid and immovable earth.

The use of one half of this wall, for horticultural purposes, would be lost unless wall-trees could be placed on both sides of it; and wall-trees cannot be placed on the outside, with any chance of utility, unless there be an *effectual fence* to protect the trees on that wall. I knew an old gentleman, one of whose garden walls separated the garden from a meadow, which was unprotected except by a common hedge. Those persons of the village who were fond of wall-fruit, who had none of their own, and who were young enough to climb walls, used to leave him a very undue proportion of his fruit, and that not of the best quality. He therefore separated a strip of the meadow from the rest by a little fence, very convenient for getting over; turned this strip, which lay along against the wall, into kitchen-garden ground, planted excellent fruit-trees against the wall, trained them and cultivated them properly; and thus, by furnishing his juvenile neighbours with onions for their bread and cheese, as well as fruit for their dessert, ever after he kept the produce of the inside of the garden for himself, generally observing (as he once particularly did to me) that he was not so unreasonable as to expect to have any of the produce of the exterior garden.

But there is no necessity for making these sorts of diversions, if you can, with the greatest ease imaginable, effectually protect the fortress against every species of attack. This protection is to be obtained by a hedge made of hawthorn, blackthorn, or, still better, with honey locust, the thorns of the latter being just so many needles of about 1½ or 2 inches long, only stouter than a needle and less brittle. The space between the wall and the hedge ought to be a clear rod, allowing, besides, 3 feet for the hedge. This hedge ought to be planted in the following manner. The plants being first sown in beds, and then put into a nursery, ought to be taken thence when their stems are about the thickness of the point of your fore-finger. They ought to be as equal as possible in point of size because, if one be weaker than the rest, they subdue it; there comes a low place in the hedge; that low place becomes a gap; and a hedge with a gap in it, is, in fact, no fence at all, any more than a wall with an open door in it is a protection to a house. Having got the plants ready; or, rather, *before* they be taken up out of the ground, you prepare the place to receive them. You make a ditch 6 feet wide, at the top, and 2½ feet wide at the bottom. I suppose the ground to be trenched to the width of 18 feet from the wall. You take all the good earth from the top of the place that is to be the ditch, and lay it upon the trenched ground to the extent of 2 feet wide, which will make a very good and deep bed of earth for the plants which are to form the hedge to grow in. Then the ditch ought to be dug out to the depth of 3 feet, and shovelled out very clean and smooth at the bottom. This bottom earth of the ditch must be carried away; for it would not do to throw it up into the border. If it be convenient, the slope of the bank ought to be covered with turf, well beaten on, and in the autumn; because, if put on in the spring, the grass would be likely to die. If not convenient to get turf, this slope ought to be thickly sown with grass seeds from a hay-loft; and, in both cases, this slope of the bank ought to be hung very regularly with dead bushes, fastened to the bank by little pegs. This bank and ditch alone, if the bushes were well hung and fastened on, would be no bad protection: few boys, or young fellows, would venture, particularly by night, to take a jump over a ditch of 6 feet, with about 2 feet of elevation on the bank; but the hedge, in addition to this ditch and bank, renders the storming literally impossible, except with the assistance of fascines and scaling ladders, which are munitions that the beseigers of gardens are very seldom provided with.

To return now to the planting of the hedge: I entirely disapprove of great numbers of plants employed for this purpose. If the plants stand too close to each other, they never can be strong: they never get stout stems: the hedge is weak at bottom; and the hedge can never be what it would be if fewer and stronger plants were put in. The time of planting is any where between September and April. The plants, when taken up, should have all their fibres taken from their roots with a sharp knife, and their main roots shortened to the length of about 6 inches; they should be planted with great care, the earth put in very finely about the roots, and, every plant fastened well in the ground by the foot. The earth should be then made smooth after the treading, and the plants immediately cut down to within a foot of the ground. The distance that the plants should stand from each other ought to be about 15 inches, and the row of plants ought to stand at about a foot from the edge of the bank. The plants should be kept perfectly clear from weeds all the summer, which is very easily effected by two or three hoeings. If plants be plentiful, and you desire to have an extraordinarily thick hedge, put in two rows of plants, one row 18 inches from the other, and the plants of one row placed opposite the middle of the intervals in the other row. The plants will make long and strong shoots the first summer. The next spring cut them down to within an inch of the ground. Go over them in June when they will have made considerable shoots, and cut off all the shoots close to the stem, except the two strongest of each plant. Let them go on through another year and these two shoots will then be about 5 feet high. Then, in winter, take one of the shoots of each plant, and *plash* it close to the bottom; that is to say, bend it down long-wise the hedge, and give it a cut on the upper side about 2 inches from the stem; cut off the top of it so as to leave the remainder a foot long; bend it down to the ground, making it lie as close as possible to the stems of the neighbouring plant, and fasten it to the ground with two pegs. When you have done this all the way along, there will be one plash for every interval between the stems of the plants. When this is done, cut down the upright shoots, which you have not plashed down, to within 4 inches of the bottom; or, rather, to within an inch or so of that part of the stem out of which the plashed shoot issues. The next October, that is to say, at the end of the fourth summer you will have a complete, efficient, and beautiful fence. This fence will want topping and clipping, in order to keep it of uniform height, and smooth on the sides. You may let it go to what height you please; but, in order to have a hedge thick at the bottom, you must trim the hedge in such a way as for the outsides of the bottom of it not to be *dripped* by the upper parts of the hedge. This is a very important matter; for, if the bottom of the hedge be hollow, holes are easily made in it, and it soon becomes no fence at all.

If the hedge be made of honey locusts, two rows of plants are better than one, the distances being the same as before-mentioned. These do not do so well for *plashing* as the hawthorn or blackthorn; but they send out numerous side-shoots, and these very strong. These locusts should not be cut down till the end of the autumn after planting; or they may be cut down the next spring, and close to the ground. Each will then send up three or four stout shoots. When these have grown through the summer, take out any little weak shoots, close to the stem, and cut down the stout ones within 3 or 4 inches of the ground. Out of these stems will come such quantities of shoots, that the fence will be complete in a very short time, and will only want trimming and clipping. The whole of the space between the two rows will be filled up by the side shoots; and the hedge will be quite impassable by any animal bigger, at any rate, than a rat or a cat; and, besides all the rest, the foliage is so very fine, that even as an ornament, it would be desirable to have it as a hedge.

With regard to the height of this hedge, it might be 6 or 7 feet; but not higher; for, if too high, it would keep the sun from part of the wall on the south side of the garden. If higher, it would give more shelter, indeed; but then this benefit would be over-balanced by the injury done in the way of shade. By the means of a hedge of this sort, you not only secure the use of the outsides of your walls; but you obtain security for the produce of the inside. For gardeners may scold as long and as vehemently as they please, and law-makers may enact as long as they please, mankind will never look upon taking fruit in an orchard, or a garden, as *felony*, nor even as a *serious trespass*. Besides, there are such things as *boys*, and every considerate man will recollect, that he himself was once a boy. So that, if you have a mind to have for your own exclusive use what you grow in your garden, you must do one of two things; resort to terrors and punishments, that will make you detested by your neighbours, or provide an insurmountable fence. This prevents *temptation*, in all cases dangerous, and particularly in that of forbidden fruit. Resolve, therefore, to share the produce of your garden with the boys of the whole neighbourhood; or, to keep it for your own use by a fence that they cannot get through, over, or under. Six feet is no great height; but in the way of *fence*, 4 feet of good thorn-hedge will keep the boldest boy from trees loaded with fine ripe peaches; and, if it will do *that*, nothing further need be said in its praise! The height is nothing; but, unless the assailant have wings, he must be content with feasting his eyes; for, if he attempt to *climb*, he receives the penalty upon the spot; and he retreats as the fox did from the grapes, only with pain of body in addition to that of a disappointed longing. I really (recollecting former times) feel some remorse in thus plotting against the poor fellows; but the worst of it is, they will not be content with fair play: they will have the *earliest* in the season, and the *best*, as long as the season lasts; and, therefore, I must, however reluctantly, shut them out altogether.

By the time that the wall-trees begin to produce anything of a crop, the hedge will become an effectual fence: the latter will go on providing protection as the trees go on in making provision for fruit. The ditch and the bank should be attended to during this time. If the earth moulder down, it should be put up again: any holes or washings that appear in the bank should be regularly stopped, and the earth carefully replaced every autumn: the prunings and clippings should be regularly and carefully performed, once every winter, and once every summer, about the middle of the month of July. This summer clipping must be earlier or later, according to the season, or to the climate: but it should take place just before the starting of the *Midsummer shoot*. All trees shoot twice in the year: the shoot that comes out in the spring ends about Midsummer, and then begins another shoot that comes out of the end of it; which is about one-third and sometimes about one-half, smaller than the spring shoot, and the pruning or clipping should take place just before this new shoot comes out: this operation causes many new and small shoots to come forth, and gives the hedge a very beautiful appearance; and also makes it much thicker than it otherwise would be. The seed of the blackthorn is a little sloe, and not easily to be obtained in any quantity: its leaf is not so beautiful as that of the hawthorn; but its wood stronger, and its thorns a great deal more formidable. A holly hedge only requires more patience; and we should recollect that it is *evergreen*: and as effectual, in a fence, as either of our thorns; for its leaves are so full of sharp prickles, that no boy will face a holly hedge of any degree of thickness. To have such a hedge, you must gather the berries in autumn, keep them in damp sand for a year; then sow them in November, and, when they come up in the spring, keep the bed carefully weeded, not only then, but all through the summer; let them stand in this bed another summer; then transplant them in rows in a nursery of rich ground; there let them stand for two or three years; then plant them for the hedge at the same distances, and in the same manner, as directed for the honey locusts; then, when they have stood a year thus, cut them down nearly close to the ground, which will bring three or four shoots out of each plant; and, with a little topping and side-pruning, carefully performed, they will, in about five years after being planted, form a very beautiful and effectual fence. Neither of the thorns is raised much more quickly; and certainly there is no comparison for such a purpose between an evergreen and a deciduous tree. And, there is this further advantage with regard to the holly, that it will flourish in any soil, from the dryest and most arid bank, to the wettest and sourest clay; and as to duration, as a plant, nothing but the yew tree equals the holly.

Edward Kemp
ROCK AND FERN GARDENS

Persons who have a fancy for a rock or fern garden, will do well to keep it somewhere in the background, and not in sight from the windows of the house or the principal parts of the lawn. It may be made very interesting if thus secluded, and be approached from the main walk of the garden, through a rustic arch, mantled with climbers, or by a kind of narrow winding passage, canopied and darkened with evergreens. Masses of rockery may even be placed fronting the chief line of walk, at some distance from the house, where a good dense screen of planting can be interposed between them and the lawn, or where they can be made to look as if they were naturally cropping out of a bank. Or they can be employed as a sort of rustic basement to a building. To grow ferns upon them, the shade of trees, or some other objects, will be indispensable; but many rock plants prefer an open sunny situation, so that rockeries should not be entirely shaded. If accompanied by a small pool of water, having a broken rocky margin, a few of the rarer aquatics and sedgy plants may be grown, and gold-fish can be cherished. The moisture exhaled from such a piece of water would be very beneficial to many rock plants; and the jutting pieces of stone, or overhanging shrubs, would afford shelter, and privacy, and shade, to the fish. Where a clear running stream can be turned through a rockery, and be expanded into a pool, trout may also be preserved in the latter; and if there be water enough to dash down a miniature rocky ravine in the shape of a cascade, another characteristic accessory will be added.

Rockeries should be formed as much as possible of natural materials. All the products of art, such as fused bricks, scoriae, and the far more vulgar constituents with which such ornaments are often constructed about towns, are nearly if not quite incompatible with any amount of rusticity. And this last should be the distinguishing element of all rockeries.

As in the material employed, so also in the mode of construction followed, rockeries should be conspicuous for a natural character. No appearance of art, and no approach to the regularity or smoothness proper to works of art, will be at all in place here. On the contrary, the surface of the whole cannot be too

Edward Kemp (1817–1891) was assistant to the famous creator of the Crystal Palace, Sir Joseph Paxton. He was a regular contributor to Gardeners' Chronicle *and his book* How to Lay Out a Garden *was described as 'The only modern book of any pretensions on the subject'.*

irregular, or too variedly indented or prominent. An additional projection must be given to some of the parts by moderate-sized bushes, or short-stemmed weeping trees. Evergreen shrubs or low trees will be particularly useful. Provision will therefore have to be made, in the placing of the stones, for planting a few shrubs, and a greater number of herbaceous rock plants in their interstices, which should be left broader or smaller according to the size of the plant that may be required in them. No rockery will ever be interesting unless well supplied with all such fittings.

For ordinary practice, the materials of which a rockery, however small, is formed, should lie on their broadest or flat sides, and not be set on edge, much less be placed with their points upwards. Little deviations may occasionally be allowed for variety; but the mass will have more appearance of solidity and strength, and be more accordant with Nature's teachings, if each piece be laid flat, with the outer edge inclining a little downwards rather than upwards.

A rock garden may, if its size demands it, be traversed or made more generally accessible by very narrow walks, just capable of admitting one person. These need not be of any uniform width, and should have no regular margin. They may be made of some quiet coloured material, and not covered with dressed gravel; the mere stones of which the rockery is composed forming the best possible paths, if they are tolerably flat.

Any great elevation should never be sought in small rockeries. This would both be inconsistent with their breadth, and would render them too prominent and artificial. They should not be carried higher than the point at which they can be well supported and backed with a broad mass of earth and vegetation. Additional height may sometimes be given, if desired, by excavating into a hollow the base from which they spring. An old quarry will supply the foundation of an excellent rockery, in which considerable height, relatively to the bottom, may be attained, and much of boldness. It should be seen, however, that in working it, masses of rock be merely wrenched or blasted off, in the most irregular manner, and no sawing or cutting to an even face be anywhere permitted. Extreme ruggedness of surface is what would be most characteristic in such a situation.

see plate 17

No collection of rocks should ever begin or end abruptly, but should *gradually* die away into the adjoining ground, by means of a few carelessly scattered groups or single masses of stone. Attention to this point will mark the difference between the practised and the unobservant artist, and will exercise a great influence over the whole composition.

Shrubs with trailing habits, evergreens, and a few of the less delicately branched weeping kinds, and those which assume a wild, and ragged, and picturesque character, are most congenial to rockeries. The first class, especially, including the Ivy, the Savin, *Cotoneaster microphylla*, *Berberis empetrifolia*, Periwinkles, common Heaths, etc., always seem in place and at home. And the more decided climbers, such as Clematis, the Hop plant, *Wistaria sinensis*, some of the better sorts of Bramble, the Ayrshire Roses, Virginian Creeper, and several others, would, if suffered to scramble over the bolder parts of rockeries, and duly pruned and regulated so as not to smother things of more value, be most important and engaging accessories.

Among evergreens, probably some of the most suitable are the green-leaved Hollies, particularly Hodgins's Holly, Box, Arbutus, *Pinus pumilio*, *Juniperus recurva*, Yuccas in groups, Rhododendrons, and common Junipers. And, if the space permits, the Yew, the Hemlock Spruce, the Scotch Fir, the *Pinus austriaca* and *laricio*[1], the Stone Pine, the black Spruce, and the Deodar Cedar are most valuable.

Grass never harmonises well with rocks, if brought into immediate contact with them. They demand the adjunct of a rougher and less polished vegetation, such as attends them in a state of nature. Common moor heath, whortle-berry, etc., cut into sods, and laid with a broken line along the margin of rocks, and interspersed, in parts, with the dwarfest trailing evergreens, will give a beautifully rustic finish, and may be particularly valuable in connecting the rocks with any dressed grass beyond. Everything like a perceptible or continued line (much more a curved line) must be distinctly avoided in the appropriation of such materials. They should join the grass in the most jagged and inartificial manner.

Rockeries can be made to answer one or two simple purposes, which will impart meaning and spirit to them, and prevent them from becoming the expressionless and pointless things which they usually are. Where there are raised banks between one part of a garden and another, rocks can be employed to face the more private side of them, and will contribute to their solidity, at the same time that they increase their propriety and interest. If, again, a walk be cut through a bank, rocks may be used to hold up the sides of the opening, when steep. Or where a walk travels along a narrow hollow between two banks, the slopes of the banks can be partially covered with masses of rock. In both these

[1] *Pinus nigra austriaca* and *P. nigra maritima*

137

last cases, an imperfect imitation of a small defile will be produced, and may be made very consistent and natural. The plan will be particularly serviceable where the hollow has to be made as narrow as possible, and the banks have, consequently, to be kept pretty upright. At any rate, such an arrangement will be infinitely preferable to having mere *heaps* of stones, thrown together without any apparent object beyond the simple creation of the mass.

In localities where stone is not easily procured, or where it abounds so much that the use of another material would be preferable, for the sake of variety, the *rugged stumps* or *roots* of old trees may be substituted, and will yield quite as much picturesqueness. Indeed, when the partially decayed and contorted trunks of aged, pollarded, or deformed oaks have been rooted out, they may sometimes, from their length, be thrown into bolder and more varied forms than could be attained with any ordinary stones; and if used as the supports of climbers, or their cavities converted into nests for trailing plants, they may be made to produce the happiest combinations.

There is an admirable example of the account to which old roots and stumps may be turned in sustaining and rusticating banks, to the north of the Railway Station in the Crystal Palace gardens at Sydenham. From the position, (which is a quiet and shaded part of the grounds, and beneath a cluster of the few fine Oaks that remain to remind us of the departed sylvan honours of Penge Wood,) and the actual construction, and the clothing of this bank of roots, some truly excellent lessons on the subject may be derived.

15   SUTTON PLACE, SURREY. 1898

The old bowling green is bordered by a high brick wall which offers shelter
and support for a variety of climbing and herbaceous plants, including fragrant
plants such as clematis and lilies. The garden has now been relandscaped by
Sir Geoffrey Jellicoe.

139

Canon Ellacombe
OLD WALLS

Henry Ellacombe VMH (1822–1916) wrote and gardened for many years at Bitton, Gloucestershire. He made fashionable many new plants and also promoted some which had been long neglected.

Anyone who possesses an old wall will find plenty of plants that will grow there as well, and in many cases even better, than on the borders; and it seems to make little difference of what material the wall is made. I have seen granite walls almost as well covered as those made of a softer stone, and slate walls soon get covered; but the best walls for the growth of plants are those made of oolite or sandstone. In many parts of the country, especially in the sandstone districts, the wall is finished with a thin layer of stones slightly projecting, and upon this projection are placed, vertically, stones of various thickness and height, which thus in time form 'pockets' of old mortar mixed with much vegetable matter arising from dead leaves and weeds, which make happy homes for many good plants.

Chief among such plants I place the Cheddar pink. In its native home on the Cheddar cliffs it grows chiefly in small tufts in projecting ledges of the cliff, and brought into the garden it is not an easy plant to grow in the open border, but it can be easily grown if its root uninjured (as it seldom is when bought at Cheddar) is inserted under the coping-stone of a wall. In that position it will flower freely, and increase by growing downwards; and such plants I have on the wall of my garden, which have probably been there for more than sixty years, and live and flower without any attention or protection; and in a garden near Bath I have seen a plant which, originally placed on the top of an old freestone wall, now hangs down in a beautiful mat, more than 5 feet in length, and 3 feet across. And I believe the same treatment is good for all the tribe of pinks. We learn this from our own wild carnation (*Dianthus caryophyllus*), the parent of all our carnations, and the gillyflower of our ancestors; this is only found wild on our old castles, and never, I believe, in hedges or fields. To me it has always been a plant of great interest, because knowing it to be an alien, and having seen it in great abundance on William the Conqueror's own Castle of Falaise, I like to think that it was introduced either by him or some of his followers; though its seeds or some plants may have been imported with the Caen stone. But I mention it now because this gives an excellent hint for growing carnations. As usually grown, they are sadly stiff, and a bed of carnations shows almost as many sticks as flowers. But in Switzerland they are grown (especially the crimson cloves) in the window-boxes of the chalets, and are allowed to hang down, and so grown they are very beautiful; and exactly the same treatment may be given to all carnations. They may be placed either on the top of a wall, or in the chinks, and will there grow naturally with excellent effect.

The hardy cacti will grow well in holes of old walls, and generally with greater vigour than when grown in the open ground without shelter. But it is well to give them some protection from snow, for snow will rot them, and the protection can easily be given by a slate or piece of glass, or by inserting them under the shelter of the coping-stones. Their chief enemy then will be the snails, who manage to get at their succulent leaves in spite of the poisonous spines with which they are protected. And, indeed, this is the chief objection to old walls; they are the favourite haunts of many enemies to the garden. In course of time the mortar decays, and the wall is full of holes; where these are at all large they are apt to get filled with colonies of snails. If the holes are in the lower part of the wall, mice will take possession of them, and I have found slow-worms even in the higher holes, but these do no harm. But it is to the insect world that all the holes in an old wall become most attractive, their warmth and dryness exactly suiting them. Alphonse Karr, in his *Tour Round my Garden* (translated London, 1855; in spite of its discursiveness, still one of the pleasantest of gardening books), has a special chapter on an 'Old Wall'; but, while he gives a few lines of praise to its vegetable beauties – "in the crevices of its top extends an absolute crown of yellow wallflowers and ferns, and at its foot vegetate pellitory and nettles in all their beautiful green" – yet his chief delight is in the animal life of the wall – the lizards, caterpillars, and spiders.

But it is for the growth of alpines that the old wall is especially useful. In many gardens it is found very difficult to grow the beautiful cobweb stonecrops (*Sempervivum arachnoideum*). But the late Mr. Wilson Saunders, a most successful cultivator of rare and difficult plants, used to grow it well on a bare stone without any soil, and in such a position I have grown it several times, till it gradually gets destroyed by the damp atmosphere. The first time I saw it growing wild was on a narrow ledge of the old bridge at Hospenthal near Andermatt, and there it was so feebly attached to the stone that the slightest touch dislodged it. I have no doubt it would grow on any wall, but if put high up on the wall its wonderful cobwebs would be invisible; yet it might be worth

see colour plate VII

growing even there if it would produce its flowers, which are of a rich crimson colour, but it is a shy bloomer out of doors in most parts of England. Many of the saxifrages are very difficult to grow out of doors, but two of the most difficult and most beautiful, *S. florulenta* from the Maritime Alps, and *S. longifolia* from the Pyrenees, are now grown successfully and easily at Kew by inserting them in the horizontal crevices of a wall-like rock-work. Another alpine that can be treated in the same way is the edelweiss. Not many years ago it was considered almost impossible to grow this plant away from its alpine fastnesses; now it is found to grow easily if raised from seed, and at the gardens at Trinity College, Dublin, it is grown as a wall-plant, in projecting hollow brackets specially used for it and other plants like it. Another alpine which is very apt to 'miff off' if grown in the open border is the *Erinus alpinus*, yet I once saw the fine old brick coped wall which bounds the garden of Denton Hall, in Buckinghamshire, completely covered with this pretty alpine in full flower, and since that I have seen it on other walls, but not in such abundance as at Denton. I have no doubt that many of the alpine primulas and androsaces would grow on old walls, but I have not tried them; and, indeed, I think that most plants which can stand drought and delight in bright sunshine would be worth trying, but it would be of little use to try bulbs, though some tuberous plants, such as the dwarf irises, would certainly grow in such positions. I say nothing of wallflowers, snapdragons, and foxgloves, for they are native plants which will sow themselves; but seeds of the better sorts are worth sowing, and I will only name one more flower which should be planted on every wall where it does not grow naturally, the wall toad-flax, *Linaria cymbalaria*. This is not a true native, and is said to have been brought from Italy, though found wild as far north as Holland, but it is completely naturalised in many parts of the United Kingdom. It is one of the most graceful wall-creepers that I know, and with me it grows naturally; but if it did not I should certainly plant it. The flowers are usually a pretty purple, but I have found it with pure white flowers, and there is a variegated form; all are lovely ornaments for any wall.

Herbert Maxwell
SOME PLANTS FOR WALLS

Everyone who, disregarding John Ruskin's *obiter dictum* that it is only people with minds of the second order who concern themselves with flowers, has given attention to his garden, must be well aware that there are many beautiful plants which, although not hardy in the open border, may pass safely through a hard winter when trained against a wall. That knowledge, however, is not so generally applied in practice as it might be. Often one sees great spaces of wall bare of all covering; in some places walls are overgrown with ivy or that wearisome *Vitis inconstans*[1] which goes commonly by the name of *Ampelopsis*; in other places they are given up to rambler roses and things of inferior merit. Many years ago I received convincing proof of the better purpose to which a wall may be put, even in the colder parts of our country. North Ayrshire – the inland parishes thereof at least – is a cold district exposed to bitter winds, yet in a garden near Kilmarnock, I found the Chilian *Desfontainea spinosa* trained against a wall and flowering freely. Now this brilliant shrub only succeeds in the open where the climate is mild and moist.

Nevertheless, one swallow does not make a summer; I must beware of generalising, lest, by recommending things on the borderline of hardiness, I mislead those whose gardens are in cold districts. Let the following remarks, therefore, be taken as suggestion for the better use of walls in our milder districts. But what considerable tracts of land fall within that limitation. Kent and Surrey, the whole of Sussex, a great part of Hampshire, all the southern and western coast as far north as Ross-shire, and nearly all Ireland, with favoured patches of climate, such as that of the Moray Firth, here and there on the east coast. I must just jot down a few plants as they come to mind, without any attempt at order, leaving out those which, like jessamine, *Wistaria*, climbing roses, honeysuckle, etc. are too commonly known and grown to require any recommendation.

It is not only against winter cold that a wall serves to protect plants not in

Herbert Maxwell VMH (1845–1937) was a distinguished politician and historian as well as author and countryman. His estate in Scotland extended to some 9,000 acres.

---

[1] *Parthenocissus tricuspidata*

143

the first degree of hardiness; even in an untoward summer it enables them to ripen their young wood more thoroughly than those of the same species in the open, thereby ensuring a fuller flush of blossom in the following year. Very well-marked examples of this may be seen in the present summer of 1923. The Chilean *Tricuspidaria lanceolata*[1] has proved perfectly hardy in the open here; but when first it came to us we were not certain how it might relish a Scottish winter and a harsh spring, wherefore we placed some of the plants against walls, where they have been allowed to remain ever since. The summer of 1922 was so dark and cold that many flowering shrubs failed to ripen their season's growth thoroughly enough to produce much bloom in 1923. Such was the case with *Tricuspidaria* in the open where large plants, 16 feet high, bore scarcely any flowers, while those with a wall at their back were densely hung with crimson tassels in June. On the other hand, *Abutilon vitifolium*, also from Chile, flowers far more profusely in the open where it has plenty of room, than it does when squeezed up against a wall. *A. megapotamicum* is not hardy here in the open, but does splendidly on a wall.

Those who knew Canon Ellacombe's garden at Bitton will not have forgotten the remarkable variety of plants trained on the long wall standing at right angles to the south front of the house. There grew and flowered the Californian *Penstemon cordifolius*, with brilliant scarlet flowers. It stood, if I remember aright, about 8 feet high against a wall facing north. The kind old Canon gave me a plant of it nearly twenty years ago; it has flowered here, but not with anything like the luxuriance it showed at Bitton, probably requiring more sunshine than prevails in our latitude. *Abelia floribunda*, however, a Mexican species, gives us plenty of its crimson tubular flowers against a south wall.

Unluckily for those who dwell in the northerly parts of Great Britain, the brilliant *Tecoma radicans*[2], from the south-eastern United States, requires a hotter sun than we can provide for it to bring out its splendid orange and scarlet trumpets. I, at least, have never seen it in flower freely north of the Trent. It grew vigorously here for many years, clinging to a house wall by its aerial roots; but, having waited in vain for a display, we removed it to make way for something better suited for our cloudy atmosphere. It is thoroughly hardy, is magnificent when in bloom, and ought to be far more frequently grown than it is in the southern counties of England.

---

[1] *Crinodendron hookerianum*   [2] *Campsis radicans*

The order of *Leguminosae* or Pea-flowers contains some splendid plants for training on walls. Of *Clianthus puniceus* mention has been made elsewhere; it has a rival for brilliancy in *Caesalpinia Gilliesii* from Argentina, which runs rapidly over sun-baked walls in districts such as Sussex, the Isle of Wight and even in the home counties, for I first saw it in flower on a south wall in Kew Gardens. Next time I came across it, the effect of its splendour was enhanced by surprise – by the unexpected – which goes so far to intensify sensation. It was in a deserted mining village of Andalusia; a long street of empty houses, mostly roofless, seemed all the more desolate because of the town hall which still stood tenantless, but entire, amid a grove of lofty Australian beef-trees – *Casuarina* – on an eminence commanding the village. No human being was in sight; goats had devoured all edible vegetation within their reach (and for them few green things are inedible); complete silence reigned under the blazing sunshine. Poking about among the ruins I came suddenly, in the backyard of a house, upon a vision of beauty. There, in this dusty, scorched solitude stood a single bush of *Caesalpinia Gilliesii* 9 or 10 feet high, laden with erect racemes of large, rich, yellow flowers, with scarlet stamens protruding full 3 inches from the corolla. This sight alone would have been ample reward for a journey to southern Spain; but why should one have to travel so far afield to enjoy it? Why does one never see this noble plant trained against some fraction of the leagues of brick wall given up to common climbers? *C. Japonica* has none of the dazzling splendour of *C. Gilliesii*, but its bright green pinnate foliage is very pretty, and when trained on a wall it bears plenty of racemes of deep yellow flowers.

Among the locust trees or false acacias *Robinia hispida* and *neo-Mexicana* are quite hardy in this country, but the branches are so excessively brittle that the plants seldom escape destruction in the open. They make fine wall shrubs with drooping racemes of bright-rose flowers. *Wistaria multijuga* was supposed at see plate 27 first to be no more than a variety of the well-known *W. Chinensis*, to which it is infinitely superior in beauty, bearing racemes of lilac-purple flowers 2 and 3 feet long; but it is now recognised as a distinct species, and should always be planted instead of the other, whereof one is apt to get very inferior forms with short, few flowered racemes.

The perennial species of *Lathyrus* being mostly herbaceous are better adapted for training to a trellis or for covering tree stumps than for growing against a wall, unless they are planted so as to run up among the branches of stronger shrubs. But *L. pubescens*, a Chilean species with pale bluish-lilac flowers, is of shrubby habit and well deserves a good place. Far superior to the common everlasting pea – *L. latifolius* and *L. grandiflorus* – is *L. rotundifolius* (syn. *Drummondi*) from Persia, not nearly so often grown as it ought to be, for its flower clusters of a peculiar shade of soft brick-red never fail to attract attention from visitors. It is quite hardy.

In all but the coldest parts of the country *Solanum crispum*, from Chile, makes a beautiful wall-plant, with a lavish display of bluish-violet and orange flowers at midsummer, exactly resembling those of the field potato. The white flowering *S. jasminoides*, a Brazilian species, is more beautiful, but more tender, suitable for outdoor walls only in favoured districts. To get this charming climber to mingle its tendrils with *Tropaeolum speciosum* so that they may flower together is to achieve the prettiest possible combination.

Like so many other Chilean plants, *Lardizabala biternata* simply revels in our west country humidity. Unluckily the hanging racemes of male flowers are not produced in fair proportion to the handsome evergreen foliage, and as we are short of wall space, and as this rampant climber was not content with covering its allowance of 20 feet by 20, but was invading room allotted to others, I reluctantly signed its death warrant. The male flowers, which are produced in midwinter, form a beautiful object in a vase. Six ivory-white stamens, monadelphously united, stand out well relieved against the broad fleshy sepals and smaller petals, both intensely dark purple, almost black, smelling of vinegar. From the same country comes *Eccremocarpus scaber*, one of the Bignoniaceae, not rampant, but of free growth, and very gay from midsummer onwards with one-sided racemes of scarlet and yellow flowers. It is easily raised from seed, which ripens in abundance.

Lapageria rosea, another Chilean climber, is not usually accounted hardy, nevertheless there are many places where it flourishes out of doors in this country, and produces its lovely waxy bells in autumn, continuing in flower till Christmas if the season is mild. It should be planted against a north wall, with a guard of perforated zinc round it as a protection against slugs, which are specially partial to the succulent shoots that spring from the roots. The majority of plants that climb by twining their young growth round some support revolve from left to right – against the sun and against watch-hands. Such is the habit of *Convolvulus*, *Wistaria*, *Aristolochia*, *Stephanotis*, *Berberidopsis*, etc.; but *Lapageria* is one of a few plants, including hop and honeysuckle, whereof the shoots revolve with the sun from right to left.

Berberidopsis corallina, mentioned in the foregoing paragraph, is one of the choicest of the treasures that we owe to Chilean forests. Even if late summer were to pass without its clusters of pendent coral-red flowers, its evergreen, heart-shaped, spiny leaves are so ornamental as to justify a good place for it on a south or west wall.

It is difficult to get away from Chile in discussing fine flowers, so rich is that land in desirable species; but I must hurry on. *Fuchsia globosa* and its hybrid *Riccartoni* are well-known as hardy shrubs in maritime districts, requiring no wall to protect them; but there are several species from South America and Mexico of surpassing beauty which I have seen trained as wall-shrubs only in Cornwall and the west, but which ought to be far more generally known and grown. *F. corymbiflora* from Peru and *F. fulgens* are two of the showiest, their long scarlet tubes making them very conspicuous among other things.

Fremontia Californica[1] is noteworthy for its bright yellow flowers set on short stalks along the branches. Though it is hardy in the open in Cornwall and the west, it requires the shelter of a wall in inland districts, and no doubt would be more commonly grown were it not for the difficulty of getting it established through its impatience of being transplanted. I have no experience of this handsome tree beyond having admired it in the gardens of others; but I understand that the surest means of propagating is to raise it from seed and plant it out of a pot. Similar treatment succeeds with *Indigofera Gerardiana*, a deciduous, leguminous shrub from the Himalayas, producing quantities of purplish-rose flowers in racemes during late summer. In cold districts it is nearly always cut to the ground in winter, but springs again and behaves like a herbaceous plant. In one respect it differs from *Fremontia*, which is short-lived and apt to die without apparent cause, whereas *Indigofera* may be relied on to endure indefinitely. Several new species have been brought from China in recent years, some of which are of much beauty.

Where the climate is too severe for it in the open, no handsomer shrub than *Abutilon vitifolium*, and none more profuse in bloom, can be given a good place on a south wall. *A. megapotamicum* is much more tender, but makes a splendid wall plant in mild districts, remaining in bloom longer than any other shrub known to me.

Due advantage is not often taken of a north wall, which is far too often surrendered to ivy or *Vitis inconstans*; but there are many choice plants which rejoice in such a situation, preferring it to any other aspect. *Lapageria* has already been mentioned as one of these; *Camellia reticulata* is another, whereof

---

[1] *Fremontodendron californicum*

147

the great loose, carmine flowers with yellow centres are so much more attractive than the prim florists' varieties which look as if they had been carved in lard, plain or coloured. Rhododendrons of the Maddeni series – *R. Edgeworthi, Scottianum, megacalyx* and others – which it is hopeless to attempt growing in the open except in very mild districts, may be successfully cultivated under the shelter of a north wall, even where winter is sometimes severe. And with what flowers they reward him who bestows this modicum of care upon them! Lily-scented, resembling lilies in shape and purity, the common run of garden flowers seem almost dowdy or aggressively gaudy in comparison with them.

In the *Clematis* family there are plants of the very highest merit for clothing walls. It puzzles visitors unversed in botany when they are told that these far-spreading, lofty-climbing plants belong to the same natural order to such diverse herbs as buttercups, anemones, larkspurs, aconites, columbines, Christmas roses, etc., and therefore are descended from an immediate common ancestor. There is indeed no such polymorphic order of plants as the *Ranunculaceae*. The beautiful *Clematis indivisa* from New Zealand can only be grown in the open by those whose lot lies in the south and west, where it is not so often seen as it deserves to be, not only for its beauty, but because it flowers in April and May. *C. Armandi*, from Western China, is quite hardy, but demands a vast space to do itself justice. *C. montana* has been in this country for nearly one hundred years, yet it is far from generally grown even now, although as a wall plant or a rambler over growing trees or tree stumps it is hard to beat. The rose-coloured variety, *rubens*, is as good as the type, and equally hardy. It was introduced by Wilson in 1900, and like the white form, flowers in May and June; while another variety, also introduced by Wilson and named after him *Wilsoni*, is described as having larger white flowers, produced in August; but I have no personal acquaintance with it yet, nor with another Chinese species well-spoken of – *C. Fargesi*, a bed of seedlings thereof here not having reached the flowering stage. *C. flammula* has probably been cultivated in this country longer than any other exotic species, having been brought hither during or before Queen Elizabeth's reign; and although the flowers are individually small they are produced in great abundance in autumn and diffuse a delicious fragrance.

Among the large flowering species – *C. patens, lanuginosa, florida, Jackmanni* and their innumerable hybrids there is plenty of choice, not for clothing walls, for these are not of the far-flung character of the kinds mentioned above, but for decorating them. They may be planted to climb among the branches of other shrubs, whether these are growing in the open or trained against walls. But they must not be starved; a good mulch of well-rotted manure is no more than their due; they all relish lime in the soil and full exposure to sunshine, provided that their roots are kept in shade. I am not competent to prescribe for the niceties of pruning appropriate for the different species, that process having been unpardonably neglected here; so I cannot do better than refer the reader to the admirable treatise by Mr. W. J. Bean, where directions founded upon experience at Kew are well set forth in vol. i. of *Trees and Shrubs Hardy in the British Isles* (John Murray, London). In the course of the present summer, nothing in our garden has pleased me better than the pure white flowers, 6 inches across, of a clematis of the *Lanuginosa* race, rambling to a height of 12 feet over a myrtle trained on a south wall. It has rejoiced us in the same gracious manner during the last fifteen summers, has never been pruned, and we dare not give it the lime which it is known to covet lest that should disagree with *Amaryllis belladonna* at the foot of the wall. Those who love *Clematis* – and who that knows the family can fail to love them? – should study for guidance the enthusiastic monograph by Mr. William Robinson, entitled *The Virgin's Bower* (London, 1912). And whereas the purpose of the present writer is to assist in rejection as the indispensable corollary of selection, let his last words about *Clematis* be to denounce all double-flowered forms of that family as abominable. No milder epithet suffices for the distortion of a perfect flower into a monstrosity that can only merit the kind of morbid attention bestowed upon a two-headed calf or a four-legged chicken in a village museum.

The passion flower – *Passiflora coerulea* – is a rapid grower and, although a native of Brazil, is quite hardy as a wall plant in all but the colder districts; but in the northern parts of our country it flowers too late in the season to form its egg-shaped orange fruit which are so ornamental on house fronts in some of our southern seaside towns. The white-flowering variety, 'Constance Elliot', is of inferior beauty to the blue-flowering type.

Lonicera tragophylla, introduced by Wilson from China in 1900, is distinguished among other honeysuckles by the size of its flowers, which are borne in heads of ten to twenty blossoms of a uniform rich yellow averaging 3 inches long. It differs also from most other climbing species in being scentless; nevertheless, it is such a handsome plant when in flower as to make it worthy of a place in the most select assemblage of plants. But let no one now make such a blunder as I was guilty of when first it came here. It was planted against a

149

south wall, where it has become a prey to a dark-coloured aphis; the proper place for it being a north wall, on a cool soil (though at Tresco it flourishes against the south face of a rock in blazing sunshine). Unluckily, we cannot now remove it, as a precious plant of *Mutisia decurrens* has wound its tendrils inextricably among its sprays. *Lonicera Standishi* and *fragrantissima* are the reverse of showy and resemble each other very closely; in fact, the only ready means of distinguishing between them is that *L. Standishi* has whitish bristles on the stalks of leaves and flowers. They both bear slender, white, very fragrant flowers in long succession through the winter months and are worth growing on that account alone.

Carpenteria Californica yields its large, white, yellow-centred flowers more freely against a wall than it does in the open; and if a tangle of *Tropoeolum speciosum* gets among its branches, you will have one of the most charming accidental effects possible, deliciously suggesting strawberries and cream.

Ceanothus rigidus and *Veitchianus* with rich blue flowers and *C. thyrsiflorus* with pale blue ones, are desirable evergreens for covering walls, though the last-named is hardy enough to stand out in the open even in cold districts, and grows over 20 feet high. *Ribes speciosus* is deciduous, but the brilliancy of its flowers entitle it to a choice corner; while *Abelia floribunda* can only be trusted to weave its long coral necklaces in such situations as the lemon-scented verbena – *Lippia* (*Aloysia*) *citriodora* – can bear it company, they being about equal in hardihood and essentially plants for the south and west.

I recommend the evergreen *Magnolia grandiflora* as noble tapestry for the south wall of a spacious mansion, where it may fill the air with perfume from its great cream coloured chalices. Unhappily for us northerners, it flowers too late in the season for our latitude; at least I have never seen it flower in Scotland; but in southern counties it is without a peer among flowering trees.

It may be observed that no mention has been made of roses as wall plants. That is assuredly not from any indifference on the part of the writer to that race of plants which, more than any other, has been the joy and pride of countless generations, but it is because to deal with them, however superficially, would lead me far beyond my purpose. Nobody will peruse these pages who takes no interest in gardening; while those who are interested in the subject will have their own taste and preference in roses, and have unlimited choice of varieties to choose from. Nevertheless, I will break the rule I have laid down for myself by naming one rose, not as the only one best fitted for a wall, but as one that has afforded us special pleasure and does not seem to be very generally grown. The rose in question is the hybrid tea Climbing Papa Gontier. Its carmine flowers may or may not be of the regulation pattern prescribed by experts; of that I am quite ignorant; but this I know, that it has grown some 12 feet high beside our dining-room window, bidding us morning greeting earlier than any other rose in the garden, while winter still lingers in the lap of May, and in chill October waves reluctant farewell to summer joys.

16   OLD PLACE, EAST SUSSEX. 1900

Carefully trained and controlled virginia creeper and flowering climbers dress
the main body of the house, in contrast to the destructive vigour of the creepers
on the wing to the left of the photograph.

Gertrude Jekyll and Christopher Hussey
OVERGROWTH

Walls should only have such coverings that neither confuse the design nor damage the structure. While ivy and *Ampelopsis Veitchii*[1] (Virginia creeper) should only be permitted in exceptional cases, and then under most careful supervision, the slower growing and flowering wall shrubs, the patine of lichen and the little growths of time are all delightful and desirable so long as they give colour and texture to a wall that they do not conceal. Ivy is particularly dangerous owing to its tight grip of surfaces and the manner in which its fine suckers, having insinuated themselves in small cracks, expand and so at last disintegrate the walls it appears to be protecting. Ampelopsis, though more easily removed, can cover a whole building in a few years. The eyes of the inhabitants grow accustomed to its presence and fail to notice the growth of the stuff. Owing, no doubt, to their preoccupation with more intellectual matters, the authorities of Oxford and Cambridge Colleges are particularly prone to this form of myopia.

Yet ampelopsis, it cannot be denied, is a beautiful plant, with its tiny tender green leaves in spring, the copper of late summer and its autumn fire. Its successful use on an architectural building is seen at Old Place, Sussex, that the late C. E. Kemp built, with such early success, in the vernacular manner. There it is under as close attention as the most precious of roses, sedulously pruned and controlled, lest it should envelop the whole building.

It may be said that all wall plants, no matter what they are, call for extreme caution in their treatment. In the selection of plants suitable for wall decoration consideration must be paid to one or two points:

(1) To the building itself, embracing its design and general architectural lines.

(2) To the plant, whether it be evergreen or deciduous, and its requirements, which include such important details as aspect, involving its need for protection from wind; whether it is a sun lover, or whether it

Gertrude Jekyll VMH (1843–1932), well loved author of Home and Garden *and other classics of twentieth-century gardening, designed more than 300 gardens. Her influence has been profound and lasting.*

Christopher Hussey (1899–1970), architect and landscape historian, was closely involved with Country Life *and with the National Trust's preservation work. His home was Scotney Castle, Kent.*

see plate 16

---

[1] *Parthenocissus tricuspidata*

prefers a moist or a dry situation; if it can climb for itself, or requires support in the way of pinning.

(3) The general habit of the plant, whether it be of upright vertical growth or is given to spreading itself laterally. In this connection the character of the structure should be considered in relation to the type of plant selected. Shrubs of upright habit should be given a position against a wall which suggests vertical treatment. On the other hand, plants, like wistaria, with long, arching, horizontal branches, lend themselves best to horizontal spaces.

(4) Its value as a decorative subject, in flower, foliage and fruit, and at what period of the year its beauty is to be witnessed.

It cannot be too strongly emphasised that position is all-important. Do not plant tender and sun-loving plants where they will receive neither sun nor protection. Planting ranks as equally important with the question of soil. It is generally advisable to take out the soil to a depth of 2 to 3 feet. It will, in all probability, be found to harbour all manner of builder's rubbish, and, if that be so, then fresh compost is required. When planting, the subjects should not be placed too closely, as in a few years' time the branches, if properly trained, will furnish the wall for a considerable distance on either side of the main stem. It is true that choice is somewhat limited, comparatively speaking, but, nevertheless, it is worth trying to accommodate species which will flower at different periods. Then, again, those shrubs which assume rich autumnal colourings should be given a position to display their foliage to the best advantage, as, for example, on a west wall in the face of the setting sun.

There are a few plants which ought to be given room on every wall: wistaria, the vines, from the many varieties of *Vitis vinifera*, with their delicate leaves of port-wine colour and feathery growth, to the large leaved *Vitis Coignetiae*, handsome in its autumnal colouring; and the pyracanthas, with their masses of red berries and evergreen foliage.

Indeed, all the ornamental vines may be said to be wall plants *par excellence*. Their rich golden brown to red autumnal tints surpass those of the ordinary virginia creeper, and their nature and mosaic habit of growth, without the disadvantages of the ordinary virginia, merit them a place in a wall collection.

All these subjects are fairly rapid and vigorous growers, and, apart from being so well adapted for wall decoration, are both graceful and charming in fruit, flower and foliage.

It is not suggested for one moment that the list appearing on pages 156–158 meets all cases or provides for all contingencies. It must be borne in mind that what will be appropriate to plant on a north wall in the south of England will not necessarily meet with success if given the same position in north-eastern Scotland. Let it, therefore, be elastic. Just a word as to the distinctions which exist between wall shrubs and true climbers. The former cannot be employed so much for clothing actual walls as for relieving monotony if they chance to be devoid of any architectural features. Evergreen shrubs will prove to be eminently suited for such purposes. If the same treatment be meted out to them as to true climbers, such as clipping, which does not tend to harshness, but, rather, produces fineness of line, then they will, after a period of growth, present a highly ornamental frontage. It is important, though, that the masses should be broken up, not only by clipping, but by controlling unruly growths, and so variety be obtained, together with the necessary subordination to the architectural background.

NOTES FOR THE SELECTION OF WALL PLANTS

PLANT	ASPECT	SOIL	DECORATIVE VALUE AND CULTURAL REQUIREMENTS
Azara microphylla	North wall. (West or south wall in northern districts)	Ordinary loam	Small dark shining leaves borne densely in shining sprays are highly ornamental. Attains height of 15–20 ft.
Buddleia variabilis ——var. *Veitchii* ——var. *magnifica*	Suitable for all aspects	Ordinary to fairly heavy soil. Prefers touch of lime in soil	Chiefly valued on account of the foliage, combined with shapely spikes of lilac to violet coloured flowers, which appear July–October. Reaches height 15ft. Advisable to cut out projecting shoots and train back to wall. A vigorous grower, suitable for large spacious walls.
*Bignonia (Tecoma) radicans	South wall	Ordinary medium soil	Large orange scarlet trumpet flowers are exceedingly beautiful. Reaches height 15–20ft. A fine wall plant for south wall.
Cleanothus thyrsiflorus ——*floribundus* ——*rigidus* ——*Gloire de Versailles*	West or south wall	Ordinary loam (preferably light)	In foliage and flowers highly decorative. Reaches 15–20ft. If properly fan-trained they provide excellent furnishing, as at Kew, where all species are being tried.
*Clematis montana ——var. *rubens*	North or east wall (West in north-eastern districts)	Limy soil	Should be selected for the beautiful white flowers of the type. Var. *rubens* bears brilliant rose pink flowers. Always well furnished with bloom from base upwards if trained and pinned to the wall.
*Cydonia japonica[1]	All aspects	Ordinary loam	One of the most useful of wall shrubs, flowering from December to March. Requires a certain amount of training and pruning.
Cotoneaster horizontalis	All aspects	Ordinary loam	Requires fan-training to be effective. The long horizontal almost sail-like branches are laden with abundant tiny red berries in autumn. May reach a height of 5–8ft.
Eriobotrya japonica	West wall	Ordinary, inclined to be heavy, loam	Foliage large dark shining green. Very decorative.
*Garrya elliptica (Male form.)	North and east wall	Ordinary loam	Should be included for the handsome tassels or catkins 6–9ins. long, of

* Denotes wall shrubs and climbers which, in our opinion, are of outstanding merit.
[1] *Chaenomeles japonica*

NOTES FOR THE SELECTION OF WALL PLANTS

PLANT	ASPECT	SOIL	DECORATIVE VALUE AND CULTURAL REQUIREMENTS
			greenish-yellow flowers which appear during the winter. Foliage of a fine grey beneath.
Holboellia coriacea	West and south wall	Ordinary loam	A first-rate shrub for covering walls with these aspects. Its dark evergreen shining foliage is handsome. The branches and leaves drop gracefully, forming a fine drapery if trained back.
*Hydrangea petiolaris	North and east wall	Fairly heavy soil	An exceedingly useful climber requiring little or no support. Both in summer, with its white blossoms, and in winter, with its reddy-brown young wood, it is very ornamental. Should certainly be included. A vigorous grower suitable for large walls.
*Jasminum nudiflorum ——officinale	All aspects (north and east preferably)	Ordinary loam	One of the most ornamental of wall plants. Its bright yellow flowers borne in the winter months are sufficiently well known to require no further praise. *Officinale* is valued chiefly for its evergreen foliage and white flowers, borne June to September.
Magnolia grandiflora	South and west wall	Rich, well-drained loam.	A fine plant and one of the most admirable for wall decoration. Its beauty is to be found in the large evergreen leaves and the strikingly handsome white blossoms. Reaches a height of 20–30 ft. Should be trained well back both laterally and vertically.
Lonicera fragrantissima ——tragophylla	South wall	Rich loam	Require a sunny position. Creamy white, sweetly scented flowers appear January to March.
*Pyracantha angustifolia ——coccinea var. *Lalandei* ——crenulata var. *yunnanensis*	North and east walls preferably, but they will do in all aspects. They withstand hard frosts with impunity	Ordinary loam	Are the finest decorative wall shrubs in fruit and foliage. *Coccinea Lalandei* should be included in every collection. With its clusters of scarlet red berries and its evergreen foliage, it is unsurpassed for wall decoration. *Coccinea* itself has

NOTES FOR THE SELECTION OF WALL PLANTS

PLANT	ASPECT	SOIL	DECORATIVE VALUE AND CULTURAL REQUIREMENTS
			orange-scarlet fruits. The other species carries dense clusters of dull red berries with attractive shining foliage which blend well together. Berries generally persist throughout the winter. The red-berried sorts should not be planted against a red brick wall, as then the red tones of the wall and the berries clash. *P. angustifolia,* with its yellowish berries, looks well against a brick wall.
Solanum jasminoides	West wall	Ordinary loam	Valued on account of its whitish-blue flowers. Requires training to be effective.
Sophora tetraptera	All aspects	Ordinary loam	Light feathery foliage. Requires to be trained well back.
Tamarix gallica	North and east wall	Prefers a rather sandy, inclined to moist soil	Attractive feathery foliage of a pleasant shade of green. Makes well-furnished bushes. Attains about 8–10 ft. Requires training back.
Viburnum rhytidophyllum	West to south wall	Ordinary to rich loam	Long handsome leaves, very ornamental. Flowers and fruit also attractive.
Vitis Coignetiae ——*Thomsonii*[2] ——*vinifera* var. *purpurea* ——*Thunbergii*	Really suitable for all aspects, although vinifera purpurea will appear more attractive on a west wall	Prefer a fairly heavy rich soil with a touch of lime rubble	The ornamental vines are the finest climbers for wall decoration. Their chief merit lies in their beautiful foliage, which assumes the most gorgeous autumnal tints. Their habit of growth, forming more or less of a mosaic, is both charming and attractive. They appear extremely well when trained against stonework of mellow tones.
Wistaria sinensis ——var. *alba*	All aspects	Prefers a fairly deep medium loam	One of the few really good wall shrubs reaching a height of 20–30 ft. Should be trained round all sides of the wall where space permits, as then its flowering period is considerably prolonged. It is a rapid grower, and can be trained on a single stem principle, with numerous horizontal branches up to a considerable height, when it is most effective in flower.

[2] *Parthenocissus thomsonii*

17   HIGHDOWN, WEST SUSSEX. 1937

In Sir Frederick Stern's garden a wide sweep of glistening chalk cliff makes a
perfect setting for the rock garden full of alpine plants which nestles at its base.

159

Will Ingwersen

BUILDING AND PLANTING
A RETAINING WALL

Will Ingwersen VMH (1905–) has an extraordinary knowledge of rock and alpine plants. For many years he has collected them from the temperate mountain ranges of the world, bred them and sold them through his famous nursery near East Grinstead, Sussex.

Walls, and especially old walls, have had a fascination for me since my early youth; ancient walls of brick or stone, etched with lichens and cushioned with moss on the shaded sides, in which certain Ferns, and the curious Wall Pennywort had found lodgment, and the sunny tops gilded with close carpets of the Wall Pepper (*Sedum acre*).

It was a marvel to me how these plants found support for their life on such starvation diet, or again on walls of old ruins, such as Conway Castle, crowned with flowering tufts of the wild Wallflower, scenting the keen sea air, or on old flint walls, too, in which the Snapdragon had found a roothold, and where it had become a good perennial plant in the meagre sustenance it could wrest from the old mortar. Here, this plant never suffers from the dread Rust disease that makes the modern Antirrhinum almost impossible to cultivate in some gardens.

Or I think of walls, once again near the coast, where the red Valerian had colonized, or in an old abbey ruin along the river Wey in Surrey, where Echium and wild Roses painted pictures of beauty against the summer sky.

All these plants seemed so happy and healthy in their self-sought homes that the thought came to my mind, why not try to create something of this kind in our gardens? Take, for instance, that steep grass slope in the garden, where the ground had been levelled to form a tennis court. It had been turfed over and required endless attention and clipping to keep it even approximately tidy. Such a steep slope became my first attempt at building a retaining wall.

I do not claim that I was the inventor of such a wall; there must have been many similar ones up and down the country, a number of which had developed a little flora of their own. Look at the many walls of this kind supporting the steep bank of a so-called ha-ha, or sunken fence, dividing the pleasure garden from adjoining parkland, where fallow deer or cattle could be watched, apparently grazing in the garden. On steeply sloping ground, too,

160

retaining walls enough had been constructed to terrace gardens at various levels, and there must be hundreds of miles of retaining walls holding up the vineyards in wine-growing countries. No, retaining walls are no modern invention, and I have little doubt but that the famous hanging gardens of Babylon were kept up by such walls.

It is evident, therefore, that there is no novelty in retaining walls, and that they can be made the happy home of many rock or alpine plants should be more widely realized. Perhaps it can become the answer to the vexed question about rock gardens in the vicinity of houses, where many purists claim that they are out of place. "No rock garden should be within sight of a house," once thundered a voice well known in horticulture. To this a witty friend of mine replied: "Many rock gardens should not be in sight of anything." But that is all long ago and need not vex us here. The fact remains that a retaining wall, if properly built, will provide ideal growing conditions for many lovely plants, some of which will colonize in such conditions and look after themselves, leaving to us only the task of keeping them in check where their colonizing capacities become obstreperous and threaten the life of less vigorous but well-loved neighbours.

Now I am not pretending that a retaining wall is inexpensive to construct where walling stone has to be bought; it is not. Suitable stone is not cheap except in such districts as the Cotswolds, where appropriate flattish stone is easily procured. Where stone has to be shaped or dressed by hand, a retaining wall can become very expensive indeed. In stoneless districts where additional costs of cartage by rail or road have to be considered, it may be best to use old bricks, which will answer quite well, especially if the topmost, finishing courses are cemented together, or if a coping of flat stones is used to finish off the work. The lower courses will be held firmly in position by the weight of those above them, but to have such comparatively light material as bricks loose in the topmost run would be inviting them to fall off during gardening operations near the top.

One of the best materials for retaining walls is the Sussex sandstone, which is easily quarried in suitable pieces as it cleaves easily and breaks at right angles. I am fond of this stone because it is porous and absorbent, and sucks up and holds water for the use of the plants inserted as the wall is being built.

In addition to the stone already mentioned, the Purbeck district provides suitable natural walling stone, and in Somerset there are quarries which produce limestone very suitable for walling, as there are beds where the natural cleavage line runs horizontally and the stones can be quarried at the desired thickness and need no further trimming and shaping. I have had similar stone from quarries on the Isle of Man, and there must be quarries up and down the country, especially in Yorkshire, where stone can be obtained that needs no costly handling nor cutting.

Now, you will ask: "Is it easy to build such a wall?" That question is not readily answered, but, as the building material is angular and need not be unwieldy or too heavy, I think that any handy man should be able to make a pretty good job of a wall as long as he understands a few simple principles and possesses a fairly straight eye. It is far easier to build a wall than a good and realistic rock garden. A wall is built on straight lines, and one starts with a shallow trench which is slightly deeper towards the solid bank of earth, and a line may be stretched along the front as a guide.

At the extreme ends drive in sighting posts at the angle to which the wall is to be built – and remember that a retaining wall should not be dead upright but must tilt slightly backwards into the bank. As the work grows up, lift your guiding line now and then and stretch it tightly between the sighting posts to check if your work is straight and level.

Remember, too, that every layer of stone put in should recede about a quarter of an inch from the front edge of the layer below it. As each course is completed, ram very tightly the soil behind the stones, and cover the stone surface you have built with a layer, half an inch deep, of fine soil. This makes a bed for the next layer of stones. Ensure also that where stone joins stone in the lower layer, the stones in the layer immediately above bridge over these joints. This makes for strength and firmness.

After three or four layers have been built to your satisfaction, you can begin to insert plants as the work proceeds. I like to use pot-grown plants for this as far as possible. Turn the plant out of its pot, remove any crocks from the base of the potball, and then place the potball on the layer of fine soil with the neck of the plant flush with the edge of the stones, and put your hand upon it and press down until it is sufficiently flattened and place a stone upon it. It is well to see that the potball is thoroughly moist, so that it will flatten out with ease and without hurting the roots embedded in it. Use trailing plants for the lower layers as you build and plant, and leave the upper layers for compact, cushion-forming plants so that the more vigorous growing plants can trail to their heart's content without growing over, and smothering, the smaller, more compact varieties.

Whilst building the third or fourth course it will be well to turn one of the longer stones into the bank here and there to act as an anchor, and I need not repeat that, as the wall grows, the soil behind it must be continually rammed as firmly as possible to avoid subsequent settlement, which might be disastrous. At the beginning and the end of the wall, tie stones must be built into the bank of course, and the same must be done if the wall is a long one and it is desired to break the run by a flight of steps to a higher level.

If the bank is a high one, I like to break the wall into sections horizontally, too; to step it back and make a convenient terrace at a height of about 3 feet. This see colour plate VII makes a very convenient bed at an easy level for a scree in which to grow some of the choicest alpine plants. Such a bed is a delight and a blessing to middle-aged or elderly people, bringing the choicest high alpine flowers of the most lowly stature to almost eye level, and conveniently easy to deal with.

To contrive such a bed it is advisable, of course, to fill it to the depth of a foot or so with a suitable mixture of scree soil. The drainage will be perfect at that height in any case. Two feet wide is a convenient width, and from that level the wall building is resumed and carries on exactly as before until the top level has been reached, or, if the bank is a very high one, another little terrace can be formed. In such a case it is advisable to bed some convenient stepping stones into the surface to enable the cultivator to get at the higher plants without tramping on the choice plants in the scree beds.

Should the wall face north, such raised little terraces could be filled with a mixture of peat and leaf-mould, which would provide good opportunities for the cultivation of the choicest small Ericaceous plants, and many other lovely peat-lovers. Great clumps of the rarer Asiatic Gentians and their fine garden hybrids would find homes here in which their great beauty can be enjoyed to the full without stooping. North-facing walls, too, form ideal homes for the lovely Ramondas, Haberleas, the choice *Jankaea heldreichii,* and the great silver Saxifrages like *S. longifolia, S. lingulata,* and the astounding hybrid between these two, *S.* × 'Tumbling Waters'.

It may come as a surprise to many people, but I have recently found that such a wall with any of the better Lewisias inserted in it as planting proceeds, makes the ideal home for these plants, which prove so tricky in some gardens, especially where the soil is chalky. On the flat surfaces, rather close against the stepped-back wall, is a good place for the charming *Calceolaria tenella,* which there becomes a mildly climbing plant, covering the stones with its dainty greenery, adangle with pretty yellow flowers. The rare *C. darwinii,* too, has been found to approve of such cool and shaded positions, as does *Omphalodes Luciliae;* and the late-flowering Saxifrages, *S. fortunei* and *S. cortusiaefolia*, are extraordinarily happy in such positions.

The dainty little Bluetts of our American cousins, also known as Quaker Ladies, or *Houstonia caerulea*, I have never been able to appreciate so much as on one of these raised peat beds. My latest triumph has been masses of *Epigaea asiatica*. Planted out as seedlings, they have spread and made themselves at home, and bring their delicious scent up to nose level, as it were.

CHAPTER V

Borders

Shirley Hibberd

HARDY BORDER FLOWERS

The hardy herbaceous border is the best feature of the flower garden, though commonly regarded as the worst. When well made, well stocked, and well managed, it presents us with flowers in abundance during ten months out of twelve, and in the remaining two blank months offers some actual entertainment, and many agreeable hints of pleasures to come, to make an ample reward for the comparatively small amount of labour its proper keeping will necessitate. Given a few trees and shrubs, a plot of grass, and comfortable walks, the three first essentials of a garden, a collection of hardy herbaceous plants is the fourth essential feature, and may be the last; for the bedding system may very well be dispensed with in a homely place, provided the hardy flowers are admitted, and cared for, according to their merits. It may be that many a reader of this will be disposed to question whether geraniums should be swept away to make room for lilies, and verbenas denied a place because of the superior claims of phloxes, but such a question we do not propose – our

James Shirley Hibberd (1825–1890) was an early specialist in urban horticulture. He wrote a number of delightful books on garden decoration and foliage plants as well as editing several periodicals.

165

business is to point out that the bedding system is an embellishment added to the garden: the herbaceous border is a necessary fundamental feature. Therefore we ask for the establishment of a collection of herbaceous plants before preparations are made for a display of bedding, and our advice to those who love their gardens and walk much in them, and find amusement in watching the growth of plants, and in contrasting their various characters and attractions, is, that they should seek to develop the herbaceous department, and so become acquainted with its full capabilities. In this pursuit enthusiasm may be manifested without incurring the reproach of season, for it is a truly intellectual pastime, and demands the practice of patience, and the exercise of thought in no small measure from those who would know more of it than appears upon the surface. Let us for a moment consider the claims of the herbaceous border to better regard than is usually bestowed upon it.

It is an important characteristic of the herbaceous border that its proper tenants are hardy plants that need no aid of glass or fuel for their preservation during the winter. Those who can be content with hardy plants alone may find it an agreeable and easy task to devote their glass-houses to the production of grapes, mushrooms, forced kidney beans, and other equally valuable delicacies, and supplement the hardy garden with a collection of Alpine flowers, a large number of which can be better grown and more thoroughly enjoyed in an airy and unheated greenhouse than when planted on the rockery in the open air. The delights of spring may thus be antedated by the aid of glass, and suitable early flowering Alpine plants and the open borders will present an abundance of flowers, from the time when the treacherous frosts have spent their spite upon vegetation until the chill of winter returns again. In the cultivation of bedding plants we may fairly reckon on a brilliant display for three months, and it may extend to four – say, from the 1st of June to the 30th of September, but the herbaceous border will be gay from the end of April to the middle of October, a period of six months, and will offer us a few flowers in February, and a few in November and December, and in a mild winter will not be utterly flowerless even in January. It would be an exaggeration to say that the herbaceous border is capable of a display of flowers all the year round, but is very nearly capable of a consummation so devoutly to be wished. To the

see plate 19

advantages of hardiness and continuity of bloom must be added a third and grand qualification, of a distinguishing kind – that of variety. It is scarcely an exaggeration to say that the varieties of form, colour, and general character, amongst hardy herbaceous plants is without limit; but, as variety may be obtained amongst ugly plants, we are bound to add that the proper occupants of the garden we are considering are all beautiful, and a considerable proportion are well-known favourites. Nevertheless, it must be admitted that with all their good claims to loving regard, the hardy herbaceous plants obtain but scant attention, and tens of thousands of persons who know that verbenas are somewhat showy when in flower, and would like to grow thousands of them, are prepared any day to ignore the whole tribe of herbaceous plants as weedy things that have had their day, and, with the exception of a lily or two, and, perhaps, a hollyhock, deserving of a place only in the unsavoury hole where grass-mowings and the sweepings of the poultry-house are deposited with a view to a 'mixen'. It ought to be needless to attempt this vindication, but we feel bound in duty to the reader to urge that every rational development of the hardy garden will prove advantageous to the lover of flowers, as tending both to lessen the expense and labour which the keeping of the garden necessitates, and considerably augment the pleasures that it is capable of affording as the seasons change and the year goes round.

As hardy herbaceous plants of some kind or other will grow in any soil and any aspect not one single square foot of ground in any garden need be utterly barren. A tuft of Solomon's seal in a dark spot where the soil is quite unfit for better plants, may be better than nothing. Sunny, shady, hot, cold, dry, moist, or even wet positions, have their several capabilities for hardy plants, and we have but to make our selections prudently to ensure a plentiful clothing of herbage and flowers for every scene. But a herbaceous border designed for a good collection of plants should consist of good deep loamy soil; the greater part of it should be fully exposed to the sunshine and the breezes, but it is well to have some extent of ground partially or considerably shaded, to provide the greatest possible variety of conditions for the greatest possible variety of the forms of vegetation. In preparing a border, in the first instance the ground should be well dug two spits deep and at the same time liberally manured. In the case of an old border requiring a repair, it may be well to lift all the plants and 'lay them in' safely while the border is trenched and manured; or it may suffice to leave the good plants undisturbed and provide sites for additional planting by opening holes and digging in plenty of manure. In any case we would earnestly advise that herbaceous plants should be thoroughly well cultivated, even if, to do full justice to them, the bedding display has to be contracted or abolished. The majority of the best herbaceous plants – the hollyhocks, phloxes, lilies, tricomas, delphiniums, pinks, chrysanthemums, primulas, pyrethrums, potentillas, anemones, ranunculuses, irises, oenotheras, foxgloves, campanulas – require a deep, rich, well-drained loam, but will grow well in clay that has been generously prepared, and need not be despaired of altogether where the soil is shallow and sandy, provided there are appliances available in the shape of manure, mulchings, and waterings, to sustain them through the hottest days of summer. It must not be forgotten, too, that if the herbaceous border is formed on a somewhat good soil – say a soil that will grow a cabbage – and in a position open to the sun and the health-giving breezes, it may be enriched by the addition of roses, stocks, asters, zinnias, balsams, dahlias, and many more good things, that 'need only to be seen to be appreciated'.

In the management of the herbaceous border details are everything, and principles next to nothing. The best time to plant is in August and September, but planting may be safely done in March and April, and with but little risk on any day throughout the year, provided the plants at the time of planting are in a proper state for planting. For example, a hollyhock may have a spike of magnificent flowers 6 feet high in the first week of September, and no sane gardener would then propose to transplant it; but the white lily, only a yard or so distant from it, may be just then in a dormant state, and, if to be transplanted at all, in a condition most desirable for the process. A great tuft of Arabis might be lifted any day from October to February, if lifted quickly and replanted with care, and in the ensuing month of April would bloom as well as if left undisturbed; but any sensible person who had struck a lot of arabis cuttings in pots in autumn would take care not to plant them until May, because little weak scraps of plants would probably perish if planted in the dark, short, cold days of the year! Leaving a fair margin for exceptions, it may be said with truth that herbaceous plants may be planted at any time, but we must return to the primary presumption, and repeat that the best time is in August or September, but if the chill November days occur before the work can be done, it is better to wait until spring, and then if possible choose a time when the wind is going round to the west and the barometer is falling. Happily, when your work is completed, soft showers will fall to help your plants make new roots quickly, to hold their own through the summer heat.

It cannot be wrong to repeat that the amateur need not be troubled about principles, but must consider the management of the herbaceous garden a matter of detail. As to watering, never give a drop if you can help it; but if it must be given, give plenty. Plants that have a deep well-manured bed to root in will rarely need water; but in some hot dry places watering is a necessary part of the routine management of a garden, and the herbaceous plants will be as thankful as any for whatever help the water-pot can give them. Some plants require stakes and some do not. Those that need support against wind should have it in time, for the storm may come and blow down half your garden wealth on the very day you have begun to talk of staking the dahlias and hollyhocks 'to-morrow'. We are no advocates of scanty planting; we rather prefer a crowded garden, but must contend always for a sufficiency of the comforts of life for all kinds of plants. The subjects we have before us require a deep nourishing soil, and plenty of light and air, which overcrowding will simply prevent them having; but a meagrely planted border has as miserable an appearance as a great dinner table with only half a red herring on it. Always plant enough to make a good effect at once, and in a year or two afterwards thin out and transplant, or give away, or sell; don't waste years in the expectation that you may obtain from half-a-dozen plants enough stock to cover an acre, because it is not well to make a nursery of a garden, and a good stock of all the best things that can be obtained will afford far more gratification than any quantity of some half-dozen sorts that you may any day buy at about a fifth, or, perhaps, a tenth, of what you must expend to produce them. Herbaceous plants are, for the most part, easily multiplied, and, generally speaking, may be increased by the very simple process of division; but it is better to plant a small plot of ground in such a way as to ensure a good effect at once than to lay out a great extent of border space with the intention of filling it 'some day' with home-grown stock. To enjoy herbaceous plants they should be left undisturbed for years, to form great masses or 'stools', as they are called, for it is only when thoroughly established that many of the best of them present their flowers profusely and show all their characters in full perfection. It is a strange thing that people who are always ready to expend money in the most liberal manner on bedding plants become ludicrously niggardly the instant they become convinced of a glimmering of faith in herbaceous plants. An instance of this has amused us lately. When inspecting a stock of hepaticas in flower in Ware's great nursery at Tottenham, we met a customer who was enraptured with them. Having, in company with some half-dozen persons, enjoyed the brilliant display of colour produced by some three or four thousand plants in a mass, this admirer ordered *one plant*, which, being drawn out at once, was found to consist of a tuft as large as a duck's egg, with two flowers expanded, and three or four leaves on the way. The attendant naïvely suggested that people should buy these things in the same way that they buy bedding plants – by the dozen, the score, the hundred.

The best way is not everybody's way. The furnishing of an extensive border by the purchase of sufficient of the very best herbaceous plants, will prove a more expensive business than every reader of this book may be prepared for. It follows that something should be said on the raising of plants by cheap and simple methods of procedure. Many good plants produce seed abundantly, and the careful cultivator may by this means increase the stock to any extent that may be desired. The best seed is that saved at home, and the best way to deal with it is to sow it, as soon as it is ripe, in large shallow pans and boxes, and keep these in cool frames until the plants appear. Some kinds of seeds remain a whole year in the soil before they germinate, and therefore it is only the patient who are well rewarded. As amateurs are apt to lose seeds that they would fain save, we shall present our readers with a rule of action that we have followed many years in saving seeds of all kinds that are likely to scatter as they ripen. Provide a lot of common bell-glasses, of various sizes, and place them mouth upwards on a bench in a sunny greenhouse. When a cluster of seeds is full grown and just beginning to ripen, cut it and throw it into one of the bell-glasses, with a label inscribed with its name. The ripening process will soon be completed, and the seed will shell itself out from the pods, and be found ready cleaned and fit for storing away with the least imaginable amount of trouble.

We have saved all kinds of seeds in this way, and may say with truth that the scheme has been worth hundreds of pounds to us. The ingenious practitioner will soon discover how to modify the plan advantageously. Thus, flower-pots, with the holes stopped with corks or sheets of paper, may be used in place of bell-glasses; but the best way will pay the best, especially in the case of amateurs who grow 'good things', and prize the seeds of choice subjects like gold-dust. As to the value of seed-saving and seed-sowing, we are bound to repeat that in the case of herbaceous plants, the matter is not of the highest importance. How absurd, for example, it would be for any one to save and sow seed of the common white arabis, when, by the simple process of division in autumn, the plants can be multiplied *ad infinitum!* What a waste of time to wait and watch for seeds of the white lily, which only needs to be taken up and parted in August or September to fill the whole garden, no matter how large, in the course of a few years. It is worthy of remark, too, that, as a rule, the plants which produce abundance of seed are those that we prize the least; the free-seeding sorts being of secondary values as regards interest and beauty.

The multiplication of herbaceous plants by cuttings and divisions, when either of these methods can be practised, is far preferable to raising them from seed. The cuttings should consist of new shoots of the season, nearly full grown and just about to harden. Old and wiry shoots are of no use; very soft, sappy shoots are no use. Large cuttings, whether from old or young shoots, are no use. The mild heat of a half-spent hotbed is to be preferred to the strong heat in which bedding plants are struck in spring; but hardy herbaceous plants may be propagated in a strong heat, or a mild heat, or without heat, and the last mode is the best, generally speaking. In the case of a scarce and valuable plant, we must sometimes adopt extreme measures to save its life or to increase it rapidly; but the best plants will be obtained from the well-managed cold-frame, and not from the hothouse.

In multiplying by division, a time should be chosen when the plant is in what we may call a dividable state; but, in truth, it may be done at any season if the operator is somewhat experienced, and can coax an insulted plant into a kindly temper by good frame or greenhouse management. When we meet with a scarce plant that we wish to possess, we secure, if we can, a cutting or a rooted shoot, or 'a bit of it', somehow, and feel bound to make that 'bit' a plant by some means. Experience has taught us, in respect of scarce and valuable plants, the best time to secure seeds, roots, cuttings, offsets, etc., etc., is, *when you can get them*, and we know nothing of seasons whatever. But in case this defining should perplex an amiable reader, we shall wind up this paragraph by saying that dividable subjects, such as violets, pansies, daisies, arabis, and primulas, should be taken up in August or September, and be pulled to pieces and replanted immediately. If the weather is showery, they will prosper without any particular attention; but if the weather is hot and dry, they must be watered and shaded until the cool, damp season returns. It is a good plan to have a plot of reserve ground in which to plant out the young stock, and allow it to make one whole season's growth before transferring it to the borders.

Many disappointments occur through mixing tender and hardy plants together in borders, and leaving them all to settle accounts with the weather. They are very straightforward in their mode of settlement. The hardy plants live and the tender plants die, and those who have to pay for the losses make long faces when summer returns and the favourites of the past season are seen no more. In very severe winters, and especially in gardens in valleys where the soil is heavy and damp, many plants, reputed hardy, are sure to perish. Losses are always objectionable; but a certain number must be borne with in every pursuit, and the herbaceous border forms no exception to the general rule. But the fact suggests that a systematic use of frames and other like protective agencies, and a reserve of plants of kinds that are least likely to suffer by severe weather, are precautions the wise will adopt without any great pressure of persuasions.

To speak of our own case for a moment, we cannot keep hollyhocks in the borders during winter, and therefore take cuttings in time, and secure a good stock of young plants in pots in autumn, to keep through the winter in frames for planting out in the month of April ensuing. The amateur must study these matters as essentials to the realization of the true joy of a garden. Borders that are kept scrupulously clean all the winter will be the most severely thinned of plants in the event of extra severe weather. There is no protective material so potent to resist frost as the dead and dry leaves of trees, as the wind disposes them, for they always gather about the crowns of herbaceous plants, to help them through the winter.

After winter comes the spring, and then the gardener will carefully dig the border, and chop up the roots of paeonies, and stamp down with his foot the pushing crowns of anemones, and by a most unavoidable accident chop up a few of the phloxes. We never suffer the herbaceous border to be dug at all, except to prepare it for planting in the first instance, or for needful repairs afterwards. Periodical digging, 'as a matter of course', such as the jobbing gardeners designate 'turning in', has for its sole object the destruction of plants; but that object is disguised by describing the operation as 'making things tidy'. When you are tired of herbaceous plants, let the jobbing gardener keep the border tidy, and you will soon be rid of the obnoxious lilies, phloxes, ranunculuses, anemones, hollyhocks, paeonies, and pansies, without the painful labour of pulling them up and burning them.

18   ENVILLE HALL, STAFFORDSHIRE. 1901

The planting of the Long Walk demonstrates the nineteenth-century
predilection for strong colour contrasts and rigid formality in bedded-out
borders. Except in municipal parks, this style of planting has seldom been used
in England since Gertrude Jekyll revolutionised the concept of the flower border.

Gertrude Jekyll
THE MAIN HARDY
FLOWER BORDER

Gertrude Jekyll VMH (1843–1932), well loved author of Home and Garden *and other classics of twentieth-century gardening, designed more than 300 gardens. Her influence has been profound and lasting.*

The big flower border is about 200 feet long and 14 feet wide. It is sheltered from the north by a solid sandstone wall about 11 feet high clothed for the most part with evergreen shrubs – Bay and Laurustinus, Choisya, Cistus and Loquat. These show as a handsome background to the flowering plants. They are in a three-foot-wide border at the foot of the wall; then there is a narrow alley, not seen from the front, but convenient for access to the wall shrubs and for working the back of the border.

As it is impossible to keep any one flower border fully dressed for the whole summer, and as it suits me that it should be at its best in the late summer, there is no attempt to have it full of flowers as early as June. Another region belongs to June; so that at that time the big border has only some incidents of good bloom, though the ground is rapidly covering with the strong patches, most of them from three to five years old, of the later-blooming perennials. But early in the month there are some clumps of the beautiful *Iris Pallida dalmatica* in the regions of grey foliage, and of the splendid blue-purple bloom of *Geranium ibericum platypetalum*, the best of the large Cranesbills, and the slow growing *Dictamnus Fraxinella* (the white variety), and Meadowsweets white and pink, Foxgloves and Canterbury Bells, and to the front some long-established sheets of *Iberis sempervirens* that have grown right on to the path. The large Yuccas, *Y. gloriosa* and *Y. recurva*, are throwing up their massive spikes, though it will be July before they actually flower, and the blooms on some bushes of the great *Euphorbia Wulfenii*, although they were flowers of May and their almost yellow colour is turning greener, are still conspicuous and ornamental. Then the plants in the middle of the wall, *Choisya ternata* and *Clematis montana*, are still full of white bloom, and the Guelder Rose is hanging out its great white balls. I like to plant the Guelder Rose and *Clematis montana* together. Nothing does better on north or east walls, and it is pleasant to see the way the Clematis flings its graceful garlands over and through the stiff branches of the Viburnum.

174

The more brilliant patches of colour in the big border in June are of Oriental Poppies intergrouped with Gypsophila, which will cover their space when they have died down, and the earlier forms of *Lilium croceum* of that dark orange colour that almost approaches scarlet.

During the first week of June any bare spaces of the border are filled up with half-hardy annuals, and some of what we are accustomed to call bedding-plants – such as Geranium, Salvia, Calceolaria, Begonia, Gazania and Verbena. The half-hardy annuals are African Marigold, deep orange and pale sulphur, pure white single Petunia, tall Ageratum, tall striped Maize, white Cosmos, sulphur Sunflower, *Phlox Drummondi*, Nasturtiums, and *Trachelium coeruleum*. Dahlias were planted out in May, and earlier still the Hollyhocks, quite young plants that are to bloom in August and September; the autumn-planted ones flowering earlier. The ground was well cleared of weeds before these were planted, and, soon after, the whole border had a good mulch of a mixture of half-rotted leaves and old hot-bed stuff. This serves the double purpose of keeping the soil cool and of affording gradual nutriment when water is given.

The planting of the border is designed to show a distinct scheme of colour arrangement. At the two ends there is a groundwork of grey and glaucous foliage – Stachys, Santolina, *Cineraria maritima*, Sea-kale and Lyme-grass, with darker foliage, also of grey quality, of Yucca, *Clematis recta* and Rue. With this, at the near or western end, there are flowers or pure blue, grey-blue, white, palest yellow and palest pink; each colour partly in distinct masses and partly intergrouped. The colouring then passes through stronger yellows to orange and red. By the time the middle space of the border is reached the colour is strong and gorgeous, but, as it is in good harmonies, it is never garish. Then the colour strength recedes in an inverse sequence through orange and deep yellow to pale yellow, white and palest pink; again with blue-grey foliage. But at this, the eastern end, instead of the pure blues we have purples and lilacs.

Looked at from a little way forward, for a wide space of grass allows this point of view, the whole border can be seen as one picture, the cool colouring at the ends enhancing the brilliant warmth of the middle. Then, passing along the wide path next to the border, the value of the colour arrangement is still more strongly felt. Each portion now becomes a picture in itself, and every one is of such a colouring that it best prepares the eye, in accordance with natural law, for what is to follow. Standing for a few moments before the endmost region of grey and blue, and saturating the eye to its utmost capacity with these colours, it passes with extraordinary avidity to the succeeding yellows. These intermingle in a pleasant harmony with the reds of scarlets, blood-reds and clarets, and then lead again to yellows. Now the eye has again become saturated, this time with the rich colouring, and has therefore, by the law of complementary colour, acquired a strong appetite for the greys and purples. These therefore assume an appearance of brilliancy that they would not have had without the preparation provided by their recently received complementary colour.

There are well-known scientific toys illustrating this law. A short word, printed in large red letters, is looked at for half a minute. The eyes are shut and an image of the same word appears, but the lettering is green. Many such experiments may be made in the open garden. The brilliant orange African Marigold has leaves of a rather dull green colour. But look steadily at the flowers for thirty seconds in sunshine and then look at the leaves. The leaves appear to be bright blue!

Even when a flower border is devoted to a special season, as mine is given to the time from mid-July to October, it cannot be kept fully furnished without resorting to various contrivances. One of these is the planting of certain things that will follow in season of bloom and that can be trained to take each other's places. Thus, each plant of *Gypsophila paniculata* when full grown covers a space a good 4 feet wide. On each side of it, within reasonable distance of the root, I plant Oriental Poppies. These make their leaf and flower growth in early summer when the Gypsophila is still in a young state. The Poppies will have died down by the time the Gypsophila is full grown and has covered them. After this has bloomed the seed-pods turn brown, and though a little of this colouring is not harmful in the autumn border, yet it is not wanted in such large patches. We therefore grow at its foot, or within easy reach, some of the trailing Nasturtiums, and lead them up so that they cover the greater part of the brown seed-spray.

Delphiniums, which are indispensable for July, leave bare stems with quickly yellowing leafage when the flowers are over. We plant behind them the white Everlasting Pea, and again behind that, *Clematis Jackmanii*. When the Delphiniums are over, the rapidly forming seed-pods are removed, the stems are cut down to just the right height, and the white Peas are trained over them. When the Peas go out of bloom in the middle of August, the Clematis is brought over. It takes some years for these two plants to become established; in the case of those I am describing the Pea has been four or five years planted and the Clematis seven. They cannot be hurried; indeed, in my garden it is difficult to get the Clematis to grow at all. But good gardening means patience and dogged determination. There must be many failures and losses, but by always pushing on there will also be the reward of success. Those who do not know are apt to think that hardy flower gardening of the best kind is easy. It is not easy at all. It has taken me half a lifetime merely to find out what is best worth doing, and a good slice out of another half to puzzle out the ways of doing it.

In addition to these three plants that I grow over one another I am now adding a fourth – the September-blooming *Clematis Flammula*. It must not be supposed that they are just lumped one over another so that the under ones have their leafy growths smothered. They are always being watched, and, bit by bit, the earlier growths are removed as soon as their respective plants are better without them.

Then there is the way of pulling down tall plants whose natural growth is upright. At the back of the yellow part of the border are some plants of a form of *Helianthus orgyalis*[1], trained down. But other plants can be treated in the same way; the tall Rudbeckia Golden Glow, Dahlias and Michaelmas Daisies. The tall Snapdragons can also be pulled down and made to cover a surprising space of bare ground with flowering side-shoots.

As it is still impossible to prevent the occurrence of a blank here and there, or as the scene, viewed as a picture, may want some special accentuation or colouring, there is the way of keeping a reserve of plants in pots and dropping them in where they may be wanted. The thing that matters is that, in its season, the border shall be kept full and beautiful; by what means does not matter in the least. For this sort of work some of the most useful plants are Hydrangeas, *Lilium longiflorum, candidum* and *auratum*, and *Campanula pyramidalis*, both white and blue, and, for foliage, *Funkia grandiflora*[2], *F. Sieboldii*[3] and hardy Ferns.

An important matter is that of staking and supporting. The rule, as I venture to lay it down, is that sticks and stakes must never show. They must be so arranged that they give the needful support, while allowing the plant its natural freedom; but they must remain invisible. The only time when they are tolerated is for the week or two when they have been put in for Dahlias, when the plants have not yet grown up to cover them.

Michaelmas Daisies we stake with great care in June, putting in some stiff branching spray of oak or chestnut among the growths and under their fronts.

---

[1] *Helianthus salicifolius*
[2] *Hosta plantagineas* var. *grandiflora*   [3] *Hosta sieboldiana*

At the end of June we also nip the tops of some of the forward growth of the plants so as to vary the outline.

There are two borders of Michaelmas Daisies, one for the earlier sorts that flower in September and the other for the October kinds. They are in places that need not often be visited except in the blooming season, therefore we allow the supporting spray to be seen while the plants are growing. But early in August in the case of the September border, and early in September in the case of the one for October, we go round and regulate the plants, settling them among the sticks in their definite positions. When this is done every atom of projecting spray is cut away with the secateur.

I hold that nothing unsightly should be seen in the garden. The shed for sticks and stakes is a lean-to at one end of the barn, showing to the garden. The roof had to be made at a very low pitch, and there was no roofing material suitable but galvanised iron. But a depth of 4 inches of peaty earth was put over the iron, and now it is a garden of Stonecrops and other plants that flourish in shallow soil in a hot exposure.

To prevent undue disappointment, those who wish for beautiful flower borders and whose enthusiasm is greater than their knowledge, should be reminded that if a border is to be planted for pictorial effect, it is impossible to maintain that effect and to have the space well filled for any period longer than three months, and that even for such a time there will have to be contrivances such as have been described.

see colour plate VIII

It should also be borne in mind that a good hardy flower border cannot be made all at once. Many of the most indispensable perennials take two, three or even more years to come to their strength and beauty. The best way is to plant the border by a definite plan, allowing due space for the development of each plant. Then, for the first year or two, a greater number of half-hardy annuals and biennials than will eventually be needed should be used to fill the spaces that have not yet been taken up by the permanent plants. The best of these are Penstemons and Snapdragons, the Snapdragons grown both as annuals and biennials, for so an extended season of bloom is secured. Then there should be African and French Marigolds, the smaller annual Sunflowers, Zinnias, Plume Celosias, China Asters, Stocks, Foxgloves, Mulleins, Ageratum, *Phlox Drummondi* and Indian Pinks; also hardy annuals – Lupins of several kinds, *Chrysanthemum coronarium*, the fine pink Mallows, Love-in-a-Mist, Nasturtiums or any others that are liked.

19   COMPTON HOUSE, WILTSHIRE. 1911

An informal atmosphere is created by the abundant mixed border which thrives
by a high brick wall in the flower garden.

Jason Hill

THE MINIATURE HERBACEOUS BORDER

'Jason Hill'/Frank Anthony Hampton (1888–1967) was a psychiatrist who was also an erudite gardener with a special gift for writing about his subject. The Curious Gardener and The Contemplative Gardener are his best known books.

The function of the herbaceous border is to provide a wealth of colour and those whose tastes set strongly in this direction may well feel that a miniature herbaceous border is no more desirable than a miniature income; but even here, smallness, though it may be enforced by want of space or money, has certain advantages of its own. The full-sized herbaceous border is usually designed to provide a blaze, riot or symphony of colour, according to the maker's taste; but, on the grand scale, the material is sometimes rather difficult to manage, whereas in miniature the effects are more easily controlled and the design can be built up with a fair certainty of success.

The herbaceous border must be accessible in all its parts for purposes of cultivation, so that a large border must take the form of a long and relatively narrow strip, but on a small scale it can have any shape, and it may be more conveniently a bed than a border. A bed has the independence of a picture that is framed and separate, and often it will have the advantage of a quiet neutral background of grass, so that we can aim at more complex, subtle or strongly patterned effects than are possible in the long border, where the different colour groups must be related to their neighbours. By diminishing the scale of operations it will be found, I think, that the choice of plants is extended, since it is no longer limited to the strong and hearty growers, that jostle one another for the rich fare of the conventional border, for in the raised and well-drained bed it is possible to grow almost any plant that suits the end in view, and even woodlanders can be accommodated on the shady side. In confining ourselves to smallish plants we shall find that we are often using the true species, which give us a refinement of form and often of colour which in many large plants of garden origin has been sacrificed for a gain in size and brilliance.

If a herbaceous border of the conventional or academic type is desired and there is no room for the towering opulence of the modern Delphiniums, Lupins and Paeonies "in Fortune's lap high fed", it is possible to find miniatures of

nearly all of them by searching through the catalogues with an eye to herbaceous plants which will not grow more than 3 feet high and will accommodate their display to a border about 15 feet long and 3½ feet wide. We have at
our disposal several wild Chinese Delphiniums (*D. grandiflorum, D. formosum*
and *D. tatsienense*) which make up for their lack of tall splendour by their light
elegant carriage and the old dolphin design of their flowers; the wild Lupins
cannot give the wide range of opalescent colour of the polyphyllus hybrids, but
Lupinus ornatus offers in exchange very beautiful silvery leaves to set off its
lavender flowers (it needs staking and appreciates a light soil) and
L. Moerheimii[1] and *L. nootkatensis* are just under 3 feet high and vary from seed;
Paeonia tenuifolia at 18 inches provides a mist of fine-cut foliage and cup-shaped
flowers of crimson-scarlet, rose-pink or white and a double red of intense
brilliance; one or two of the colour forms of *P. arietina* can be accommodated
without throwing the other plants out of proportion, and the rare *P. Cambes-
sedesii* is a jewel in flower and leaf for a sheltered corner – all these flower a little
before the hybrid 'Chinese' Paeonies.

'Thora Perry', 'Peter Pan' and 'Fortune' are refined miniatures of the great
Oriental Poppies; *Kniphofia rufa* and its hybrid *K. corallina* are slender and early
flowering Red-hot Pokers; *Campanula punctata*, pale pink and freckled with
crimson, is in effect a more subtle Canterbury Bell, and, if it cannot be provided
with a very light soil, may be replaced by its hybrid *C. van Houttei*. *Verbascum
phoeniceum* and *V. Weidmannianum*, *Hemerocallis Dumortierii* and *Solidago
brachystachys*[2] can take the place of the large Mulleins, Day Lilies and Golden
Rods with no loss of anything but stature. *Inula ensifolia* and *I. grandiflora* are
distinguished substitutes for the tall sunflowers, and the blue of Anchusa is
reproduced (but with greater intensity) in *Cynoglossum nervosum* and, at 7 or 8
inches, by the biennial *Borago laxiflora*.

The plants cited above indicate merely the lines along which a small
brilliant herbaceous border of the orthodox kind can be built up, but if we are
working within the compass of one or two small beds it is possible to
experiment with different themes, for failure is not so difficult to repair in the
bed as it is in the big border, when the Lupins drop their buds or slugs have
demolished the Delphiniums, since small plants can be transplanted easily and
there are many good bedding plants to call upon in case of need. By grouping
formal, stylistic flowers together we can obtain the effect of a French flower

[1] *Lupinus polyphyllus* 'Moerheimii'   [2] *Solidago virgaurea* (of gardens)

painting or a Victorian posy, and the material for such a design may be found among such plants as Sweet Williams (including the dwarf double crimson), striped Snapdragons, double Potentillas, the magenta *Geranium sanguineum*, the double wall-flower 'Harpur Crewe', the golden-leafed Valerian (*Valeriana Phu aurea*), the striped grass 'Gardener's Garters' (*Phalaris arundinacea*), double Columbines and quilled Daisies. For the end of summer there are the pompom Chrysanthemums and pompom Dahlias.

Turning aside from the primary consideration of colour and indulging a little in form, we can devote a bed to plants whose leaves and flowers have a strongly marked design, and with sweeping curves and bold volutes, build up another kind of stylistic picture, with a fantastic, slightly rococo effect. The material may be drawn from the Funkias[1], *Mertensia virginica*, *Hemerocallis*, the Megasea saxifrages[2], *Ranunculus amplexicaulis*, *Podophyllum emodi*, *Tradescantia virginiana* and, since all these plants like a cool soil, a few bold ferns.

It is possible, if we like, to be naturalistic, for Nature presents a kind of great herbaceous border in the alpine meadows and on the slopes of the sub-alpine valleys, and we can make a compressed version or excerpt of it by a selection of the larger plants which are offered to the rock-gardener. The meadow grass may be represented by dwarf tufted grasses such as *Festuca glauca* and *F. crinum-ursi* and small sedges such as *Carex baldensis* or even our native Wood Rush (*Luzula silvatica*) and suitable plants are *Campanula barbata* and *C. glomerata*, *Crepis aurea*, *Phyteuma Scheuzeri*, *Jasione perennis*, *Lychnis flos-jovis*, *Anthericum liliago*, *Iris xiphioides*, *Ranunculus gramineus* and many others, including *Anemone alpina* and *A. sulphurea*[3], which like a deep soil and close company and do not often flourish in the rock garden.

Those who have only the smallest area that can be called a garden, or even no garden at all, need not be quite helpless in their envy of the sumptuous fell-dress herbaceous border, for there is a good handful of jewel-bright little herbaceous plants which can be composed into a picture in a tiny bed, a stone sink, egg-crock or a stout packing-case gaily painted. A few of the plants which offer themselves for this kind of embroidery are: *Lupinus confertus* (4 inches), *Sisyrinchium angustifolium* (Blue-eyed Grass), *Papaver alpinum* (in lemon-yellow, orange, white and sometimes pink), the double *Saxifraga granulata* (the 'Pretty Maids' of Contrary Mary's garden), *Lychnis alpina*[4], *Geranium cinereum*, Campa-

---

[1] hostas

[2] bergenias   [3] *Pulsatilla alpina* and *P. a. sulphurea*   [4] *Viscaria alpina*

nula glomerata acaulis, Campanula Warleyensis (semi-double)[1], *Anomatheca cruenta*[2] (cerise pink barred with crimson), *Veronica spicata nana, Myosotis rupicola,* and *Iberis* 'Little Gem'; all these like a sandy soil. They may be edged with the quilled Daisy 'Dresden China' and, if a background is required, the shrubby Thymes, such as *Th. nitidus* or *Th. carnosus,* can be clipped into a dense formal hedge; and, before apologizing for indulging in such doll's house gardening, it is legitimate to remind oneself that fifteen or twenty varied plants provide a good deal of interest, whether they are large or small.

The most obvious way of using a small herbaceous border, that of building up in it a design or pattern of colour like an impressionist painting, has been left for consideration till the end, for the range of colours available is so wide that the imagination and taste of the gardener have free play, and suggestions are almost impertinent. It is, therefore, only by way of illustration and as a record of experiment that an example is offered. A circular bed was made with a background of grey-leafed plants (*Artemisia canescens, Anaphalis nubigena, Anthemis cupiana,* the white form of *Agrostemma coronaria*[3]) into which a rather steely, purplish blue was worked with *Clematis integrifolia, Amsonia tabernae-montana, Campanula Burghaltii, C. raddeana* and *Eryngium Violetta*; this was lit up with one or two dwarf Red-hot Pokers, toned with the light clear yellow of a dwarf Evening Primrose and *Anthemis tinctoria* Buxton's variety.

[1] *Campanula × halyodgensis* 'Warley White'
[2] *Lapeyrousia cruenta*   [3] *Lychnis coronaria*

20   HIDCOTE MANOR, GLOUCESTERSHIRE. C.1930

A border of peonies may take two years to become established, but this bed of
Paeonia officinalis varieties makes the most of their superb form.

Margery Fish
THAT PATCH OF SILVER

Although Gertrude Jekyll realized long ago the value of silver foliage plants, I think it is only in the last few years that the vast army of ordinary gardeners have made a point of including silver subjects in their schemes.

I remember about 1939 a local nursery appealing to me for a bit of *Stachys lanata*, and suggesting that if I hadn't the plant I might be able to get a piece from one of the villagers. That now deservedly popular king of the silvers was then only a despised cottage garden plant, and did not figure in nurserymen's catalogues. If I could have only one grey plant in my garden that would be my choice. The texture and colour of the foliage is the best of all. It is indifferent to climate or soil, and is happy wherever it happens to be planted. I have it in walls and in paving, falling over banks and great chunks of it in borders. It makes an excellent border between bed and path, and for this purpose can be trimmed to an even band and not allowed to flower. Everywhere else its tall branching flower spikes of softest pink are a welcome feature, and I could not do without them in the house – alive in the summer – and dead in winter-time.

The next on my list used to be *Senecio cineraria*. I thought it was the most silvery of all the silvers until I met *Senecio* 'White Diamond', and that is so silver as to be almost white. Its leaves are not unlike the *S. cineraria* but they are wider and more substantial, and it makes a sturdier and more compact plant. I had not realized how good it was until I met a plant I had given to the Oxford University Botanic Garden. One gets used to the plants in one's own garden, and when one meets them elsewhere they take on a new personality. I came home and apologized to my own unappreciated plants. As well as being better to look at, it has the estimable quality of being more reliable. My poor *S. cineraria* has the regrettable habit of dying on me sometimes; always when I don't expect it, and I always take a yearly batch of cuttings. I like plants that I can rely on, and I discovered many years ago that though my friend *S. cineraria* may live happily for several winters one particularly hard frost will turn that smiling beauty into a pathetic wreck that offends the eye; so I learned never to plant it in such a position that should this happen my whole plan would be

Margery Fish (1892–1969) made a major contribution, through her writing and broadcasting, to horticulture in the years between the end of the last war and her death. She drew on her experience at her garden at East Lambrook Manor in Somerset where she moved in 1937. Her books include Cottage Garden Flowers, A Flower for Every Day *and* Ground Cover Plants.

ruined. I think I could risk 'White Diamond' in a key position, but so far have always put her where she has a little protection to her back, such as a wall or some steps. I don't allow either of these poor things to open their flowers, as those tight little golden flowers do detract from the lavenders, pinks, and lemon shades that look so well with silver.

I find *Centaurea gymnocarpa* hardier than *Senecio cineraria*, but not so dead certain that I would dare risking a winter without a nice little collection of cuttings in the frame. I would hate to lose those long fern-like leaves that are so very graceful. Although park gardeners use it in little tufts to temper brilliant bedding effects, it really looks best grown in a mass. I always remember how Mrs. Clive at Brympton d'Evercy used it in a great frothing mass against purple rhus and red dahlias in her famous red and silver scheme. If my plants are not very big I use three or four together, with the front ones at the edge of a wall or path so that they cascade over the side. The dull mauve thistle heads are quite unworthy of such a handsome plant, and are never allowed to see the light of day.

Another good grey plant is *Senecio leuchostachys*, and it has the added attraction of ivory-coloured flowers, which need not be removed. There is no question that it is tender, and even in Somerset does not get through the winter unless it is trained to a south wall. Another reason why I like to grow it against a wall is because it looks better this way, or poised horizontally on top of a raised bed. It is rather more feathery than the others and has not as much substance, so I like to grow it where its lack of body is not revealed.

Helichrysum angustifolium is a good plant and effective when it gets big enough. This, of course, is the famous curry plant, and there is no mistaking it when you get near it. I hadn't realized I had it in the garden until one day I was bending over a bed and had an unmistakable whiff of curry. I 'acquire' a vast number of new plants and cuttings each year, and I must have struck this little soul and planted it out without realizing what it was. The leaves are narrow, and it grows rather like an abandoned lavender. The first flowerings are flat corymbs of dull gold at the top of each stalk, and afterwards little side shoots appear down the long stalks, each topped with a small cluster of golden flowers. This is really a very good gold and silver plant, because the gold is soft and burnished and has none of the harsh crudeness of *Senecio cineraria* and the santolinas.

I am rather frightened of giving the name of a neat bush helichrysum that is one of the joys of my life. I was given it in the beginning as *H. trilineatum*, and I think most of the nurseries call it that, but I have been put right by a knowledgeable friend who insists it should be *H. alveolatum*, and the name *H. trilineatum* belongs to a plant I call *Helichrysum plicatum*. I know I shall be corrected again, but I think it is safer to follow the lead of the nurseries and keep the names I know. So I continue to call my neat little bush with its narrow leaves and tiny flowers of yellow plush *H. trilineatum*. It is a most comfortable plant, never gets too big, and there is never a hair out of place. It just sits there complacently smiling whatever the weather or the time of year.

Helichrysum plicatum is definitely more elegant, but its long, narrow silver leaves come on brittle stems and it does get rather dishevelled in the wind. And I have a suspicion that it can be affected by heavy frost. With me it comes and goes. Sometimes I have a beautiful rounded bush, then I notice part of it is dying off, which spoils the symmetry, and next year there is very little life on its skeleton limbs, and I am faced with a gap until the next child grows up. The flowers are as elegant as the leaves and as slender. They come on foot-long stems, are in flat open corymbs, and are very small in a thin greenish gold. I cut them for drying, but take care to protect them as they are brittle.

Those are all the large silver plants apart from shrubs that are good all the year round. There are legion artemisias, but they are only good in the summer. Some keep their form in the way of bare arms and legs, but none of them can be considered good all-the-year-round silver plants. I used to think *A. ludoviciana* was the best of the tall thin silver artemisias. It is still the whitest, but is almost too slender to be effective by itself and looks best when it is hemmed in by herbaceous plants about the same height. *A. gnaphalodes* is much more sturdy, and a good clump can look quite well without backing, so long as it is staked early and has grown up as straight as possible. *A.* 'Silver Queen' was heralded as an even better plant, but I have two complaints. They all ramble, but 'Silver Queen' is the worst of the lot and can't keep herself where she is put but comes up in the middle of irises and peonies a long way off. She is bushier than the other two, but has a weak backbone and I have never succeeded in making her hold herself up, however well and early I stake. Whatever I do she goes at the knees and flops into a feathery mass, which looks all right from the distance but is distressing close at hand.

My best artemisia is a good form of *A. absinthium*, not nearly as woody as the usual one, and making a beautiful low clump of delightful feathery foliage on stems strong enough to keep their shape. I don't know where it came from and I have never seen it elsewhere, so to distinguish it I call it *A.* 'Lambrook

Silver'. It doesn't look too attractive in the winter, but is better than the first three, which should really be cut down in the autumn. Some people leave the flower spikes on all through the winter after the foliage has disappeared; but they don't really stand up well to inclement weather, and the slender grace that charmed us in the summer looks untidy and shabby after being buffeted by winter wind and rain.

There are many other artemisias. I like the pewter-coloured *A. pontica*, that is said to look like a little cypress but quickly becomes a grove with me. *A. stelleriana* is lovely for the front of the border when its long skinny arms have their complement of white, chrysanthemum-like leaves, and as for the feathery ones, such as *splendens* and *canescens*, *discolor* and *valesiaca*, it would take someone far cleverer than I am to discriminate between them. They are all lovely and all help the garden scene. Some of them wander somewhat, but never enough to be a nuisance.

Not so fashionable as it used to be, *Lychnis coronaria*, late agrostemma, is a good silver maid-of-all-work. I wouldn't put it in a place of honour, but I do think it is worth growing in those odd places such as one finds near the back door or round the sheds, where it is pleasant to have something that looks nice and gives no trouble. It makes fine rosettes of silver leaves which cover the ground and look pleasant even when it is not in flower, and when the flowers start they don't stop. *L. c.* 'Abbotswood Rose' is the one best known; there is a white version which is delightful and a dainty pink one, but neither of the last two are as vigorous or as generous as the purple form.

Another plant that makes a good silver rosette, but rather smaller this time, is *Anaphalis triplinervis*. There is another very much like it called *A. nubigena*, perhaps a little taller. Both make neat tight clumps of silver and increase slowly. In the summer both produce sprays of little ivory daisies which are not unlike the popular French *immortelles*, and can be regarded as 'everlasting' flowers for winter drying. *A. margaritacea* is taller and has a different habit. Instead of tight clumps, it sends out feelers which show only a tiny silver rosette above ground before they grow into stalks about 18 inches tall in a very pleasant grey-green. This plant really needs a little backing, and if one does not stake it I think it should be grown between tall perennials. The flowers are the same ivory and very good for drying as are the two-foot *A. yedoensis*, grey-green again and with the same kind of flowers.

There is really nothing so silvery as the foliage of *Verbascum broussa*, and it is delightfully downy as well, so it is beautiful even before it sends up those tall

188

spikes of soft yellow flowers. It does appeal to caterpillars, alas, and I find
V. haenseleri, which is silver too, but not downy, escapes the depredations of
these marauders. *Salvia argentea* is another silver-foliaged plant, even more
downy than *Stachys lanata* and with a silken sheen to its down which makes it
most vulnerable to winter wet, and I give it a pane of glass in the winter.
Another way to grow it is vertically or under an overhanging rock, anything to
keep the pitiless winter rain from beating down on its defenceless head.

Achillea clypeolata is a first-rate silver plant. It comes from Greece and has
the best foliage of all the achilleas. It is almost white and cut with fern-like
delicacy. Flat heads of pale yellow complete the picture, and it goes on
flowering with great faithfulness throughout the summer.

A good way to get a silver effect without actually using a silver-leaved
plant is to have a big clump of *Catananche caerulea major*. The flowers, of course,
are blue, but the buds are silver, and give the effect of a silver cloud as they
sway about in the summer air. I saw this effect in a good herbaceous border
at one of the big nurseries, and I have been striving to enact it myself.
Unfortunately catananche doesn't much care for my heavy clay, and I have had
a hard time getting her going.

The hawkweeds are inclined to be persistent, but there is one whose
persistence one can tolerate as it will introduce a silver carpet for us. All that is
necessary is to plant one small rosette of *Hieracium pilosella*, and it will do the
rest. Out come its little feelers, with a rosette at the end of each. Down they go
and there is another little plant. The flowers are typical hawkweed, but in a pale
shade of lemon that blends with everything and they come on 6 inch stems.
There are two other silver hawkweeds which are not at all venturesome, both
make neat little plants and increase themselves by discreet seeding. *H. villosum*
is, as the name implies, woolly, and *H. waldsteinii* has attractive wide leaves.
Both have yellow flowers.

I have one little silver plant that came from one of the expeditions, and I
have never had a name for it. I was told, when it was given to me, that it was a
pyrethrum, but I was not even given a number. The leaves are small and look as
if they were made of light grey flannel, and each cut to the centre along each
side to give a fringed effect. It is one of those plants that everyone notices, and I
grow it at the edge of a supporting wall and let it hang over the side. I can't
remember if it has flowers; if it has I have no doubt they are the usual dull
yellow. It is not unlike *Chrysanthemum praeteritum*, but much more silvery and
flatter in growth. I see that another of these silver chrysanthemums,

C. ptarmicaeflorum, is now being called a pyrethrum. Two small silver teucriums for growing among stones are *T. aroanum* and *T. polium*.

It is a great pity that one can't make more use of that arch silver carpeter, cerastium, but it can't be trusted. The only place where it is safe to use it is on a wall or some bare place where it can ramp to its heart's content and not swamp more worthy plants. The villagers call it 'snow-in-summer' and prize it highly, so I have to fight a losing battle with it, as I do with the village cats.

I use the silver potentilla, *P. nitida*, in paving and in my walls, and *Achillea clavenae* in the same way. The dianthus family introduce a pleasant blue-grey, and for a sink *Helichrysum marginatum* is shining silver, but it hates winter rain. Two creeping artemisias are shining silver, *A. glacialis*, which is by no means easy, and *A. lanata* (syn. *pedemontana*), which, as its name implies, walks – and it does, too, over stone or path, but not enough to be a nuisance. I have seen it used as a carpeting plant with red-foliaged dahlias and lobelias, and the combination was very good.

I wish there were more silver shrubs we could plant in our gardens. Of course there is *Senecio greyii*[1], a real stand-by, which keeps its leaves and doesn't seem to mind where it grows. It flowers well, too, not such strident yellow flowers as some of the silver plants but yellow enough, and I know many people who cut them off before they come into flower. The buds are beautiful, practically white, and because they are usually mixed up with the open flowers, I don't often cut off either.

But *Senecio greyii* has, I think, one fault, and that is it grows too fast, at least it does for me. I grow it in one of my terraced beds, and I cannot let it take up too much room so I cut it back savagely every year, but there comes a time when the wood is too thick for beauty and one has to start again. Cuttings taken in July root very easily, and I think there should always be a few little plants tucked away to put in when the poor old grandmother has to go. Four or five little ones will be needed to fill the space she occupied, and as they grow one or two can be removed at a time until only one remains, to wax stronger and stronger until she in her turn has to go.

There are three other senecios on the same lines. I believe *S. compactus* is a neater form of *S. greyii*, but I haven't managed to get hold of it. *S. laxifolius* is very similar and is, I believe, said to do better by the sea. *S. monroi* is not so silvery, although the crinkle-edged leaves have a silver lining. It makes a low,

[1] *Senecio* 'Sunshine'

190

sprawling bush, good for informal work, and again is said to be a good shrub to grow by the sea.

I would not call *Phlomis fruticosa* a silver plant. The foliage is a pleasant soft grey-green, and the woolly texture makes a nice change among other plants.

I couldn't do without santolinas, and in the right place I think *S. neapolitana* is the most effective of them all. I like *S. chamaecyparissus* and its neat dwarf form, and enjoy its neat mop-heads at strategic points in the garden. I have never used it as a hedge, but have seen it used most effectively this way and I think it would be pleasant in a formal herb garden. But I think *S. neapolitana* is more graceful and feathery, and it is certainly much whiter. It looks best posed against a wall or filling up a sheltered corner. I cut off the yellow button flowers of these two santolinas most ruthlessly, but luckily I have several with sulphur flowers; but, alas, they are not quite so white and feathery as *S. neapolitana*.

I am warned that *Elaeagnus argentea* will make a big tree in time. It is taking a long time doing it. I have had it for several years and it remains about 2 feet tall. It has large glistening leaves like grey satin which shine as they blow in the wind. *Artemisia tridentata* is a silver aromatic bush which, I believe, grows to about 3 feet, although it isn't as tall as that with me yet.

Occasionally a grey-leaved tree looks well against a dark background. I have a white poplar, a whitebeam, and, at the end of the little path through the terraced garden, a kind of weeping pear, *Pyrus salicifolia argentea*, with narrow grey leaves that flutter in the wind.

21   HIGHDOWN, WEST SUSSEX. 1937

Short-lived but magnificent borders planted with clusters of bearded irises in
different shades. A broad ribbon of white pinks is used as edging; fox-tail lilies
(*Eremurus* spp.) and Japanese cherries interplanted with lilacs, provide background.

Percy Cane
SPECIAL BORDERS

When spring and early summer trees and shrubs have finished flowering and the delicate fresh greens of spring foliage have turned to the more sombre tones of midsummer, gardens should not become masses of dark rhododendrons and dull-looking shrubs. They should continue lovely with colour into and through the long summer days and well into the autumn, and this is when roses and herbaceous plants come into their own.

Percy Cane (1881–1976) was a prolific garden-designer and author. Among his creations are the gardens at Dartington Hall, Devon, Hungerdown House, Wiltshire and Hascombe Court, Surrey.

Flowering plants can be used to give the final glory of colour to gardens in many ways. Herbaceous borders can be in various shades of one colour, say from cream to deepest yellow or orange; blue borders are refreshingly cool in appearance and clear blues in a green setting can be delightful; a border of grey-foliage plants with perhaps only pink and white flowers could be charming; blue, purple and grey, too, would be distinctive, and borders of strong colours – reds, purples and oranges – could be striking in their almost oriental brilliance. Plants and flowers can be used to give endless harmonies of colour.

When space allows some plants, paeonies for instance, could be given a border to themselves. Paeonies take two years to become established, but a paeony border in all shades of white, cream, from pale to deep pink, reds and crimsons, can be lovely. Even after they have finished flowering their bronze-green foliage is decorative and fairly wide borders could be planted with two or three rows of paeonies in front and two or more rows of some later flowering plants behind them. Aster (Michaelmas daisies) in all their shades of mauves, blues, pinks, crimsons and purples, will by themselves make lovely colour schemes, soft but rich, and they could, in a wide border, be planted behind the earlier flowering paeonies.

see plate 20

Irises, too, can be grown by themselves either in an iris border or in a separate garden. Their grey-green, swordlike leaves look particularly well against flagstones and a paved iris garden can be a joy when the irises are flowering, and even later their foliage is decorative. Like most plants with grey foliage they grow best in soil with a high lime content, but the basic nature of the soil is of no great importance as lime can always be added. Blues, as distinct

see plate 21

from mauves and purples, are particularly useful and have a colour value entirely their own. Mulberry-coloured irises are distinctive and tone especially well with pale yellow and chrome varieties. Of yellow iris, 'Lady Mohr', 'Pinnacle', 'Rocket', 'St. Crispin', 'Yellow Hercules' and 'Xantha', this last with large flowers of rich deep yellow, are all good. But there are so many excellent varieties that it is invidious to name a few. Skilfully planted there are more than enough to make an iris border or garden a charming sight. Iris should be planted with the upper part of the rhizome exposed to sun and air.

Delphiniums in all shades of blue and purple are the glory of midsummer flower gardens. Their stately spires, planted at regular intervals down the length of an herbaceous border, give an idea of order that can be very satisfying and blue in its many tones goes happily with most other colours. A border of delphiniums only can be charming and they can, too, be planted in groups amongst shrubs, but planted in this way there should be sufficient to make an impact, say a dozen or more to a group. As an example, their blue shades seem to take on an added loveliness against a background of *Cotoneaster franchetii*, the grey, not very exciting flowers and downy undersides of the cotoneaster leaves being a perfect foil for the blues of the delphiniums.

In yellow or golden gardens, yellow anthemis with the taller creamy-white *Artemisia lactiflora* behind it would be charming. *Thalictrum glaucum*[1] with plumes of greenish-yellow flowers; *Helenium autumnale pumilum magnificum*, a deep butter yellow; and coreopsis, of which there are several good varieties, could be included. Such a garden should be in full sun as in sunlight yellows and golds gleam like silk. Yellow and white hollyhocks, too, if white may be admitted into a yellow garden, are lovely together. Their flowers are a kind of paper white rather like *Romneya coulteri*. Both the single and double forms can be included, although personally I like the single ones better. Hollyhocks look their best against a tall hedge or wall and they need lower plants in front of them to hide their bare stems. For this purpose, in a golden garden, floribunda roses, such as Allgold or Poulsen's Yellow, both of which tone beautifully with almost any other colour and flower continuously, would make charming colour harmonies. Sunflowers and solidago or Golden Rod – the strong growing variety Golden Wings and the newer shorter kinds Leraft and Lemore – prolong the flowering season of yellow or golden borders or gardens. Groups of *Lilium testaceum* or *L. tigrinum*, too, would heighten the colour values and

---

[1] *Thalictrum speciosissimum*

there are the shrubby hypericums which produce their pleasing yellow flowers over a long period.

One scarcely realises how many shades of white there are until one comes to use them. Of lilies, *L. candidum* and *L. regale* are unrivalled for scent, as, too, for the delicate beauty of their flowers, and once established they are easy to grow. As backgrounds there could be philadelphus in its many varieties, most of them fragrant and lasting in flower well into the summer. The paper-white *Romneya coulteri* with the loveliest shade of soft yet deep gold centres; Shasta daisies, single and double; and hostas (funkias) could be included, both for their grey-green leaves, which go so beautifully with white flowers and for their silvery-lilac blooms. Hostas make an excellent foil for white lilies. Amongst shrubs with white flowers there are *Cytisus albus*, *Cistus cyprius* with a maroon blotch at the base of the petals, and *C. corbariensis* with a yellow flush. There are, too, *Escallonia iveyi*, evergreen with white flowers, and *Choisya ternata*, the glossy evergreen foliage of which is fragrant when crushed. And there are spiraeas and white roses for the back.

A border of phlox in their many shades from pale to deepest pink, orange, scarlet, deep purple, mauve and white give rich masses of colour and they are at their best during August and September when delphiniums and the earlier herbaceous plants have finished flowering. Phlox, which like a cool, moist soil but plenty of sun, planted in herbaceous borders, would lengthen the flowering season.

To save work a number of shrubs could well be included in herbaceous borders. The shrubs should be if possible summer flowering and they must fit harmoniously into the colour scheme. For this purpose grey foliage is particularly useful. Because of its grey leaves *Senecio laxifolius*[1] with yellow flowers tones happily with most colours, and it has a delightful habit of growing down over a wall face when planted in raised pockets or on the top of a retaining wall. *Phlomis fruticosa* is somewhat similar, only with flowers of a slightly orange shade. Floribunda roses, too, are useful and can be chosen to fit into any colour scheme. They continue to flower throughout the summer and being permanent, save a lot of work. Groups of Floribunda roses should be proportional to the size of the border, but it is essential to have enough plants in each group to seem an integral part of the planting. Yet another effective way of using these roses is to plant a part of a border with perennials using the roses and other

see colour plate IX

---

[1] *Senecio* 'Sunshine'

shrubs towards one or both ends. In this case the change from herbaceous plants to more shrubs or roses should not be too abrupt.

Amongst summer-flowering shrubs suitable for inclusion in herbaceous borders is *Abelia chinensis* with clusters of white flowers flushed with pink and flowering from July onwards. Abelias should be given a reasonably sheltered place. The silvery-grey foliage of *Artemisia arborescens* would earn it a place in any border, particularly with a grey or blue colour scheme. *Buddleia alternifolia* with its long racemes of mauve flowers would be distinctive with purple delphiniums or I often plant it next to the pink flowered *Escallonia* 'Apple Blossom' or the newer *E.* 'Peach Blossom'. *Buddleia alternifolia* is free growing and should be at the back where its pendulous habit would show beautifully. Ceanothus, too, in their charming shades of powder and deeper blues are suitable and *Ceratostigma willmottianum* with bright blue flowers from July onwards is indispensable for the front. *Choisya ternata*, the Mexican orange blossom, would give a useful touch of evergreen and its white flowers would be right with any colours.

Cistus in their different varieties could almost furnish a border but they are at their best on a dry wall or bank in full sun. To name two or three only, *Cistus corbariensis*, white with a yellow flush, is one of the hardiest; *C. purpureus*, red with a deeper red blotch in the centre, has large flowers and is one of the finest; while *C.* 'Silver Pink', although not quite so hardy, is a gem that should be in any collection. *C. cyprius*, the finest of the tall hardy varieties, grows to a height of from 6 to 8 feet and flowers continuously. There are, too, *C. loretii*, white with a crimson blotch; and the cistus relative, *Halimium ocymoides*, which produces small bright yellow flowers with a chocolate ring at their base.

Cytisus battandieri with yellow flowers, unusual both in colour and shape, is tall and at its best against a sunny wall. *Spartium junceum*, the Spanish broom, produces clouds of flowers of a pleasing shade of yellow during summer. Hibiscus, in shades of blue, mauve and white are distinctive, and the newer variety 'Woodbridge', a large-flowered single red, is well worth a place. There are, too, hypericums, the choicer varieties of which are some of the best of summer-flowering shrubs. *H. patulum forrestii* has large golden yellow flowers and its autumn foliage, a rich deep shade, is very decorative. *H. moserianum* is dwarf and spreading, a useful plant for the front, while *H.* 'Rowallane', attaining a height of up to 4 feet, is one of the finest of the genus.

Growing up to 5 feet in height, *Olearia haastii*, decorative itself, is useful because the grey-white flowers with which it is covered enhance the values of any flowers near it. *Olearia macrodonta* grows well near the sea and *O. scilloniensis* is another good variety. Perovskia, the Russian Sage, which should be planted in full sun, has blue flowers, very silvery deeply cut foliage and is invaluable. *Phlomis fruticosa* is another shrub with grey foliage that may be planted in such a border as I am describing. Like *Senecio laxifolius*, it has the useful habit of growing down over a wall face. Potentillas, too, of which there are several good varieties, produce their flowers in all shades of yellow and white over a long period. *Romneya coulteri*, the Californian Tree Poppy, can be included in any border, shrub or herbaceous; its paper-white flowers with yellow centres against very grey leaves and charming with the powder-blue *Ceanothus* 'Gloire de Versailles'. *Romneya coulteri*, which is at its best against a south wall, also seems to enhance the value of any flowers near it.

The grey-green aromatic leaves of rosemary entitle it to a place both in herbaceous borders or with shrubs. *Santolina chamaecyparissus*, another dwarf shrub with very grey foliage, is useful for the front, rather more for its grey foliage than for its flowers, a not very pleasing shade of yellow. For the back of fairly wide borders *Holodiscus discolor ariaefolius*, attaining a height of 9 or 10 feet, produces drooping panicles of creamy-white flowers in midsummer. And there are several of the shrubby veronicas or hebes, amongst them *H.* 'Autumn Glory', low and with deep violet flowers; *H. traversii* producing a cloud of greyish-white flowers over its not particularly attractive foliage, is useful for the way in which it intensifies the value of adjacent colours. A border may be planted chiefly with suitable shrubs and yet give very much the effect of an herbaceous border. The advantage of this predominant use of shrubs is that the planting is permanent and labour-saving as practically no staking would be necessary. To give rather more the effect of an herbaceous border a few groups of, say, delphiniums and phlox, both of which are, for their colour values, outstanding, might well be included.

H. E. Bates
PLANTING FOR LATE SUMMER

*H. E. Bates (1905–1974),
immensely well known for
his novels and short
stories, was also an
enthusiastic amateur
gardener and
countryman. His garden
writing is informed and
typically elegant.*

I am not a purist where borders are concerned. My sole purpose is to achieve the longest possible display of colour – virtually for nearly half the year – with the minimum of labour. My border therefore must be totally uncluttered by subjects which, however beautiful, have short lives. For this reason such things as lupins, geums, pyrethrums, paeonies, poppies, aquilegias, doronicums and irises are ruthlessly excluded from it; I want no glaring gaps in July and August left by things which have bloomed for a mere fleeting fortnight or so. My search is for things which begin to bloom late and then persist in flower for five, six, eight weeks and even for three months and more. In this way my border is never ready for display until the first week in July but is thereafter of increasing interest and beauty, reaching its peak in August and September and even holding its own, as Miss Jekyll's celebrated borders did, in October, when the angle of light, together with its soft autumnal distillation, is the most gracious and kindly of the year.

When I hear gardeners proclaim dismally that their gardens are virtually finished in August, as in fact many all too often are, I am prone to congratulate myself that the main feature of my own has almost another richly rewarding three months to run. The lesson in all this was, I must hasten to add, neither quickly nor easily learned. It took some years to introduce the ruthless hand that finally banished the ephemeral beauties of spring and substituted for them subjects of greatly prolonged life, many of them, such as grasses, hostas and grey leaved things, grown more for foliage effect than flower. With horror, I am aware, the border purists will recoil from me when I declare that dahlias are permissible too in this long four-month pattern, but permissible they are and have long been and will long continue to be.

Contrasts of foliage – a lesson long ago learned from Miss Jekyll – are of as great an importance in the border pattern as continuity of flower. The Northern end of the border therefore begins with that wholly admirable hosta, *H. lancifolia*, which, as I have already said, not only hides every centimetre of soil with its thick, bright green, graceful leaves, but for good measure flowers from July to September, thus being the longest flowered of all the desirable hosta family, its tender rose-mauve stalks of bells, almost like enlarged hyacinths, being of infinitely seducing loveliness. This hosta's density of foliage contrasts admirably with the fluffy fern-like grey of the old, common but wholly desirable southernwood, and both in turn contrast still more effectively with a 4 foot high pink and silver grass whose name, I am ashamed to admit, I do not know. In this way the eye is led into the heart of the border gently and without shock, the first colours to strike it being whites, pinks and mauves before the strong central masses of orange, crimson and scarlet begin. In this introductory space three other wholly admirable plants provide a long and rewarding feast: first, the delicate little *Penstemon* 'Evelyn', of which I am immensely fond; and second, *Aster frikartii*, which I mention yet again since it is surely the most desirable and possibly the least known of all the family of michaelmas daisies, a plant of such marvellous value that it deserves a paragraph to itself.

I call a plant excellent when it has the following virtues: that of being able to stand on its own legs without stakes, of producing flowers of great beauty for weeks on end and of showing incontestable grace of form. All this *Aster frikartii* does to perfection. Yet one rarely sees this hybrid between *A. amellus* and *A. thomsonii* and it seems to me that one possible reason for this is that it has suffered from unintentional ill-treatment and is thus suspected of being difficult and short-lived. This ill-treatment simply consists of splitting it up in autumn, immediately after flowering. This should never, never be done, since there is no adequate time space left for the roots' re-establishment. Always, therefore, *Aster frikartii* – which, by the way grows stiffly to a height of 3 feet or so and has big star-like flowers of purest mauve – should be divided in spring, as growth re-starts, when it will positively present not the slightest difficulty.

The third plant in this portion of the border's threshold to deserve the company of *Aster frikartii* is also too rarely seen and for the life of me I can never think why. *Verbena venosa* is, to my mind, easily the finest half-hardy perennial that can be raised as an annual from seed. When I say half-hardy perennial I should immediately qualify this by saying that in the mildest of winters – that of 1966–67 being an immediate example – it will survive unscathed and as an extra reward will sow itself freely. The plant is stiff, about 15 inches high and has rather spare foliage that is crisp and almost rough. Its myriad heads of pleasing purple, not at all unlike that excellent lavender, 'Hidcote Purple', begin to appear in June and persist until the severest of frosts, growing denser and denser as summer fattens into autumn, until the whole plant – it needs to be planted in generous masses – is a great royal sheaf that has also the supreme virtue of doing almost as well in a rainy season as in a hot one, this virtue being a fourth to add to my three listed above.

Verbena venosa also has a taller relative, *V. bonariensis*, which has the same family virtues: easily raised from seed, long-flowering, almost hardy. Though growing to a height of almost 5 feet, its own crisp rough stems need no staking and are, to my eye, of pleasing architectural form, the stems spreading in a stiff angular fashion, but lightly, so that the whole plant can be seen through. In some ways it is not at all unlike one of those fragile modern designs in wire or ironwork that have invaded the realm, if one can call it that, of sculpture. It too has purple flowers which, like those of *V. venosa*, are equally happy in rain or sun. I am fully aware that there are horticultural fuss-pots who recoil from this plant, even hate it, but for me it stands high on the list of desirables and I am even tolerant of its habit of seeding freely and in totally unexpected places, when it adds a sort of careless informality to groups of other things without upsetting them.

At intervals along the first and second rows of the border *Cineraria maritima* lights up the crowded pattern of summer with silver, a cool foil for such reds as the old-fashioned but lovable bergamot, *Monarda* 'Cambridge Scarlet'; but the plant that at this point really takes the eye is a comparatively new one, *Phlox* 'Norah Leigh', a lady who, in the words of a Swiss friend of mine, ''is worth to have''. (I note, by the way, a growing habit among gardening writers of using the detestable word 'cultivar', which always sounds to me like an ugly Russian cross between 'samovar' and a collective farm. I consequently consign it to the muck-heap with such contemporary horrors as teach-in, fenestration, escalate, proliferate, reflation, where I hope it will rot.) Miss Leigh is a variegated phlox in light green and cream, an old plant re-discovered in a cottage garden, not grown for her flowers, which are of a rather insipid pink, but purely for foliage effect, which endures for weeks and weeks from May onwards. She is thus yet another highly valuable addition to the growing family of foliage treasures who need neither staking nor dead-heading but provide elegance and illumination without difficulty or fuss.

Standing not far behind her, as a sort of stouter, taller reflection, in almost precisely the same light green and cream, is another plant all too rarely seen, *Scrophularia nodosa variegata*. This accommodating four-footer would, I am sure, have brought forth scorn from Reginald Farrer, for whom its thick strong leaves, dappled as if with broken light, would no doubt have seemed as coarse as some wayside nettle. But, as I have remarked elsewhere, we have today learned to look on leaves in a different way and to use them bountifully and for contrasting and even dramatic effect. I yield to no-one in my affection for such celestial miniatures as soldanellas (to see them flowering by the thousand in the spring alps is the purest of joys) but at the same time I am bound to agree with whoever it was who once said that "one cannot live for ever on quince jelly". So the scrophularia will continue to be very much a plant for me.

Even at the risk of seeming to burble on and on about these leaf variegations, which I find not only useful but vastly attractive, I must nevertheless call attention to yet one more beauty, *Veronica variegata* (the pundits, like the gods playing with the ill-fated destinies of Hardy's Tess, have been having sport with the *Veronica* family, having decided to divide the house into two, calling the other half *Hebe*. I confess to being irritatingly confused by these changes and still prefer and insist on the soft elegance of *Veronica*). This plant is a sub-shrub, and unfortunately, like many veronicas, not quite hardy, but so easily wintered in cool houses or frame and so readily struck from cuttings that it need cause no heart-burnings in that direction. Its parma violet bottle brushes of flower in the second half of summer give added enchantment to the green and cream stripes of the typically narrow veronica leaves and I use it constantly in all manner of places. If you need a perfectly hardy relation of it *Veronica* 'Midsummer Beauty', taller and unvariegated, is your answer.

I am constantly struck by the behaviour of visitors who stand and stare at some long-known, long-loved plant as if it were some newly discovered treasure only recently acquired from the exclusive slopes of some horticultural Parnassus. Such a plant is the old *Catananche coerulea*, commonly called Cupid's Dart, which I put in the front row of the chorus at the border's other end. It is perhaps best described as a sort of everlasting cornflower: flowers of charming delicacy, classic mauve, held in cups of rustling *Immortelle* silver. From about mid-June it flowers with a fussless prodigality that constantly enchants. Perhaps its fragile-looking stalks need the lightest of support, but on the whole it is self-sufficient. It is readily raised from seed (this is the best way of acquiring it, since you must have good generous groups of it and not mean and measly dots-and-carries) and though I have seen discouraging advice given as to not allowing it to flower after August for fear of its early demise, I have never found this to be in any way true. There is also a white variety and a variety *major*, an improvement on the type. Farrer, by the way, generously called it "the noble blue cupidore with the darker eye, very beautiful in wild rough places in the South of France", a splendid tribute, absolutely right.

This reference to "the darker eye" and the South of France instantly serves to remind me of another marvellously good plant all too rarely seen – and again I simply cannot think why. When one thinks of all the labours that are every year expended by gardeners raising such horrors as tagetes from seed (always pronounced by jobbing gardeners to rhyme with 'sweets') and various other dingy things known as 'bedding subjects', it becomes even more of a mystery why *Dimorphotheca ecklonis* is not better known. I playfully mock this South African treasure by calling it the Government Plant, since it opens up its flowers at nine in the morning and closes them promptly at four in the afternoon, a characteristic shared by numbers of other South African beauties, gazanias among them. The common *Gazania splendens* with its strong golden daisies and black central ring, has long been known to us, but I rather fancy the newer grey leaved introductions, called Wisley Hybrids, have so far escaped wide attention, which is a great pity. One of the most ravishing sights I have ever seen was provided by these grey-leaved gazanias along the Rivieras of France and Italy in May (and to be continued, I presume, all summer) where great silver mats of fern-like foliage were starred with dense galaxies of orange, cream, lemon and tangerine for mile after mile, of the intensest brilliance in the baking sun. Such ravishing displays of glory cannot, alas, be hoped for in our fickle northern summers, since gazanias thrive only in perpetual sun, but happily we have here yet another instance of the saving grace of foliage, for if a wet or cloudy summer should frustrate your gazanias' flowers you may safely bet that the fine cut fern-like foliage will give continuous pleasure until the summer's end. Just before this comes it is the easiest of tasks to pull off cuttings from the parent plants, wintering them in batches under glass, to be kept well dry until repotted in spring.

But here I seem to have done an injustice to *Dimorphotheca ecklonis*, the white beauty with the darker eye, by turning my back on her in temporary favour of her South African cousins. Let me immediately remedy this by saying that there are few plants in my garden with which visitors fall more readily in love, and understandably so. There is a celestial purity, grace and subtlety about this lady – the plant is incontestably feminine in appeal – which few others share. The wide daisy-shaped flower is of perfect whiteness, not starchy, not harsh as in certain of the commoner varieties of chrysanthemum maximum, not exactly milky, but of a glistening purity that contrasts superbly with the vivid blue eye and its delicious and delicate sprinkling of brightest orange dust. Mad dogs and Englishmen traditionally go out in the midday sun and how wise they are if their reward is to see a mass of *Dimorphotheca ecklonis*, in full glory. The plant may, by the way, be raised from seed with no more difficulty than stocks and asters and once you have mature plants the rest is child's play: you simply take autumn cuttings, winter them under cold glass and plant out in spring. Old plants may also be lifted, potted up and over wintered in the same way, when they will also flower at the first touch of sun and lengthening light in February. Miss Jekyll, by the way, refers to a twin sister of *D. ecklonis*, namely *D. pluvialis* (the opening and closing of the flowers were said at one time to indicate rain) and most happily describes the backs of the flowers as being "of that pleasant quiet colour that is like diluted ink".

Two more good plants are joined in modest embrace on the borders' farthest boundary: the one, *Ballota pseudo-dictamnus*, merely offering its curious crimpeld half-grey, half-green foliage in dense 2 foot masses all summer (an excellent foil, by the way, to *Helleborus argutifolius*, as it would also be to any of the bergenias) and *Sedum* 'Autumn Joy', a sturdy, tough but highly rewarding so-called ice-plant (a term I have never cared for very much) which holds back its splendid reddish bronze heads of flower until the threshold of autumn and then stoutly carries them on and on over the very threshold of winter, there to be harvested and dried, if you care for that sort of thing. Inclining to the view that it is, like wool-gathering, an art for country spinsters, I am not sure if I do. All I know is that I now let the flower heads of *Sedum* 'Autumn Joy' remain on the plants all winter, my reward being that sometimes, even on December or January afternoons, a touch of sun seems to set them on burnished fire.

CHAPTER VI

Roses

William Paul

THE FORMATION
OF THE ROSARIUM

In the formation of the Rosarium, it appears to us that the simpler the forms of the beds the better. The plants of which it is composed are for the most part budded on stems, and decidedly artificial objects; and parallelograms, squares, circles, ovals, and other regular figures, are in perfect harmony with the character of the plants; admit of the most perfect arrangement; and display the Roses to greatest advantage.

When the Rosarium is intended to be of large or even moderate size, there should be two compartments; the one for the summer kinds exclusively, the other to contain the autumnals. The boundary of each may be defined by planting a single row of Pillar-Roses at intervals of a yard apart. When they reach the height of 5 feet, each alternate plant may be removed, and small chains be fixed from pillar to pillar, hanging in graceful curves the entire length

William Paul VMH (1822–1905) was a hybridizer, nurseryman and rose specialist. His Chestnut nursery was an important source of roses during a vital transitional period of their development.

of the line. Over these some of the branches may be trained to form elegant festoons, two or three shoots being allowed to ascend the pillar until they reach such height as circumstances or taste may point out as desirable.

If Pillar-Roses are not approved of to form the line of demarcation, the same end may be accomplished by a rustic fence, which should be covered with some particular kind of Rose suited for the purpose. It should be a good, free flowering, hardy variety, whether a summer or autumn bloomer: if the latter is preferred, the Bourbon or Noisette offer the best kinds. Or again, this would seem a fitting opportunity of introducing the sweet-briar, which should abound in every Rosarium; for the delicious fragrance of its young leaves in the earliest of spring, the delicacy of its blossoms in summer, and the gay appearance of the scarlet hips it produces in the autumn, must recommend it to every observer.

The walks of the Rosarium should be invariably of grass, which sets off the plants, when in flower, to much greater advantage than gravel. Grass walks are objected to by some because unpleasant to walk upon early in the morning, or after a shower of rain; but they give such a finish to the Rosarium, and lend such a freshness and brilliancy to the flowers, that it were a pity to forego these advantages solely on this account. And if the grass is kept closely mown, the force of this objection is greatly abated.

When the walks are of grass, it is perhaps not desirable to plant edgings to the beds. When they are of gravel, it is decidedly necessary to do so; and Box, slate, or fancy tiles may be used. In many instances, too, the Pompon and Fairy Roses may be introduced as edgings, with a very happy effect, to form a complete hedge, of less than a foot in height, covered with their miniature blossoms; the one variety blooming in summer only, the other throughout the autumn.

It is desirable that the Rosarium should have a raised spot in its vicinity, from which a bird's-eye view of the whole may be obtained during the season of flowering. A mound of earth thrown up is the simplest plan; and some burs and stones may be placed upon the surface. The sides of the mound may be planted with Ayrshire, Sempervirens, and other running Roses, or climbing plants of various kinds: on the top may be formed a Rose Temple, or a cluster of Pillar-Roses. From this spot we obtain, in the flowering season, a view of the Roses *en masse*, as they lie beneath us, the effect of which is agreeable and striking; and indeed every one can appreciate the beauty of the picture thus submitted to him. It needs neither the knowledge of the Florist nor the refined

see plate 23

taste of the connoisseur; the beauty and effect of the *coup d'œil* thus obtained is acknowledged alike by the skilled and unskilled in these matters. This we regard as one important point gained in the formation of the Rosarium; but there are others deserving of attention.

When the amateur forms a Rosarium, he does not usually plant for effect: he views his plants individually, rather than collectively. And we should suppose that, to meet his approbation, the Rosarium should be so formed that he may attend to, and examine, each plant, without risking an injury to the rest. He may be delighted with viewing his collection as a whole; and, in addition to this, the knowledge that his friends, who may be less skilled in floriculture than himself, would derive the highest gratification from such a sight, would induce him not to neglect this point. But he finds greater pleasure in looking at his favourites separately. What would be tedious and uninteresting to them, is to him highly amusing. Each of his plants has a name by which he distinguishes it. He regards them as so many friends or acquaintances, every one of which has a claim upon his attention. He therefore wishes them so disposed that he may attend to each in turn, without annoying the rest. How often have I seen, in large beds of Roses, the soil round a favourite tree trodden as hard as a gravel walk! I have also seen the adjoining trees, whose beauty was only dimmed by the presence of a brighter gem, seriously rubbed and broken, being altogether unheeded in the eager haste to inspect more inviting specimens. It would seem desirable, then, that the beds be so formed that each see plate 22 plant may be seen from the walks. No one who really loves Roses will be content with viewing a plant placed in the back of a bed some 6 or 7 yards from a walk. To fully appreciate its beauties – to be satisfied – one must have it directly under the eye, or how can he mark the exact colour, form, and various characters, and last, but not least, inhale its perfume? If the plant is so placed that we cannot do this from the walks, the beds must be trampled on; the temptation is too great; we cannot resist it.

When forming a Rosarium, it is at the option of the cultivator to set apart a spot for growing plants from which to save seed. If he desired to raise seedlings, this should be done; for the plants become impoverished by the ripening of the seeds, and therefore those from which he wishes to obtain large and perfect flowers should never be suffered to seed. He should select the sunniest spot in the garden in which to plant the seed-bearers, in order to secure every possible advantage for accelerating the period of maturity. Autumn pruning should also be adopted, as a means to this end, by inducing an early development of flowers. Our climate is not the most favourable for this branch of Rose-culture: we therefore must not waive even the slightest advantage which may be obtained either naturally or artificially.

Let us now proceed to make a few remarks on planting. We will suppose the beds ready formed and prepared, and the order of planting arranged. There is a sufficient number of plants at hand of the required heights and kinds to fill them. If it be a Rosarium or a series of beds we are about to plant, we may suppose that each group will have a bed to itself; or if our plans are not sufficiently extensive to admit of this, each bed should be planted with varieties of one group only, or at furthest with a combination of such as resemble each other in external characters. We are speaking now of planting the Rosarium, or a series of beds: in a single bed or clump it is desirable to mix the groups.

The disposing of the plants will vary so much, according to the plan of the Rosarium or the taste of the individual, and is withal so simple, that it does not appear necessary to enlarge on this particular point. One thing in planting should be borne in mind – Never suffer the roots to lie exposed to the sun and wind, not even for an hour. I fancy I hear, as I have heard some say, Nonsense! the Dog Rose is so hardy that you may expose it for a month to all weathers, wind, frost, or sunshine, without fear of injuring it. I have often heard this asserted, and have tried experiments, which it is not necessary to record here, to convince myself of a simple fact, which it may be said no one ought to have doubted. One experiment I will relate. In planting some French Roses, two plants of the same kind were left out of the ground for two days and two nights in December. They were budded on the Dog Rose. The days were sunny, the nights were frosty, the mercury falling to about 28° Fahrenheit. Numerous other plants, whose roots were kept covered, and which were planted at the same time, grew and flourished without one exception. And these two *did not die*; but for three years they have maintained a miserable existence, neither growing as the others grow, nor producing any creditable flowers; and yet they were as robust and vigorous as any, if, indeed, not more so.

If there are two employed in planting, the one may dig the holes at proper distances, mixing the soil taken out with some well-pulverized manure, and laying it on the sides of the holes ready for use in planting. If the soil be light, he may, notwithstanding the dressing it may have previously received, add a few spadesful of loam for any very choice kind: if the soil be heavy, he may add a few spadesful of leaf-mould. This latter substance is an excellent addition to heavy soils, and almost indispensable when the Tea-scented Roses are planted there: it tempts them to root vigorously, and strong well-flowered plants are the result.

If Standards only are planted, 3 feet apart is a good distance; and if there is an objection to planting Dwarfs among the Standards, and it is still thought desirable to cover the ground below during summer, this may be accomplished by planting Annuals, such as, Mignonette, *Viscaria oculata*, *Campanula stricta*, and any others of slender growth. These cannot injure the Roses: in hot dry seasons we believe they prove beneficial, by the partial shade they afford; but they should be planted very thinly, and those kinds chosen which are of the most slender growth. When Dwarf Roses only are planted, from 1 to 3 feet, according to the vigour of the kinds, is the distance usually chosen.

A few words on arranging plants in single beds may not be misplaced here. We first take the centre of the bed, where we place the tallest plant, and which should be a robust grower, an abundant bloomer, and an attractive Rose. In reference to this plant, whatever may be the shape or size of the bed, the others are disposed. They should incline gently from it in any or every direction, till the plants at the edge be on very short stems or perfect dwarfs. An inclination of 1½ feet, from one row to another, admits of a very pretty arrangement. Supposing the centre plant to be 5 feet, the next row may be 3½ feet, the next 2 feet, and so on. Let it be borne in mind, that the strongest growers should be planted nearest to the centre; and in consequence of their more vigorous growth, greater space should be allowed from plant to plant there than at the circumference of the bed, where the smaller growers are planted. When the holes are opened for planting, throw a little manure in the bottom, and mix it with the soil there; then place the plant in the hole filling in with the manure and soil laid ready above, treading them firmly about the roots. After planting, give each Standard a stake, to secure it from the action of the wind, and the operation is finished. Be it remarked, that planting deep causes Roses to throw suckers: if the roots are from 3 to 6 inches under the soil it is quite enough.

The Tea-scented, Chinese, tender varieties of Noisette, and Lawrenceana[1] Roses, should never be planted in the autumn. Let the beds or places which they are intended to fill remain open till spring. The plants of these groups are sometimes small and delicate, and if put into the ground in autumn they often suffer fearfully from the winter's frost. But plant them in spring; if they are a year old, in March; if younger, in May or June; and they have the growing

---

[1] Fairy Roses (see next page)

season before them: they get a firm hold of the ground by winter, and are more gradually hardened to, and better capable of supporting, the changes and severities of that season.

It is important that the ground be in good working order at the time of planting, for on this depends greatly the measure of success. If it be wet, it hangs to the spade and to the heels of the operator, and prevents him from doing the work well. But worse than this: the moving of ground when wet causes the particles to combine more intimately: it becomes close and dead, and, if thrown about the roots of a tree in this state, acts most prejudicially. Choose, then, a dry time, when the earth bounds clean and free from the spade; and if subsequent dry weather points out the necessity of using the watering pot, by all means do so: far better this, than to plant when the ground is in bad order.

*   *   *

I believe pruning to be the most important practice in Rose culture, and, at the same time, the most difficult to obtain the mastery over, and to apply with success.

The difficulty arises chiefly from the extensiveness of the genus, which is made up of varieties differing so much from each other in habit and character. What a striking contrast does the tiny Lawrenceana[1], which does not usually exceed 18 inches in height, present to the other extreme of the genus, the Ayrshire[2] and Sempervirens, which will form shoots 15 feet long in a single year! And there are kinds of every intermediate degree of vigour and character, and hence the difficulty – the great variation required in the application of pruning.

But, beyond this, the manner of pruning is partly determined by the object the operator has in view, or by the condition and health of the plant. A rose intended to form a standard would require different pruning to one wanted to form a Pillar Rose, although the variety were the same. When flowers are desired of the largest size, as for exhibition, the plan should differ from that pursued to obtain masses of flowers. Again, a Rose in vigorous condition, when healthy and full of sap, requires *less* pruning than when, owing to soil,

[1]*Rosa chinensis* 'Minima' also known as
Miss Lawrence's rose – parent of the group of miniatures called Fairy Roses.
[2] *Rosa arvensis*

situation, or other causes, it is of moderate or weakly growth. The same degree of pruning applied to each condition would produce opposite results. Close pruning would be the means of improving the health and flowering of a weak tree: it would induce a vigorous one to form wood-shoots only, no flowers.

From the above remarks it will be seen, that after the fullest and most careful examination of the subject, pruning depending so much on circumstances, a great deal must be left to the judgment of the operator: a certain degree of practice is necessary before any great attainment in this art can be arrived at, and I would not advise the uninitiated to trust himself too far, before he has well marked the manoeuvres of some skilful friend or practitioner.

I know many instances in which amateurs, who take delight in attending their own Roses, mar the beauty of their trees for want of considering the principles of Rose pruning. Many trees, from too much pruning, grow most luxuriantly, but shew little disposition to flower; others, from too little pruning, produce an abundance of flowers, but they are poor in quality. These are known facts of everyday occurrence; and what are the consequences? Probably the varieties are condemned as worthless, though of first-rate merit, and only requiring a skilful application of the knife to cause them to flower perfectly, and in gorgeous abundance.

But it is not a question of flowers only. On pruning depends the formation of the trees; whether they be handsome, or irregular and misshapen. Regarding this branch of cultivation, then, as one of primary importance, I shall give myself full scope in discussing and illustrating it.

There are two seasons of the year at which pruning is usually performed; November, which is termed autumn-pruning; and March, or spring-pruning. Winter-pruning cannot be recommended, as there is a risk of the trees being injured by the action of wet and frost upon the fresh wounds. Thinning in summer is advocated by some; and of this we shall have occasion to speak by and by.

Which is the better season for pruning, spring or autumn, is a point concerning which Rose-cultivators are not altogether agreed. To enable our readers to judge for themselves, it may be well to state the condition of the trees at each season.

In November, Roses may be said to be at rest; for although there is always a circulation of the sap, at this particular time it is less active than in spring or summer.

As a proof of this, if we removed a Rose in autumn, the roots are then, to all appearance, inactive; but if we remove the same in March, or often, indeed, earlier, we shall find numerous white rootlets, which have been newly formed, and which, sponge-like, are continually sucking moisture from the earth, thereby favouring the circulation of the sap, and promoting growth. Hence the different state of a tree in autumn and spring is, that at the former period it is sinking into or at rest; and in the latter rising into life and action. Now, it is evident, that the greater the quantity of nutritious matter that can be collected in the immediate vicinity of the buds intended to remain for bloom, the more vigorous will the growth be, and the finer the flowers. Autumn-pruning favours this storing of the juices of the plants; for by cutting away the superfluous shoots in autumn, the buds on those left behind are placed in contact with a greater supply of food, by the lessening of the number of the channels through which the sap has to pass: they increase in size, become plump, and, when spring arrives, vegetate with great vigour. An earlier bloom is also produced than when pruning is deferred till spring; and the shoots and flowers are formed with more regularity, and in greater abundance. It may, however, appear that many of the summer kinds, being more disposed to produce growing than flowering-shoots, autumn-pruning is calculated to favour this tendency. But, to counteract this, the operation should be performed with less rigour at that season than when deferred till spring.

But autumn-pruning has its disadvantages, the greatest of which is this: – a few mild days in winter often excite the buds of autumn-pruned Roses, and they push forth; severe weather follows; the young shoots are frosted; and the bloom injured. This is more particularly the case with the Chinese, Noisette, Bourbon, Tea-scented, and the Hybrids of these kinds, which we shall term *excitable*, because they are quickly excited to growth. The Provence, Moss, French, Alba, and others, rarely suffer from this cause, as they are not so readily affected by the state of the weather. Be it remarked, however, that the quickness with which buds are roused into action depends much upon how far the shoots were matured the previous autumn: the less mature the more excitable. It will be perceived, then, that there is a difficulty in the way of autumn-pruning, when applied to the excitable kinds, which can only be remedied by affording them protection from frost, should a mild December or January be succeeded by severe weather. But this would entail great additional trouble, and cannot always be done. Let us now turn to the other season.

The chief advantage gained by deferring pruning till spring is, that the flower-shoots are placed beyond the reach of injury by frost. If, during winter, any buds push forth in unpruned Roses, it is those at the ends of the branches, and they will be removed by pruning. But there is an evil attendant on this apparent advantage. When pruning is put off till spring, the buds placed at the extremities of the shoots are often found in leaf, and in the operation we cut off some inches from a shoot in this state. The tree is denuded of its leaves, and thereby receives a check; the sap, being in active motion, exudes from the fresh wounds. The lower buds find themselves suddenly in contact with a great supply of food, by the cutting away of the buds beyond them. There is a pause. Soon one or two buds at the extremity of the pruned shoots take up the work: they swell, and are developed apace, but all below remain dormant. Thus spring-pruning is unfavourable to an abundant and regular development of branches and flowers, and, consequently, to the well forming of a tree. The flowers are also usually produced later in the season, and of less size.

Thus it may be said that each season has its advantages and disadvantages; but is it impossible to draw from both? We think not: and would strongly recommend that all but the excitable kinds be pruned in autumn: thin out these at the same time, but leave the shortening of their shoots till spring.

For pruning Roses two instruments are necessary, a knife and a saw. The knife I use is one with a straight blade: the saw is a double-toothed one, small, with a handle about a foot long and a blade of rather less length: the point is narrow, to admit of its being easily worked among the close branches. Armed with these we are ready for action; and it is necessary to bear in mind that they should be kept very sharp, in order that the work may be well done.

In France it was formerly the practice to clip the heads of the Standard Roses with shears; but I believe this practice is now abandoned there, and scissors used in their stead. I have tried the latter, but find, in my hands, the knife executes the work better, and more expeditiously; although, as to the latter point, something may depend on use. The scissors are, however, very convenient for gathering flowers, and for cutting off the flower-stalks when they grow shabby, or begin to decay.

There are three principal ends sought in Rose pruning, each of which carries with it a degree of weight, and should be kept distinctly in view; and let it be borne in mind, that on the judicious use of the pruning-knife their perfect accomplishment more or less depends.

Our first end is to maintain a tree in full health and vigour. We are told that the extraordinary vigour and beauty of some plants on which goats had been browsing first gave the ancients the idea of pruning. Certainly no one in the present day would dispute the advantages of it. Cultivators can only be at variance as to the mode of action, and the season at which the operation should be performed. If we leave a Rose-tree unpruned for one year, a great number of buds will burst forth, producing a vast quantity of blossoms, but both shoots and flowers will be comparatively thin and puny. If such tree be left unpruned for two or three successive years, it will become greatly enfeebled; the ends of the yearling shoots will die back for want of nourishment, and thus are reduced the number of buds capable of development during the subsequent year. Here we see one end of pruning naturally accomplished. But it is not sufficiently so. The flowers continue to degenerate, till at length they can be scarcely recognised: the tree dwindles, presents an unhealthy appearance, and pruning must be the first means applied for its restoration.

Secondly the formation of a tree is a point deserving of the closest attention; for if the form is inelegant it cannot but displease, however healthy and vigorous it may be, or what the degree of beauty the flowers it produces. Should the latter be forming small, their size may be increased by lessening their number, or by a timely application of manure-water; but for the improvement of the form of a tree there is no such ready remedy. The flowers, too, are but transitory: the shape of the tree is lasting; it remains to view after they are gone. To form a handsome tree, it is necessary to take it in hand when young: it is then easy to fashion, as taste, or a view to its permanent weal, may require. But if it has become straggling, from unskilful management or other causes, it is often difficult to re-model, sometimes requiring the patience and skill of two, or even three seasons. Before we commence the pruning of a Rose, whether it be a bush or a tree, it is therefore well to determine the shape it shall assume, and then frame all our operations with a view to its accomplishment. Perhaps a form at the same time pleasing and advantageous is that of a half oval; for in such all the shoots and branches get a due portion of air and sunlight, and the under ones are not excluded from view, which they often are in round-headed trees. The varieties of spreading growth are most easily brought into this form, but the principle is applicable to all.

The next aim in Rose pruning is to secure an abundance of fine flowers. If the health and vigour of a tree are affected by pruning, the flowers, depending so much on these conditions, must also be affected by the same operation.

When about to prune a Rose, I first look to the name, that I may know the habit and character of the variety I have to deal with. I must know whether it is a summer or perpetual bloomer; a strong or weakly grower; and whether the flowers are produced fine from low, middle, and top eyes indiscriminately, or not. It is only by knowing and considering these points that we can prune with accuracy, and ensure full success.

It is an axiom in Rose pruning, that the more vigorous in habit a plant is, the more shoots should be thinned out, and the less should those which are left be shortened in. This has in view, in particular, the production of flowers in the most perfect condition. The eyes near the base of those kinds which form short shoots (especially the autumnals), usually produce the best flowers; and in the vigorous growers we prefer, for the same reason, the eyes about the middle of the shoot, or nearer its summit if the wood be well ripened. But there is a question arising here which it may be well to glance at before proceeding further. All Roses make two growths in the year; first in spring, and again in summer shortly after they have flowered. Some of the autumnals start afresh at short intervals throughout summer and autumn; but we wish at the present time to speak of the spring and summer's growth only, and to ask which we should look to as calculated to produce the finest flowers.

When the shoots formed in summer are well ripened we should prefer them, and for these reasons. The growth at that season is generally more rapid, and, in consequence, the shoots, although usually of less strength, are freer in the bark; the eyes are more plump and prominent, and well stored with the juices required to supply nourishment and promote growth. Nevertheless, it is only a question of flowers that would induce us to prefer the summer wood; for when we look to the forming of the tree, we shall find it necessary, in most cases, to prune back to the growth of spring, to keep the form elegant. Still it is well to bear in mind that the wood grown during summer usually produces the finest flowers, that we may make the best of the materials beneath our hand; for it does sometimes happen that we may prune to the summer's growth with advantage to the tree, and it is often a matter of indifference whether we do so or not.

22   ENVILLE HALL, STAFFORDSHIRE. 1901

The design of this formal rose garden, with its narrow beds, gravel paths,
box edgings and absence of underplanting, allows each plant to be seen and
fully appreciated.

S. Reynolds Hole

A NOTE ON MANURES

And now, to be practical, what do I mean by farmyard manure – when and how should it be used?

By farmyard manure I mean all the manures of the straw yard, solid and fluid, horse, cow, pig, poultry, in conjunction. Let a heap be made near the Rosarium, not suppressing the fumes of a natural fermentation by an external covering, but forming underneath a central drain, having lateral feeders, and at the lower end an external tank, after the fashion of those huge dinner dishes whose channels carry to the 'well', the dark gravies of the baron and the haunch (here that fastidious reader collapses, and is removed in a state of syncope), so that the rich extract, full of carbonate of ammonia, and precious as attar, may not be wasted, but may be used either as a liquid manure in the Rosary, or pumped back again to baste the beef.

How long should it remain in the heap before it is fit for application to the soil? The degree of decomposition to which farmyard dung should arrive before it can be deemed a profitable manure, must depend on the texture of the soil, the nature of the plants, and the time of its application*. In general, clayey soils, more tenacious of moisture, and more benefited by being rendered incohesive and porous, may receive manure less decomposed than more pulverised soils required. Again, the season when manure is applied is also a material circumstance.

I have made many experiments, but I have come back to the plan which I adopted first of all, and I believe it to be the best – namely, to give the Rose trees a liberal stratum of farmyard manure in November, leaving it as a protection as well as a fertiliser through the winter months, and digging it in in March. For some years I manured the plants heavily in the spring, after hoeing or digging, and let the manure remain through the summer. This system succeeds in a very hot, dry season, but makes the ground sodden when the weather is wet, and at all times is an obstruction to the sunlight and the air. I therefore prefer the

Dean Samuel Reynolds Hole VMH (1819–1904) was an energetic and dedicated rosarian and organised the first National Rose Show in 1858. His A Book About Roses, *went into more than twenty editions.*

* see the article on Agriculture in *Encyclopaedia Britannica*.

217

course which I have named, to be supplemented by liquid manure, or some slight surface dressing of guano (that which comes from the dovecot is still almost as precious as it was in the siege of Samaria) or bone-dust, when the buds are swelling into bloom; so that, as the lanky schoolboy is placed upon a regiment of boiled eggs and roast-beef, Allsopp, Guinness, and Bass – so the Rose trees (those nursing mothers of such beautiful babes) may have good 'support' when they want it most. "It is believed," writes Morton, "by observers of nature, that plants do no injury to the soil while they are producing their stems and leaves, and that it is only when the blossom and the seed require nourishment that they begin to exhaust it."

A very effective surface dressing was communicated to me many years ago by Mr. Rivers, who afterwards published it, as follows: – "The most forcing stimulant that can be given to Roses is a compost formed of horse droppings from the roads or stable" (he says nothing about a fire shovel), "and malt or kiln dust, to be obtained from any malt kiln, equal quantities. This, well mixed, should then be spread out in a bed one foot thick, and thoroughly saturated with strong liquid manure, pouring it over the compost gently for, say, two days – so that it is gradually absorbed. The compost is then fit for a summer surface dressing, either for Roses in pots, in bed, or standard Roses. It should be applied, say, in April, and again in May and June, about an inch thick, in a circle round the tree, from 12 to 18 inches in diameter. This compost is not adapted for mixing with the soil that is placed among the roots, but is for a summer surface dressing only; and care must be taken that it is not placed in a heap or ridge after it has been mixed, for then fermentation is so violent that the smell becomes intolerable."

So powerful is this confection, that I have found one application quite sufficient; and this I apply, when the Rosebuds are formed and swelling, towards the end of May, or, in a late season, the beginning of June. I wait for the indications of rain, that the fertilising matter may be at once washed down to the roots; and it never fails to act as quinine to the weakly, and as generous wine to the strong. During the extraordinary drought of the summer in 1868, I watched day after day – nay, week after week – with a patience worthy of that deaf old gentleman who listened for three months to catch the ticking of a sundial, or of him who undertook the tedious task of teaching a weather-cock to crow; and at last, feeling sure of my shower, wheeled barrow after barrow with my own hands, not seeming to have time to call for help, over the little bridge, and spread it over the parched soil. Soon the big rain came dancing to the earth, and when it had passed, and I smoked my evening weed among the Rose trees, I fancied that already the tonic had told. At all events, it is written in the chronicles of the Rose shows how those Roses sped.

Again, Mr. Rivers, whom I have just quoted, and to whom we must still give precedence, remembering what he has done in the Rosarium, writes: "I have found night soil, mixed with the drainings of the dunghill, or even with common ditch or pond water, so as to make a thick liquid, the best possible manure for Roses, poured on the surface of the soil twice in winter, from 1 to 2 gallons to each tree: December and January are the best months: the soil need not be stirred till spring, and then merely loosened 2 or 3 inches deep with the prongs of a fork. For poor soils, and on lawns, previously, removing the turf, this will be found more efficacious. Brewers' grains also form an excellent surface dressing: they should be laid in a heap for two or three weeks to ferment, and one or two large shovelfuls placed round each plant, with some peat-charcoal to deodorise them, as the smell is not agreeable."

I will quote in alphabetical sequence the other distinguished public Rosarians who have expressed their opinions, or proved their skill at all events, in the matter. There is, of course, a very large number of other nurserymen, who grow Roses most extensively and in their fullest perfection – such as Bunyard at Maidstone, Dicksons at Chester, Dickson at Newtownards, Harkness at Bedale, Mack at Catterick, Merryweather at Southwell, Mount at Canterbury, Smith at Worcester, Walters at Exeter, but I may not extend my quotations.

Mr. Benjamin Cant, who, from his rich soil at Colchester, produced a larger number of pre-eminent Roses than any other exhibitor, recommends that in planting Roses, a hole should be made about 18 inches deep, and large enough to contain half a wheelbarrowful of compost; two-thirds of this should be strong turfy loam, and one-third well-decomposed animal manure. These should be thoroughly mixed together.

Mr. Cranston writes in his *Cultural Directions for the Rose* (Derby, 1857), which may be followed by amateurs with a sure confidence: "I have found, after repeated trials for some years, that pig dung is the best of all manures for Roses; next night soil, cow dung, and horse dung. These should stand in a heap from one to three months, but not sufficiently long to become exhausted of their ammonia and salts. Pig dung should be put on the ground during winter or early spring, and forked in at once. In using night soil, mix with burnt earth, sand, charcoal dust, or other dry substance. Apply a small portion of the mixture to each plant or bed during winter, and let it be forked in at once. Soot is a good manure, especially for the Tea-scented and other Roses on their own roots; so are wood-ashes and charcoal. Bone dust or half-inch bones forms an excellent and most lasting manure. Guano and superphosphate of lime are both good manure for Roses, but require to be used cautiously."

Mr. Keynes of Salisbury recommended "a good wheelbarrowful of compost – two-thirds good turfy loam, and one-third well-decomposed animal manure." He adds – and the words of one whose Roses, in a favourable season, could not be surpassed in size or colour, should be remembered practically – "It is difficult to give the Rose too good a soil."

Mr. Lane of Berkhamsted wrote: "The best method of manuring beds is to dig in a good dressing of stable or other similar manure, this being the most safe from injuring vegetation in my soil, and it never does more good to Roses than when it is used as a surface-dressing. When placed, about two inches deep, over the surface in March, the ground seldom suffers from drought; but this is, perhaps, by some considered unsightly."

Mr. George Paul advises that "in planting the ground should be deeply trenched, and well-rotted manure be plentifully added. If the soil is old garden soil, add good loam, rich and yellow; choose a dry day for the operation, and leave the surface loose. Stake all standards, and mulch with litter, to protect the roots from frost."

Mr. William Paul, in his interesting work, *The Rose-Garden* (London, 1848), gives, in the Introduction, the results of his experiments with manure. "In the summer of 1842," he writes, "six beds of Tea-scented Roses were manured with the following substances: (1) bone dust, (2) burnt earth, (3) nitrate of soda, (4) guano; (5) pigeon dung, (6) stable manure, thoroughly decomposed. The soil in which they grew was an alluvial loam. The guano produced the earliest visible effects, causing a vigorous growth, which continued till late in the season; the foliage was large and of the darkest green, but the flowers on this bed were not very abundant. The shoots did not ripen well, and were consequently much injured by frost during the succeeding winter. The bed manured with burnt earth next forced itself into notice; the plants kept up a steadier rate of growth, producing an abundance of clear, well-formed blossoms; the wood ripened well, and sustained little or no injury from the winter's frost. The results attendant on the use of the other manures were not remarkable: they had acted as gentle stimulants, the nitrate of soda and bones least visibly so, although they were applied in the quantities usually recommended by the vendors. . . . I think burnt and charred earth the best manure that can be applied to wet or adhesive soils."

Mr. Prince says: "My plants on the cultivated Seedling Brier do not require so much manuring as other forms of stocks. I do not recommend any manure at time of planting, unless the ground has been greatly impoverished by trees and shrubs or Roses, in which case a portion of the soil should be removed, and a fresh supply given, which should consist of the top-spit from a meadow of heavy loam, well decayed; but it should not be forgotten that after the Roses have been planted for two years, and are well established, they will require a liberal supply of manure. I have found that the worst attack of mildew first made its appearance on young plants in land which had been manured at the time of planting."

Mr. Turner of Slough did not show his cards, but when he came to play them on the green cloth or baize of the exhibition table, no man dealt more fairly, knew the game more thoroughly, held more trumps, or scored the honours more frequently.

Messrs. Wood of Maresfield, at one time the largest growers of the Rose in the world, commend a mixture of well-seasoned animal manure, with the top-spit of an old pasture, deep trenching, thorough draining, and a free use of the pruning knife the first year after planting.

To conclude, I would earnestly assure the novice in Rose growing that there is only one exception (and that in Egypt) to the rule, *Ex nihilo nihil fit*. If he really means to make the Rose his hobby, and to enjoy the ride, he must feed him liberally and regularly with old oats and beans. The Rose cannot be grown in its glory without frequent and rich manure; and again, I recommend that the best farmyard dung be applied towards the end of November, when the ground is dry and dug in in March, and that the surface dressing prescribed by Mr. Rivers, or some other stimulant, be administered at the beginning of June. And if neighbours, who are not true lovers of the Rose, expostulate, and condemn the waste, quote for their edification those true words of Victor Hugo, in *Les Misérables*, "the beautiful is as useful as the useful, perhaps more so."

Nevertheless, I must warn the young Rosarian that he may be too lavish in his application of manures. The enthusiastic tyro has been known to plant his Rose trees in a composition, made up half and half, of raw reeking manure and soil. The results have been disastrous; and when an explanation of the debility outside has been sought within the soil, it has been sadly seen that the little tender rootlets have been sore let and hindered by their rank unsavoury surroundings, and have made but a feeble growth.

Nor must the amateur keep the sunshine and the rain from the soil by covering it continuously with solid manures. One liberal application from the farmyard, laid on late in November or early in December (when the first frost makes a hard road for the wheelbarrow), and dug in about the middle of March, is ample, with the addition of some fertilising liquid, when the buds expand for efflorescence, and some slight thin mulching in times of excessive drought.

The novice must not expect that his Roses will always maintain their integrity even in the kindliest of soils, and with a most anxious and clever cultivation. Sooner or later they will deteriorate, and must be replaced by a younger and stronger growth from the nurseries or the budding ground.

Nay, the time must come, when the soil itself will give manifest intimations that in horticulture as in agriculture it is expedient to change our crops; and he who would maintain his supremacy as a Rosarian must seek "fields fresh and pastures new".

I exhausted three Rose gardens of considerable extent, and should have joyfully continued the process of exhaustion, had I not reached my boundaries, satisfied my ambition as an exhibitor, and become more and more inclined to distribute my admirations among the manifold beauties of the garden, rather than to concentrate all my devotions upon the Rose. Of course, she was to remain for ever my Sovereign Lady, the Queen.

23 CLAREMONT PARK, SURREY. c.1920

Old fashioned climbing roses trained in decorative swags give a delightful
rococo air to the Lily Pond in the school's garden.

Reverend Joseph Pemberton
A GUIDE TO PLANTING

Joseph H. Pemberton (?–1926) was an enthusiastic cultivator of hybrid musk roses. Those of his crosses which survive today, are renowned for their fragrance and vigour. He was appointed President of the National Rose Society in 1911.

Some people have an idea that roses will grow almost anywhere, and so they may if they are hardy sorts; but even the most robust will be all the better if planted in a place that suits them. Now roses are very sensitive to cold, heat, wind, and close confinement. A cold north-easterly wind in early June will, if it gets at them, destroy the promise of April and May, the first crop of flowers coming rough, green centred, or otherwise malformed. Again, a strong wind the day before a show, or the rose garden party, will play such havoc with the blooms that hardly one perfect rose can be found.

Therefore, in selecting a situation for the roses we should, if possible, choose ground that falls slightly towards the south or south-west, since the least inclination of the land in that direction will effect considerable protection from the north or north-east winds, the latter being the worst, because it is usually more laden with moisture. In sloping ground the wind touches the highest part, and passes over level, so that the plants situated under the hill escape the strong blast. As an instance of wind direction, observe the movement of long grass in a meadow possessing even a gentle slope as the wind sweeps across the field, and see how protected is the grass half-way down the slope. And what is true of a field is also true of a garden; a garden with a southern aspect just below the crown of a hill is invariably earlier than another in the same neighbourhood which slopes in the opposite direction. Therefore we should, if possible, select a situation for the roses where the land slopes however slightly towards the south or south-west.

Roses are particularly grateful to the shelter afforded by tall trees. The late spring frosts are intensified by cold north-easterly winds, which frequently prevail at this period; they are especially injurious after the buds are formed, and although we cannot wholly escape them, we can at least mitigate their severity by choosing a spot for the roses where high trees will break the force of these winds. And, if you can, select a position equally protected from the south-westerly gales which the experienced amateur will admit often occur on some days during the blooming season. Roses dislike wind at all times, but a hot dry wind when the flowers are in their beauty is particularly harassing; not only will the blooms be battered – we might obviate that by tying them down – but if not absolutely bruised, the hot air blowing upon them will cause the young flowers after cutting to shrink rather than expand; and no variety feels this more than Alfred K. Williams. Therefore look out for protection from the hot winds of summer.

If yours is an open situation it would be advisable to plant a hedge. A beech hedge is good because the beech retains its leaves in the brown state for some time. Likewise a hedge of *multiflora* roses is recommended, since the species *simplex*, together with some of the hybrids, retain their foliage green until it is pushed off by the new growth in spring, and are therefore almost evergreen. Or a hedge of any other strong-growing rose, Reine Olga de Wurtemburg, Madame Alfred Carrière, or a Penzance Brier, for instance, would similarly serve to break the wind.

But a word of caution. Although tall trees are the best protectors from wind, there is this disadvantage; if near the bed their roots will soon be in it, and then, especially if ash, with its crowd of small fibrous roots, good-bye to the roses. Nor should roses be planted too near to hedgerows. And so here comes the difficulty; roses like an open space admitting plenty of air and sunshine, yet at the same time they must have shelter; if planted too near large trees, laurels, or other shrubs, the rose will be robbed of moisture; if planted in the open it is exposed to wind frosts. With the exception of strong growing species and hybrids of such kinds as *sempervirens*, never plant roses near a shrubbery, or a border of laurel, privet, or indeed near anything of rooty, fibrous habit. They may exist, but they are not really at home even in a herbaceous border; they like to be by themselves.

And as to shade. Well, roses like shade from the afternoon but not from the early morning sun. It is very convenient, when growing for exhibition, to have the long shadows from distant trees come creeping over the bed about half-past four in the afternoon, because as soon as the roses are shaded we can commence cutting for the next day's show. But more of this hereafter.

And now to summarise these remarks. The best situation for a rose garden is land tilted towards the south or south-west, with tall trees in the distance on the north-east; the next best position is a level, open spot, surrounded on all sides but the south with a rose or beech hedge; the worst site is a northern slope with trees and a hedge in close proximity.

Having decided upon the site, the next thing is to choose the roses. This brings us to our second point.

*   *   *

Selecting roses is by no means a simple matter. As a rule the more inexperienced the amateur, the more rash he is in his selection. He has perhaps just made up his mind to grow roses. He goes to a rose show, sees a fine specimen bloom, possibly one that has obtained a silver medal as the best rose in the show; attracted by the colour or size he at once decides to grow it, quite regardless of its habit or constitution. Now, that flower may be what is technically termed 'a catch bloom', that is, a flower of a very uncertain, shy, blooming variety; or one that can only be brought to this perfection when grown on a maiden or yearling plant; or has been cultivated under a shade or in paper; or a variety that yields but one crop of flowers annually and for the remainder of the year the plant is flowerless. Now, of what use is such a rose as that to the man who wants roses for the garden?

But possibly the amateur may be quite aware of the risk attached to selecting his kinds from the serried ranks of wired-up and dressed-out specimens in the exhibition boxes, and he turns his attention to the roses exhibited in bunches, 'garden roses' as they are called. Here again there are many traps to catch the unwary, and will be unless the number of stems to a bunch is limited. Our amateur sees a large and doubtless very beautiful bunch of some decorative variety, but what he fails to notice is the great number of sprays cut to form the bunch. He may likewise, unless he carefully studies a catalogue, overlook the fact that the bunch on which he set his mind is of a rampant growing, summer flowering rose, which would be quite out of place on lawns or beds. Roses suitable for bedding purposes should possess three principal qualifications: they should be hardy, dwarf or moderately so, and free-flowering, giving a constant succession of flowers from early summer until late in autumn. Therefore to all beginners I would say, state your requirements to a friend who is an expert, and leave the selection to him, or else visit the rose grounds of some leading nurseryman, and see them growing.

Order your plants in the height of the rose season. Visit a nursery, an amateur's rose garden, or a rose exhibition, make notes of what you would like to get; compile your list with regard to the capacity of your garden, and despatch the order at once. While the rose fever is at its maximum is the best time to order roses; do not delay until the autumn, or you may have cooled down – at least this is my experience. By sending the order early you will probably obtain better plants, and also be more likely to get what you want; you can always add to your first order later on. It is the usual practice of the trade to execute orders in the order in which they are received – first come first served; thus by ordering early is ensured early autumn delivery.

On the arrival of the plants the bundle should be carefully unpacked, and the roses 'laid in by the heels'. To do this dig a trench in some more or less protected spot, say in the kitchen garden, and lay in the plants side by side, the removed earth from the trench forming a back on which they may slightly lean. If there are more roses than will fill the first trench, or indeed in any case, dig another trench parallel to the first, and turn the earth as it is taken out into the first trench, covering the roots of the roses already laid in. See that the soil covers the roots both back and front, so that they do not lie hollow, tread slightly, and repeat the process as often as there are plants to lay in. Here the roses will remain without injury until required for planting even if planting is deferred for some weeks. Should the bundle arrive during a hard frost take it into the potting-shed and leave it there for a few days just as it is. It would, however, not be advisable to leave the bundle unpacked much longer than a week, for the sooner the plants are in the ground the better. In the process of unpacking see that the roots do not become dry, and if they do, dip both roots and wood in a tub of water before laying them in the trench. Some trade growers invariably dip the roots in clay puddle before despatching them to their destination. This coating of clay effectually prevents the roots from becoming dry, and therefore when this is done dipping in water on arrival is unnecessary. It sometimes happens, when the roses are sent early, before the wood has quite ripened and the leaves fallen, or when the plants have been long in transit, or when carelessly packed, that the bark of the wood is found on arrival to be shrivelled. Where this is the case the plants should be placed in a tub of water deep enough to cover both roots and wood, and left there for a few hours before laying them in the trench. Some authorities recommend that the whole plant should be buried in the soil a few inches deep, and well watered, when they will soon plump up again.

*   *   *

The time of year most favourable for planting depends upon these conditions, viz.: (*a*) the condition of the plant; (*b*) the texture and condition of the soil; and (*c*) the temperature of the ground.

(*a*) *The Condition of the Plant.* – Lifting and replanting checks growth, and therefore transplanting, unless it can be done quickly, should not be carried out when the rose is in full vigour. Sometimes and under certain circumstances we can remove a plant in full bloom from one part of the garden to the other; but it is a risky proceeding, requiring great care and much after-attention. If a rose is transplanted whilst in full growth, the sudden stoppage of sap supply will cause the wood to shrivel, and copious watering will be required before it will again plump up. And it is not only that the sap is checked, but leaves, being the lungs of the plant, if they are left on, the moisture in the plant will speedily evaporate unless the foliage is watered as well as the roots.

A rose to be in good condition for removal should be in an advanced stage of ripening; the signs of ripening being when the leaves at the base have been shed, and the wood and prickles hard. It is not advisable to transplant a rose until the leaves have fallen naturally, or have at least been stripped off by hand. The rose is in the best condition to plant when it is at rest; during the sleeping period, a period which begins in September and ends in March; the greatest depth of its inactivity being from November to the end of January. Although said to be sleeping, the rose is nevertheless alive, and where life is, there must be a certain amount of activity; a rose never stops growing altogether. This being the case, our aim should be so to time the planting that the rose has as long a period as possible in which to establish itself before nature calls upon it to awake, and therefore we should plant it as soon as possible after sleep has ensued. In other words, the rose will be in the best condition to plant during the months of October and November; the beginning of October if the ripening season is an early one.

(*b*) *The Condition and Texture of the Soil.* – This is the next consideration. The rose may be fit, but the soil may not, and successful planting depends greatly on the condition of the soil; as much if not more so than on the condition of the rose. In the process of planting, our chief care should be to pack the earth around and among the roots as closely and as firmly as possible. Firm close planting engenders growth, loose planting hinders it, and, as has already been stated, the smaller the particles of earth, the easier it is for the plant to obtain supplies of food. We, therefore, require the soil to be in such a condition that it may fall closely among the roots and be trodden firmly about the plant, without

228

losing its friableness; but this cannot be done when the soil is wet, especially heavy soil. Treading a clayey, wet soil causes the particles to adhere to one another, becoming a solid lump; and a rose planted when the soil is in this condition will never thrive.

From this it is evident that the land is in the best condition for planting either in the autumn before the sun loses its power to dry it, or in the early spring whilst the ground is fairly moist and the sun's power is increasing; in the depth of winter, the sun has little power, and especially for some time after a frost the soil is adhesive and heavy. We, therefore, arrive at this conclusion: that the soil is in the best texture or condition to receive the plants either in the autumn or spring, and is at its worst during the winter.

(c) *The Temperature of the Soil*. – This is our third point. To the newly planted rose, a warm soil promotes growth and consequent speedy establishment, whereas a cold soil means inactivity; and therefore we ought to plant whilst the ground is warm. Now, it is obvious that the soil will be of a higher temperature in autumn than in winter, and is warmer in autumn than in the corresponding months of spring; that is to say, the temperature of the soil will be higher in October and November than in February and March. And there is also this point to be considered; it is essential that during the winter as much warmth as possible should be preserved in the soil. Now, it sometimes happens that a sudden cold snap is experienced in October, and we certainly get hard frosts in most Novembers. When this is the case, all planting operations should cease for a while. Never be tempted to plant when the crust of the bed is frozen, or when there is snow on the ground, however slight the fall may be; because, be as careful as you may, some of the frozen earth or particles of snow will be certain to get in the hole or trench, and being buried, will remain in its frozen state for some time, chilling the surrounding earth, and thus lowering its temperature. For this reason all digging operations should be suspended in frosty weather, whether the ground is required for immediate or for spring planting.

From these considerations we can see that October and November are the best months for planting, because the rose is then in the best condition. It will also have time to establish itself before spring awakens it; the earth is then more friable, and above all the soil is warmer.

Failing these months roses may be planted during the first fortnight of December provided winter has not set in, but if unable to plant before Christmas, defer it until February when the sun begins once more to exert its influence. Nothing is gained by planting in January, even if the weather is open, for, as has already been said, the temperature of the soil is then very low, and an unestablished plant feels the frost acutely. But frosts or no frosts, roses planted in February or March will give better results than when planted in the depths of winter. Roses may be planted as late as April or even May; but they will need special care lest they suffer from drought, and we must not expect to see good blooms until the autumn.

E. A. Bunyard
OLD ROSES

Edward Ashdown Bunyard (1878–1939) grew up in a family of horticulturists. He was a highly respected rosarian and wrote extensively about roses and about fruit growing.

The great interest now shown in the old Roses is an encouraging sign that flower lovers, in general, refuse to accept any standardizing of their tastes.

There are indeed some Rose enthusiasts who refuse to see any beauty of form save in the long pointed bud of the Hybrid Tea Rose of today, just as the ideal of beauty for their grandparents was the buxom Hybrid Perpetual. Everything in those days tended to the buxom; furniture, feminine figures and flowers: such were the canons of mid-Victorian taste.

Some of us, however, fail to see why there should be but one standard of beauty for the Rose, or for that matter, any other flower. If we admire a Poet's Daffodil, must we despise a Cyclamineus? If the incurved bloom of a Trollius is lovely, why not the same form in the Rose? Those who preserve the old Roses are, besides ministering to their own enjoyment, preserving for gardens in general the forms and colours which gave delight to a past generation and which may equally do so to a future one.

Some happy Rosarians can find beauty in both ancient and modern forms and colours, and in both there are, of course, the good, and others less good.

As I have given a short résumé of the history of the Rose and especially those groups which we know as 'Old Roses' in my recent book *Old Garden Roses* (Country Life, London and New York, 1936), I propose here to deal with them more particularly as garden plants and to add some notes to help in their identification.

One of the first questions we ask of an unknown plant is the height it naturally attains. In Roses it is difficult to answer this very definitely as by pruning we can keep a plant in a dwarf form or by allowing it to grow at large the same plant may attain many feet in height and width. Our 'dwarf' H.T.s are now grown in some gardens unpruned and thus reach some 6 feet or more in height.

When pruning is abandoned growth begins again at the end of last year's wood. If the plant makes 3 feet in the first year, it will probably make 2 or 3 feet on the top of the unpruned shoot next year and so on. By pruning back hard each year, as we do in our dwarf H.T.s, we merely repeat the first year's growth again from the base and we call this plant a dwarf, but it is only an artificial dwarf produced by pruning. A natural dwarf makes a few inches each year – there are but few of these among the old Roses and I have suggested that where the flower and leaf are of normal size but the annual growth very short this is a true dwarf.

Where leaf and flower are much reduced in size from the normal, as 'Spong'[1] in the Cabbage Roses and 'Rouletti'[2] in the China group, I suggest that we call these Miniatures.

Height is therefore determined by the natural growth and the presence or absence of pruning, leaving for the moment the true climbing Roses which make, say, 6 to 10 feet of growth a year, we can group the various families in order of height, thus:

Tallest, 6 to 12 feet.	White Rose. (*R. alba.*)
Medium, 5 to 8 feet.	Damask. (*R. damascena.*)
	Cabbage. (*R. centifolia.*)
Short, 3 to 4 feet.	French Rose. (*R. gallica.*)
Very short, 2 feet.	Miniature of all classes. Some Scots Roses.

ROSA ALBA

These give us the strongest growing of the old garden Roses and were in fact known as 'Tree' Roses in the last century.

Their place in the garden is therefore at the back of the border in woodland glades, or as climbers on walls.

---

[1] *Rosa centifolia* [2] *Rosa chinensis* 'Minima'

Among the hardiest of all Roses, they thrive in the northern climates of our country and, not minding shade, on north or east walls.

Their great vigour enables them to look after themselves in places where the roots of other trees penetrate and the check to their growth is in fact an advantage, tending to more flower and less growth.

If left unpruned the strong branches will become bare and look rather coarse. It is well to cut back to 1 foot or so all branches three years old and over in order to get fresh growth from below and flowers at eye and nose level.

In most soils manure is not required but, like all Roses, an occasional sprinkle of potash and phosphatic manure will be repaid by better health and quantity of flower.

All this group can be trained up pillars and pergolas, but as their flowers are held upright they are better seen on walls or as bushes; they should be looked 'into' rather than 'up at'.

The Italian painters have shown us the way to see them at their best by training them on low trellises bounding the small gardens of those days. All the Renaissance paintings that I have seen show *R. alba* thus used and never the darker and dwarfer *R. gallica* which from its low growth would obviously have been unsuitable.

Lovely as the flowers are, this Rose is always welcome to the eye on account of its fine silvery foliage which firmly resists black spot, mildew and such disfigurements. The scent is distinctive, having an Eau-de-Cologne sharpness, quite different from the Cabbage and Damask scents.

The pure white varieties we have today are as follows: semi-double, double white, and large double white, and the small 'Pompon Parfait'. The first three are of great antiquity and can be found in the Herbals of the sixteenth century and in the works of early Italian painters such as Botticelli and Crivelli.

Of the pink varieties our 'Maiden's Blush' is best known and there is also the large 'Maiden's Blush' which I think I have now recovered.

The semi-double 'Celestial' is certainly one of the most lovely of all pink semi-double Roses and can be distinguished from the others by its cupped leaves and the curious metallic sheen of these when quite young.

THE AYRSHIRE ROSES

It is now a little difficult to draw a line between these and the Evergreen varieties, and there are few in catalogues today. They are very robust and long-lived and as the descendants of a native Rose (*R. arvensis*) they make the best of our climate.

'Dundee Rambler', double white, and 'Bennetts' Seedling' are sometimes seen in gardens and probably a good many more lurk unsuspected.

I should like to find 'Splendens', a pale pink, buds crimson before opening and smelling of Myrrh.

THE BOURBON ROSES

These take their name from the Island of Bourbon (now Reunion) and are most probably a China-Damask cross.

They retain the perpetual flowering of the China Rose and its distinct foliage.

The best two are 'Mme Pierre Oger', a dainty shell-petalled flower of Cabbage style, pale pink but deeper in the sun, showing the China character in this respect, and 'Louise Odier', lilac-pink, of the same form and equally well scented.

Both have the valuable character of not allowing their petals to fall when dying; they quickly close up and so remain, a joy to those to whose care the vases are entrusted.

Two other old varieties, now nearly centenarians, are 'Coupe d'Hébé' and 'Blairi No. 2'.

These are more of the H.P. style, both are rose-pink, very fragrant, and should be allowed to make free bushes when they will attain 6 feet or so.

'Mme Ernst Calvat' must be counted one of the moderns, having been introduced in 1888, but it has an old-fashioned air and indeed is one of the most distinct of all garden Roses. At first glance it is often taken for a Tree Paeony. The large flowers, not very double, have the silky texture of the Paeony and the dark claret foliage helps the illusion.

The general foliage effect of the Bourbons is well seen in the best known variety of today, 'Zéphirine Drouhin', an oldish Rose (1868) rescued from oblivion by the seeing eye of Miss Jekyll. The curious milky-green and the claret tinge on the young growth are, as far as I know, quite distinct marks of the Bourbon Rose.

All of them are admirable for large bushes for pillars but not, I think, for hot walls. Red Spider and the ever-present Leaf Hopper damage the foliage in many seasons. All should be boldly pruned to get strong shoots from below.

THE BOURSAULT ROSES

These are the offspring of the Alpine Rose (*R. pendulina*) and the China Rose (*R. chinensis*) and once famous, but they are now seldom found in gardens.

I have, in the last two years, found one or two varieties, and 'Elegans' is semi-double, purplish-red and showing a white stripe in the petal.

The 'Blush Boursault' is the second variety now available and here the flowers are larger than 'Elegans' and blush-pink, very attractive and free in flowering.

No Roses do better in town gardens and it is to be hoped that Rose hybridizers will again turn their attention to this very distinct group.

The strong shoots are thornless, or nearly so, like the parent 'Alpina' and the leaves very distinct. In winter the shoots might very well be taken for Raspberry canes.

THE CABBAGE ROSES (*R. centifolia*)

The Cabbage Roses are the largest and most fully petalled of all the old Roses and received their not very pleasing name from the shape of the flowers, the incurving petals overlapping as in the Cabbage.

Since their arrival in Northern Europe at the end of the sixteenth century they have won a favoured place in gardeners' hearts, first for the scent and secondly for their noble and massive contours so appropriate to the seventeenth century. We may indeed think of them as the Rubens among Roses.

Of the large number grown in the early nineteenth century we have now but few, but those that remain are fortunately the classics of their race.

The original Cabbage Rose, beloved by the Dutch flower painters, still remains, as do its sub-varieties 'Prolifera', which bears a bud in the centre of its flowers, a Rose in Rose, and the remarkable 'Cabbage-leaved', whose large leaves are crisped and curled in the best Cabbage Lettuce style.

'The Crested Cabbage', often wrongly called 'Crested Moss', is remarkable for the winged edges of its sepals. This was formerly known as the 'Chapeau de Napoléon', a suggestion which is easily recognized before the bud opens.

A group with smaller flowers and growth is worth a place in any garden of Old Roses – 'Duc d'Angoulême', a pale pink anemone-shaped flower, 'Duchess de Montebello' in the same manner, 'Anaïs Ségalas' remarkable in that the lilac rose petals are contributed in the manner of a Zinnia and a very distinct and charming variety.

The White Cabbage Rose known as 'Unique' still stands alone to-day as it did on its introduction in 1775. It is large and pure white, save for a flake or two of red on the outside petals, faintly scented. The large leaves are very striking when young by reason of the brownish-red tints they then possess. Growth moderate.

All this group make fairly large bushes and respond to manure and fairly hard pruning. But, as many an old garden shows, neglect does not discourage them and it is for this reason that they have survived so many generations of less hardy successors in the fleeting fashions of the day.

CHINA ROSES (*R. chinensis*)

This group is easily distinguished by the characters well known in the Tea Rose – pointed leaflets, often a little undulating at their edges; wood usually red, with thorns and no bristles; a dwarfish habit generally and where the flowers are pink or red they get darker as they grow older, unlike the Cabbage Roses which get lighter in colour. There are miniatures in this family of which 'Rouletti', which will be found under the heading of Miniature Roses, is best known to-day.

The oldest is our still-favoured 'Blush China', which can be traced in Chinese pictures a thousand years back. 'Hermosa' is a modern edition dating from 1840. The two are often confused, but the 'Blush China' has a loose open flower and 'Hermosa' has many more petals like a small Cabbage Rose. One of the most beautiful is the dark crimson 'Semperflorens', beautifully illustrated on page 89 of Miss Willmott's *Genus Rosa* (London 1910–14). The cupped flowers, dainty foliage and general look of distinction make this one of the most attractive of all the China Roses and I am glad to have found it, after a long search, at Nymans, the home of so many rare and lovely Roses.

The 'Crimson China' is a larger form of this.

Another remarkable variety is 'Lemesle', also known as 'Vesuvius'. The flowers are the size of the common China, the outer petals dark crimson and when opening the centre petals are blush-pink. As they expand they gradually turn a pale crimson like the outer petals, an interesting example of this habit, possessed only, so far as I know, by the China Rose.

Resembling this in size and colour of flower is the curious 'Serratipetala'. The petals are cut at the edges and fluted with pink and white when grown outdoors. This makes a large spreading bush, quite different in habit from the type of China Rose.

'Chinensis purpurea' is the darkest of all, often reaching plum colour, and is semi-double.

Among the singles is 'Miss Lowe', probably the old single 'Red Chinensis'. This is also figured in Miss Willmott's book.

Finally we must add the remarkable variety known as 'Tipo Ideale' and also as *R. turkestanica* and *R. mutabilis*. Its varying tones of pink, rose, red and buff in its single flowers account for the 'Mutabilis' but the 'Turkestanica' is, I imagine, a geographical error; it is obviously a China Rose.

EVERGREEN ROSES (*R. sempervirens*)

Of the Evergreen Roses the best known is the old 'Félicité et Perpétue' which was named after the two Carthaginian Martyrs, St. Félicitas and St. Perpetua.

This bears clusters of faint blush flowers fading to white and of the most perfect petal arrangement. The smaller central petals lie back in the large ones and produce a true imbrication. As the leaves are almost evergreen there is nothing better for covering a screen or trellis or to run over an arbour if such exists to-day.

'Little Pet' is a dwarf edition of this old favourite and makes a neat cushion of 18 inches, save for an occasional ambitious shoot which wishes to climb and must be removed. Not less beautiful is 'Adélaïde d'Orléans', raised by Monsieur Jacques, gardener to the Duke of Orléans and introduced in 1829. The flowers are the same colour as 'Félicité', but loose and excellent for a pergola as the flowers hang downwards.

Both of the above are admirable for climbing up old trees but for 'Félicité' they must not be too old as the great weight of branches in ten years' time will need substantial support.

THE GALLICA ROSES (*R. gallica*)

Taking this group and excluding for the moment the striped ones, the type is the 'Red Gallica' which is our 'Rosa Mundi' in the striped form.

I have noticed that 'Rosa Mundi', when on its own roots, produces the unstriped flowers on shoots which come direct from the roots, so it is evidently a chimera.

The name 'Red Gallica' is a little inaccurate as it is a bright rose – Tyrian rose to be exact. This was long known as the 'Red Damask' but this is obviously wrong, as its short stature, 3 to 4 feet, its round – not elongated – hip, and the foliage all proclaim it a 'Gallica' pure and nearly simple. The 'Apothecary's Rose' is very double, medium, rose-pink fading paler at the edge of the petals, a neat flat little flower and an equally neat dwarf plant. This name has been disputed and some would have it that the true old 'Apothecary's Rose' is the 'Red Gallica' named above. As the name is now so well established for the double variety it is perhaps best to leave it and remember that all Roses at one time were subject to the apothecary for various healing medicines.

Perhaps the most striking of this group is the well-known 'Tuscany', whose colour might well be matched with the Chianti of that country. The flowers are semi-double. A good semi-double variety is known as 'Gallica Splendens', the flowers are a deep rose with a hint of scarlet and are followed by a profusion of bold red hips. A hardy variety which will hold its own in shade and on the driest of soils.

All of this group and the striped ones as well should be pruned after flowering and so no scruples need be felt in gathering them freely for decoration. They quickly make new wood in July and from this better flowers will come than from unpruned bushes.

However treated the Gallica Roses refuse to give way to neglect, and often a bush growing in a neglected spot will be found to mark the site of a destroyed cottage. Its free seeding quality has made it spread widely on the Continent, even as a weed in cornfields, and thus it has been considered as a native of Europe, but I think this very doubtful, despite the authority of many botanists for a century or two.

The striped Gallicas are best known by the well-known 'Rosa Mundi' and we may presume that this was the parent of them all. As later on they were crossed with the Centifolias or Cabbage Roses we find two groups, those with the flat Gallica flowers and those with more globular ones resembling the typical Cabbage Roses.

Taking the Gallica class first we have 'Tricolor de Flandre', a little more double than 'Rosa Mundi', with broad and narrow purplish-red stripes and of Camellia-like form, a most striking variety. 'Panachée Double' resembles it but is darker, the darkest of this group I have yet found. 'Panachée de Luxembourg' is a deep crimson and though I condemned it in my *Old Garden Roses* I find since then it must be reprieved as it greatly improved as the bush grew older.

'Georges Vibert' is a Carnation-like flower, much smaller than the above, pale pink, with darker but not broad stripes. This makes a neat dwarf bush of true Gallica proportions.

'Belle des Jardins' is a purplish-crimson, only faintly striped, but it must come into this group and will please those who like this colour.

'Oeillet Flamand' as its name suggests is another Carnation-like flower, lilac-rose striped with lighter colour. This name I advance with some hesitation as in olden days three Roses bore it, a fact by no means unique among the old Roses, and there is obviously a great difficulty in verifying such names, especially when no good descriptions or pictures are to be found.

Turning to the Striped Roses of Cabbage forms the old 'Village Maid' is typical. The large pale pink flowers are lightly striped with rose. This is usually the first of its group to flower and continues for a long time.

'Perle des Panachées' has almost the shape of an H.P.; the stripes are broad but not numerous, rose-pink or pale, almost creamy-white, a very effective combination. 'Commandant Beaurepaire' is more cupped in form, brilliant carmine with darker stripes and the reverse of petals pink with darker stripes, the only striped Rose I know which shows this character.

'Panachée Double' is a dark lilac-purple with white stripings, the most distinct of all by its very small amount of striping. 'Dometille Beccard' is very near to 'Village Maid' if we have it correctly named, but so far I have to keep a query after this name.

All these striped Roses benefit by good cultivation and vigorous pruning; in fact the same generous treatment we give the modern Rose, if we are to have them at their best.

MINIATURE ROSES

The Miniature Gallica known as the 'Burgundy Rose' is notable for its small dark flowers and its upright compact habit. This is the *R. parvifolia* of many botanical authorities. No Rose pays better for a severe pruning after flowering. It is always willing to break from below and then the plant is kept dwarf and free from the leggy appearance an unpruned bush will develop.

The Miniature China Roses have had a recent renaissance due to the interest of rock gardeners, and some of them are of quite ancient ancestry.

Whether 'Rouletti' is one of the old Lawranceana varieties or not I cannot pronounce – there were many varieties a century ago.

'Indica Pumila' and 'Pompon de Paris' are much alike, having small rose flowers produced throughout the summer. The latter makes a round neat bush but occasionally sends up a strong shoot which over-balances the tree. Such growths must be removed if a dwarf bush is to be preserved.

There are two Miniatures we should like to find again, a Damask 'Bifera Pumila', illustrated by Redouté – the dwarf 'Pompon de Bordeaux', a low-growing Cabbage Rose which evidently became a weed by its suckering habits.

Possibly both may yet turn up in some old garden where such things are cherished.

THE NOISETTE ROSES

These result from a cross of the Musk (*R. moschata*) and China Roses (*R. chinensis*), and this valuable group has very distinct characters.

I have never seen the Musk Rose or its descendants showing any trace of mildew or black spot, and as nearly all of this group are autumn- as well as summer-flowering varieties this quality is of great value.

The first to open is 'Boule de Neige', very white and Camellia-like in shape and also in the very solid substance of its petals; tea-scented. The foliage is also stout and hard.

Closely following comes the summer-flowering 'Mme Plantier', for some time known provisionally as 'Miss Rhodes'. Here the flowers are pure white and very freely produced. Both of the above can be allowed to grow and ramp as free bushes and in this way show themselves at their best. If pruned as the H.T. for dwarfs they will submit gracefully and fill a place well in a back row.

'Mme Alfred Carrière' is usually used on a wall and will do well even facing north or east, but it can also be allowed to grow into a free bush. The very white flowers have at first a blush tinge but finally turn paler.

'Aimée Vibert' is an old favourite, the double white flowers being produced in clusters right up to the frost. Admirable for a wall, pillar, or free bush where space allows. All of this group flower throughout the summer and into late autumn except 'Mme Plantier'.

No Roses are more tolerant of neglect and hard living than the Musks and they are often the last survivors of a neglected garden. Their virtues are shared, it may be stated here, by the modern Musk hybrids of the late Mr. Pemberton which have added new colours to this group.

QUEEN OF DENMARK GROUP

This family was known of old as 'Belgic Roses' and as so few, I fear, exist to-day, we must group them under the name of their best known representative. Their origin is a matter of guess-work, but I suggest that Alba × Damask may be likely.

I know no old Roses which have more distinction in the garden, aristocrats in every line.

'Queen of Denmark' is often known by its German name 'KönIgen von Denmark' and has been grown in England since 1840.

The flowers are rose-pink, very double with no anthers, leaves rather dark and flat. It makes a bush of medium height about 4 to 5 feet.

Additions to this short list would be very welcome and there were many in cultivation a century ago which it would be most interesting to reintroduce into our gardens.

H. C. Andrews' *Roses* (London, 1805) figures a 'Blush Hip' and one or two others which evidently belong to this group.

SCOTS ROSES (*R. spinosissima*)

The great day for the Scots Roses was a century or so ago when a hundred or more varieties were raised. Some few of these have come down to us to-day, but lacking good descriptions it is very difficult to be sure as to their names.

This Rose has a wide extension across Northern Europe and Asia and is

see plate 25

thus very variable. We have the tall-growing 'Altaica' down to the very dwarf garden forms, like 'Bicolor Nana' which does not exceed 2 feet in height.

Colours run from pure white to cream and yellow and from pale rose-pink to a deep purplish-red and to the red of 'William III'.

Many can only be referred to by colour names, lacking their original ones. Of the pure rose-reds 'William III' is best known. This makes a compact upright bush rather like the 'Burgundy Rose'. The flower is small, semi-double, paler on the outside of the petals.

Of the mottled crimsons – perhaps claret is a better term –' Bicolor Nana' is the dwarfest, reaching only 2 feet. 'Lady Hamilton', 'Berwick' and 'Staffa' are very much alike. 'Lismore' is to be preferred being more rose-pink. These all make rounded bushes from 3 to 4 feet.

Among the rose-pinks I think *Andrewsii* is the most beautiful of all, a large semi-double, cupped, pale rose-pink lighter in centre. Miss Willmott's illustration in the *Genus Rosa* (p. 263) shows this lovely Rose to perfection. Another in this section is more upright in growth and is known as 'Double Blush', this is a cupped flower of medium size.

Whites or more properly pale creams are found in two forms to-day, one a dwarf round bush not more than 2 feet in height and another which makes a tall spreading bush of 6 feet in favourable positions. Both have small cabbage-like flowers.

Of the double yellows I have only found the well-known 'small double yellow' in colour very near to the hybrid *Harrisonii*, but there were several large double yellows known a century ago which may perhaps yet turn up in some old garden.

Of the singles I know only the pretty red form grown at Nymans where it makes an admirable small hedge, a single yellow, and of course the dwarf wild form well known to all who golf in Scotland.

Into this group we must place the well-known 'Stanwell Perpetual', probably a hybrid between a Scots and a Damask, which alone has the quality of flowering the whole summer and autumn and often in the south till Christmas. It has the Damask scent and the habit of *spinosissima*, making a bush of 6 feet or so. For a Rose hedge nothing can be more fitting; pruning does it good, producing stronger growth and therefore larger flowers. It is, in my estimation, worthy of a sheltered place in every garden as I know of no other flowering shrub which will produce scented flowers from May till Christmas, and were I limited to one Rose this would be my unhesitating choice.

SWEET BRIERS (*R. rubiginosa*)

The modern hybrids of this much-loved Rose which Lord Penzance raised and introduced in the nineties of the last century are well known to modern gardeners. These are all singles.

Perhaps the most beautiful of all this group are 'Janet's Pride' and 'Hebe's Lip', both remarkable for the fact that the flowers are edged with rose-pink. 'Janet's Pride' is semi-double, about 2½ inches across, creamy-white edged rose-pink.

'Hebe's Lip' is larger, of the same colour and probably a Damask-Sweet Brier hybrid. The foliage is darker and the flower stalk smooth; in 'Hebe's Lip' it is glandular. This forms an easy method of distinguishing the two varieties.

There were many double forms known a century ago, and recently I have found two of these, both pink.

No Rose is better able to look after itself than the Sweet Brier, and pruning should be limited to an occasional branch-thinning to get fresh growth from below and thus prevent the leggy appearance often seen in unpruned plants.

SEMI-DOUBLES

Of the semi-double forms of the species, some of them favourites in old gardens, one of the best known is the double rose-pink form of the Cinnamon Rose (*R. cinnamomea*), a native of Northern Europe and Asia. This was known to Gerard in 1597. Most of the herbalists of the sixteenth century include it as *Rosa majalis* – the 'Rose of May'. The flowers are 2 inches across, with about thirty-five to forty-five small petals, curved and twisted.

The bush grows about 5 feet in height. It can be distinguished at once from others by its thorns, which are in opposite pairs at the base of each leaf and no more.

The next, which is sometimes confused with it, is the double form of the Virginian Rose (*R. virginiana*, formerly *R. lucida*) and known as 'St. Mark's Rose' and 'Rose d'Amour'. It is only semi-double and the shining leaves serve to distinguish it at once from the Cinnamon Rose.

Very pretty is the double form of the Alpine Rose (*R. rubrifolia*), a cupped flower like a small China Rose and of a purplish-pink. This can be distinguished from those named above by the claret-coloured leaves.

24   THE HILL, HAMPSTEAD. C.1910

Plants and architecture blend to maximum effect in this garden designed by
Thomas Mawson. The noisette rose and jasmine soften and scent the pergola.

243

Graham Stuart Thomas
ROSE SPECIES IN NATURE
AND IN THE GARDEN

*Graham Stuart Thomas VMH (1909–)
trained at the University Botanic Garden, Cambridge. He began to collect old roses after World War Two, and his knowledge of the subject remains unsurpassed. He is Gardens Consultant to The National Trust.*

Wild roses might be described as prickly deciduous shrubs, with pinnate leaves and usually fragrant flowers borne singly or in clusters, from yellow and white through pink to dark red, normally with five petals; the achenes, or seeds, are contained in a fleshy, usually reddish hep. But how little can be conjured up from those bare phrases; how little they depict the wonderful and varied beauty to be found within the genus!

According to conservative botanists about a hundred and forty species occur in the Northern Hemisphere, from as far north as Alaska and Siberia to Abyssinia, and Mexico, but the greatest number come from China and neighbouring countries, and with very few exceptions all are hardy in the southern half of the British Isles. If we take our native Dog Brier, *Rosa canina*, as a yardstick we find about fifty species which are deserving of cultivation in our gardens. The Dog Brier is not usually grown as a garden plant; the reason being, I suppose, that it is too common in our hedgerows and too thorny to be manageable. Nobody will deny its beauty of flower, delicate fragrance, and colourful heps, but even so I would venture to say that other species roses can make a greater appeal to us, either through their flowers or their heps, or both, for inclusion in our gardens. Many are just as thorny and unmanageable as *R. canina*, but their display makes them more valuable.

Some may ask why we trouble to grow wild species of rose when we have so many gay garden hybrids; others may exclaim that the modern bedding roses are so overweening and vulgar that it is a relief to turn to nature's unadulterated beauty. In some districts and on some soils species will grow where Hybrid Teas will not; in some gardens anything but species would be out of place. Fortunately there is such a wide difference between the extremes of taste in gardening that there is enough demand even for the more obscure roses to warrant nurserymen growing them, although it is probably equally true that for every species that is sold, a hundred or more modern bedding roses find sales.

Some of us are brought up on Gilbert and Sullivan and develop later in life a taste for Bach. Whether the obvious is thrust on us or not there comes a time in most people's lives when the discerning mind needs more than the obvious for its refreshment, and I know many gardeners who have graduated from dahlias and nasturtiums to species of flowering shrubs and lilies. But I should not like it to be thought that I have no use for the obvious, nor that I want all gardeners to grow species roses. When we are confronted by such variety as we find in the genus *Rosa*, only then can we say that there is a rose for every taste and every garden; and there is abundant latitude for all tastes.

As we study and seek to appreciate all kinds of roses so does our appreciation become deeper, finding more and more delight in colour, form, shape, scent, and all other characters that are spread before us, and gradually roses fall into fairly clearly marked groups in our minds – groups which are not botanical, nor of colour, nor of size, but which bring together certain styles of roses. These styles become associated with styles of gardening and the gardens with styles of houses, and of course with types of people. Then there are the different areas of each type of garden to be considered. Thus, putting forth a few generalizations – however dangerous they may be – a small modern house in a new estate may suit Floribundas very well; but if the garden is large, the farther away from the house one goes the less prim one's ideas can become, and at the end of the plot wild species might not come amiss. Species can easily predominate in a country garden of large size, but I feel they are not happily placed near the house; that is where the Hybrid Teas can go, or China Roses; and to link one group with another there are the roses of sophisticated colouring, modern in tone, but gay and perpetual-flowering, such as the Hybrid Musks, which can link the moderns with the species. And of course there is the period house around which only the Old Roses look well, with species appearing more and more frequently as one recedes farther into the depths of the shrub borders. I hope this does not sound fanciful. In my opinion, in this country today we are far too fond of collecting plants and not nearly careful enough over their placing. Our gardens are frequently like a junk shop where a bit of Old Chelsea lies cheek by jowl with a Japanese fan, an elephant's tusk, a piece of modern pottery, or a Roman coin. We are far too prone to go round the garden looking for a site for a new acquisition than to sit quietly and think out the best plant to give effect in a certain place. In the first instance the

245

gardener is a *collector* and in the second he is a *selector*, and may well be an artist. Occasionally these two qualities are found in an individual.

Putting it simply, I like a slight sense of orderliness and prefer my Hybrid Teas, my Floribundas, or my Old Roses fairly near the house; they are man-made and assort well with seats and paths, vegetable plots, formal lawns, and flower beds. At the other end of the scale are the species roses, breathing of fresh air and freedom and the wild countryside; appealing but not perhaps showy; of a beauty which needs other natural things around it in herbaceous or woody plants. Between the two extremes we are lucky in having today an ever-growing new category of roses, those which have perhaps modern colours but are big shrubs.

Having indicated the place in the garden generally that the wild species roses might occupy, let us now examine these roses and see what they have to offer us for our garden furnishing. No sweeping statements can be made. There is as much variety among them as is found in the majority of garden genera – in fact *more*. For they vary from little bushes of a couple of feet to climbers achieving a height of over 50 feet. They may grow into stalwart shrubs of 12 feet or may lie prone on the ground, exceeding that figure in length. They may make shrubs with a single woody stump giving off branches, or may colonize the ground with a thicket of ever-increasing suckering stems, and roots that travel as fast as couch grass. Some will do best climbing up into bushes and trees, others seem more at home sprawling downwards. Some are impossibly prickly; a very few are devoid of all thorns. Their lovely colours we have already sounded, and theirs is also the beauty of fruit; the heps may be tiny and round or long, bottle-shaped, and bristly. Given reasonably well-drained soil and freedom from dense overhead shade, there is not a position in any garden where a species rose would not thrive. Certainly they like full sunshine, but they will be beautiful in light shade, often taking on in such conditions a grace and delicacy not otherwise shewn.

I have felt it best to group the species botanically, following Mr. B. O. Mulligan's key to the species in the Royal Horticultural Society's *Dictionary of Gardening*, incorporating recent changes in nomenclature from the eighth edition of Bean's *Trees and Shrubs Hardy in the British Isles* (1980). Every now and again one receives a jolt and finds that two species which one had always considered were alike belong in fact to widely separated botanical groups! However, this once again demonstrates that gardeners and botanists do not think alike; it also demonstrates that the botanists' presupposed idea that all wild species should fall conveniently into botanical compartments is a hope without foundation. After all, why should they? They have been evolved through hundreds of thousands of years, and were successfully established denizens on this planet before mankind had invented anything, let alone a botanical 'key' to the species. Various groups of species, shall we call them, had established themselves over the earth; as an example we may cite the Musk Roses which extend from Madeira through the Himalayas to Japan, and, when introduced by seed from their native habitats, usually breed true to type. Geographical segregation is one of the factors which break up such an array of related plants into local species. When these 'species', separated in nature by a varying terrain, are brought into cultivation and propagated by seeds over a generation or two, they may lose their identity; they may become one, or become totally different roses by hybridization with an unrelated species or garden hybrid.

This is what makes the study of species so difficult. Few of us can afford the time to refer to a pressed specimen in the British Museum, for instance, collected by a plant hunter in western China, and have to be content with knowing the plant as grown in cultivation. Fortunately variation of this kind can seldom be blamed upon the nurseryman. His long-practised method of reproduction has been by budding; he may be maligned when – on a wayward Dog Rose seedling that prefers a suckering life, or when his budding has been effected too high upon the 'neck' of the stock and thus allows the latter to start life on its own – a rose comes up which is nothing like the plant that was sold; but he can at least claim that all his propagation has been to maintain the *status quo*. Much confusion has been caused in many genera of plants by the distribution of open-pollinated seeds of plants that inter-hybridize freely. One can sympathize with the keen amateur gardener who, having received seeds of some species from a noted botanical source, finds out after years of proud distribution of resulting plants to his friends that he had given away hosts of hybrid individuals none of which is the true species which he tried to acquire. Roses interbreed so freely that seed-raising is not recommended; yet, let us remember the numerous seedlings that have been raised deliberately or under nature's care; I need only cite *R*. 'Highdownensis' as an example.

To return, as I have already devoted some trouble to the grouping of the species botanically, I think this is the place to examine them horticulturally, so that when the artist goes into a brown study to find the right growth for his given spot he may perhaps be helped by the following notes, always remembering, however, that two seekers for quality in plants seldom see eye to eye. The beauty of plants is so infinite in its variety when nature has alone been the artist that we each discern different beauty on contemplation.

It may be as well to start our review with a few completely prostrate roses, among which none is so flat and flowing as *R. wichuraiana*, and it has an added advantage among species: it is late-flowering. In the south of England the month of August usually arrives before the first flowers open. The dappling of creamy-white small flowers over the close carpet of tiny, glossy leaves is a sight well worth waiting for, to say nothing of the fragrance. This is a rose which thrives well in sandy soil; it grows well at Wisley and at Talbot Manor and is a dense carpeter for any sunny slope or flat ground. Slightly higher off the ground is a hybrid between it and *R. rugosa*, 'Max Graf', which is a splendid colonizer, rooting as it goes. The next most important low ground-coverer is the vigorous and prickly *R.* 'Paulii'; this will cover 12 feet square in a few years, and not exceed 2½ feet in height. Various of the true Wichuraiana Ramblers such as 'Albéric Barbier' and 'François Juranville' are also excellent when allowed to grow flat. The former is particularly effective near the Japanese temple at Nymans. But lovely as they are when grown in this way, they are not sufficiently dense to smother weeds, and it is not an easy or pleasant job hand-weeding among their prickly trails. So long as a rose can make a dense mass to exclude weeds I class it as a ground-cover plant; less dense roses are best used as ramblers and trained on supports.

There are several more rather higher growing sprawling roses which make a dense covering; among the best are *R. macrantha* and its form 'Daisy Hill', 'Raubritter', and *R.* × *polliniana*. They all make wonderful hummocks of blossom, the first two being considerably stronger than the last two. One of the loveliest annual sights that I know is the flowering of a huge planting of 'Daisy Hill' at the back of a flower border. Practically no pruning is required. In the foreground of shrub borders, and on the fringe of woodland or grassy slopes and to cover low walls, these sprawling roses are invaluable. Many of them root as they go, and thus when suited will cover large areas of ground.

In some gardens one sees an area given to heathers, which finish abruptly and give way to shrubs or other plants. As heathers are essentially plants of the wild, their surroundings should be made as harmonious as possible, and this is best done by planting dwarf rhododendrons, of which there are many that enjoy full sunshine, prostrate junipers, and dwarf brooms. Where the heathers are winter-flowering varieties or hybrids of *Erica carnea*, the ground may be limy and the rhododendrons must be excluded, but dwarf shrubby potentillas and some of the dwarf roses then come into their own, although they will of course do equally well, perhaps better, where there is no lime. The two really dwarf roses that are ideal for the heather garden and the outskirts of the rock garden are *R. nitida* and *R. pendulina* 'Pyrenaica'. They grow to only about 18 inches in height and are free colonizers, with single pink flowers and red heps, and with autumn colour from the first named. Slightly taller and of similar uses are three little species, the first two with aromatic foliage: *R. glutinosa, R. serafinii,* and *R. nanothamnus.*

Rather taller and suitable for use where the heathers merge into shrubs proper, some of the bigger colonizing roses, so thrifty on sandy soils, may be used; these are notably *R. pimpinellifolia* (*R. spinosissima*) in its many forms and colours, *R. virginiana, R. × reversa, R. foliolosa,* and *R. rugosa.* One or other of them would be flowering from the end of May till the end of September. I must repeat here a warning I have given under *R. pimpinellifolia* (*R. spinosissima*): that if you plant these roses you must be prepared for the nuisance of running roots. *R. rugosa* is considerably bigger than the others, but both thrive on light soils which are not usually given to roses, and even when the soil is really sandy – dunes or heathland – all these species will thrive amazingly. And in their likes as well as in their size and habit they are very suitable for the heather garden area. Many other species increase steadily at the root.

Many rose species will withstand the salt of the sea, but none makes so excellent a windbreak even on the dunes as *R. rugosa.* This hardy species in its typical forms is one of the best hedging roses we have. Its naturally bushy habit can be enhanced by clipping it every spring, and the clipping will result in a longer display of flower, for the best flowers are produced on the strong young shoots of the current year. Others which are dense and bushy and make good windbreaks are *R.* 'Coryana', *R. × micrugosa,* and 'Frühlingsanfang'. *R. virginiana* is lower and also excellent. Equally bushy is 'Felicia', a Hybrid Musk, and the great 'Nevada' is as good and dense as any. To create a really dense screen the first three and 'Nevada' should be planted at 4 feet apart, and the others at 3 feet, and they will all attain 5 to 7 feet in height. If greater sturdy height is needed from roses, I should interplant them at every 8 feet with one of the much taller types such as *R.* 'Highdownensis'. The riot of colour from such a mixture – and thorny tangle! – would be superb.

While on the subject of hedges I may perhaps call attention to some of the upright Gallica roses – 'Officinalis' and 'Rosa Mundi', 'Charles de Mills' and

'Tuscany Superb' – all will stand annual February clipping and will reach to about 3–4 feet. 'Great Maiden's Blush' comes to mind for an informal hedge and many of the Hybrid Musks; in fact any bushy rose is admirable for hedging. But let us return to the species.

It is not generally realized what a big part roses can play in the colour schemes of the garden from the foliage point of view. *RR. alba, murieliae, fedtschenkoana, soulieana*, and *beggeriana* have grey-green leaves and white flowers. When they are in flower they give a nearly all-white effect. By grouping them with silvery foliage of other plants, santolinas, artemisias, *Elaeagnus argentea*, and the Cardoon, interspersed with white lilies, galtonias, and perhaps white phloxes and the rose 'Gruss an Aachen', a spread of cool colours can be achieved with very little trouble. To come upon such a planting round a bend in a path after a rich Byzantine mixture would startle the most phlegmatic mortal. The two colour schemes could be linked together by another rose, *R. glauca* (*R. rubrifolia*), whose leaves are greyish-green, overlaid with coppery-mauve. This is an invaluable species in the garden, being quite dusky and purplish in full sun, but pale and greyish in the shade. Other species have leaves which are variations in greens, though with considerable variety in shape, size, and texture, from the tiny foliage of *R. elegantula* (*R. farreri*) and *R. pimpinellifolia* (*R. spinosissima*) to great limp leaves of *R. centifolia* 'Bullata' and *R. brunonii*. But they all conform to a fairly regular pattern except *R. sinowilsonii*, which grows well on a wall at Kew and in the open at Wakehurst. It has wonderful lustrous, dark green leaves which are shining red-brown beneath, and if I had a sunny wall available, it would have an honoured place. There is one variegated-leaved rose, *R. wichuraiana* 'Variegata', not very vigorous but producing dainty sprays of tiny leaves of shrimp pink turning to creamy white, with a few green flecks which become more prominent as the leaves age.

The genus is not noted for its autumn foliage colour but there are a few species and varieties which make a decided contribution. Best known perhaps is the clear yellow of *R. rugosa*. The American species *RR. virginiana, foliolosa*, and *nitida* can be brilliant in their red and orange, especially the first named. For more subtle and long-lasting tones 'Morlettii' should be planted; its coppery-pinks and soft orange will sometimes last in mild autumns until December.

Having combed out the dwarfs, the trailers, the dense low-growers, and foliage roses, we now have left all the usual big bushes from 6 to 10 feet high and wide. The group headed by *R. moyesii* – *R. moyesii* 'Fargesii' and the forms 'Geranium', 'Sealing Wax', and others; *R. setipoda, R. davidii, R. sweginzowii,* and *R. macrophylla* – are all noted for their rather gaunt growth and magnificent flagon-shaped heps, which are at their best from August to October. Rather more bushy are three hybrids, *R.* 'Highdownensis', *R.* 'Hillieri', and *R.* 'Autumn Fire'. All of these must be expected to exceed 10 feet in height and it is useless trying to keep them bushy by pruning. The more they are pruned the stronger they grow, and the less flower will be produced. It is best to encourage them to grow upright, and to make a wide ferny canopy over one's head, through which will appear the glowing flowers. The weight of the fruits will cause the branches to arch gracefully and at that time nothing can surpass them for beauty in the garden. Small clematis species like *C. macropetala* and *C. alpina* can be planted to grace their gaunt stems, and to add colour and interest in the spring.

This great group does not exhaust the fruiting roses. One of the most glittering and brilliant is *R. webbiana*, a very pretty, bushy, wiry shrub. And *R.* 'Andersonii', *R. eglanteria (R. rubiginosa), R. glauca (R. rubrifolia), R. × alba* 'Semi-plena', and some of the Hybrid Sweet Briers also are very good, but this group has the usual oval heps, not the striking flagon-shaped kind of *R. moyesii.* The main difference in the shape is that while both groups have oval heps, those of *R. moyesii* and its relatives have a persistent calyx which adds the flange, as it were, to the flagon. *R. rugosa* also has a persistent calyx, but its heps are rounded like tomatoes; *R. soulieana* has small orange heps. And apart from the species several other roses are noted for their autumn fruits. 'Wilhelm' and 'Will Scarlet,' two Hybrid Musks, hold their colour through the winter; 'St. Nicholas', a Damask, and 'Cupid', 'Düsterlohe', 'Scarlet Fire', and many others come to mind.

From their size alone the big species would not be suitably placed in conventional beds. The fringe of woodland is an excellent place for them, or the back of wide shrub borders. They assort well with other shrubs and bring to a collection good late colour, just at a time when shrubs are looking most dull. I remember seeing a particularly happy grouping of *R.* 'Highdownensis' used behind *Senecio* 'Sunshine', the arching sprays of red heps weeping over the grey-leaved hummocks of *Senecio*; I have used *R. sweginzowii* behind the silvery grey of *Atriplex halimus*; the dark red of 'Europeana' Floribunda coupled with *Clematis* 'Royal Velour' is wonderful when lightened by the orange-red sprays of heps of *R. moyesii* 'Geranium'. Their period of beauty is so much longer when in fruit than when in flower that it comes to me more naturally to arrange schemes for that period. In May and June one welcomes every flower that comes to fill that glorious time, and all flowers contribute to the gaiety of the garden. But a display of certain colour in August and September is worth catering for: the weeks in the garden stand still, the flowers of the period are lasting, and all is poised in a quiet maturing way for the final autumn pageant. Even in July and August certain late-flowering species with only the one normal flowering period are at their best, notably *RR. multibracteata, foliolosa, virginiana, davidii, setigera,* and the prostrate *R. wichuraiana* mentioned earlier.

25   HIGHDOWN, SUSSEX. 1937

The white-flowered Scotch rose, *Rosa pimpinellifolia altaica,* grows well on chalk soil, making an ideal hedge about three feet high.

F. C. Stern

GROWING ROSES ON CHALK

Roses are most beautiful garden plants and are valuable as they begin to flower in April, and some go on flowering all the summer until the frost in autumn. There is hardly any other genus of plants that has such a long period of flowering, and they are all so attractive that naturally we were anxious to find out which would do well on chalk. We began planting different sorts – hybrid teas, the old-fashioned roses, the species and others, and found that many of them, especially the Chinese species, had no dislike of lime. The roses were mulched fairly heavily in March with the old mushroom soil thrown out by the nurserymen. Those with *R. foetida* 'blood' in them do least well; the variety *persiana*, the Persian rose, with double yellow flowers just exists but has never made a good plant. Many of the hybrid teas require a better soil, although some of the stronger-growing ones, such as 'Etoile de Hollande', 'Peace', and some others grow well.

The first rose to come out at the end of April is the double yellow Banksian rose *R. banksiae lutea*; there is nothing more delightful on a fine spring morning than to pick the little bunches of double yellow flowers from outside one's bedroom window. It is a strong climber, and here on a south wall it has gone up to the top of the house. The single white form also does well in a warm situation on the south side of some beech trees, going up high into the trees. The single yellow form is not so strong and is temperamental, flowering well some years but not in others; yet it is the only one of these roses to go to seed here in one of its good years. The last two roses were raised from seed from 'La Mortola' garden in north Italy. The next to flower, also a climber, 'Ramona', a *laevigata* hybrid, is delightful with beautiful large single red flowers. This rose takes a little time to settle down, but when it gets going it is a strong grower, now high over the stable roof. Some of the *gigantea* hybrids also do well. 'La Folette', that charming pink-flowered hybrid, so beautiful in the south of France, is not too hardy here and has never shown itself to the best advantage, but on the other hand another *gigantea* hybrid, 'Sénateur Amic', is quite hardy and the double

Frederick Stern VMH (1884–1967) established a remarkable chalk garden at Highdown, Sussex. He wrote for several botanical and horticultural journals and is famous for his Study of the Genus Paeonia *and for* Snowdrops and Snowflakes.

deep red flowers are very decorative on a wall or growing through some tall evergreen shrub like *Feijoa sellowiana*.

R. primula, one of the earliest bush roses, coming out at the end of April, becomes a mass of open single yellow flowers. One of the attractions of this plant is the scent of incense from the small fern-like leaves; it is especially strong when one stands rather away from the bush on the windward side, and on a hot summer evening it scents all the garden around. This rose came from the Arnold Arboretum near Boston, USA, as a quite small plant which we brought back in a sponge bag in 1929, and is now about 10 feet high and about the same in diameter. It was discovered near Samarkand by F. N. Meyer in 1911. Another fine bush rose flowering in April is 'Earldomensis', the first of the 'hugonis' hybrids to come out; it has open yellow flowers. The hybrids, with *R. hugonis* as one of the parents, open their flowers more satisfactorily than the parent plant. *R. hugonis*, bought at Veitch's sale in 1912, has grown into a large bush, flowering in May, but the yellow flowers never seem to become fully open. Another good *hugonis* hybrid, 'Cantabrigiensis', makes a tall shrub with light yellow flowers in early June. One of the best of all the single yellows, *R. xanthina* var. *spontanea*, usually known as 'Canary Bird', has arching stems with large deep yellow flowers opening wide and very graceful in May.

Several forms of *R. omeiensis*[1], sent back by collectors from China, are attractive with their fern-like leaves and early flowers of white or yellow, and their amusing and decorative little bottle-shaped fruits. One variety raised from Forrest's collectors' seed comes out very early with rather insignificant flowers and is the earliest of any rose in this garden to form its scarlet bottle-shaped fruit, ripe about 1 July; in 1936 it received an Award of Merit in fruit and was named *R. omeiensis* var. *praecox*.

Towards the end of May *R. ochroleuca* has yellow single flowers on a large bush, but it is not very satisfactory as the flowers go over too quickly. At the same time the two fine hybrids of Messrs. Kordes, *R.* 'Frühlingsgold', with a mass of large fragrant yellow flowers, and *R.* 'Frühlingsmorgen', with cream flowers edged with pink, are out, both wonderful plants making big bushes. These two and 'Nevada', also a large bush, are the best of the modern shrub roses grown here. The large cream-coloured flowers of 'Nevada' cover the entire plant, so that not a green leaf can be seen, a grand sight and it often has a

---

[1] *Rosa sericea*

second flowering in July. It is said to be a cross with *R. moyesii*, which seems hardly credible.

'Zéphirine Drouhin', with red flowers, and its pink sport, 'Kathleen Harrop', are early semi-climbers. They are both charming plants, but 'Kathleen Harrop' makes the finer bush; the large delicate pink flowers are beautiful and it often has a second flowering in July.

The late E. A. Bunyard encouraged us to grow the 'old-fashioned' roses of which he was so fond. Some people criticise them because they only flower once a year; they should be used as flowering shrubs, for most of these only flower once a year. The lower-growing ones are useful to plant in the herbaceous border. The 'Cabbage' rose, *R. centifolia*, said to have been grown by the Greeks and Romans over 2,000 years ago, is one of the earliest with red flowers and the sweetest scent, only equalled by 'Celestial', whose charming light pink flowers have also a divine scent. In the garden of an old almshouse dating back to the time of Queen Elizabeth I, there are two rose bushes with deep red flowers sweetly scented, both unknown to the experts that have been consulted. They are probably old hybrids; we have named them 'Miss Murray's rose' and 'Lucas' rose', as these names are connected with this old almshouse. It is in such ancient gardens that these interesting and unusual old roses may be found. 'Stanwell Perpetual' is covered with white flowers from May to the autumn, one of the earliest and latest to flower; it is said to have been discovered in a garden over a hundred years ago. Another old American hybrid, 'Harison's Yellow' rose, now known as *R. harisonii* (which is the correct spelling of this name), is reported to have appeared in a garden in New York about 1830. It makes a bush about 8 feet high, and in early June has a mass of golden double flowers – one of the most beautiful bush roses in existence. An excellent bush rose, *R. chinensis* var. *mutabilis*, is in flower in early June, about 6 feet high with flowers pale pink when they first come out, but they die a good red, hence its name; it is particularly useful as it goes on flowering till July, and it starts again in August, going on to the end of September. It used to be called *R. turkestanica*, and there seems to be some doubt whether it is a hybrid or a species. There are many other June-flowering roses, but it is not possible to mention them all, only a few we like best. *R. macrantha* is charming with large single pink flowers over the entire bush. At this time a low-growing trailing rose, known here as *R. repens*, has large deep pink single flowers in a mass over the whole plant, good for the front of the shrub border. It is said to be hybrid with *R. arvensis*.

Many of the 'rugosa' hybrids are in flower now. They mostly grow into large strong bushes. 'Dr. Eckener' is the first, with creamy-yellow flowers, then a little later the two forms of 'F. J. Grootendorst', one with red and one with pink flowers. These hybrids are decorative when in full flower, but we often wonder if they do not take up too much room. The hybrid climber bred by Pedro Dot of Barcelona, 'Madame Grégoire Staechelin', with double rosy-pink flowers, is splendid for a wall or over some old trees; one of the prettiest of all climbing roses. Many of the species come into flower in June. *R. rubus*, one of E. H. Wilson's introductions, has white flowers which are after the style of a 'rubus', and makes tremendous shoots each year and has to be kept in check. One of the pleasantest of the species, Farrer's 'Threepenny-bit rose', as E. A. Bowles used to call it, *R. farreri* var. *persetosa*[1], has innumerable small pink flowers which look enchanting against the thin fern-like foliage, making a bush about 6 feet high, and the leaves turn a reddish brown in autumn.

see plate 25

The different-coloured forms of the Scotch rose, *R. spinosissima*[2], are useful for this chalk soil, even growing on the rubble of the cliff. The variety *altaica* makes an ideal hedge about 3 feet high and is very attractive when full of white single flowers. Some of the forms have double pink flowers, and the variety *lutea*[3], with single butter-yellow flowers, is the best of all.

R. moyesii has most attractive reddish single flowers. The colour of the true species is quite unique and indescribable. A number of plants have been raised here from this species, but none of them has ever had the same unique colour. The original plants were sent out by Messrs. James Veitch (raised from seed sent back by E. H. Wilson from China) and it may be possible that out of a large number of seedlings Veitch selected the best and propagated that one. A seedling raised here differed from its parent by having many more flowers to a cluster, about eight or nine instead of the usual three or four, and the flowers and fruit a deep red. It grows into a tall bush and is valuable both in flower and, later on at the end of August, in fruit. It was named *R. × highdownensis*.

R. laevigata is a fine species with its large single white flowers and glossy green leaves. It has grown here for many years on a hot dry border in front of some beech trees, and has only once been cut by frost, during the winter of 1955–6, but soon recovered. This rose came to us originally as Cooper's Burmese rose, and has had a number of names, but appears to be the true *R. laevigata*. Near by, growing up the beech trees, is a rose of Kingdon Ward's

---

[1] *Rosa elegantula* 'Persetosa'   [2] *Rosa pimpinellifolia*
[3] *Rosa × harisoni* 'Lutea Maxima'

introduction (No. 6309) from the Tsangpo Gorge in Tibet; it has many large single white flowers and grey-green leaves. In his notes Kingdon Ward says it grows 30 to 40 feet high. Some people call it *R. brunoni*, but it is quite different from Farrer's form (No. 1084) of *R. brunoni* which he collected in China. Farrer's rose has grown high over a tree in the chalk pit and is fine with masses of white flowers in July. It has golden-brown seed, and seedlings sow themselves; one has made a large and beautiful plant on the chalk cliff. There seems to be much to be done to disentangle the correct names of these great white-flowered climbing roses of eastern Asia.

At the same time that *R. laevigata* is in flower, the strange Persian rose, *R. persica*, comes out with its small yellow flowers with red markings at the base of the petals; it makes a small bush with small grey-green leaves. Kew sent us seed which came from Persia in 1933. A bed was made for it in a cold greenhouse. This greenhouse fell to pieces by blast in 1942, and since then the rose has grown without protection, but was hit by the severe winter of 1955–6. It is still growing but not so well as it used to. It never flowered very well till, reading a book about the Persian mountains where it said that the Persians used these small bushes as fuel, cutting them to the ground each year, we followed their example and the little bushes then flowered freely. There is an interesting article about this rose and an illustration in the *Botanical Magazine*, vol. 116, t. 7096, of 1890 by Sir Joseph Hooker, in which he says that Sir Joseph Banks introduced it into England in 1790, and adds that it has never become common as it is so difficult to propagate. That is still true today, and the only sure way is to raise it from seed, although the article mentioned above suggests that it may be propagated by suckers. There is an excellent illustration of this rose by Redouté in his book, *Les Roses*, vol. 1, p. 27 (Paris, 1817), under the name of *R. berberifolia*.

R. sinowilsoni is unusual, with bronze-coloured stems and the back of the large leaves also bronze with clusters of white single flowers; it grows into a strong bush in the open border but is a shy flower. We thought it might be useful to cross it with *R. moyesii* in order to get a hardier plant with pink flowers and bronze stems and leaves. When the seedlings germinated there were two quite distinct forms among them: one much like its parent with pink flowers, a strong climber, which was named 'Coral'. This is not a worthy garden plant as it does not flower enough, only having clusters of fairly large pink flowers here and there. The other form from the same cross made a massive bush and was covered with apricot buds which opened white with the stems a light bronze.

From seeds of the latter a good number were raised and all were strong growers but all somewhat different. The best was named 'Wedding Day', as it flowered for the first time on 26 June, our wedding day. It is a very strong climber and has now completely covered a cherry tree; the flowers made a mass over the whole plant, buds being apricot, opening pure white and dying pink with stems bronze. 'Coral' seldom had any good seed and, being examined, turned out to be a triploid. It occasionally had a seed or two and one germinated, which is also a tremendous climber and has pale pink flowers.

One of the most lovely shrub roses out now is 'Souvenir de Claudius Denoyel', with deep red double flowers and the sweetest scent. Here it grows as a bush about 5 feet high. In early June it is covered with flowers and if these are cut back they will come out again later, carrying on to the autumn. Another modern bush rose with wonderful scent and double red flowers, rather lighter in colour than the last, is 'Gipsy Lass'. It is not very vigorous, and would probably do better on a wall, but should be grown for its scent alone, although the flowers are charming too. There are many other fine bush roses well worth a place in the garden; 'Gipsy Boy' ('Zigeuner Knabe') makes a good bush with double red flowers, but is not so good as 'Gipsy Lass'. A low-growing hybrid, R. richardi, a wild hybrid from Abyssinia (Ethiopia), has pretty shell-pink flowers with prominent yellow stamens. Among the larger hybrids R. andersoni, said to be a cross with R. canina, has big pinky-red flowers and makes a bush about 5 feet high and will grow anywhere. The white-flowered R. duponti grows up to about the same height, and a fine old rose 'Janet's Pride', which is the same as an old rose called 'Clementine', becomes a tall thin bush about 7 feet high with attractive semi-double red flowers with a white centre.

One of the most satisfying low-growing old roses is 'Rosamundi', which really is old, as it was thought to be named after 'Fair Rosamond', the mistress of Henry II; it runs about on its own roots with delightful flowers, sometimes red and sometimes streaked with white.

The hybrid Musk roses raised by the Reverend Joseph Pemberton are excellent garden plants, especially when grown on their own roots. A gardener's life would be much easier if all roses were grown or would grow on their own roots, and if no unpleasant suckers appeared. These 'Pemberton' roses become large plants, and if the old flowers are cut off they will flower a second time. The first to come out in this garden is 'Nur Mahal' with crimson flowers, and later 'Penelope' with pale pink flowers with a sweet scent. These two are not so vigorous as some of the others such as 'Vanity', with light red flowers,

see colour plate XI

258

and 'Prosperity' with white flowers. They are all good, and a bush of 'Vanity', about 6 to 7 feet high and the same in diameter, in full flower with its large red flowers, is a sight which will gladden any gardener's heart. Some say that these Musk hybrids never get disease.

The new so-called Floribunda roses are most useful and do splendidly on this chalky soil. They are easy to grow, and if the old flowers are cut off they go on flowering all the summer long. One of the oldest and one of the best is 'Nathalie Nypels'. This rose has grown here for over twenty-five years, and is in flower from early June till the frost in autumn. The clear pink flowers are delightful and excellent for cutting as decoration in the house. 'Nypels Perfection', a sport from the last, has deeper pink flowers and is just as good a grower. The yellow 'floribunda' which does best in this soil is 'Goldilocks', a delightful rose, lower growing than most. The climbing sport from this rose is very attractive. There are now any number of these roses with many different colours. The violent-coloured scarlet-flowered ones are avoided as they do not blend with the more delicate-coloured forms which are so charming. The deep red-flowered 'Alain', with fine green foliage, comes out rather later than most and is outstanding. Some people do not like 'Masquerade' with its red and yellow flowers on the same bush, but it seems to us amusing and well worth growing.

At the end of June or early in July the climbing roses are in full flower. Many are crosses with the wild *R. wichuraiana*, which was discovered in Japan in 1861 and introduced to the United States in 1890, where it was crossed with other roses – and so arose many lovely plants that decorate our gardens today: 'American Pillar', 'Dorothy Perkins' and 'Dr. W. van Fleet' were some of the first to be produced. From the latter arose a sport 'New Dawn', with charming pink flowers. One of the pleasantest of these 'wichuraiana' hybrids, 'François Juranville' covers an old tree and has unusual coloured flowers, a sort of apricot-pink. The comparatively old climber 'Albéric Barbier' will grow in any soil and always looks pretty with its creamy-yellow buds and white flowers against the deep green leaves. Another strong climber, 'Silver Moon', said to be a cross between *R. wichuraiana* and *R. laevigata*, has grown over another old tree and has large white single flowers, but it only has one flowering. 'Mermaid', a wonderful plant, has grown up the wall of the house to the first-floor windows, and the large single yellow flowers come out in early July. This is a cross with *R. bracteata*. The latter attains about 8 feet on a south wall, and the pure white single flowers are out usually in August. This rose is one of the oldest introductions from China; Lord Macartney led a commercial delegation to China in 1792 and his secretary collected plants during their stay, and among others he introduced this rose to England in 1793, hence the other name of the 'Macartney Rose'. One of the best of the July climbers, *R. filipes*, was introduced by E. H. Wilson from China. On the wall of the house facing east it grows luxuriantly up to over 20 feet, and is covered from top to bottom with white flowers.

There are a number of large bush rose species from China which are particularly useful as they flower in July. *R. multibracteata* makes a large straggling bush with branches up to 10 feet high, and is covered with light pink flowers all through July and has a mass of red berries in autumn. The unusual small round leaves separate it from other species. Severe pruning is sometimes necessary, but beware, as the long sharp paired thorns are everywhere! Another delightful rose, *R. willmottiae*, also makes a large bush but keeps its shape better than the last; the fairly large light pink flowers are very fine. *R. soulieana*, also a strong grower coming out now, has single white flowers and silvery-green leaves making a pleasant combination.

Among the lower growing late flowering species is *R. roxburghii*, which was raised from seed from China. It is a shrub about 4 to 5 feet high with rose-coloured single flowers in July. This wild form does not produce enough flowers at one time to be a worthy garden plant, but a cross between it and *R. rugosa* has made a good shrub, more robust than *R. roxburghii*, with semi-double pink flowers. This is named 'Micrugosa', as *R. roxburghii* was originally named *R. microphylla*. *R. roxburghii* has a curious character of the calyx and sepals being covered with bristles. It is said that only alternate sepals are bristly, but on the wild plant each sepal has bristles, though the alternate ones have fewer than the others.

All these late-flowering roses come from China, but there is one from Mexico worth a place in the garden, *R. stellata* var. *mirifica*, low growing with pink flowers. The hips are like green berries with sharp bristles, which has given it the name of the 'Gooseberry Rose'.

This is just a short list of the types of roses which will grow well on chalk soils.

260

CHAPTER VII

The Fragrant Garden

Frances Jane Hope
PLEACHED ALLEYS

I wish every garden had its summer and winter 'Pleached Alley'. The Summer one, consisting of the orthodox Shakspearian Roses and 'Lush Woodbine', commencing with the early white and very sweet *Lonicera fragrantissima*, Sweetbriar, and Scotch Roses (attracting early bees), and ending with the evergreen *Lonicera glabra* and Gloire de Dijon – tempting sunning places for the latest butterflies (Red Admiral) – both of which, if the season be favourable, would flower far into December. Among the Honeysuckles I would also include the delicious *Lonicera flexuosa*[1], *Lonicera xanthocarpa*, and *Lonicera parviflora*[2], that form fine clusters of yellow and red berries; and I would decidedly have a single Persian-yellow and copper Austrian Briar up the trellis for the sake of their refreshing and fragrant early foliage.

The Sweetbriar would be as a hedge outside the whole length, and all

Frances Jane Hope (18??–1880) was an enthusiastic amateur who lived and gardened at Wardie Lodge near Edinburgh. She contributed regularly to the Gardeners' Chronicle and other journals.

---

[1] *Lonicera japonica ripens*   [2] *Lonicera dioica*

261

varieties of Scotch Roses in a row on the other side. With the tiny *Allée* of Rose (Scotch), and the huge Gloire, extremes would meet, and make a long season for the 'Beatrices' to 'run like lapwings' to their 'woodbine coverture'. A light pair of steps should be kept at hand to reach the late Roses, that one may never fancy them 'sour grapes'; the dwarf Scotch bushes are convenient to hover over and select from, each dainty bud more tempting than the other.

But the Winter Alley would, I am confident, be the most pleasant resort in a close Summer's day. I would make it entirely of these four Poplars – Balsam, Aspen, Italian, and Abélé.

The first, with its aromatic fragrance in earliest Spring, would form principally the sides, and the roof would be arched over with the sweet tinkling Tremula and Italian. All these Poplars have a more or less flattened foot-stalk set at right angles to the leaves, which form the special charm, particularly in the two last-named species. I would have two or three Abélés, for the sake of their white under-leaves, to give light as well as air to my high roomy Alley, and a wand of Willow here and there, of all those sorts that have early and pleasant catkins, and bright red, yellow, and purple barks within reach of eye and hand.

I would make the entrance through an arch of Rosemary, and the exit through one of *Salix caprea*, whose early flowers would attract innocent flies of various sorts, and please me when I came out to watch the stirring of the Balsam buds, and see if the resinous sap was showing. There should be a hedge of Rosemary on the one side of this Alley, and a bed of evergreen Thymes, Lavender, and all sorts of sweet Aromatic green Herbs on the other, all collected together safe under my eye. But it is as an Alley 'of the Winds' that I would principally advocate this Poplar, and I am sure popular, covered walk. Some of the endless and beautiful effects produced by a breeze, could conveniently be studied, and we do not in planting take this sufficiently into account – the bad effects of wind we are always keenly alive to. We are sure to have wind, therefore let us see the white under-leaf of wild Raspberries in the hedges, Bay-laurel in shrubberies, planted in the direction of the prevailing wind. Abélés, and *Acer dasycarpum*[1], and the purple colour of the under-surface of the leaf in *Acer pseudoplatanus purpureum*, in our plantations and woods, and in particular Lombardy Poplars, for their peculiar and beautiful swoop in a breeze.

[1] *Acer saccharinum*

Let them have plenty of room, so that from any quarter that the wind may blow we can admire its graceful sweep unimpeded, unlike that of any other tree.

In the Alley not a 'catspaw' will be lost; long before one feels it, it will be seen in the gentle quiver of one or two leaves (not always at the top or on one side of one branch); it will be heard first in the sweet tinkle of the Italian, more sensitive than the Aspen, and of a completely different sound. How instantaneously does the Aspen stop at times, or, may be, go on pattering like rain for a few seconds; no two airs giving the same sounds. I always fancy Poplars make the best trees for hot weather, as they multiply and utilize the slightest breath. The mere rippling sound cools one, and they certainly keep off flies, which heavy-shade trees like Sycamore and Horse Chestnut do not, for insects cannot settle upon their restless foliage, which in July, methinks, is no small advantage. After a thunderstorm or steady rain, when the Summer-flower Alley will be dripping and strewed with Rose petals and Honeysuckle flowers, the Poplar leaves will have 'merrily danced' themselves dry, if ever they were wet. No trees. authorities tell us, suffer so little from storms.

In Spring the Alley would be bright yellow with the young Balsam leaves, and rich gold in Autumn with the old foliage of the Aspens, beautiful to look at as well as to hear at that season.

As all Poplars have suckers more or less, a succession crop can be selected to have tops on a level with the eye; the leaves on the young rank suckers do not twitter so well as those on the older wood. We have all paused to listen to the soft hushed sound of the young deciduous needles of the fragrant Larch in spring, or the louder 'soughing' of the hard evergreen ones of the Scotch Fir in winter, and the brittle rattling of Beech leaves in autumn; but for summer sounds there are no trees like the Poplar, as sensitive as an Eolian harp; but not made by man – they are perfect, and never go out of tune.

William Robinson
SWEET-SMELLING FLOWERS

In placing sweet-smelling plants, some attention is due to their habits. Some are lavish of fragrance and give it spontaneously. Of these, in the shrubbery, we have Lilacs, Mock Orange, Azaleas, Sweet Briers, double Gorse, various Brooms and Thorns, Acacias, and Honeysuckles. In the borders, Tulips, Hyacinths, and Daffodils, Triteleias, alpine Auriculas, Musk, double Rockets, Lupines (annual and perennial), Fraxinella, White Lily, Musk Mallow, Phloxes, Mignonette, and Sweet Peas, with several kinds of Scotch and other Brier Roses. For wilder parts, common Gorse, Broom, and Hawthorn, wood Hyacinths, Cowslips, Agrimony, Meadow Sweet and Marsh Marigold. A peculiar and delightful fragrance rises from a sun-baked bank of Heather in late summer, and who does not know the sweetness of a Clover field, and of a warm breeze perfumed with Pine trees, and, better still, though perhaps less commonly known, an April night full of the sweet breath of the young Larch trees? All these are plants and trees that give off their sweetness bountifully, and even from some distance, but the fragrance of many others can only be enjoyed by touching, or, at least, by closely approaching them. Of these the most important are Myrtle, Lavender, Rosemary, Balm of Gilead, Southernwood, *Escallonia macrantha*, Bay, Bog Myrtle and the Fernleaved Gale (*Comptonia adiantifolia*), Juniper, Thyme, Marjoram, and other sweet herbs. A good plan would be to plant these in a wilderness, with narrow walks or spaces of turf between good groups of each, so that one would brush against the living masses of sweetness, the turf being full of Thyme and the free-smelling shrubs and trees beyond. What a delight it would be to take a blind person into such a garden!

The Gum Cistus in autumn gives off a pungent and agreeable smell, though its flowers have none, and in early winter the foliage of Violets and Woodruff and the dying Strawberry leaves are sweet good-byes of the garden year. There are many of our smaller treasures, to enjoy whose sweetness we must either bend low to, or gather. *Linnaea borealis*, whose tiny twin-flowers smell like Almonds, the New Zealand Mayflower (*Epigaea repens*), *Polygala*

Willi
(1838
great
garde
book.
The
Gard
own
Mar
desig
inclu
near

Chamaebuxus, also Almond-scented Pyrolas, the sweet-scented Orchid (*Gymnadenia conopsea*), like white Lilac blossom, and the Butterfly Orchis, fragrant in the evening; Iris graminea, whose flowers hiding low among the grassy leaves, have exactly the smell of ripe Plums. The Water Hawthorn (*Aponogeton distachyon*) is strongly perfumed. The Lily of the Valley need hardly be mentioned. Of other sweet border flowers there are Chinese Paeonies, delicately Tulip scented; Grape Hyacinths, the Musk Hyacinth, Snapdragons, Salvias, including the variegated-leaved Yuccas; the large white Plantain Lily, as sweet as the white Lily and more delicate, but faintly delicious, smells like those of Crocus, Water Forget-me-not and Pansy. The Rose family give a whole scale of sweet notes. The wild Roses have a scent as tender as their colouring. The Burnet Rose and its descendants, the whole race of Scotch Briers, have a delicate smell quite peculiar among their kind, as have also the Austrian and Persian Briers respectively though in their case it is less agreeable. It is distinct again in the Damask Rose and in the sweet old Provence; while in Hybrid Perpetuals we have at least three distinct types of perfume, and as many in the Teas, the most marked type among the latter being that of Gloire de Dijon. The scent differs again in China Roses, and again in the clustered climbing kinds. In Moss Roses the very peculiar and delightful smell seems to come mostly from the viscid matter on the mossy calyx and stalk. This is also the case with some of the garden Brambles, notably *Rubus speciosus* and with *Fraxinella*, *Escallonia maracrantha*, and Gum Cistus. Among sweet-smelling plants we must not omit those of the wholesome aromatic character, such as Wormwood, Chrysanthemum, Chamomile Santolina, and Tansy.

26   ARLEY HALL, CHESHIRE. c.1980

A variety of scented plants including honeysuckle, lilies, thyme, stocks,
heliotrope and mignonette fill this corner of the garden, which was created by
Viscountess Ashbrook in 1977.

Jason Hill
THE INVISIBLE GARDEN

No gardener, however prince-like, can have a garden large enough for all the flowers that he would like to grow, and most of us are compelled to make our choice of plants conform to the exigences of a mere acre or two, and so we are compelled to do all we can to get the most out of our limited space. Saxatile plants are encouraged to accept out little walls for cliffs and the edge of the gravel path is allowed to be a temporary bed for self-sown seedlings; for spreading trees we substitute fastigiate columns and we plant the roof of the garage with House-leeks. But there is a way in which we can add another dimension altogether to the garden – and that is by thinking in terms of our sense of smell. The Cinderella of the senses opens the door upon an aspect of reality which most people ignore a little contemptuously, yet the scent of flowers is no small part of their beauty, and by giving a little special attention to it we can have a garden within a garden, an invisible garden not much less rich and various than the other which appeals to the eye.

The right of fragrance to be considered as an independent form of beauty is justified on two grounds: firstly by the tendency of many scents to drift away from the plant that produces them, and, secondly, by the frequent disparity between a plant and its scent. The scent which seems, more than all others, to have an independent existence is that of 'strawberry leaves dying with an excellent cordial smell'; in fact, when I met it for the first time, as I was walking along a country lane in winter, I felt sure that some violets were flowering before their time in the hedgebank, and when I found nothing among the dead leaves to account for the unexpected scent, I was inclined to put it down as an hallucination. There is a distinct note of violet, or rather of orris root in it, together with cedar wood and something like the dry, earthy fragrance of ambergris; and, because all scents of the musk and violet group fatigue our sense of smell very quickly, it seems to fade away almost as soon as you peceive it. This natural elusiveness enabled old Lady Ludlow, in Mrs. Gaskell's story, to maintain that it was perceptible only to the members of certain old and aristocratic families, while a later generation, failing to find it in their straw-

'Jason Hill'/Frank Anthony Hampton (1888–1967) was a psychiatrist who was also an erudite gardener with a special gift for writing about his subject. The Curious Gardener *and* The Contemplative Gardener *are his best known books.*

267

berry beds and reluctant to write themselves off as hopelessly plebeian, seems to have decided that the scent of dying strawberry leaves is a myth. But it is there, for anyone who cares to look for it, in the Wild Strawberry, the Alpine Strawberry and the Hautbois, which were the only varieties known to Elizabethan gardens; and it may even be extracted from their brown leaves, though in confinement it loses a little of its October morning freshness and acquires a hint of Russian leather. The best way to have it in the garden is to let the double form of the Wild Strawberry carpet the ground under some trees, which it will do with the greatest willingness, or to make an edging of one of the improved varieties of the Alpine Strawberry in the kitchen garden.

The scent of dying strawberry leaves is nearly matched by the fragrance which *Veronica cupressoides* gives off in damp weather or when it is wet with dew; but here the note of cedar wood predominates, and the effect is almost exactly that of Vetivert or Khus-khus, the grass-root which they weave into mats in India. There are two plants in commerce under the name *Veronica cupressoides*; one is dwarf, scentless and with rather yellowish foliage, the other is glaucous, scented, and grows into a neat ovoid bush about 4 feet high. But it is difficult to say which has the better right to the name until these New Zealand Veronicas have settled down and been sorted out in the new genus *Hebe*, which has been created for them.

A variation on the violet theme is played by Mignonette, which introduces a note – a dusty odour of antiquity – that is almost peculiar to itself, though it occurs again, I think, in the subtle chord struck by the flowers of the Vine and of the Climbing Asparagus, *Asparagus tenuifolia*, which wreathes the groves of Oleander and Lentisc on the shores of the Mediterranean. These plants not only throw their scent far abroad, but seem to disclaim it by the inconspicuousness of their minute greenish flowers.

The best known of the detached scents is the sharp apple smell given off by Sweet Briar after a shower of rain. Everyone likes it, yet you do not meet the plant very often in modern gardens, perhaps because its less fragrant, but more handsome descendants, the Penzance Briars, detract attention from it in catalogues. In Germany they call the Sweet Briar not inappropriately 'Weinrose', for its scent has something in common with the clean brisk bouquet of the Rhine wines; but it is not so obviously vinous as the heady smell of Elder flowers or the heavy, stale vinosity of *Calycanthus floridus*. It is one of the very few scents that are more soluble in water than in oil or alcohol, a quality that makes it elusive to the perfumer, but increases its carrying power in the garden when it is dew- or rain-wet in summer. We meet it again in the flowers of that excellent climbing rose 'Dr. Van Fleet' and in the leaves of *Santolina pinnata*; and it is particularly desirable, for it is the only scent with a sharp tang which, as far as my experience goes, is dispersive in northern gardens.

There is a trace of sharpness in the scent which drifts, on a hot day, from the glandular stems of *Rubus odoratus*; but here the impression is chiefly that of a mixture of resin and cedar wood with a slight hint of pineapple. This Rubus from North-West America is a really fine thing and, as it seems to me, undeservedly neglected. It is a giant Raspberry, with canes up to 8 feet high and enormous vine-shaped leaves; the flowers, which are freely produced from June to October, are about 2 inches across and open in deep magenta crimson, set off by a tassel of straw-coloured stamens and fading to a curious tone of crushed raspberry.

A cool freshness, which suggests the smell of earth after rain in summer, is a peculiar merit of the Sweet Pea, and, in spite of forebodings, it is well maintained in the modern varieties, except, perhaps, in the orange and scarlet departures. In the perennial *Lathyrus tuberosus*, sometimes called 'The Fyfield Pea' from its one site of naturalisation in this country, the freshness is enhanced by a hint of lemon, giving us a scent that is far more delicate than the rather coarse carmine pink of the flowers. This quality of freshness occurs again in the scent of the Bearded Irises, which Huysmanns called *'une odeur de miel et d'herbe fraiche'*, though most of us would think of orange blossom rather than honey, especially for the *Pallida* group, whose scent blends so well with the rain-washed sweetness of Sweet Peas.

The most powerful and far-reaching scent in the garden by daylight is given off by *Humea elegans*, not only by the flowers – plumes of chestnut-coloured Pampas grass – but also by the stems and leaves. It resembles incense so closely that it once caused a country vicar to be suspected of ritualistic practices; and one day, as I was walking down Victoria Street, some hours after handling a leaf of it at Vincent Square, a friend who was with me remarked, "What a long way the smell of incense carries from Westminster Cathedral!" *Humea*, for all its old-world hieratic smell, comes from Australia, and is a tender biennial for summer bedding; in a small garden it can be overpowering, but it may often be appreciated gratefully in the London parks.

The intense sweetness of vanilla, which comes from the minute yellowish flowers hidden beneath the leaves of *Azara microphylla*, is almost as unexpected in the garden as incense; it would be over-sweet in summer, but it comes early in Spring when the air is often chilly, and it is welcome then, if only because it recalls the little dark, vanilla-scented orchid *Nigritella* and the high Alpine pastures. An even more characteristic reminder of the Alps comes with the wafts of rose and peaches from the Alpine Clover, *Trifolium alpinum*, whose value in the Alpine lawn is to be measured by its evocative fragrance and not by the rather dingy pink of its flowers.

The disparity which sometimes exists between a flower and its scent, enables us to make a tropical garden out of hardy plants. *Asclepias syriaca* (syn. *A. Cornutii*), a North-American in spite of its name, is a gawky plant with faded purple flowers, but its rich and sumptuous scent is almost exactly that of the old stove plant *Hoya carnosa*. *Clerodendron foetidum* must have been named by someone who always looked on the worst side of things, for, although its leaves smell of beef extract and elder leaves when they are bruised, its flowers are almost excessively sweet with a mixture of Tuberose and Honeysuckle. If it is given a warm and sheltered corner it may be relied upon to open its large heads of deep pink flowers before the frost catches them, but, for my own part, I prefer the less showy but equally fragrant species, *C. trichotomum* and *C. Fargesii*, for their flowers are set off by dark red bracts, and they sometimes produce magnificent berries of indigo blue.

A scent with the intense, penetrating sweetness of some tropical orchid comes from the tiny, greenish-yellow flowers of *Valeriana celtica*. This is the 'Speik' of the Styrian Alps, and it is valued there for its roots, which smell like those of the true Spikenard, though not quite so pleasantly. The true Spikenard, *Nardostachys jatamansi* from Nepal, is only a curiosity, and has no beauty above ground, where it would pass for an unremarkable Valerian with small, dim lilac flowers, but its roots, which were once worth far more than their weight in gold, exhale a powerful, disturbing scent of patchouli blended with a trace of musk. This mossy, ferny smell is not exactly sweet, but it is curiously pleasant and indefinably attractive: it would be described, I think, as typically eastern, a category which would embrace also the smell of pepper and ginger from the roots of *Asarum europeum*, an unassuming carpeter with dark, round, shining leaves for any shady spot.

Pride of place in the tropical garden belongs to *Viburnum Carlesii*, which some of us are disposed to reckon the best hardy plant introduced during the last fifty years. Its scent, of the Tuberose type, is lightly touched with a suggestion of Clove Carnation, which gives to it a finish of perfection, matching the faint pink that warms the waxen white of its petals. I am inclined to place *Viburnum Carlesii* above *V. fragrans*[1], which seems to fall just short in its smaller flower-heads and in its habit of flowering sporadically from November onwards*, as well as by lacking the aromatic note in its scent.

Something of the complex, unforgettable scent of the *maquis*, that typically southern smell of the Mediterranean coast, can be caught in the garden from a bank of *Cistus creticus*, Rosemary, Juniper, Bay, Thyme and Fennel during a spell of really hot, dry weather; but one of its sweetest components, the suave, balsamic smell of labdanum, is reproduced almost exactly by the sub-Arctic Poplars (*Populus balsamifera*, *P. trichocarpa*, *P. candicans* and others) when their leaf buds are opening in the spring.

The smell of the Spice Islands also has its northern counterpart: I have smelt it on the Surrey Downs from the Clove-scented Broomrape, and in a cold white cloud on the Julian Alps from a sheet of *Dianthus Sternbergii*. In the garden it is produced most lavishly by the super-abundant petals of 'Mrs. Sinkins', but at the price of a blowsiness that is almost dissolute, so that many of us prefer the smaller and more refined *Dianthus fimbriatus albus*[2], the old white Pink of cottage gardens, which 'Mrs. Sinkins' has supplanted. The Pinks have their forerunner in the Golden Currant, *Ribes aureum*, whose rather dull yellow flowers give us a hearty clove scent in the spring. It comes forward again in the autumn, when its leaves die in a splendour of luminous gold; but you seldom see it, except in the background of old shrubberies, for its modest merits are eclipsed by the brilliant, acrid American Currant, *Ribes sanguineum*.

Flowers, in the quality of their scent, neither observe the times nor regard the seasons of garden convention. Spring begins at any time between November and February with the primrose and pansy scent of *Iris stylosa* (properly, but seldom, called *I. unguicularis*) and with a perfect replica of Lily of the Valley from the long yellow racemes of *Berberis hyemalis*[3]. In mid-winter *Chimonanthus fragrans* distils a rich cinnamic fragrance, which recalls the bean fields of June. In February, or even earlier, spidery yellow flowers break out of the leafless branches of *Hamamelis mollis* with a scent of soft autumnal richness; it is one of the most delightful scents of the garden, for its hyacinthine sweetness is combined with a fresh, delicate perfume of ripe fruit, a chord that we meet, though with a slightly different effect, in its contemporary *Corylopsis spicata* and in the Primulas *P. sikkimensis* and *P. chionantha*.

---

* This is a fault of youth. Flowers tend to appear later and simultaneously as the plant ages.

[1] *Viburnum farreri*

[2] *Dianthus orientalis* [3] *Berberis japonica hyemalis*

The fruit-like quality appears almost unmixed in the orange and lemon of *Tulipa Batalini*; it is again quite pure, but now almost unflowerlike, in the ripe greengage smell of *Iris graminea*, *Akebia quinata*, *Muscari neglectum* and *Clematis heracleifolia*. *Calycanthus floridus* carries ripeness a stage further with brownish purple flowers and a smell like that of an old wine barrel; while *Veratrum nigrum* goes right on to decay, with black flowers and a smell of vinegary fermentation.

The suggestion of ripe fruit is developed very elaborately by *Aquilegia suaveolens* from the Himalayas; this is a very beautiful Columbine, with wide, intricately sculptured flowers in creamy-yellow, and its scent is a blend of peaches and *Lilium auratum* with something of the musky quality of a Canteloup melon. It is almost too luscious, a Château-Yquem among perfumes, but rare and exquisite of its kind. At very close quarters this delicious scent becomes nothing but the violent smell of Black Currants, and on further concentration it degenerates into the suggestion of a delinquent cat; this remarkable change is shown also by *Humea elegans* and it is one of the many unexplained problems of the sense of smell.

Some of the richest scents are designed to attract night-flying moths, and they have in common a certain quality of sweetness which makes the odorous night-garden, with its Honeysuckle, Evening Primrose, Jasmine, Night-scented Stock, Tobacco Plant and Double Rocket appropriate to the cool air and different from the sunlit nosegay of Rose, Lavender and Mignonette. The jewel of the night garden is the dwarf Evening Primrose, *Oenothera caespitosa* (syn. *eximia*), whose enormous white goblets pour out a tropical scent of lemon and Freesia. It likes a hot, gravelly bank, but not for long, unfortunately: for it is a great wanderer and is often lost in small gardens after a year or two unless it is transplanted.

A recondite garden is enclosed in those plants with scented leaves that are 'fast of their smell', and it remains imperceptible until we call it out with a touch. Several of these plants, such as Rosemary, Rue, Southernwood and the bushy Thymes, can be used for low hedges, where they will disengage their scent as one brushes past them, and lightly touched in this way they are sweeter than when they are bruised in the hand. One of them, our native Chamomile, *Anthemis nobilis*, makes, – I will not say a good substitute for grass, since it does not wear so well, – but a close green turf, pleasant to the eye and the nose, on any path that is not subject to constant traffic. It has a brisk, sharp smell like an apple with a suggestion of resin, and the form that is grown commercially to provide Chamomile tea (thirty years ago there were a few stony fields of it near Sutton in Surrey) has neat little double white flowers. *Mentha citrata*, which combines the Bergamot orange of *Monarda* with the coolness of Spearmint, is allowed to grow lush here round the tap at which we fill the watering cans; it came to me from an old garden on the border of Wales with the legend that it was the first scented plant to be created, and that its virtue was such that it would enhance the fragrance of any scented plant in its neighbourhood; but its merits are more firmly enshrined in the composite bouquet of Chartreuse. *Mentha gentilis*, the 'Cow Basil' of Gerard, has a similar scent of mint and bergamot, and is even more cool and delicate. A form with yellow-veined leaves was grown a hundred years ago as a window plant in the cottages of Cheshire and Somerset, a precursor of the pot of scented Pelargonium, which, in its turn, is becoming obsolete. *Mentha rotundifolia* varies the theme with apple in place of bergamot, and *Acorus calamus* one of the plants that were used to strew the stone floors of mediaeval living-rooms, develops the apple motive aromatically with a suggestion of Cox's Orange Pippin and cinnamon.

The Lemon-scented Edelweiss, *Leontopodium haplophylloides*, is a new scented plant of solid merit, which redeems the family from the slur of spurious romance cast over it by *L. alpinum*, for its leaves give off a delicious scent of fresh limes when they are lightly stroked, its flowers smell of honey and its roots are perfumed like those of the true Spikenard with orris, musk and patchouli. It was introduced by Farrer, under the name *Leontopodium aloysiodorum*, from the river shingles of the mountains of Kansu, and it grows easily in any well-drained sunny soil.

Near the Lemon-scented Edelweiss I have an old plant of *Micromeria corsica* now reduced to a wiry mat and tagged with tufts of hair by the cats who come to roll upon it at night in transports of erotic ecstasy. Its scent of lemon, menthol and ozone is more pungent to the human nose than alluring, but its peculiar note of ozone (which is pure and unmixed in the leaves of *Phlomis umbrosa* and *Mertensia maritima*) appears in at least one recent and subtle example of the perfumer's art.

The Thymes have developed many different scents, and all are pleasant except one, that of a hybrid of *Th. herba-barona* which smells of sassafras. Most of them are well known, but *Th. vulgaris* var. *fragrantissimus*, which was discovered in a cottage garden and put into commerce by Messrs. Thompson & Morgan, is less familiar than it deserves to be, for its delicate lemon scent is softened with a hint of Sweet Marjoram and sweetened with a suggestion of something like Rose Geranium. Mr. Lofthouse has recently collected some fragrant Thymes from the Spanish mountains, which will be very welcome in the garden when they are distributed.

A scent is very seldom peculiar to one species of plant (the scent of Lavender is the only one that I can think of which seems to stand quite alone), but is nearly always repeated elsewhere, sometimes identically, but far more often with interesting variations or re-combined with other scents. This tendency to repetition with a difference affords a slight excuse for occasionally using metaphors borrowed from music in attempting the difficult business of describing an invisible garden and hinting at its possibilities; for in reality there is no close association between the sensory impressions of smelling and hearing. But the tendency also makes it difficult to describe scents accurately, and in describing one scent in terms of another I am conscious that I am often stressing a likeness and neglecting a difference. I may say, for example, that Rue, if it is lightly handled, smells of coconut; but the comparison is by no means exact, and the reader may consider it more like gorse, ripe apricots, or cowslips, for all these scents have something in common.

In our appreciation of smells we are strongly influenced and sometimes hindered by associations. The smell of pigs, for example, is not, I think, unpleasant in itself: it is the pigsty rather than the pig smell that we dislike, for most people find the almost identical smell of celery seed pleasant enough and do not object to the warm suggestion of pig that lurks behind the fragrance of the border Phloxes. There is room in the garden for smells that are interesting rather than purely fragrant: for the rough pungent suggestion of Elliman's embrocation in *Perovskia atriplicifolia* and some of the Artemisias, for the dusty woody smell of the flowers of *Hamamelis arborea*[1], the resinous smell of the common St. John's Wort, and even for the vigorous goatiness of *Hypericum hircinum*.

The plants that have been described in trying to illustrate an invisible garden have been chosen, therefore, rather more for their distinctive character than for their excellence; and, when all is said, I suppose that the Rose is pre-eminent among them all for the delicacy and unwearying charm of its scent, but this is so complex and varied that it needs separate consideration.

---

[1] *Hamamelis japonica arborea*

27

PYRFORD COURT, SURREY. C.1965
A secluded and fragrant shelter beneath
a mature wisteria arbour.

E. A. Bowles

FRAGRANCE: AN APPRECIATION

Edward Augustus Bowles VMH (1865–1954) was a great gardener who specialised in bulbs; he created a remarkable garden at his home, Myddleton House, Enfield, Middlesex. His books include: A Handbook of Crocus and Colchicum *and* A Handbook of Narcissus.

There is a general outdoor fragrance which is one of the most delightful of the experiences that make life worth living. Take, for instance, the first time that you really smell spring in the air. It is hard to define what sort of scent it is, but it conveys the idea of fresh and young growth, and when we get it we feel that we have got rid of the winter.

Later there is the fragrance of a newly mown meadow. Grass, when freshly cut for hay, has a delicious scent of its own, suggesting almonds or Gorse blossom, and if the meadow is close to the garden, this is added to the general fragrance.

Again there are plants which scent the air. There is a passage in Bacon's essay *Of Gardens* which may be familiar to you all, but I should like to remind you of it:

> And because the breath of flowers is far sweeter in the Air (where it comes and goes, like the Warbling of Musick) than in the hand, therefore nothing is more fit for that delight, than to know what be the flowers and plants that do best perfume the Air. Roses, Damask and Red, are fast Flowers of their Smells, so that you may walk by a whole row of them, and find nothing of their Sweetness; yea though it be in a morning's Dew. Bays, likewise, yield no Smell as they grow; Rosemary little, nor Sweet Marjoram.

Among those that scent the air Bacon mentions Musk Rose, dying Strawberry leaves, Sweet Briar and Lime trees; I think that he would have mentioned, had he known them, *Rosa Primula*, *Veronica cupressoides*, Helichrysum and Balsam Poplar.

Rosa Primula does not always scent the air, but after a shower it diffuses a most delightful scent like Russian leather that can be enjoyed from a distance in the garden; but on dry days you must bruise the leaves to obtain the scent. Bacon mentions Sweet Briar as 'not fast of its scent', and most people know its delightful widespread fragrance after a shower.

276

There is also what I call the curry plant – I do not know whether I invented the name. It is a Helichrysum, I think *H. angustifolium*. It gives out a most extraordinary smell like curry, and not only curry but a very good curry too with mango chutney in it. During the Kaiser's war I thought it might be useful to chop it up and put it into ordinary minced beef to turn it into a curry, but the flavour does not compare with the scent, and is unpleasantly bitter. This strong scent, however, especially as I pass by on a hot day, still makes me feel hungry.

Scents which delight some people do not please others. One of the plants that I grow which scents the air most is the wonderful Jasmine from China, *Jasminum polyanthum*, which has white flowers in the spring and early summer. It will not grow out of doors here, but I like to open the door of the conservatory, where it grows, and let the scent into the drawing-room. I enjoy it when it pervades the whole house but my housemaid thinks it a horrid sickly smell. There is an old saying 'different people have different opinions. Some likes Apples and some likes Inions', but I like both.

Another invasive scent is that of *Calycanthus floridus* which in a newly opened flower has the powerful scent of a pineapple but in an older one resembles grapefruit, and when fading has a slightly alcoholic savour like that of cider. This Chinese species with its maroon flowers looks like a nearly black miniature Magnolia, whereas the American *C. occidentalis* has bright red flowers and only yields its scent to a nose which is within a few inches and then the scent is not at all pleasant resembling that of a wine that has turned sour. Both species, however have pleasantly aromatic leaves which have won them their English name of 'Allspice' trees.

Thus far scents have been dealt with according to the way they are borne. Now let us consider some of the flowers which will make a sequence through all the months of the year, beginning with January.

If on New Year's Day there is no snow on the ground but mild, open weather, you may expect to find *Iris unguicularis* which people will persist in wrongly calling *I. stylosa*. 'Stylosa' means that it has a very long style reaching down to its underground seed pod. Surely we ought to learn to call it by its oldest and correct name. The broader-leafed form is usually the earliest to flower and in some seasons I have gathered a few on Michaelmas Day. After that they come at intervals all through the winter and I like to have a bowl of them on the table for Christmas Day instead of Holly and to keep up a succession until the Daffodils come to replace the Iris. It is a good plan to pick them before the bud is open and put them into tepid water to open on the following day and then they will last for two or three days, but no more. I described the scent in one of my books as having "the real essence of spring". It is a mixture of all sorts of good scents, but chiefly that of Primroses.

It is difficult to put these Iris flowers in a vase in such a way as to make them quite happy and comfortable, and I should like to pass on to you a good tip. They look best with clippings of Lawson's Cypress, but then are over-powered by its unpleasant scent, and the best thing to use is clippings of Box. I am lazy and do not like having to change the water in my flower vases every other day. The Box will go on for three weeks if you tip out the water, leaving the Box there, and put some fresh water in, and the Iris flowers stand up better among the short stiff sprigs than among anything else I have so far found.

In January you ought to be able to find some of the later flowering forms of *Crocus laevigatus*, especially the variety *Fontenayi* which flowers so late that it connects Autumn Crocuses with those of spring of which C. *chrysanthus* is generally the first, and on New Year's Day on the way home from church I am usually able to pick one and to enjoy its honey-like scent.

We can begin the New Year well, therefore, with Iris and with Crocuses. Another wonderful plant which you can sometimes pick right through the worst of the winter is Winter Heliotrope or winter-flowering Coltsfoot (*Petasites fragrans*). A small bunch will scent a whole room with a scent resembling that of almond paste on a bride cake. It is not beautiful to look at but for the sake of its fragrance it is worth growing, especially if you can find it in your neighbour's hedgerow. It has been advertised and sold as Winter Heliotrope at a high price. I do not know whether any purchasers brought lawsuits against those who said that it ought to be in every garden, because once it is in the garden it is difficult to get it out again. I have managed to keep it in check by digging down as far as possible and then covering the broken root with a pinch of sodium chlorate and leaving that to poison it.

There is no sweeter scent among winter flowers than that of *Chimonanthus praecox*, of which there are now several varieties, some much more brightly coloured than others. I used to think the sweetest of all was the old rather transparent grey-petalled one, but the newer bright yellow ones flower quite as early and are more beautiful to look at, with their yellow outer petals and dark purplish-red centres to the flower. As it is wasteful to cut a long spray and thereby destroy many unopened buds, you can pick off individual open flowers to float on a very little water in a saucer and they will scent the whole room.

Viburnum fragrans[1] flowers throughout the winter and is one of the best of Reginald Farrer's introductions. It took me a long time to persuade others of its value. I showed it for several years before a committee would give it any award. Even now that people are beginning to realize what a fine thing it is, I believe that we have not yet learned the full beauty of large and old specimens. In this garden it has improved in beauty of outline and freedom of flower year by year. It is capable of flowering in October, which I do not care about, because the flowers are then packed in close heads and hidden by the leaves; but if you can induce it to wait and to flower in January or February, when the leaves have fallen, it will be covered by a cloud of blossom and on sunny mornings will scent the air for quite a distance around. It is a beautiful shrub and if planted where its roots can find some moisture it will do very much better.

Farrer first knew it as a garden plant in China and wrote about its edible fruit but did not mention it as flowering throughout the winter. Later he described finding it in the high foothills in April and wrote enthusiastically about the beauty of its flowers. In those high altitudes it evidently waits to flower until the end of winter and then makes a remarkable show instead of flowering intermittently and sparingly through the winter months. In Edinburgh and elsewhere in Scotland it adheres more closely to its native habit, but even here in some seasons it can provide both a lovely show and fragrance on a sunny day in January.

There are two winter-flowering Honeysuckles, *Lonicera fragrantissima* and *L. Standishii*. The latter is the more valuable because it comes earlier and I have been able to pick bunches of it before Christmas. Their small white flowers are not much to look at but they are so fragrant that they scent a room for a day or two before dropping off. *L. fragrantissima* ought to be the most fragrant of all, judging by its name, but it is no sweeter than the other. It has the virtue, however, of coming out a fortnight or three weeks later.

I remember the celebrated Henry Elwes causing quite a sensation at a show here at the Royal Horticultural Society many years ago when he shouted out "Where's Bowles? He's the only man with a nose!" People expected to see someone with a nose like that of Cyrano de Bergerac and may have been disappointed. He wanted me to smell the difference between two things which he said were totally different, though nobody else could detect the difference between them. Perhaps I find it easy to notice differences in scent because I do not smoke.

[1] *Viburnum farreri*

I have not mentioned Snowdrops because not many people have Snow-drops in January, but there is one which is going about now as *Galanthus caucasicus*. I have grave doubts about what it really is but that is the name given by Baker, a great botanist at Kew, to a Snowdrop which he described as a large form of *G. nivalis*. The few I have found were mixed with collected bulbs of *G. Elwesii* or *G. cilicicus*. It has a remarkable fragrance, smelling more strongly of heather honey than other Snowdrops. Very often I get a few flowers out before Christmas and others follow over a long period up to the end of March.

There are forms of *Daphne Mezereum* which will flower freely if planted in a cosy corner, but cannot be relied upon to flower in January.

However, there is a tree which strictly adheres to the calendar for its time of flowering. This is *Hamamelis mollis*, one of the most valuable shrubs or small trees that have been introduced during my lifetime. I call it the Epiphany Tree because it is always at its best on January 6, the feast of the Epiphany, the old Christmas Day, although it begins to flower a little before. We associate the Epiphany with the visit of the Magi and the gifts which they brought, and this shrub brings the gold in its flowers, the frankincense in its wonderful scent, like Primroses, and myrrh in the stringent quality of the bark. 'Pond's Extract', 'Hazeline' and other useful household remedies are made from the Autumn-flowering American species, *H. virginiana*, but if the mediaeval monks, who invented so many pleasant but inaccurate legends about plants, had known this Chinese species, they would have called it the Epiphany Tree. I advise all those who can do so to grow as big a bush or tree of it as they can find room for.

In February we can rely upon many Daphnes both to scent the air outside and also to provide fragrance in the house. *Daphne odora* is sweetest of all, and in some years it has scented the air in February. One grows here by the side of the house, and if I come out on a warm evening at the end of February I smell it strongly from the front doorstep on the other side. It is sometimes said to be a very tender plant. I would not plant it in a windswept place where nothing early-flowering ought to be asked to grow, but if you have a corner outside by the kitchen chimney, the sort of place where the cat goes to lie and where blue-bottles sit on the wall in the late autumn, put in a *D. odora*, making sure that you have the one with a slightly golden edge on the leaf, and it will be a real pleasure to your nose in February. (Many people say that the wild Spurge Laurel of our woods, *D. Laureola*, has no scent, but that is probably because they do not go out after dark.)

A lovely old Tazetta Daffodil 'Grand Soleil d'Or' which was figured 200 years ago has a delightful scent. It appears on the market about Christmas, but you cannot expect it to flower in our eastern counties before February. If you plant it in a corner against a wall you can sometimes pick the flowers in February. The scent is very sweet and strong and reminds me of a good pancake with brown sugar and a squeeze of lemon.

During March we have Violets which have always been celebrated, and I need not describe to you the delightful scent. *Skimmia japonica*, especially the male forms, provide delightful fragrance in the open air and as cut flowers for the house. A large-flowered form which I brought from Mt. Usher many years ago is my best and I rely upon it for a bowl of fragrant flowers at the same time that I start picking Daffodil buds for the house.

April is the great month for Primroses and April 19th is Primrose Day, when they are worn in memory of Lord Beaconsfield. Very few trumpet Daffodils are pleasantly scented, but a Dutch-raised seedling named 'Vanilla' lives up to its name. *Osmanthus Delavayi* flowers in April, a good evergreen bush with hanging flowers and a fragrance like Lily of the Valley, but a month earlier. It is not, however, a good thing for cutting; the flowers do not seem to smell when you bring them into the house.

Viburnum Carlesii is highly praised, and rightly so, but it frequently happens that the flowers are damaged by an April frost. When Easter comes in April it may be accompanied by the lovely flowers of *Magnolia stellata*. I like to stand under my tree and enjoy the bean-field scent which is so distinctive of summertime.

May is the best month of sweetly scented flowers – Lilac, for instance, and Cowslips. If you pick a bunch of Cowslips and put your nose into them, you will agree that it is the most delightful scent of the whole year. I believe that if heaven smells of anything it will be of Cowslips. There are Lilies of the Valley in May, and you know what a lovely scent they have. Some people get bored with Lilies of the Valley, because, like the poor, they are always with us. That may be true of the forced and almost scentless blooms but a large bunch picked from the open ground in May is so refreshingly delicious that few flowers can equal them.

Of the Japanese Wisterias, *W. floribunda* has little scent, but *venusta* with its short bunches of white flowers strongly scents the air, especially in the evening. The old *W. sinensis* must not be overlooked in both its lilac and white varieties, although its scent may be a little too overpowering when coming through open windows on a warm night. *Staphylea colchica* has a scent like see plate 27

281

coconut, much like that of Gorse. It reminds me of coconut ice which I thought delicious as a child but have outgrown now.

However, there are strongly scented flowers in May which are not so pleasing and among those I class most Hawthorns. Many people say that they like their scent, but I do not. Now and then at a distance you get a rather pleasant scent from them, but too close it is like a fish shop. In the last two or three years I have also become conscious of the horrible smell of Pear blossom when you put your nose to it, and the worst smell of all is *Cotoneaster multiflora*, which smells like a fried fish shop, and one that uses bad oil at that.

In June we have bearded Iris and Philadelphus. Most people say that they love the scent of what they call Syringa, which is the common name for Lilac. The so-called Syringas all belong to the genus Philadelphus and they have a variety of scents. The old *P. coronarius* is an enemy of mine as it gives me hay fever and I have destroyed all the old bushes, except the golden and the silver variegated forms and I like to get someone to cut off all their flower buds before they open and annoy me.

Some Roses and Pinks, of course, scent the air, though Bacon did not recognize this. When he mentioned the single and double white Violas as doing so he must have meant white Stocks as the name white Viola was used in his day of varieties of Matthiola instead of Viola.

No house ought to be without a Japanese Honeysuckle (*Lonicera japonica*). It does not take up much room and it is one of the most fragrant things that you can grow; but do not grow the golden netted form of it, which does not flower sufficiently freely.

There are Lilies and Phlox in July. I do not care much for Phlox, which smells like a combination of pepper and pigsty. The scent of newly opened Evening Primroses is superb. A good kind is the *Lamarckiana* variety, which we have now to call *Oenothera erythrosepala*. If you can hit off the right time for it to open, you can watch it do so as the little calyx springs back and the flower unrolls and opens. Jasmines must also be included in the delights of July.

In August one of the finest scents is that of *Genista aethnensis* from Mount Etna. This has a luscious exotic scent such as that we associate with plants grown in the most costly greenhouses, but it blooms in the open air. *Cytisus Battandieri* is a remarkable plant as the nature of its fragrance changes every few minutes. Sometimes it reminds me of strawberries, and at others of grapefruit and lemons, or of a fruit salad with a dash of maraschino or kirsch. You can get all these scents from the same bunch of blooms at different times of the day.

Clematis Rehderiana comes in September. It not only looks like a Cowslip but smells rather like one. Belladonna Lilies have one of the nicest scents, and one which I grow, *blanda*, has a delicious scent with a touch of lemon in it. As it fades the odour changes very much, like dying Hyacinth flowers or some Daffodils which acquire a fishy smell before they die.

We have also Daffodils for September and October, and I have brought here the North African and Southern European *Narcissus serotinus*, which has a strong Narcissus scent. Heliotrope gives us one of the most delightful of autumn scents. By October, moreover, we can have some very sweetly scented Crocuses, such as *longiflorus*, which is so strongly scented that it was at one time called *odorus*.

There is a Greek Snowdrop, *Galanthus Olgae*, which in a suitable season will flower before its leaves appear. It is wrong to say that Snowdrops have no scent for that means that people have no noses. When freshly gathered and brought into a room they emit a delightful scent. These winter-flowering Snowdrops follow one another in a constant succession from the end of September into the first weeks of January. Thus I have shown you that if you have a well-stocked garden you should be able to find some flowers to provide fragrance in each of the twelve months of the year.

However, we need not depend entirely upon blossoms because there are so many plants which have sweetly scented leaves. One of the most delightful and refreshing scents is that of the Lemon but there are few places in England where they can be grown in the open air, and even there they require some form of shelter such as glass screening. I have a Lemon tree in my conservatory which I am sure that I never planted. Someone may have spat out a lemon pip which has grown into a fair-sized tree, and although it has not yet flowered I frequently bruise a leaf as I pass by to enjoy the incomparable fragrance.

There are many plants which we call lemon-scented but none of them so good as *Citrus Limonum*. The runner-up to the true Lemon in respect of fragrance is *Aloysia citriodora* which is only hardy in a favoured climate. Where it flourishes it is always known as Lemon Verbena, and grows into a large bush or small tree on the south side of many a cottage in South Devon. The leaves wither quickly when picked but as they retain their scent for a long time it is one of the most precious ingredients for pot-pourri or to push to the bottom of a handkerchief pocket. Among other tender plants are many Pelargoniums, which are worth growing for the sake of their lemon scent, even though they must be housed in winter.

Now we come to the different Thymes. There are two varieties of Common Thyme, one which gives the flavour to veal stuffing somewhat resembling Sage; the other is preferable as it suggests the addition of lemon. There are also two varieties of the true Lemon Thyme, one called 'Silver Queen' on account of its beautiful variegation, and one with golden leaves. Every herb border should contain all the forms of Balm that can be collected. The old form, known as Bee Balm, was widely grown and the crushed leaves used for rubbing the inside of the old straw skeps to disguise the lingering smell of the sulphur with which the bees were smothered the previous autumn.

A plant that can be placed among those whose fragrance suggests that of lemon is *Dictamnus Fraxinella*, commonly known as Burning Bush. The whole plant is aromatic but if bruised it is rather too strong to be pleasant. When in flower or bearing young seed pods that English name is justified if a lighted match is put to the base of the spike on a still warm evening when the essential oil is held among the closely packed flowers. If the experiment is successful a flickering flame will run up to the top and a very strong and delightful odour will be borne on the surrounding air. If there is too much breeze at the time the volatile oil will be dispersed and the result will not repay the expenditure on matches.

There are many strong-scented Mints of which the best known is *Mentha piperita* or peppermint, a wild but uncommon British plant and too seldom grown in gardens. Its flavour used to be widely enjoyed when met with in bulls' eyes, brandy balls and mint humbugs in the good old days. *Mentha viridis* or spearmint is the one generally used for mint sauce and is the best for drying or boiling with new potatoes. *Mentha rotundifolia* is known in some parts of the country as Apple Mint but I call it Lamb Mint as it was given to me with that name many years ago from a garden in Norfolk. *Mentha Pulegium* provides the Pennyroyal of chemists. It is a pleasant carpeting plant for a damp spot, especially where it can be trodden on and scent the air.

Mentha Requienii from Corsica and Sardinia is not only the smallest of the Mints, but has an odour of peppermint as powerful as any. It is probably the smallest herbaceous plant grown in gardens and if it can be accommodated in spaces between paving stones and can be protected from invading hordes of *Poa annua* and *Oxalis corniculata* will proclaim its presence with its fragrance although we may not be able to see it.

In contrast one of the largest hardy evergreens with aromatic leaves must be *Laurus nobilis*, generally called the Bay Tree. The value of its fragrant leaves seems to have gone out of favour but in my young days they were much used in cooking for flavouring custards and milk puddings and also for 'soused' herrings and mackerels.

I have left the Californian Bay, *Umbellularia californica*, for the end. It is the most powerfully scented in leaves and stem of all evergreen trees which we can expect to flourish in the colder districts of Great Britain. The fragrance is as pungent as cinnamon sticks but never seems to be air-borne unless the plant is bruised. The fallen and dried leaves still retain their powerful odour and when weeding or gathering up fallen leaves I can recognize the remarkable aroma if I happen to touch one. My tree is planted on the south side of a trimmed Holly hedge which has protected it so well from our harsh north-east winds that it is now about 12 feet high. It is a self-sown seedling of the fine old specimen which used to grow, and I hope may still do so, at the right-hand side of the porch at Bitton Vicarage, where in some seasons it freely bore its characteristic black berries. Umbellularia unfortunately has an evil reputation, for if the fragrance is inhaled too much it has strong soporific consequences.

28   HATFIELD HOUSE, HERTFORDSHIRE. c.1980

The fragrant walk in the Lower West Garden. Aromatics, planted where they can easily be rubbed, combine with the heady scents of pinks, roses and nicotiana.

285

Arthur Hellyer
THE SEARCH FOR SUMMER FRAGRANCE

*Arthur Hellyer VMH,
(1902–) began his
career as a nurseryman
but by 1946 was editor of*
Amateur Gardening. *He
is a plantsman,
Vice-President of the
Royal Horticultural
Society and has many
publications to his credit
including a regular column
for the* Financial Times.

One compensation for the miserable summer we have so far endured[1] is that the cool, damp air has brought out the full fragrance of many flowers. Honeysuckles have never smelt richer, especially on those oppressive evenings preceding thunderstorms and I have become aware of several scents that I had completely missed before.

It is not so many weeks ago that I was recommending *Syringa velutina*[2] in this column as a miniature lilac suitable for small gardens but regretting that it had no perfume. Then one day I was busy in the garden when I became aware of a particularly strong and unfamiliar scent that assailed me every time I passed a particular point. At first I thought it must come from a genista that grows nearby but the scent of genista is sharp and lemony whereas this was sweet and rather heavy. It took me a little while to be convinced that it came from *Syringa velutina* for every time I sniffed the small blue-lilac heads of this bush the scent disappeared. But then some plant perfumes are like that; they carry on the air and are at their most powerful a few feet or even yards away from the flowers that produce them but seem to anaesthetise the nostrils if one approaches too close.

Anyway there is no doubt that it was *S. velutina* that was scenting the air that day, a fact confirmed by a knowledgeable friend who described it as "really too scented" and so I hasten to make amends to a delightful and useful shrub which I had slighted unwittingly. Incidentally in nurseries it is just as likely to be found labelled *S. palabiniana*, an old name still much in use. It comes from Korea and is bone hardy.

One of the problems in writing about flower scents is our pitifully inadequate vocabulary so different from the rich array of adjectives available

---

[1] This piece appeared in the *Financial Times* on June 25th, 1977.
[2] *Syringa meyeri* 'Palibin'

for colours. I suppose that perfume experts must be better endowed but whatever language they use does not seem to come the way of ordinary folk and the literature on flower scents is negligible. Catalogues give no more help, usually stating no more than that a plant is 'scented', or if they want to be particularly complimentary, 'sweetly scented'.

But part of the charm of flower scents is that so many of them are not sweet. The host of mock oranges are at this moment enveloping the garden in a variety of sharp lemony scents for which I know of no individual descriptions. They certainly vary greatly in power and quality, one of my own favourites being *Philadelphus microphyllus*. It makes up in numbers what it lacks in individual flower size and, since it rarely exceeds four feet in height, is much better for small gardens than the big popular favourites such as 'Virginal', *P. coronarius* and *P. intectus*. Another little known but very beautiful kind is *P. delavayi calvescens* which has white flowers backed by purple calyces and is arguably the most powerfully scented of all mock oranges. Unhappily, though it was introduced from China nearly a hundred years ago, it remains a scarce plant and few nurseries are able to offer it.

I suppose that roses offer the widest range of scents, which is not surprising when one considers the vast range of species and the complex parentage of the garden races. From the old Damask roses they inherit the richest and most heady perfume but, as was pointed out by that great and wise rose grower Edward le Grice (whose death recently is a great loss to rose lovers) it is a scent which seems to be brought out by the underlying magenta pigment in some pink, red and crimson roses and is also inextricably linked with weak flower stems. Roses such as 'Etoile de Hollande' and 'Crimson Glory' have it in full measure but the rose buying public rejects these because they hang their heads. Mr. le Grice suggests that ways of overcoming this are to breed roses such as 'Josephine Bruce' with no more than 29 petals or to be satisfied with a somewhat diminished damask scent as in big blooms such as 'Alec's Red'.

He distinguished and described a number of rose scents in addition to damask. One he tentatively called nasturtium, though agreeing that this was not really an accurate description for the peppermint spicyness of 'Pink Favourite' and 'Peer Gynt'. Orris-violet was his name for the slightly sharp, lingering scent associated with some orange and salmon roses such as 'Orange Sensation' and 'Elizabeth of Glamis' though it also occurs in other shades including 'My Choice', 'Dearest' and 'Blue Moon'. Then there was apple, found in 'The New Dawn' and 'Elinor le Grice', lemon in 'Ophelia' and 'Sutter's

Gold', clove in *Rosa* 'Paulii' and the sweet yet slightly musty perfumes of some musk roses such as 'Buff Beauty'. Oddly enough people can be extraordinarily insensitive to the scent of some flowers. I once received an angry letter from a reader asking why I and other writers kept on say that 'Fragrant Cloud' was a scented rose.

The pea family is particularly well endowed with scents though not all are acceptable to everyone. *Cytisus* × *praecox*, the first bloom to flower, has an extraordinary heavy smell which I am at a loss to compare with anything else. I once carried a bunch of it on a train and had to discreetly throw it out of the window when I realised that other passengers were eying me suspiciously. Yet in the garden I rather like it so long as I do not get too close and the same applies to the distinctly foxy smell of the Crown Imperial, *Fritillaria imperialis*. For sheer penetration I can think of nothing to surpass a field of broad beans which can fill a car with their distinctive sweetness even when one is travelling at speed along a highway and would otherwise be quite unaware of the proximity of beans. *Cytisus canariensis*, the genista of florists' shops, has the same refreshing quality but is not sufficiently hardy to be safe in winter in cold gardens. *C. monspessulanus* and *C.* 'Porlock' are hardier but do not fill the air so well with perfume. *C. battandieri* smells as pineapple but one has to approach quite closely to be aware of this. *Spartium junceum*, the Spanish broom, is also sweet scented and a useful later flowering shrub which will grow freely on chalk or limestone soils and is a first rate cut flower.

Finally if you want to fill a sheltered patio with the richest of perfumes and set your friends guessing where it comes from, plant either *Trachelospermum asiaticum* or *T. jasminoides* against a wall. The leaves are evergreen, the flowers small and half hidden but the scent is superb. *Asiaticum* is the hardier of the pair.

CHAPTER VIII

Woodland and Shrubbery

Jane Loudon

TREES AND SHRUBS IN PLEASURE-GROUNDS

In all places sufficiently small to be managed by a lady, without the aid of a regular gardener, the trees and shrubs should be of the choicest kinds. It is quite the fashion of the present day to plant arboretums; and though a place of the kind I mention would not admit of a complete one, a lady might take some genus, or some small natural order to illustrate (as for example the genus *Ribes*, or the order Berberideae), and fill up the rest of her grounds with hollies or other evergreens, so as to form a background to the ornamental trees. The genera *Magnolia* and *Liriodendron* form the hardy trees of another small order, which it would be easy to cultivate, taking care to plant *M. conspicua*, and any other kind that produces its flowers before it does its leaves, with a rich background of evergreens. The almond, which flowers in the same manner,

Jane Loudon (1807–1858) was as keen a gardener and writer as her husband, John Loudon, and achieved great success with Gardening for Ladies.

289

should be placed in a similar situation; and standard roses may also be so placed as to have the unsightliness of their long naked stems greatly lessened by a mass of evergreens behind.

Another very interesting mode of arrangement, where the ground will admit of it, is to plant particular situations with certain trees, which are not to be found in any other part of the grounds; and thus to form what the landscape gardeners call 'scenes'. Thus, for instance, there might be an American ground, formed in some shaded hollow, and planted with rhododendrons, azaleas, and kalmias. All these plants require a light peaty soil, and a shady and somewhat moist situation. In another part of the pleasure-grounds there might be some alpine scenery, with pines and firs, and particularly larches, interspersed with a few birch trees, planted in dry sandy soil, on hilly ground. The deciduous cypress and weeping willow should be near water, as should the common willow, nearly all the poplars, and the alders. In another place might be a thicket of the different varieties of hawthorn, with a few of the fine large-fruited foreign thorns planted in striking situations.

In short, there are no limits to the numerous and beautiful scenes that might be laid out by a woman of cultivated mind, who possessed fancy and taste, combined with a very slight knowledge of trees; and I think I may safely add, that I do not know a more delightful occupation than this kind of landscape gardening. It is landscape painting, but on the noblest and boldest scale; and it is a source of constant enjoyment, from the daily improvement that it displays. What a difference it makes in the pleasure we have in returning home, if we have something to visit, that we know has been improving in our absence. We regard the trees and shrubs we have planted, and the scenes we have laid out with almost a parental fondness; and a new and daily increasing interest is given to life. I would, therefore, most earnestly entreat my readers to study trees and shrubs; and I do assure them that they will find themselves amply repaid, not only by the pleasure they will have in landscape gardening, but in the additional enjoyment their accession of knowledge will give to every country walk and ride that they take.

There is, however, one great drawback to the pleasure that may be anticipated from planting an arboretum, or even an illustration of any particular order or genus; and this is the very great difficulty that exists in procuring plants true to their names. Nurserymen put down a great many more names in their catalogues, than they have different kinds of plants; and thus the same plants, like the actors in a country theatre, are often made to perform under a great many different names in the same piece. I have heard of instances where 12 or 14 species were named in a catalogue, though the nurseryman only possessed three or four, which, when wanted, were made to do duty under all these different names. Almost all nurserymen are alike in this respect, and the only real cure will be an increased knowledge of trees and shrubs on the part of the purchasers, which will render it impossible to impose false kinds upon them. In the mean time I may mention that Mr. Loudon has found the trees and shrubs in the nursery of Messrs. Whitley and Osborn, at Fulham, more correctly named than in most others.

In planting masses of trees and shrubs, great care should be taken to hide the dug ground around them, which always forms a scar in the landscape. The best way of doing this is to cover all the space between the shrubs with grass, and to tie down the branches of the trees to pegs or stakes fixed in the earth, so as to make the trees feather down to the ground. Where this cannot be accomplished, on account of the expense of clipping the grass, for it cannot be mown among the trees, ivy may be pegged down over the dug ground, or evergreen trailing roses, of which there are many kinds especially adapted for this purpose. There is one general rule relating to the planting of trees and shrubs, which can never be too often repeated, or too strongly enforced – it is, never to suffer them to be planted too thickly. This may appear a very simple rule, but it is one, which it is very difficult to put in practice, as all the persons employed in planting are generally opposed to it. The nurseryman, of course, wishes to dispose of his plants, and the gardener to produce a good effect as soon as possible, nay, even the proprietor cannot help feeling the bare and desolate appearance of a new plantation, where the shrubs are placed at proper distances. There are but two remedies for this: either planting so as to produce an effect at first, and then thinning out half the plants, beginning the second or third year; or planting the shrubs at the proper distances, and covering the ground between them with some trailing plant pegged down.

Nothing can look worse than a row of tall trees, which were evidently planted for a screen; but which, so far from answering the intended purpose, admit the light between their slender naked stems, which afford no more concealment than the open rails of a paling. Mr. Loudon observes, in one of the numbers of the *Gardener's Magazine*, that the quickest way of thickening a plantation in this state is, if the trees are deciduous, to cut every alternate tree down, in order that the stools of the fallen trees may send up young shoots; but if any of them have branches within six or eight feet of the ground, by taking off the tops of the trees, and tying down these branches, the plantation may be thickened, without cutting any trees down.

A weeping ash is a very ornamental tree on a lawn, but unless it is well trained, it loses its effect. When trained to a wooden frame, the hoops and rods of which it is composed are seldom strong enough to sustain the weight of snow which falls on the summit of the tree in severe winters, and if they give way in any place, the boughs are frequently broken. In the arboretum which Joseph Strutt, Esq. has lately most liberally presented to the town of Derby, there is a very fine weeping ash, for which Mr. Strutt has had an iron frame-work made. The iron rods are light and elegant, and yet so strong that they are in no danger of giving way under any weight of snow that is ever likely to fall on the tree. The iron frame work has been coated over with gas tar, to preserve it from rust, and it looks exceedingly well.

William Robinson
THE WOODLAND GARDEN

William Robinson (1838–1935) was the great exponent of the wild garden. Of his many books, the best known is The English Flower Garden. *Apart from his own garden at Gravetye Manor, Sussex, he designed many others including Shrublands, near Ipswich.*

In several country places I have lately seen woods of singular tree beauty – woods with all the natural advantages of soil, air, and country, and well placed near the house – a charm which does not always occur. There was all the dignity and grace of trees planted with loving care by past owners; but such woodland is very often neglected until ugly plants such as Nettles, Dog's Mercury, and, most hateful of all, the Common Elder and Privet take possession.

In such woods covert is sought for game, shelter and other ends, and there is no reason why it should not take a beautiful form. No situations about a country house offer such opportunity for beauty as these woodlands, where we can mass and enjoy many of the most beautiful of native and other shrubs for which there is not always room in the garden. They would be far better in the woodland garden than in the usual mixed shrubbery; and while good wholesome undergrowth does not interfere with the trees, but rather helps them, the growth of weeds and Grass rankling over the ground is hurtful in many ways. Some of the finest natural woods have a natural undergrowth of evergreen shrubs, as for instance in the Californian forests with their undergrowth of lovely evergreens, the trees rising with clean stems far above them.

The first aim should be to get rid of the weedy and noxious enemies by light grubbing, and then plant in bold free masses things that will fight the weed. I know of nothing that cleans the ground below it more thoroughly than the Red Dogwood; its foliage is so close and it gives bright winter-effect in wet places beside streams and ponds, and will also grow away from water.

Our native Holly, Box, and Yew make much more beautiful and effective groups than the weedy shrubs which usually have possession. The common evergreen Barberry is a beautiful covert shrub, with its foliage all through the winter and its fragrant blooms in spring, but it should be held together in natural masses, and close enough to keep the ground clean. The common way of having coarse Laurels clipped down to one level is ugly, and there are so many things that give a very fine undergrowth without clipping. The large Partridge-berry (*Gaultheria Shallon*) of North America, as it may be seen at Coolhurst – what an excellent undergrowth it makes, and yet how little grown!

Evergreen Barberries might alternate with our common native Barberry, so brilliant in fruit, and wide masses of Aucuba and Yellow Azaleas, now so easily raised. Such excellent evergreen covert plants as Cunningham's White Rhododendron can be brought on their own roots. Rhododendrons are a host in themselves, but there is too much of the dull *ponticum*. We should encourage the bright-coloured kinds such as *Jacksonii*, and never put in a grafted plant. There are splendid kinds in the country if people will only layer them, or even allow them to layer themselves, as they often will when let alone. Kinds good in colour can be picked out in flowering time at the lowest rate the nursery trade offers. Only hardy things should be used, and in southern places we may have a little more variety of evergreen undergrowth. Some of the new Bamboos would help very much for effect, such as *palmata*, which keeps the ground clean and is fine in habit. In open and poor soils the Heaths would tell well, such as the Cornish Heath, and the Common Heather in its stoutest varieties. Sweetbriers, Wild Roses, and Brambles, would naturally be welcomed, and it would be well to encourage native bushes like Viburnum, Sloe, and the beautiful Spindle-tree (*Euonymus europaeus*), and plants such as Solomon's Seal and the Ferns, which often form a pretty undergrowth in woods. Wherever natural covert exists, as it often does in large woods in the shape of tall evergreen Sedges like *Carex paniculata*, or masses of Bracken, it should be kept, as there is no better covert.

The planting of covert had better be done from early autumn until March or April, but much may be done throughout the year in clearing the ground and getting rid of weedy plants. That is even better done in summer, as we are then more certain to make an end of them than in winter. When planting Holly in places overrun by rabbits it will be necessary to wire, and if we plant in large, bold masses, as we ought, the wiring is easier. Happily rabbits do not attack Box, which is a great gain when seeking covert for hungry soils or poor dry bluffs.

29   BODNANT, GWYNEDD. 1920

Looking over the Lily Pool Terrace towards the Woodland Garden. In addition
to the superb formal gardens, Bodnant has one of the most interesting woodland
gardens in Britain with special collections of trees and shrubs introduced by
plant hunters during the early years of this century.

Charles Eley
HEDGES

Charles Eley VMH (1872–1960) was a successful amateur gardener who specialised in growing rhodo-dendrons and other Himalayan plants at East Bergholt in Essex. He subscribed to George Forrest's plant hunting expeditions and was closely associated with J. C. and P. D. Williams of Caerhays and Lanarth in Cornwall.

It is obvious that hedges will be required for different purposes and will be of several kinds. I propose to deal briefly with them under three headings: as boundaries, as screens, and solely as objects of beauty.

Few things are more important to the appearance of a garden than a suitable and definite boundary – gardens that slither away into the surrounding land have, at best, an unfinished appearance. Sometimes a sunk fence can be successfully used as a boundary, but in many cases, where I have seen it used, a hedge of suitable height would, to my mind, have been preferable. When considering a boundary hedge the first matter to be decided is whether or not it is required as a defence against stock and possibly other marauders. For this purpose, choice is very limited.

The best 'all-rounder' is unquestionably Common Thorn (*Crataegus monogyna*). It thrives in almost any soil, and possibly was called 'quick' because it rarely dies, no matter how brutal may be the mistreatment of it. With little care it is quite impenetrable and it can be well kept at any reasonable height. But in replacing or mending up an old hedge of 'quick' it is inadvisable to use the same species: there is an ancient warning against 'putting quick on quick'. For this particular purpose the Cherry Plum (*Prunus Myrobalana*)[1] or Blackthorn (*Prunus spinosa*) is probably the best choice. But most gardeners will be anxious to possess for their garden a hedge that appears to have more claim to beauty and to be less 'ordinary' in appearance than 'quick'.

Beech (*Fagus sylvatica*) makes a beautiful and effective hedge on medium soils and on those that are chalky, and its rich brown leaves – long retained – produce in winter a deliciously warm contrast to chilly surroundings. On heavy soils, for example London clay, Hornbeam (*Carpinus Betulus*) should be used instead of Beech, and indeed the Hornbeam, except that its yellow leaves in autumn (retained like those of the Beech) are not quite so attractive, makes a more accommodating and denser hedge than Beech, for which, indeed, it is

---

[1] *Prunus cerasifera*

often mistaken. Unfortunately it is less easy to get and is more expensive. Hornbeam will not thrive on chalk, in which peculiarity it is in direct contrast to Beech.

If the bark of Hornbeam is scraped on one side and bound to another branch similarly treated they readily unite, and in this way a veritable criss-cross barricade can be created. To effect this most easily, the plants can, in the first instance, be planted crossing one another at a suitable slant. Hornbeam is more twiggy than Beech and lends itself to topiary work of an unusual character.

Loudon calls attention to the extensive use of Hornbeam for hedges in France and in Germany, and declares that the density and height at which a Hornbeam hedge can easily be maintained gives protection equal to that of a wall.

Unfortunately, both rabbits and horses eat and gnaw Hornbeam greedily.

Hornbeam is easily raised from seed, and if anything like a reasonable demand arose it would soon be obtained at sizes and prices that would suit everybody.

To repeat, the deciduous plants most suitable for a defence against stock are these three – Common Thorn, Hornbeam and Beech, the latter two being the more ornamental. To these might be added the Cherry Plum (*Prunus Myrobalana*) and the Sloe (*P. spinosa*), but the former takes longer to get solid and the Sloe even longer still, and when established is prone to spread laterally – a great inconvenience.

Of evergreen plants the only plant that can be recommended for use against stock is Holly (*Ilex Aquifolium*), but it must be borne in mind that Holly does not thrive in cold stiff soil and that rabbits are fond of it. Contrary to popular opinion, a Holly hedge does not take very long to grow nor need it be costly if, as is best, quite small seedling plants are obtained, which was easy and cheap enough before the war and will be so again before long. But in every case it is obvious that a temporary protection will be required at first and this is most easily and most cheaply effected by a wooden post and wire fence or post and rails, which can be quite neat. The posts need not be rough and unsightly, and, at any rate to me, such a fence is preferable to iron hurdles, whether of the ornamental variety or otherwise.

Chestnut close pale fencing is cheap and affords a certain amount of valuable shelter, but it is hideous to look at and its associations with allotments do not quicken one's sympathy towards its use.

This question of a temporary fence in connexion with hedges brings me to what, to me at any rate, seems to be one of the most important problems in connexion with hedge planting under the conditions that usually prevail. Whenever a house is built in a town, or near one, or indeed far away from other dwellings, it is natural for the owner to desire to make at once the boundaries of his property. This is usually achieved either by a wall, high or low, or some sort of close fencing – often a combination of both – and to it a hedge is added. The important thing to remember is that any live fence should be planted a proper distance – at least 2 feet – from the erection that marks the boundary. And 3 feet is far better than 2 feet. But this question of distance *must* be governed by whether the fencing is to be a permanent erection or whether it is intended to remove it as soon as the live fence is fit to take its place. Hundreds of thousands of miserable looking barriers testify to the fact that this essential point was never considered, and if one discovers a case where the correct steps were taken in the first instance, it is frequently apparent that the fencing has not been removed at the right time: it is left there to crowd and destroy the beauty of the hedge and to make the task of putting things right, even if possible, a long and unsightly business.

This question of distance brings me to the consideration of the proper shape of a hedge, since it is clear that all questions of measurement hinge upon shape. Leaving rough or 'wild' fences out of account, there is indeed only one shape that a good hedge can be allowed to assume. It must be substantially wider at the base than at the top: in section it should assume the shape of a capital letter 'A' with a square or rounded top.

No plant will successfully stand clipping for any length of time unless it is allowed at least 6 inches on each side of the main stem. Therefore, when established, the top of the fence will be at least a foot wide, and since the sides must take the form of a gentle outward slope right down to the base, it follows that the desired height of the fence, when established, will govern the distance that the plants must be placed away from any fence or barrier near which they are to be planted.

Also it must be remembered, when making these measurements, that a living plant cannot be maintained at an exact width, but that some slight addition to the width will have to be allowed at each clipping if good appearance is to be maintained. To repeat in another way, it should be clear that a fence that is to be maintained at 4 feet 6 inches, since the top must be 1 foot wide, will require the base to be about 3 feet – that is to say, 18 inches on each side of the main stem. If the desired height be 6 feet (or more) then the allowance for the width of the base must be correspondingly greater. Moreover, the question of maintenance should be considered, and there is no doubt that whenever possible sufficient room should be allowed between the fence and the plants to enable clipping and cleaning to be performed.

Perhaps I ought to add that the reason for insisting upon a distinct outward slope to all hedges is that, without it, it is inevitable that in course of time gaps will appear at the base and in the sides owing to the drip and shade caused by the overhang of the top, and weeds and grasses will then more easily encroach at the base to the detriment of the health and appearance of the hedge.

Far too often the attainment of success is greatly delayed by indifferent preparation of the ground. For reasons given above, hedges are often too hastily planted, and such haste does not mean speed. It is a good plan to trench the ground in the spring at least 2 feet in width – but the wider the better – and keep it clean until the plants are put in during the following autumn. It is helpful to make the trenched ground wide – say 5 feet – and to plant it with potatoes.

The crop will compensate to some extent for the extra labour, and the resultant benefit to the soil is considerable. Another good procedure is to sow the trenched area with mustard and to dig it in green. When planted and until such time as maturity has been reached, a hedge should be kept absolutely clean from weeds, and in this connexion I will add flowers also, since newly planted hedges are frequently seen being almost checked by greedy annuals and herbaceous plants. If the owner feels that brown earth is a sight that cannot be borne, then he should content himself with a few bulbs – the fewer the better. The plants should be small and well-rooted, the smallest obtainable will give the best and quickest results.

There is room for some argument when considering the distance that the plants should be apart. I will content myself with saying that they should not be less than 1 foot apart: it must be borne in mind that no plant will develop quickly if its roots have not adequate room to expand, and if adjoining soil is robbed by the roots of others. Obviously, the larger the plant the more room should be allowed at the start. Of this, more later. However, if the trenched ground is really wide – say 5 feet – then, if it is desired to plant closely for appearance's sake at the start, larger plants can, without much risk of being checked, be planted closer together as the roots will have a chance to expand laterally.

Remember that for good and rapid results the plants must be kept quite clean of weeds until maturity is reached, after which very little annual attention will be needed.˙

To many these remarks will, I fear, seem absurdly obvious, but I have made them because one so often sees hedges planted in small and shallow trenches. The planters seem to have forgotten that they are really planting *trees*.

As regards the cutting back of Quick, Beech, and Hornbeam, if deemed necessary, the best results will be got by cutting back to about 5 inches two years after planting. The principle of cutting back the young plants at the time of planting is detrimental to a vigorous start. As a general rule, the tops or leaders should not be touched until the desired height has been reached: the side-shoots being kept to proper shape with a knife.

Passing on to the consideration of hedges, within or around the garden, which are not required to afford protection against stock, but as screens or as shelter or as an object of beauty, one plant – the Yew – most clearly will rightly claim to be considered first. I assert this boldly because it is a fact that a well-kept Yew hedge will attract more attention and more admiration from that type of casual visitor who regards a garden as he or she would a room that should be furnished beautifully. Such critics have a peculiar value and should not be disregarded.

It is a common delusion that Yews are of slow growth. If kept clean, and, as soon as they have got going, given a handful of nitrate of soda mixed with sand (the application being made when the soil is damp in April, May and June), the result is astonishing. Care must be taken not to dust the mixture on, or too close, to the stems. A single leader should be maintained and the sides pruned just enough to promote even side-growth. With this treatment, and plants about 6 inches high, a good hedge 4 feet 6 inches high can be achieved in about seven years.

To Holly (*Ilex Aquifolium*) the second place must be accorded, but Holly never produces the 'finished' effect that one associates with Yew: it is more cheerful but lacks the severity that makes Yew so effective. In the dry eastern counties, where self-sown Holly grows freely in the hedges, it is unquestionable that the best time for planting it is at the end of September or early in October while the earth is still warm from the sunshine of summer. In other localities it may be wise to follow the books and to plant in May; I do not know, but I will add that I am confident that many evergreens transplanted in October that are large enough to be wind-rocked are lost from that cause rather than the time of planting being at fault. A little thought at the site will suggest several methods by which this danger can be guarded against.

Of Hollies the big-leaved varieties make glorious hedges, and if taste demands a gold or silver one then 'Golden Queen', 'Handsworth Silver', or *argentea marginata* will be found to give good and speedy results.

Box (*Buxus sempervirens*) makes a good hedge and is particularly useful where the soil is damp and shady. There is a variety of *B. sempervirens* the young growth of which is of a blue-green colour that makes a pleasing contrast to Holly or to Yew.

Oval-leaved Privet (*Ligustrum ovalifolium*), invaluable in smoky districts, and *Euonymus japonicus* both make useful hedges, but both have been used to excess and the latter is prone to a disfiguring disease.

Lonicera nitida is now being used extensively, and I plead guilty to having recommended its use in *Gardening for the Twentieth Century*, (London, 1923) but a hedge planted about ten or twelve years ago is now 3 feet high and 8 feet wide at the base, and this in spite of clipping it three times a year. Moreover, as might be expected with a plant of such vigorous growth, it now begins to show signs of getting into holes in spite of sides sloping at about 45 degrees. My verdict would now be: 'Altogether too much of a good thing'.

Berberis stenophylla is a good garden hedge plant, especially where it can be allowed a certain amount of freedom, but it requires care to keep it into a shape that will enable it to display its bloom without getting bare at the bottom.

Berberis Darwinii is even more showy, but tends to get leggy and bare at the base and is not easy to control.

Escallonia macrantha forms a superb hedge and seems hardy on light land if given a quite dry situation.

When a large hedge is required within the garden some careful consideration (except in very cold districts) might well be given to Laurustinus (*Viburnum Tinus*). It has been well described as a plant without a fault, and makes a fine barrier and background if allowed plenty of room and knifed back just enough to keep it in shape. It must be planted in October to avoid serious losses.

Phillyrea angustifolia makes a very pleasant hedge and is valuable in that it succeeds well on cold heavy land.

Bay (*Laurus nobilis*), and its variety *angustifolia* are recommended for cool land: the latter clips particularly well.

Probably only very large gardens will desire to venture upon a hedge of Holm Oak (*Quercus Ilex*), but with time and care a hedge – dense to the ground – of almost any height can be obtained with this tree. Small plants from pots should be used. This tree likes a hot dry situation.

I am assured, and can well believe, that admirable hedges can be made with *Elaeagnus pungens* or *Cotoneaster Franchetii*.

Conifers, such as Douglas Fir, Scotch Fir, Common Spruce, *Thuja plicata*, *T. occidentalis* and *Cupressus macrocarpa* are frequently used for hedge purposes by planters impatient for effect.

None of them can be said, for varying reasons, to be satisfactory in the long run.

Of these, if their use is decided upon, the best selection would be *Thuja plicata*. Prudence will suggest that it should be regarded as a temporary measure only and the plants removed as soon as their duty is done. *Cupressus macrocarpa* commits almost every crime except that of laziness.

Such thorny and comparatively thin deciduous plants as Sweet Briar or Rose 'Conrad F. Meyer' are most difficult to keep clean after they have attained any size.

Before I close I suppose I shall be expected to make a few suggestions from amongst the plants of recent introduction.

Of evergreens, I will cite – *Griselinia littoralis* on heavy land; *Berberis verruculosa*, if both time and space be allowed (I know a plant now 8 feet high); *Ligustrum Delavayi*, a privet of character and distinction.

Amongst deciduous plants – *Berberis Vernae* and *Cotoneaster divaricata*; with a suitable amount of knifing back both these plants would give a very handsome hedge of wide and ornamental character and dense to the ground, but plenty of room would be required.

I have almost certainly left out many things that I ought to have mentioned, and in the favoured West of England numerous splendid plants are turned into amazing hedges. My remarks must not be regarded as applying to cold districts in the North of England.

In conclusion I would urge that there is little consolation in using a plant of rapid growth unless it results in a permanent hedge of the first class.

Above all, remember that hedges should never be cramped for room nor treated as mere indications of a boundary, but regarded as objects of great beauty that are worthy of every attention.

Gardeners, whom fate or temperament impels to become migrants, should make it a matter of virtuous pride to leave behind in each of their gardens some worthy mementoes of their transit.

Such a memento may well be a hedge.

30   SCOTNEY CASTLE, KENT. 1928

The view over Castle Hollow, showing the wonderful contrasts of shape and texture created by skilled woodland planting around the romantic ruins of a fourteenth-century moated castle. The original planting in 1842 was on advice from William Gilpin and the castle is Christopher Hussey's birthplace.

303

M. Haworth-Booth
PLANTING, FEEDING
AND WEEDING

*Michael Haworth Booth
(1896–   ) has designed
over seven hundred
low-maintenance
gardens, where a
foreground of vivid colour
harmonises with a longer
view of the countryside.
He is the author of three
books on shrub
gardening.*

There are few pleasanter tasks than the unpacking of a newly arrived bale of flowering shrubs. Yet at times this keenly awaited event is marred by curses and imprecations as needlessly smashed branches and mutilated roots come to light, apparently betraying that either a shortage of skilled shrubmen has led to unskilled labourers having to be employed, or that we have been supplied by some travel-worn importation from a foreign nursery.

How easily, when watching men at work among plants, one tells at a glance the hopeful from the hopeless. For there is a great gulf fixed between the cruel, jerking, thoughtless, flapping hand and the tender, knowing hand that moves precisely, governed by the mind, gentle, even at speed, in smoothness and sensitivity. And all is yet not altogether plain-seeming for, judged in movement alone and among tender things, it may be slender lily fingers that appear brutish and cruel and Hodge's gnarled paw a poem of gentleness and grace.

Carefully, then, let the strings be cut and guardian stakes removed, the wrappings eased away until, after yet another cutting of strings, the shrubs may be severally lifted forth and duly appraised. If they are not to be planted forthwith they must be 'laid in' in a shady sheltered spot, the roots well covered with earth or leaves until planting time.

Only small deciduous trees with bare roots may, of course, be carried by the stem. An evergreen, with proper ball of soil as all such plants need for certain re-establishment, will have the main weight of the ball taken with a hand underneath whilst the other supports the stem. When too large for this the ball is placed on a sack and two men can then manage it well enough. For the largest size or 'four-man' plants, such as big Rhododendrons, we use two 3 foot by 1 foot builder's planks each with a rope lug at each end. The plant is first levered over on to its side and the planks then pushed under so that when lifted the four lugs will take the weight evenly. Usually such a monster is mostly slid to his destination along planks on the ground.

If the ground is not frozen and the time propitious, the next stage toward planting, that of the selection of the site, can now be proceeded with. In dealing with flowering shrubs, matters are not at all the same as in the vegetable or herbaceous garden, whose inhabitants are much more inured to unnatural conditions. We need to know something of the natural habitat of our species if we are to place it where conditions give it the best chance of growing freely to perfection. It may be an inhabitant of either the desiccated scrub-desert or 'Maquis', the sheltered but sunny forest clearing, or again the shadier, damper depths of the forest. Yet so great is the amazing variation of climate between the various parts of even quite a small garden that once we understand the habitat-requirements of a species and know the points of our own ground we can place it with vastly increased prospects of success. One is apt to forget that while we are lying snug and warm in our beds within the house, the plant must fight the howling wind and frost all through the winter.

A few feet this way or that may make all the difference, and as, before planting, it is often a case of 'now or never' it is well to consider carefully the incidence of sun and wind upon the site proposed for a tender shrub. It is best to place it a little above a clearer space of lower ground, so that the heavy frost may slide down and away below rather than sit, like some baleful broody hen, upon the victim helplessly stuck in a hollow.

In the old type of mixed shrubbery border I have seen *Buddleia alternifolia*, a desert plant, placed next to *Rhododendron Falconeri* from the dampest forest depths. When, simultaneously, the Buddleia expired from damp and the Rhododendron from drought there were surprised and angry grumblings and talk of 'pernickety miffs'. Yet only a few yards away from the discomforts of the arbitrary bed there was a little hot, sandy bank on which the Buddleia would have broiled happily, whilst on the other side, a dank overshaded corner would have provided the dim humidity craved by the Rhododendron.

After aspect comes the question of soil and, here again, all is changed, for shrubs, strangely enough, care little for the kitchen-garden mixture that old beds and borders provide. In former times the system was to mound up these beds with richly manured, and even frequently limed, heavy soil and trust that none of the shrubs would object to taking this *table d'hôte*. Actually such soil tends at the best to produce excessive soft growth with dearth of bloom and, among the autumn leaf-colouring shrubs, a tendency not to colour properly, whilst the lime-haters, which are legion, dislike it as intensely as would be expected. Consequently whenever, in making-over old gardens, such beds are found there need be no question of feeling bound to fill these results of *quondam* hard labour with shrubs, but they can be turfed over without the smallest compunction. For whereas in the ordinary garden Nature is too often looked upon as a monster to do battle with, in the shrub garden she should be rather the presiding deity never to be outraged or flouted, but rather wooed as a powerful friend and ally.

The natural soil of the particular spot selected can be made quite as suitable and probably more so. For, now that we group our shrubs together properly, we can take a leaf out of the rock gardener's book and feed each species of shrub *à la carte* with a mixture suited to its exact requirements. This was of course almost impossible with the old mixed beds, where many kinds were jumbled up together.

It can safely be said that there is no better soil for a shrub garden than a sandy loam rich in humus. Sand even of the poorest is much to be preferred to clay, for it is easily worked and enriched and hardly any shrubs object to it. Indeed "Possession turns sand into gold", as the Ascot gardener remarked as he put the finishing touches to his planting of *Azalea* 'Unique'!

A generous-sized hole must be taken out and the soil thoroughly broken up to a good 2 foot depth*. No manure is really needed except in naturally very poor soils or those whose fertility has been exhausted by gardeners yearly sweeping away the natural food of fallen leaves, but the addition of leaf-mould, and a few inverted meadow-turves chopped up in the bottom of the hole, is always a good plan. When planting a Rhododendron, if leaf-mould is not available a generous dosage of peat mixed in with the soil, and a few shovelfuls neat around the actual ball, are of the greatest advantage. Furthermore the plant should, it will be remembered, be set a little lower in the ground than before to prevent suckering of the stock. The saucer thus formed makes watering, sometimes necessary in dry spells, a much easier matter than it would otherwise be. Indeed in making any bed for Rhododendrons or Azaleas the soil of the bed should be kept slightly lower than the surrounding ground rather than humped up in the ordinary manner.

* In ill-drained clay soils it may be necessary to plant young trees on artificial mounds, no hole being dug but the roots merely covered with soil from roundabout.

As regards the size: a forest tree needs a hole 6 feet in diameter even though the turf may be replaced afterwards up to 2 feet from the bole all round, whilst a 2 foot Azalea bush will be satisfied with a 4 foot hole. The roots must be spread out evenly all round when planting, and the depth of the tree or bush in the ground neither deeper nor shallower than it evidently grew before. If there is burlap round the ball of roots and soil, unless it can be removed without in any way disturbing the soil on the ball, it is best to leave the covering under it to rot away buried in the soil.

For a young tree a strong stake, about twice the thickness of the bole, should be inserted, preferably with an iron crowbar, before the soil is replaced around the roots. Before starting to put back the earth it is as well to make sure that the stake, whilst set at a sufficient distance from the bole to avoid chafing, yet approaches it closely enough at a suitable height for the tie. This matter of tying is worthy of some little thought, for nearly as much damage is done by bad or broken ties, causing the stake to gore the tree, as by the wind rocking unstaked trees and so breaking the fine feeding roots. By far the best method I have tried is the 'hose and wire' system, although even this is not absolutely fool proof. To secure a young tree, take a piece of an old, worn-out rubber hose pipe about 8 inches long, and a piece of strong galvanized wire about a foot long; thread the wire through the pipe, and then wrap the middle portion closely round the stem of the tree; then cross the ends over, finally twist up the loose ends of the wire round the stake till it is quite tight. If there is any movement cut off a little of the rubber hose and twist the wire up further. This will hold the tree firm so long as the stake holds and, when the tree has grown enough for the tightening band to cause a groove in the young bark, it is usually sufficiently strongly rooted to stand on its own and the tie and stake can be removed and used again elsewhere.

TRANSPLANTING

There is no branch of gardening in which care and skill are more strikingly rewarded than in the moving of established flowering shrubs. Forethought and preparation, extra pains taken and gentleness in the operation, followed by after-care of the patient whilst convalescing, make the whole difference between striking success and total failure. Once the decision to move a shrub is made there should be no delay in getting ahead with the first steps – for every season passed makes the operation more troublesome and perilous. The best course is to prepare the shrub in March one season beforehand by severing the outlying roots all round, at a distance slightly nearer the bole than the diameter of the 'ball' of soil and fibrous roots which it is intended to move. Then a mulch of well-rooted manure may be applied close around the bole. By this means I have sometimes made the roots of a cherry appear to turn back toward the stem in the most extraordinary manner, providing an easily moved mass of fibrous roots of the happiest augury for a successful shift.

With most deciduous trees and shrubs, such as Cherries, Viburnums, Mock-oranges, Deutzias, Roses, Crabs, Laburnums, and Maples, it is purely a question of obtaining sufficient fibrous roots to enable the subject to take hold quickly in the new position, as it is not necessary to move a ball of soil when the plant is in a suitably dormant condition. With the evergreens, as they are never entirely dormant, a ball of soil, with their root system almost intact, must be moved. The compact roots of Rhododendrons and Azaleas make the problem purely a mechanical one and, if slightly prepared beforehand, the same may be said of Camellias.

Pines and Hollies are more difficult in that their roots are coarser and more straggling. Yet, if the fibrous roots can be secured, and the plants are always replanted the same day as they are unearthed and not allowed to dry out for an instant in transit, they can be moved with a surprisingly low percentage of loss.

The mortality of moved Magnolias is notorious, yet again if an adequate root system can be secured and the operation performed at the right moment (such as a showery period in late April) they will often survive well enough. But even the deciduous Magnolias are better moved with a goodly ball of soil, as if the roots are much cut or broken they are very likely to rot back.

As regards the time for moving, this depends largely on type of soil, climate, and moisture. Whilst the optimum time generally speaking is probably late August or September for evergreens, in districts where the soil is cold and heavy equally good results will often occur with plants moved in April. On the other hand, in hotter, drier places exposed to the desiccating spring north-easters, plants are apt to get windrocked and dried out before the new root-hairs can grow and start to support the plant in the new position.

Deciduous shrubs when dormant, that is to say, when growth has ceased and they are hibernating, can be moved at any time between the middle of October and the beginning of April, weather permitting, north-east winds, frost, and waterlogged conditions, needless to say, being avoided when planting.

FEEDING AND WEEDING

It will be noticed that Nature always feeds a shrub by placing the plant food on the surface of the soil. The plant's own anchor roots provide part of the mechanism required to transport the provender to within reach of the deeper roots. I noticed this action very plainly displayed when I had occasion to cut away the ground to a 14 foot deep face of soil in making a tennis court. A big Larch was growing at one point, revelling in the rich 8 inch top strata of humus which was overlying two feet of white sand, below this being another strata of orange sand, and then our normal subsoil of yellow, sandy clay and stones. One could follow the stain of the black humus descending along each of the deep roots of the Larch down the whole depth of the face to the fibrous roots below. It looked as though the almost imperceptible movement of the big roots whenever the tree was rocked in a breeze made a way for water to seep down alongside, carrying food particles from above with it.

When feeding our shrubs the natural method is the best, and food is thus most effectively applied as a mulch in the autumn* and spring. Shrubs that manufacture a lot of flower and leaf material obviously need feeding much more than those of thinner and more parsimonious habit, yet this is all too often ignored. Roses are commonly rather overfed, whilst Rhododendron and Azaleas, which have as insistent appetites as any (and no wonder), are almost invariably starved.

Of all plant-foods for shrubs, leaf-mould is the most invaluable and universally acceptable. At the same time, although some of the more delicate feeders, such as Heaths and Kurumés, often like it well rotted, the Rhododendron, Azalea, and Camellia seem to extract the greatest advantage from it whilst the rotting is actually taking place, apart from the benefit of physical moisture-conservation. That is to say, the dish is best served as mere dead leaves, and indeed this is the most convenient method for all but the tiny shrubs, which are apt to be embarrassed by the size of dead leaves as opposed to a shorter compost. As soon as the leaves fall these need only to be swept directly on to the beds and over the roots of specimens growing in turf. For this work the new rubber-toothed rakes are very effective.

Unless there is a large number of big old trees close by, this food supply

---

* That is, when fresh-fallen leaves are used; for by the following spring they will begin to yield soluble food particles to the soil below.

will, of course, have to be augmented by extra quantities obtained from wherever possible. So little is the value of dead leaves understood, however, that their provenance seldom presents much difficulty. Lawn mowings contain but little nourishment, but are more useful in dry springs as an early summer mulch to retain moisture and prevent weeds than nothing. They must never, however, be looked upon as an effective substitute for dead leaves in the feeding of Rhododendrons. Many hundreds of these unfortunate plants starve a little nearer death annually because some professional gardeners, whose hearts are perhaps in the kitchen garden, remove even the natural mulch of leaves and leave these unused, to rot in some distant forgotten place. In such cases there is a general accretion of happiness all round when the owner takes over the shrubs himself, personally, and leaves his gardener free to attend his preferred kitchen garden. It is certain that no amount of neglect could be as harmful as the rake or broom that starves the plants instead of feeding them. Some shrubs, of which Brooms, Crabs, Cistus, Laburnums, Heaths, and Mimosas are examples, are easily overfed, the effects being decreased hardiness and excessive growth of wood and foliage at the expense of flower. Other kinds, such as Roses, Camellias, and hardy Rhododendrons, can hardly be too well fed.

If a mulch has a tendency to blow about this is often a sign that it is not thick enough. If, after a good foot's depth of leaves is applied and patted down with a fork, then green lawn mowings added over all, there is still trouble from wind, it shows that the bed is altogether too exposed, and the addition of extra shelter at the threatened points should most certainly be considered. Such feeding also eliminates weeding, for few weed seeds can germinate in the mulch of leaves.

Among the Heaths, Daphnes, Kurumés, and miniature Rhododendrons, where only a lighter mulch of peat, pebbles, or even a growing carpet of moss can be allowed, weeds will, however, unless lawn mowings are used, spring up in abundance. Resort had better not be had to the hoe; it is a dangerous instrument in unskilled hands among flowering shrubs, for the damage it can do to surface roots and tender stems is greater than that possible by the action of any number of annual weeds whatsoever. In such places weeds are better lightly forked and hand pulled. If it is true that the amateur uses the fork for weeding and the professional the hoe, then it is only another proof of the adage that no man will dig another's cabbage patch as he digs his own. If weeds continue particularly troublesome in some spot where small seedlings are being grown the effect of a top dressing of 3 or 4 inches of proprietary peat may be tried; this usually discourages the germination of weed seeds and is in no way objected to by the little shrubs. In the wildest form of wild gardening the grass is simply scythed once a year and put over the roots of the shrubs as a combined smother weed-killer and mulch, and it is really amazing how well the larger shrubs will do with no more attention than this.

31   HIDCOTE MANOR, GLOUCESTERSHIRE. C.1930

The Rock Bank showing how sensitivity to scale and growing habits can produce
a well-balanced border from a combination of conifers, shrubs and alpines.

A. T. Johnson
RHODODENDRONS IN WOODLAND

Arthur Tysilio Johnson (1873–1956) was a plantsman who pioneered the style of 'natural' gardening with its use of low spreading plants and ground cover. He gardened in North Wales during the first half of this century. He wrote several gardening books including A Garden in Wales, A Woodland Garden, The Mill Garden *and also wrote for the little magazine* My Garden *many times.*

Rhododendrons have always been treated as woodland shrubs by planters of discretion, but our steady drift towards natural gardening – not due only to economic causes – suggests the desirability of a clearer focus upon these plants from that particular angle. The first lesson we have to learn is that the Rhododendron must be subservient to the wood. We may, if we would, use trees incidentally as shelter or sun-screens, but I am referring to the more definite operation of so introducing Rhododendrons into a wood that, while harmonizing sympathetically with their environment, and enhancing its charm as well as their own, they lend their aid in so enriching a woodland that it remains above all else restful in its native simplicity.

It may be urged that if, in selecting Rhododendrons for such a purpose we exclude the more highly coloured and ornate, so apt to emphasize the exotic note we wish to avoid, we are placing a serious limitation upon our choice. But consideration will soon reveal that this is not so, that we have an abundant assortment of suitable plants. Even if we were to confine our attention to species, many of which, in foliage as well as flower, are more in accord with our aim than the average hybrid, there would be no difficulty in securing any number of appropriate kinds.

In an endeavour to set forth some personal conclusions on this matter I make no apologies for suggesting that *R. ponticum* might give us the clue as to what our objective should be in woodland Rhododendrons. Though we may seldom plant that old species now, there is no denying its charm, more especially when distance lends its enchantment, and this charm, acclaimed with enthusiasm by most authorities during the last half-century and more, has not been shaken by that of recent introductions. What, then, is the secret of its appeal? No one can regard unmoved those long-naturalized colonies of *R. ponticum* which impart such a tender loveliness to miles of some westerly shires. Whether they are staining the high moors with heather-purple, filling the wooded glens with a haze of violet or being mirrored in the oak-girdled lake, these Pontic Rhododendrons blend so sympathetically with the scene that their colour is not less in keeping with our landscape than the wild hyacinth's mist of woodsmoke blue. And it is just this quality in *R. ponticum* which leads to other blues, ranging from a wash of methyl violet to the purple-blues of, say, *R. × 'Blue Diamond'*.

The natural landscape effect referred to may be attempted on any lesser scale by deliberate selection and planting. And in taking the blues – using the term in its widest significance – one might make a start with any good form of *R. catawbiense*, which is better in foliage than *ponticum*, and generally more pleasing in the flower colour. *R. campanulatum* is a fine species and, at its best, a good blue, but I do not place it before the American here, not only because it is so often a bad blue, but it so commonly has a way of looking unhappy and ill-conditioned that I have come to regard it more as a specimen shrub for good cultivation rather than one for the rough life and often rooty soil of woodland. But I must in passing accord full marks to a plant bought many years ago as *R. campanulatum* 'No. 15'. Where it came from I have forgotten and what its origin is I do not know, but it may be what is called 'Williams' Campanulatum Hybrid' and comes very near to 'Susan', if the two are not identical. That it is not typical of the species in foliage or flower is admitted. But it is the best plant under that name that we possess, the medium trusses being a charming harebell-blue in woodland shade and it is very prolific and always looks contented.

To return to *R. catawbiense*, this, like *ponticum*, can be deplorable in colour, but there are some charming blues – or mauves, if you will, and one of these is the old *R. c. fastuosum*. (I have a feeling that to add *plenum* to its name is a redundancy). With a good bold foliage, plenty of vigour in growth and prolificacy, this old stager is decidedly worthy of every woodland planter's consideration. The somewhat lax trusses are more blue than mauve, the doubling of the blossoms is only partial and it is such a good doer that a plant on a dry slope is over 12 feet high, 20 feet across, brimful of health, still increasing in size and providing plenty of layers for extension. Yet it is not so much these more vivid blues – seen also in some forms of *R. Augustinii* and in *R. × 'Electra'*, that I would go in for had I the opportunity of spacious woodland grouping offering a distant effect. This may be a personal whim, but the gentler shades, producing a melting softness of tone, which is the other end of the pole from the metallic and strident, would be my choice. Further, we must be guided by constitution and the problem of obtaining plants. Thus it would be of little use directing the average planter to species or hybrids which are only rarely to be

313

seen in the nursery lists, if at all. As for reliability, it would never do, taking a broad view, to suggest such as *R. Augustinii* and the hybrid, 'Electra', with its *chasmanthum* blood. We must place our money and our hopes on those more likely to do well under conditions not exceptionally favourable and which will prosper with a minimum of care.

Thus in hybrid blues, their colour ranging from a thin sky-blue to lavender and mauve, there is every prospect of realizing our objective, including a quiet life, by using in detached groups such as 'Lavender Girl', 'Susan', 'Distinction', 'Blue Peter', 'Goethe', 'A. Bedford', 'Blue Ensign' and 'Countess of Athlone', always, where possible, checking colour descriptions by the actual plant in the nurseries or at the shows. Then, not forgetting a personal leaning towards paler hues, there are the bluest of the blues, those crosses from *RR. Augustinii, intricatum, impeditum*[1], 'Augfast', and 'Intrifast', including 'Bluebird', 'Blue Diamond' and 'Blue Tit'. There is also that allied variety called, I think, 'Sapphire', which deserves to be better known. These hardy and easily satisfied shrubs, some of which will ultimately make at least 6 feet, are most delightful and great bloomers. But they seem to need more openness than most and I like them best along the margins of sunny woodland walks, or among widely-spaced small trees, like birches, and in such places they rarely fail to do well.

RR. scintillans and *hippophaeoides*, may also come in here among the smaller blues and for similar treatment. With the limited exposure of woodland they will gain in height what they lose in compactness, but they always make charming features when widely grouped. They are early bloomers, especially *scintillans*, but if a Rhododendron planting of any size is to give the fullest possible pleasure and interest surely we must have, not so much great beds of one kind, but threes, fives or larger groups so arranged that one or other will be in flower for four or five months, those in bloom being framed by the foliage of those which are over or yet to come.

Blue is so much a courtesy term in this connection that it is an easy step to rosy-lilacs, blue-pinks, amaranth and kindred tones, all coalescing one with another. Thus, in colour at all events, we have in *RR. yunnanense, caeruleum*[2], *oreotrephes, Searsiae,* and *concinnum,* to name but a few, a range of shrubs which in colour drift from palest blue-white, or mauve-tinted white, to silver lavender and rose-lilac. These of the *Triflorum* Series should be valued very highly for the

---

[1] Probably *Rhododendron Fastigiatum*   [2] *Rhododendron rigidum*

purpose in view, for among them are many of the easiest of all Rhododendrons. They are all prolific bloomers, even under adverse conditions, some are deliciously scented, they are a useful size for limited spaces and do not flower too early. Then in colour those mentioned, even if they do vary, should associate agreeably with the blues on the one hand and the pinks on the other.

Among the smaller Rhododendrons, having in view subtle shades of silvery blush to rose, those of the *R. racemosum* group deserve the fullest consideration. As individuals they may not amount to much, but let them be massed and we can enjoy a delightful combination of delicate tints, one that covers an unusually long period and the plants will carry on indefinitely even under the most trying conditions. A selection should include variations of the type as well as those of Wilson's and Kingdon-Ward's introduction, some of the 6–8 feet rose-pink forms of the latter being very desirable, though smaller in flower. Yet another group which we regard with the fullest admiration is that of which the white *R. mucronatum* is typical – if I may poach in Azalea territory for a moment. Here you have a low-growing, but widespread, bush with a foliage of moss-green which bears large snow-white, sweet-scented flowers in prodigal profusion about mid-May, a willing doer in most soils. But this valuable shrub excels also in colour, its variety, *ripense*, bearing flowers in a most charming rosy-mauve, fresh and silvery. These flowers, moreover, are produced in incredible abundance and nothing, even in Azaleas, can exceed them in their far-reaching fragrance. Of this species there are in currency some poor forms with meagre, starred blossoms to be avoided, and this applies to the coloured as well as the type. In addition to *ripense*, there are several varieties with rose or lilac blotches or streaks, and we esteem them all so highly that we have a considerable number coming on from cuttings expressly for woodland planting.

It is a short stride from the pale bluish-rose tints to pinks, and here in this widely used term we are confronted by an array of varieties which extends from a thin blush to cyclamen-rose, and so on we go to the reds, orange-reds, salmons and scarlets. But I dare not attempt to offer suggestions in the way of Rhododendrons covering so great a multitude of colours. Indeed, that is not my purpose here, for it is not colour *per se* but its use and effect in woodland landscape which is my theme. Colour in itself, as Gertrude Jekyll once said, "is not a positive matter, but one of relation and proportion" – relation to its environment, and this was never more true than in connection with the subject under discussion. Thus the early-flowering *R. mucronulatum* and *R.* × 'Praecox' on close inspection may to many of us possess an aniline hue which is almost hurtful. Yet, let there be a group of the latter away among the grey boles of trees, or within eye-shot of that plum-purple which comes to the Alders in early spring, and that acidulous colour will melt into the scene with a vaporous softness and become a kindly contribution to its most touching qualities.

I have seen much the same result from the use of larger shrubs, such as *R. sutchuenense* var. *Giraldii*, as well as from that admirable woodlander, *R. Fortunei* – its off-white bells palely rouged – from *R. Fargesii* and *oreodoxa*, the shell-pink forms of *RR. decorum* and *discolor* and hybrids of a like kind. But while one's inclination ever turns to the less assertive colours, I would not rule out the distinguished *R. orbiculare*, with its shriller note, nor hesitate to give such a shrub some commanding position, provided it were spared a clash with neighbours by a preferably green or neutral surround. And this applies also to, let us say, the magnificent *Loderi* group, though their most striking quality is size of bloom rather than colour. It is largely a matter of avoiding the error of turning the woodland into a garden. I do not question the right of anyone to do this if they wish, but, as I have said at the beginning, we are concerned here with the more delicate operation of keeping the woodland as a woodland. We must not risk disturbing it with arrogant diversions. Nor may we bring in confusion by overcrowding, remembering always, as Gertrude Jekyll again so rightly says, that "The simpler effect obtained by means of temperate and wise restraint is always the more telling."

There is, perhaps, more jeopardy in the use of those scarlets and hot-reds, now coming into cultivation in ever-increasing numbers, than with any other colour section. Insisting on their prerogative to a place in the dress circle of the border, they are too liable to thrust their demands upon the woodland with cataclysmic results. And if you were to begin making exceptions, as most of us will, in the case of such species as *RR. Thomsonii, barbatum, Hookeri, haematodes, euchaites*[1] and *strigillosum*, it will be difficult to stay the flood. Other colours – deep rose, purple and white – have been recommended by way of assuaging their intensity, but when all has been said, and we have heard of colour sequences leading up to these triumphant high notes – which I should abhor – one comes to the conclusion that they are at their best placed singly in detached positions with a surround of green, using for preference the species as suggested.

---

[1] *Rhododendron neriiflorum*

I once saw a clump of the vivid old crimson-scarlet 'Doncaster' which had for stable mate an equally large planting of 'Sappho', the object being either that of allaying the ferocity of the former or of creating a contrast. But in a wild woodland it failed in both, and the impression gathered was that something in a milky-ivory like 'Dr. Stocker', 'Lady Bessborough' or the rosy coffee-cream of 'Unique' would have been more agreeable than the sharp black-and-white effect of 'Sappho', that is if the red fellow were to have a companion at all.

Yellow, so near to green, is a most valuable colour in woodland Rhododendrons, and I may include those 'whites' just suggested and others which are infused with cream or ivory. These will be appropriate in almost any company, especially within touch of those blues, mauves and blue-pinks. And in yellows and allied tints there is a wide choice from the early *R. lutescens*, an ideal woodlander in habit and leaf as well as colour, to *R. campylocarpum*. From the latter a number of hybrids have been raised, notably the clear yellow 'Lady Primrose' and 'Letty Edwards'. Then there are 'Unique', 'Dairy-maid', 'Mrs. W. C. Slocock', 'Souvenir of W. C. Slocock' and 'Goldsworth Yellow', all of which, and there are others, are some shade of rosy-yellow or apricot maturing to ivory, cream or primrose. Because of their general reliability under any circumstances, their free flowering and restrained colours I would place these hybrids before the typical *campylocarpum*, even its variety, *elatum*, before also such yellows as *R. R. Wardii*, *croceum* and *caloxanthum*, lovely as they un-doubtedly are.

It will have been gathered that I have in these notes steered clear of strong colours, sharp contrasts and other diversions likely to promote a disquieting effect. For this attitude I do not feel that personal idiosyncrasy need be pleaded. Nature in our land – and I have had in mind all along woodland natural and uncultivated – exercises so much restraint in the employment of colour, leaning towards the subtle and suave rather than the garish and spectacular, our senses are more sympathetically attuned to that lower scale.

So in the case of foliage do we find a parallel, though here it is obviously more a question of form than colour. Assuming the undergrowth to consist largely of other shrubs, these breaking up the groups of Rhododendrons, some harmony should exist between each. Thus, while I have never been quite happy in the presence of Bamboos and Rhododendrons, a combination one may see even in some botanic gardens, such shrubs as Hazel, Viburnums, Heaths, Yew, Holly, *Gaultheria Shallon*, Vacciniums, Stewartias and Enkian-thuses, will be in keeping with the majority of Rhododendrons referred to here. As to the big-leaved kinds, ranging from *RR. calophytum* and *sutchuenense* to *R. Falconeri* and those of the *R. grande* Series, these are hardly likely to come within the orbit of the average grower. But should they do so it is manifest that some degree of isolation be accorded them, and I like them best in colonies of one class with nothing more about them than trees of maturity with a nobility to match their own – a reservation in line with the suggestions already made regarding the large-flowered and the more brilliantly coloured.

While foliage, in a general way, need not offer many pitfalls, that it is a matter of great importance in Rhododendrons will be admitted when it is realized that we have it alone for company during the greater part of the year. And in its infinite degrees of colour, dimensions, shape and poise, whether in the off-season or during that period when the young leaf shoots are in many species and hybrids so eminently beautiful in colour and texture, we have a choice without limit. It is to be regretted that foliage may be weak in some of those woodland Rhododendrons recommended for flower colour – in the ponticums and the *campylocarpum* hybrids, for example – but even in the latter some are better than others. Thus *R.* × 'Unique' is as good in foliage, perhaps better, than *RR. oreodoxa* or *Fargesii* in similar style. In the days of the old *catawbiense* and *arboreum* hybrids the general foliage effect was depressing compared with that of today, with the soft moss-greens of many *Griersonianum* crosses, the glaucous-olive of the cinnabarinums and racemosums, the steely blue of many of the *Thomsonii* Series, the full-toned grass-greens of the Fortuneis, the gleaming metallic deep greens of the big-leaved sorts and the curiously attractive mat-surfaced leaden-green, lit by rusty-red, of say, *R.* × 'Sir Charles Lemon', an all-round woodland Rhododendron of the highest merit. And, without touching upon the little alpine species, there are tones in addition of infinite variety, and none of them will be other than in harmonious accord with the average woodland. Not forgetting the part played by that under-leaf and young growth indumentum, ranging in colour from a frosty, lichenous silver and yellow, through fawn to mellow browns and chestnut, they will blend with native hardwood trees as pleasantly as do the conifers of many colours which, with very few exceptions, have entirely lost any exotic appearance they may have possessed.

32 COBHAM HALL, KENT. C.1930

Once belonging to the Earls of Darnley, these exotic and abundant gardens are
now partly owned by a girls boarding school and the National Trust.

319

Patrick M. Synge
COLOURED BARK IN THE WINTER GARDEN

Patrick M. Synge VMH (1910–1982), horticulturist and plant collector, was for many years editor of the Journal and other publications of The Royal Horticultural Society. His books include Collins Guide to Bulbs, The Gardens of Devon and Cornwall, *and* Mountains of the Moon *which describes plant hunting in East Africa.*

One of the factors rarely considered in planning the garden is the beauty of bark in some trees and shrubs and how such plants can be used as focal points at the end of grass walks or near the house. Yet the bark is an interest that will be with us throughout the year. It is not really seasonal, although in some maples and birches it does vary slightly at different seasons as the older bark peels off to show the young bark, which is more brilliant in colour. The placing of these trees and shrubs with beautiful bark requires care, so that they stand out on their own where the sun shines on them and lights them up against a dark background, if the bark is white or scarlet. Those with mahogany bark are best where they have an open light background or one of green grass. Good bark is complementary also to good form and foliage in the garden, although unfortunately there seem to be very few plants which combine these characteristics. Perhaps the arbutus come nearest to it. We have quite a selection to choose from, arbutus, birches, cherries, dogwoods, maples, rubus and willows, so it seems best to discuss them in order.

Acer (Maples). One of the finest of all trees for its peeling bark is *Acer griseum*, the paper bark maple. The old bark peels off in large flakes to reveal the young bark below which is a bright cinnamon-mahogany. The whole effect is of a rather shaggy warm reddish-mahogany trunk. Young trees should be pruned early so that they develop a tall stem free of side branches. I have seen some with very tall straight trunks drawn up by the surrounding bushes but they do not usually show to best effect in such a situation. The autumn colour of the foliage is also good, a strong reddish-orange, enhancing the bark.

Another first-rate small tree or large bush for winter colour is *Acer palmatum* 'Senkaki', the coral bark maple. The young twigs are a beautiful coral-scarlet, very bright in effect when the sun shines on them in front of a dark background. The effect is only developed in early autumn but lasts throughout the winter. It is unique among the maples and a bush that I would hate to omit from any good garden, where there is space. Even quite young plants are effective. The snake bark maples, particularly *A. grosseri* var. *hersii* and *A. pensylvanicum*, are unusual trees. In these the bark is a yellow-green with wavy longitudinal silvery stripes running up and down the trunk. These are particularly noticeable in young trees, and again a clean trunk should be developed. Others in the same group are *A. capillipes*, *A davidii* and *A. rufinerve* and these are all desirable where there is space, although their garden effect is not very different. If there is only room for one, probably *A. grosseri* var. *hersii* is the best. There is also a red-twigged form of *A. pensylvanicum* called 'Erythrocladum'. I have occasionally seen magnificent plants of this but they are rare and it is often of rather weak constitution. Great care must be taken of the graft when young. I have lost two through damage to the graft in its young stages. All of these have good autumn colour also in the foliage in varying shades between butter-yellow and orange-crimson. They make excellent small trees for the smaller modern garden.

Arbutus (Strawberry Trees). These are useful for their winter-flowering and their fruits, but even more distinctive and valuable are the colour of their bark and their curving and twisting way of growth; it is always a delight to look up into the branches of an old strawberry tree outlined against the sky and for these features the common *Arbutus unedo* is pre-eminent. For bark the hybrid *Arbutus × andrachnoides* is among the best, the trunk varying in shades of silvery-pink and cinnamon-red and peeling to reveal fresh tones melting into each other. Once they have seen them few will forget the venerable specimens of this tree on one of the upper terraces at Bodnant. In the western American Madrono tree, *Arbutus menziesii*, the bark adds to its reddish-mahogany an ochreous tinge which makes a young tree very striking in its native forests and also in the garden. In all cases one wants to be able to approach the trunk and even help in peeling off the old bark, so they should be planted near a walk and not surrounded by other bushes since the colour goes right down to the base.

Betula (Birches). These are some of the finest trees for coloured bark of any genus, both in the creamy or silvery-whites and in the orange-mahogany range, and when well grown make most striking effects. Intending planters should, however, be warned that the full bark colour is not developed in very young trees, but gradually spreads from the base upwards. As in arbutus and *Acer griseum*, the colour can be helped by a little judicious peeling or rubbing off of the old bark when it seems ready to come. Our own native silver birch *B. pendula* is very variable in the colour of its trunks but it is usually a beautiful

see colour plate xiv

and graceful tree, sometimes with a fine silvery-white trunk; even more strikingly silver is *B. papyrifera* the paper birch of North America. This in time makes a big tree up to 60 feet and it is surprising that it is not grown more freely. The bark peels off in thin paper-like layers, leaving a smooth stem beneath. These two are quite different in the quality of their whites from those with creamy-white stems which may often have a slightly pinkish undertone. The best of these are *B. jacquemontii* and *B. utilis*, the Himalayan birch. The two are closely related and have some of the most striking bark in the genus. In this connection white is a colour. It is usually better to plant a specimen standing forward near the beginning of a glade since if planted as a focal point at the end, as indeed is often done, it tends to make the glade seem shorter since the eye is immediately attracted to it. This doesn't apply to the mahogany stemmed species. Both the species mentioned, however, are variable and trees of *B. utilis* have been found with light mahogany-brown bark rather than the creamy-white that is much the more desirable. The bark seems to get darker as the origin goes eastwards towards China. Another species with rather similar characteristics is *B. ermanii* which usually has a beautiful pinkish-white trunk merging into darker mahogany colouring in the branches. *B. platyphylla* var. *szechuanica* can also be very beautiful with a conspicuous creamy-white bark. For planting there is probably not much to choose between these Asiatic birches, but it is important to get a good form. Occasionally one sees large trees of them, but more often they make small but graceful trees.

Among those with pinkish or orange-mahogany stems the best is probably *B. albo-sinensis* var. *septentrionalis* and a mature specimen of this with a clear trunk is one of the most beautiful of trees. The trunk is covered with a silvery-grey bloom, and the tones underneath of pink, orange and mahogany seem to melt into each other.

Cornus (Dogwood). The dogwood for winter colour is *C. alba*, named for the colour of its berries. It is a strong grower making thickets of bright crimson stems, especially where it has been cut back and there are plenty of young twigs. The finest form is 'Sibirica', sometimes known as 'Westonbirt'. In this the twigs are a brilliant sealing-wax scarlet growing up to four feet from a pollarded base. It is not so vigorous as the ordinary form but the colour is so much better that it is certainly the one to choose; several clumps of it should be planted to form a group and there will be no brighter colour in the garden all the winter. Once established, it should be cut down nearly to the base in spring. With it may be grown *C. stolonifera* 'Flaviramea' which has bright ochreous-yellow stems and should be treated in spring in the same way. Groups of the two contrasting colours are very striking. Such a planting may be seen at Wisley beside the round pond. Both these cornuses are unsuitable for dry places and do well by the edge of a pond or where the soil remains moist.

Prunus serrula. This cherry usually makes a small tree but it has perhaps the finest shining dark reddish-mahogany of all barks. It is like a finely polished piece of old furniture, and an old trunk kept peeled and rubbed over occasionally with a duster is a very fine sight. It must be planted where the sun will light up the trunk. This tree used to be known as *P. serrula tibetica* but apparently there is no other variety and so the third name is not required. It has inconspicuous flowers but some enterprising nurserymen have top grafted more interesting flowering cherries, such as *P. sargentii*, on young specimens so that one can have the advantage of both bark and flower, an ingenious idea but the results are still uncommon and rather expensive.

Rubus cockburnianus. This is a bramble of great vigour in which the dark purplish stems are covered with a silvery-white bloom which makes a thicket of them a very conspicuous sight in winter. It is not, however, a plant for the small garden, but looks well at the edge of an open woodland or in the wild garden where it can be placed against a dark background. This plant is more often found in older books and catalogues under the name *Rubus giraldianus*. It should be cut back hard in spring so that it makes plenty of young growth, a prickly job. The flower and fruit are not particularly decorative but the foliage is fernlike with a number of leaflets which are white or silvery-grey beneath.

Salix (Willows). There are several willows with very decorative bark. The brightest are forms of *S. alba*. The scarlet-twigged willow is *S. alba* 'Chermesina', often known as 'Britzensis'. A pollarded group of these can make a very brilliant winter spectacle. I well remember one such near the entrance to the Savill Garden in Windsor Great Park, standing up like flaming fires out of the snow. They will grow into quite big trees but to get the most brilliant scarlet effect from the young twigs they are best kept to a short trunk and cut back hard each spring. The yellow-twigged *vitellina*, the Golden Willow, is also very conspicuous. In late February or early March the yellow twigs and freshening green growth of the best of the weeping willows, *S. × chrysocoma*, is a sight to which we always look forward and one which heralds the beginning of the change from winter to spring. It is a hybrid between *S. alba* and the ordinary weeping willow *S. babylonica*. Willows with a white mealy bloom on their young stems are also decorative in winter and the best of these is *S. irrorata*, which also has good catkins. A group of these contrasted with 'Chermesina' can be very effective and such a planting has been made in the winter garden of the Cambridge Botanic Garden. *S. daphnoides* also has an attractive white bloom on its bark in winter and also has large furry catkins. The willows are so easily propagated from cuttings, or even from large slips taken in autumn and plunged in the open ground, that they should be planted much more freely for their colour in winter.

CHAPTER IX

The Wild Garden

William Robinson

NOTES ON THE WILD GARDEN

This term is especially applied to the placing of perfectly hardy exotic plants in places, and under conditions, where they will become established and take care of themselves. It has nothing to do with the old idea of the 'wilderness', though it may be carried out in connection with it. It does not necessarily mean the picturesque garden, for a garden may be highly picturesque, and yet in every part be the result of ceaseless care. What it does mean is explained by the Winter Aconite flowering under a grove of naked trees in February; by the Snowflake growing abundantly in meadows by the Thames side; by the perennial Lupine dyeing an islet with its purple in a Scotch river; and by the Apennine Anemone staining an English wood blue before the blooming of our Bluebells. Multiply these instances a thousandfold, illustrated by many different types of plants and hardy climbers from countries as cold and colder than our own, and one may get a just idea of the wild garden. Some have erroneously represented it as allowing a garden to run wild, or sowing annuals

William Robinson (1838–1935) was the great exponent of the wild garden. Of his many books, the best known is The English Flower Garden. Apart from his own garden at Gravetye Manor, Sussex, he designed many others including Shrublands, near Ipswich.

promiscuously; whereas it studiously avoids meddling with the garden proper at all, except at attempting the improvements of bare shrubbery borders in the London parks and elsewhere; but these are waste spaces, not gardens.

I wish the wild garden to be kept distinct in the mind from the various important phases of hardy plant growth in groups, beds, and borders, in which good culture and good taste may produce many happy effects; distinct from the rock garden or the borders reserved for choice hardy flowers of all kinds; from the best phase of the sub-tropical garden – that of growing hardy plants of fine form; from the ordinary type of spring garden; and from the gardens, so to say, of our beautiful native flowers in our woods and wilds. How far the wild garden may be carried out as an aid to, or in connection with, any of the above in the smaller class of gardens can be best decided on the spot in each case. In the larger gardens, where, on the outer fringe of the lawn, in grove, park, copse, or by woodland walks or drives, there is often ample room, fair gardens and wholly new and beautiful aspects of vegetation may be created by its means.

* * *

In passing through Sussex in March I came upon several fields of Daffodils, and was charmed with their beauty. It was at the time of harsh east winds, and yet not a speck or trace of decay of any kind was visible among them. They were not in tufts or groups as in some woods, but scattered through the Grass, as if they had taken their chance in the struggle for life with the other vegetation, and perhaps been mown down repeatedly. They were somewhat smaller than usual, perhaps owing to this fact, but in point of beauty I have seen nothing to surpass them, as they danced in the sun and realised Wordsworth's poem to the full. Having passed through several parks soon afterwards, and not seeing any of this glorious flower life in its wide breadths of turf, I asked myself why, if this occurs by accident in secluded farms, it should not be made a feature of in our parks here and there? Nothing would be more easy, and no effect of the whole floral year would be more bright or cheering. These Daffodils are fitted to our climate in a peculiar way, and as no other flowers are. Harsh winds or rains may disturb others, but the Daffodil seems regardless of them. The little hardy Hepatica of the mountains of Europe is brave enough, and yet it will be almost destroyed, flowers and all, if much exposed to a long-continued east wind, of which the Daffodils take no notice. Therefore we say to those who have means to enjoy this bold and noble phase of gardening – Consider the Daffodils. It is see plate 34 not only the old and common kind which we may establish, but a variety of other kinds no less beautiful and distinct from the common one. They will prolong the season of bloom, and give a fine variety of form. Of the bolder kinds suited for park scenery I should name *Narcissus maximus*, *N. incompara- bilis* and its forms, *N. poeticus* and its varieties (they succeed each other in blossoming), *N. odorus* (the large Jonquil), and the common kind itself is now obtainable in several forms. Some of its allies, too, are very fine.

*   *   *

Whoever has seen the Snowdrop at home, in the copses and thickets of many parts of England, must have felt a pleasure totally different from that of seeing it in gardens and shrubberies. About a mile from where I live is a large wood, with a green drive up its centre. A stony-bedded brook crosses a portion of it and runs through a park. In one of the wildest parts of this wood are a few clumps of Snowdrops, and although I have as many of these plants as most people, I always go every year to see these Snowdrops in the wood. Now there are hundreds of miles of woodland walks and drives in the kingdom where one simply walks among trees. How interesting such places might be made by planting them with Snowdrops and similar plants. We have all heard of the Lily of the Valley woods at Woburn, and how jealously they are guarded. But plant such things in profusion, and they need not be guarded. Some imagine that flowers of this or any other class never ought to be out of a garden. They may as well imagine that a bird never looks well except in a cage. If all surplus stock of Snowdrops, Crocuses, and even Hyacinths were distributed in the woods and copses, and by path sides in grounds, a fine feature would be added to many of them. The great fault to be found with most of the places in England is that no matter how great their capabilities may be, gardening only begins at the garden gate. What I have said in reference to the Snowdrop also applies to the summer Snowflake (*Leucojum aestivum*). This has some claim to be considered indigen- ous. It is a very hardy, somewhat stately-looking plant (that is, compared with the Snowdrop), and its introduction into damp spots in woods and groves would provide a charming feature.

*   *   *

Even in the smallest gardens there are places under deciduous trees where the Grass grows thin all the year round, and where it is useless trying to renovate it. These are the very spots for Snowdrops, Aconites, Jonquils, Daffodils, Anemones, Scillas, and similar flowers. Take out a good spade's depth of earth, and, if poor, put in some rich soil, then the roots, and then fill up with the old soil. They will make these bare spots look beautiful in spring, and as the trees put on their verdure in summer, the bulbs will go to rest out of sight, and in the autumn the fallen leaves should be left as a protection for them. The worms will draw most of them into the ground, or, if in very conspicuous places, where on the score of neatness they must be removed, put them in pits, and the following year spread them in a decayed or leaf-mould state over the bulbs. There are, however, plants that require a lighter position to bring them to perfection – that look better springing from the turf than in any other way, such, for instance, as *Bocconia cordata*[1], Solomon's Seal, *Acanthus latifolius* and *mollis*, the hardy Fuchsias, like Riccartoni, which are cut down annually like herbaceous plants, *Heracleum giganteum* with its noble foliage, and many others. On mossy banks beautiful effects may be produced by planting various coloured Primroses, single and double Polyanthuses, Oxlips, Hepaticas, Auriculas, Gentians, Cyclamens, Dog's-tooth Violets, Lily of the Valley, Colchicums, and similar plants, all of which will have a better effect so situated than in beds of freshly dug earth, there being no splashing of the blossoms with heavy rains; and there is no need to remove the plants, as is too often the case when used in connection with ordinary spring flower gardens.

see colour plate xv

*   *   *

For every beautiful native plant, like the Foxglove, many exotics are equally suitable, because there are many countries with a larger and more varied flora than our own, while quite as hardy. Some of our most charming flowers occur everywhere, and cannot indeed well be left out of the Grass, as in the case of the Primrose and Cowslip. The Snowdrop is, apart from gardens, frequently naturalised in England and Scotland and supposed to be truly native in the western counties, and it would be strange if it did not occur in gardens too. The Lily of the Valley is a true native plant, said in Hooker to be wild from Moray to Kent and Somerset. Yet, lovely as this plant is, I never saw a deliberate attempt

[1] *Macleaya cordata*

to make it, in a wild state, one of the permanent ornaments, so to say, of a country seat till Mr. George Berry planted out a good deal of it at Longleat some eight years ago. The Vernal Crocus is so freely naturalised in meadows, as to be by many considered a native. The Narcissus is common as a native plant. I have seen meadows of it fairer than any collection in garden or nursery. What I urge is, if so much is done by Nature herself, how much more might be done if Art stepped in and that due attention were given to the many charming things that come from the vast cold regions of the northern world – Europe, Asia, and America. Our own wild flowers are so beautiful and so common about us that their presence is not so important to secure as that of plants equally hardy, equally beautiful, but wholly distinct. For example, wherever the Wood Anemone grows wild, there can be no reason for putting it in the Grass; whereas, the addition of the Apennine Anemone would add a new charm. The subject is a most important one; in this way alone the great question of spring gardening might be for ever settled. Unhappily, the rule is bareness and shaven or naked surfaces everywhere. Not only are there few, except native, flowers in the Grass, but the very borders avowedly made for flowers are bare, and not in winter or spring only, but even at midsummer.

*   *   *

With care in the selection of positions, a good deal of very charming work might be done in Pine woods with such material as the following: The Twin Flower (*Linnaea*), Winter Greens (*Pyrola*), Partridge Berry (*Mitchella repens*), Oregon and Winter Greens (*Gaultheria Shallon* and *procumbens*), Cornish Money-wort (in shady and moist ditches), yellow Peruvian Lily (*Alstroemeria aurantiaca*), *Lithospermum prostratum*, Sun Roses (*Cistus*), and Rock Roses (*Helianthemum*). Of course we are assuming there are open sunny places as well as shady ones. The Mayflower (*Epigaea repens*) does best in a sandy wood under shade; Hellebores will do with goodish soil and the 'pan' broken up. No doubt there are many other plants, but almost all of the above have been tried to my own knowledge and found to succeed. *Cypripedium spectabile* will do well in the bogs, and the showy *Asclepias tuberosa* on the sand hills. A whole world of beauty exists in the varieties of hardy Heaths perfectly suited for this kind of gardening.

*   *   *

In our climate, it is well to have some shady walks near the house on sunny days. So, too, it is delightful in taking a walk around the grounds on warm May days to do so on a sunny Grass walk, just a strip of the turf mown without any further preparation going here and there through the shrubbery, and by groups of Lilacs and fragrant bushes. Even where a bold and well-planned walk goes around the garden or pleasure ground it is easy and desirable to have this. In these days when people begin to see the advantage of putting flowers to grow in the Grass, such walks would be all the more delightful. Not less precious is the shady Grass walk, which is of course cool in hot weather, and which enables us to grow Ferns and shade-loving plants, offering a complete relief to the open sunny walks just alluded to.

33   GRAVETYE MANOR, EAST SUSSEX. 1918

The Lake, an old hammer pond, is the home for many varieties of water lily.
The banks were planted by William Robinson with ornamental waterside plants
and hardy shrubs such as giant heracleum, willow-herb, irises, polygonum
and scarlet balm.

34   GRAVETYE MANOR, EAST SUSSEX. 1918

Daffodils on a grassy slope below the house. William Robinson's principal
legacy to the wild garden must be the naturalising of narcissi and
daffodils in grass.

Walter P. Wright
WORKING WITH NATURE

Walter Page Wright (1864–1940) who came from a large family of horticulturists and writers, was editor of The Gardener *and* Popular Gardening *and horticultural adviser to Kent County Council.*

In many gardens it happens that there is a certain area of ground which does not fall in with the general design. It is perhaps so rough, uneven, and shaded that cultivation on 'full dress' lines presents serious difficulties. Of course, there is no condition which could not be overcome by the application of sufficient labour, skill, and capital. When a railway engineer comes to an obstacle that he cannot level he either cuts through it, climbs over it, or burrows under it. The one thing that he does not do is to give up his railway because of it. A garden maker is not bound either to give up a piece of troublesome ground or to carve at it with slow and costly labour. For him there is always a way round. He can let this be his Nature Garden – his bit of wild, and it is quite likely that he will get as much pleasure out of it as he will out of the fully cultivated parts.

It is not in large gardens alone that these rough, tree-shaded areas exist; they are often found in small ones. But large or small, something has to be done with them. Here, if ever in gardening, is a case for joining hands with Nature, and, partly coaxing, partly coercing, improving on her handiwork.

The paths in the wild garden could not be, and should not be, neat, dressed paths of gravel or turf, which would entail a great deal of labour, and still be incongruous. In sandy or peaty districts the low, heathy growths will suffice for a footing, and practically all that is needed is to clear rambling branches away. The paths should be narrow and winding – losing themselves,

see plate 35

so to say, in the tangled vegetation. In the case of wet, clayey land, some sort of made path must be provided, otherwise the garden would be impassable in wet weather. A couple of inches of unsifted ashes on a layer of broken clinkers or rubble will suffice. In wet or marshy spots a few large stones may be laid as steps.

It must not be supposed that because we are going to make a covenant with Nature in this matter we intend to tolerate a mass of weeds and ugly growths. A wild garden that is a mere waste of Cow Parsley and Crowfoot will not be satisfying. Hence it is that the first step, in the rough as in the cultivated area,

332

may be the clearing away of noxious and objectionable growth, and some amount of shrub thinning and tree trimming. Then will come the introduction of fresh plants. For the most part planting must be done in scattered, informal groups. Plants must grow as if they had originated in the places they occupy, not as if they had been put there.

The Foxglove is a valuable plant for the wild garden, and comes readily from far-flung, uncovered seed. Its tall spikes have a very good effect when rising here and there without rank or order. The Honesty, *Lunaria biennis*, loves to naturalise itself in partly shady places. It is more than tolerable when in bloom, but its main beauty lies in the transparent seed pods which clothe it in the autumn. Violets and Primroses will be charming in the spring. The common yellow Primrose attains to a size, both of plant and bloom, in damp clays that it never reaches in impoverished woodlands. A faintly coloured bloom is sometimes found – a sort of refugee from cultivation – but it is rare, and there is no reason why some of our coloured Primroses should not be naturalised.

The little Hepatica is never so happy in a cultivated border as in a home of its own under trees, and the same may be said of *Cyclamen Coum*, which has a lovely effect when naturalised on a bank. Snowdrops and Daffodils love the grass. The naturalisation of Narcissi has developed apace these latter years, in spite of some failures. Thin, gravelly, and chalky soils do not offer such promise of success as deep loams and clays. Daffodils luxuriate in heavy land, where their roots can strike down and find moisture. In such places they develop immense growing force. In turfing a piece of ground where a colony of Van Sion had been established the author was interested in observing, not only that he had signally failed to extract all the bulbs, but that those which had been overlooked came through the thick turf as early as, and stronger than, plants in the bed which the turf surrounded.

The Winter Aconite is a little early bloomer which may be established under trees, and is very cheerful in the winter. The Dog's-tooth Violet, Lily of the Valley, and Poet's Narciss, may also be named. Amongst taller plants we have the Mulleins (Verbascums), Meadow Sweet (*Spiraea*), Canterbury Bells, Golden Rod (*Solidago*), Monkshood (*Aconitum*), Evening Primrose (*Oenothera*), Snapdragon, and Solomon's Seal.

Bold groups of good, selected plants will be better for the purpose in view than odd representatives of a great many kinds, but if more variety is wanted such things as Borage, Columbines, various hardy ferns, Heaths, Winter

Heliotrope (*Petasites* or *Tussilago*), Sea Hollies (*Eryngium*), Loosestrife (*Lythrum*), Lupins, Mallows, Meadow Saffron, Monkey Flowers (*Mimulus*), Ox-eye Daisy, Plantain Lily (*Funkia*[1]), Rocket, Penzance Brier Roses, St. John's Wort (*Hypericum*), and Wood Anemone may be employed. Periwinkle (*Vinca*) will be valuable for covering bare ground spaces, and Wichuraiana Roses for rambling over banks. As creepers, Clematises, Honeysuckles, and Everlasting Peas will be as useful as any.

In such a rough, shaded spot as is indicated earlier the author founded a wild garden that proved very attractive. It was separated from the garden proper by a row of pole Roses, including such vigorous sorts as Crimson Rambler, Félicité et Perpétue, Dundee Rambler, Ards Rover, Rampant, Euphrosyne, and Dorothy Perkins. At early morn, and in the cool of evening, the wild garden drew many wandering feet from the lawns and borders, and kept visitors lingering long in its cool paths.

---

[1] *Hosta*

35   NYMANS, WEST SUSSEX. 1932

Maze-like paths wind through the heather garden, made by Ludwig Messel.
The scale of planting and combination with gorse, feathery trees and shrubs
make the heather appear more natural than in most smaller gardens.

Sir Arthur Hort
WILD CORNERS

Arthur Hort VMH (1864–1935) was a botanist and gardener with academic as well as practical interests. He edited Theophrastus and translated Linnaeus. His own books drew on his experience of chalk soil.

Wild corners give an opportunity for growing plants desirable in themselves, but whose manners and customs make them troublesome to manage where order and discipline reign. Local and individual circumstances must determine where the line is to be drawn, both as to what is to be admitted to beds and borders, and as to what may be tolerated in less formal surroundings. There are some plants however which may be termed 'cautions', by which I mean plants often grown in and recommended for gardens, which the small gardener at all events will be wise to eschew. If one's plot is of small dimensions and unnecessary labour must be avoided, it is almost as important to know what not to grow as what to grow.

The English winter, despite the trials and disappointments which it inflicts on gardeners, has yet at least one advantage over that of more even climates; its length gives time to reorganize the garden, to get it really tidy, to shift plants about in order to produce newly conceived effects – and to get rid of undesirable aliens. In this class must be placed not only weeds, properly so called, but the things once planted, perhaps by a former owner of the garden, if not by ourselves, but no longer cherished. To garden successfully, unless one has unlimited room, one must sometimes deliberately harden one's heart and endeavour to exterminate what once were treasures. A cynical speaker in a play of Sophocles lays down the principle that one should regard a friend as one who may some day become an enemy, and conversely an enemy as one who may eventually become a friend. The first part of the advice is doubtful ethics as regards the relations between man and man, but it may be usefully followed as between grower and plant. Of course, in every garden writs of ejection are served every year, as the collection improves in quality and good plants have to make way for better. And every year it is wise to divide some overgrown clumps, replanting only pieces. But the question just now is of plants which should be dug out for no other reason than that one cannot afford to grow them.

Take, for instance, that handsome horror the Japanese knot-weed, *Polygonum cuspidatum*. There was once a man who, having come into possession of a nice garden overrun with this frantic wanderer, and having taken suddenly and furiously to gardening, spent several November afternoons in eradicating the pest, whose name he did not know, but whose character he had observed. He then bought a gardening book in which, in a list of perennials suitable for the back row, he found *Polygonum cuspidatum*. In childlike faith he sent his order; and the next spring, as he proudly noted his peonies and delphiniums pushing through, there among them were the ruddy shoots of his old enemy smiling at him again. Now, if he had been better advised, he would have ordered instead *P. campanulatum* or *P. polystachyum*, two beautiful autumn-flowerers of more compact growth, which need, it is true, some keeping in order, but are not, like their kinsman, hopelessly unamenable to discipline. It should be noted that these two exemplary knot-weeds are impatient of drought. There is a form of *P. cuspidatum*, distinguished as *compactum*: but the compactness is only relative: indeed some say that it is an even worse offender.

I am trying too late to harden my heart against *Convolvulus tenuissimus*, the acaenas, and the strawberries. The first-named, which is generally sold as *C. althaeoides*, is a most beautiful bindweed with silver-grey leaves and rose-pink flowers. Others may take warning: were my heart as hard as flint, I could not get rid of it now. It is in very truth a terrible ramper, and, if grown at all, must have a place where small neighbours will not be strangled in its embraces. It is fair to add that it does not climb high, like the bindweed 'of the hedges', *Convolvulus sepium*, but only some few inches: it is easy to pull off the part above the ground, and, if you from time to time tear away all that you can see, there will always be plenty left. Being now condemned to live with it I console myself with quite unaffected admiration of its charms and with reflecting that *C. sepium* and *C. arvensis* (the bindweed 'of the cornfields') are far worse weeds. *C. arvensis* in some parts of the country is called 'lilies', a euphemism which does not mitigate the nuisance.

The acaenas are carpeters of the rose tribe and come from New Zealand. Their close, flat tangles of delicate ferny foliage are pleasant to the eye, but so dense that few things can struggle through them. For the same reason they save some weeding, as only such invincible intruders as the creeping buttercup get much chance. A rough bank may be given up to them, but they should not come anywhere near the choice rockery.

By 'strawberries' (another rosaceous tribe) I mean here wildings such as *Fragaria vesca*, of which there is a pretty semi-double form; or *F. indica*, which has yellow flowers and inedible fruits set in a quaint green collar. I have spent hours and hours in trying to eliminate both of these pretty crawlers: the place for them is hardly even the wild garden, but the wilderness, unless one is prepared to spend unlimited time in curbing their luxuriance. There is however an attractive red-stemmed species with shiny leaves, *F. Daltonii* which I find does not run nearly so fast, and which, for the present at least, I encourage.

There are not many campanulas of which the gardener need be shy; but, if you have not already *C. rapunculoides* (different from *C. rapunculus* which, if not very interesting, at least knows how to behave), pay your vows thankfully to the goddess Flora, and let nothing induce you to acquire it: if you have it, you can but cultivate the Stoic temper. It is comely enough, but it never knows where to stop. I am, I trust, quit of it now, not because I have succeeded in eradicating it, but because when I moved house I left it behind. In Hooker's *Flora* it is said to be a weed of the fields of Fifeshire: there let it stay, and if tall native bell-flowers are desired, let us have *C. latifolia*, purple or white, a fine thing, the Russian form of which, called *macrantha*, is yet finer.

A warning against Winter Heliotrope (*Petasites fragrans*), so euphemistically called from its delicious 'cherrypie' scent, would not be necessary if a more altruistic spirit pervaded horticultural literature. I have seen it in Devonshire growing just outside a garden by the roadside, and it struck me that this was the very place for this incorrigible knave.

In these few, possibly superfluous, admonitions I have had the small rockery much in mind, and I cannot close them without suggesting that the creeping toad-flaxes, if not 'cautions' in the worst sense, should only be planted with full knowledge of their behaviour. *Linaria hepaticaefolia* and *L. pallida* (there are others of the same character), quaint and interesting little creatures, will run for yards among and under stones: they are so small and keep so flat to the ground that they perhaps do no more harm than the native *L. Cymbalaria*, the Ivy-leaved Toad-flax, which scrambles about on old walls. But, if one introduces them, the thing is done once for all: there they will be, and also everywhere thereabouts, till the rockery is taken to pieces and re-made.

Some of the commoner sedums love the rocks only too well: if it were not too late, I would refuse admittance to *S. acre* and *S. album*, not for their lack of charm, but because they ask too much. By all means let them scramble about on the rough bank to which we have relegated so many plants: for the rockery proper there are plenty of good, nicely behaved stonecrops, such as *spathulifolium*, especially the purple-leaved variety, the fine orange *obtusatum*, and, of taller kinds, the white *populifolium*, and the glaucous, yellow-flowered *Palmeri*: while, if something is wanted to run about between steps, *S. dasyphyllum*, a rare native, is prettier when out of flower than the common Britisher *S. acre*.

Christopher Lloyd
MEADOW GARDENING

The idea of allowing areas of grass in your garden to take on the appearance, at certain seasons, of a hayfield, either horrifies or appeals. If you are horrified, you had better not read on, for I shall offer no sort of comfort to the trim minded; I shall not tell them they can safely cut their grass as soon as the daffodils have faded and keep it like a lawn for the rest of the year. They can carry on like that if they wish, but it has nothing to do with my message, which, on the contrary, enjoins you to delay cutting your grass to the last possible minute and a little longer after that – perhaps not till late July or even August, when everything has had a chance to run to seed except the tufted vetch, meadow cranesbill and meadow-sweet. And you will have enjoyed the best from even these.

Gardening in a meadow is a relaxed pursuit. There are no obligatory planting programmes or deadlines; you can do as little or as much of this as suits your inclination. Your first aim is to create the kind of old-fashioned English meadow that was the norm not so long ago when a great preponderance of pasture was permanent; nobody even dreamed of using fertilizers on them. Fertilizers encourage a few plants (useful as fodder, perhaps, but not to our purpose) at the expense of others, which get crowded out. The richest tapestry can be achieved by a starvation diet.

In the valleys of much of Scotland, Ireland, Wales and the less farmed parts of England, you can still find meadows that in late spring and early summer are the greatest delight with buttercups, moon daisies, a variety of handsome (and less handsome) thistles, red and white clovers, bird's foot trefoil, orchids, grasshoppers and bees. The many other insects include butterflies like the

Christopher Lloyd (1921–) lives and works at Great Dixter in Sussex. He is interested in a wide range of plants and has written a regular weekly column for Country Life *for over twenty years. He is the author of many garden books and has an enthusiastic following.*

common blue, the silver-washed, high-brown and pearl-bordered fritillaries and flopping members of the brown family like the ringlet and grayling, that used to be common in the south and east but have become scarce in recent years.

Having first created your meadow with a preponderance of perfectly common 'weeds', not forgetting the grasses themselves, you can then add to the turf other plants, including bulbs, that are not necessarily natives, at least to your district, but that will look appropriate. You can extend the length of season when your grass garden is flowering. In many cases the ingredients will increase their range without encouragement, usually by self-sowing. This is what is meant by naturalising. You give the plants a start, they take the hint and from then on they will do the work for you.

There are, however, certain disciplines that you must observe if you are to achieve the best in this form of gardening. If the turf becomes coarse and tussocky with great lumps of cocksfoot that are only useful for wiping your boots on before you bring the rest of their mud into the house, then the turf will give little pleasure and it will be too rough and barbarous to accommodate, in comfort, small bulbs like winter crocuses or the hoop-petticoat daffodil. Cocksfoot is fine, if you cut it reasonably often and so are other strong-growing grasses; even couch matters little.

If you are unlucky enough to be starting with a coarse, rank piece of turf with a good many docks and nettles and the only flowering plant of any consequence, cow parsley, it may be wise to rid yourself of certain weeds – the nettles, bindweed and creeping thistles, for instance – with a selective weed-killer; and of certain others, notably docks, by repeated and tight mowing for the first year or two. You will reduce or eliminate the coarsest elements in turf by treating it like an ordinary lawn, which is the negation of what I am writing about and aiming at in the long term but it is only a start and this is a difficult though common situation. Turning this situation upside down, it is worth observing that the best kind of meadow can be created from a lawn, already composed of the finer grasses, simply allowing it to grow and to flower.

Another treatment of the area that you find composed of all the most undesirable elements, is nowadays offered by the non-residual chemical, Glyphosate, which is offered in the retail trade as Tumbleweed but is more cheaply wholesaled as Roundup. It can either be applied, selectively, by hand from a small sprayer or dabbed on from a dispenser. Alternatively, apply a spray (in still weather when it won't drift) to the entire area. But the plants to be killed must be growing vigorously. Wherever the active ingredient may touch the plant it will be taken into the entire plant system, root and all. Don't be impatient for results; they take time to show up. With ultra-persistent weeds like ground elder, a second spraying may be necessary some weeks later, where renewed growth has shown up. If you claim that this chemical "doesn't work", it is because you have not used it correctly. Some people think they are being clever by applying a double-strength dose. This is counter-productive. The plant's top growth is "burnt" off instead of absorbing the chemical into its whole system. Always follow the instructions.

A meadow may need to be started by sowing a piece of bare ground. Most of our seed houses are offering wild flower mixtures but these are unsuitable for meadows, where 80% of the mixture should consist of grasses. Better, then, are the specialists in this field such as John Chambers (15 Westleigh Road, Barton Seagrave, Kettering, Northants) and Suffolk Herbs (Sawyers Farm, Little Cornard, Sudbury).

Mixtures that include fine grasses are what you need. They are charming in flower. Red and white clover are also important ingredients but the strains found in mixtures that have been prepared for farm leys usually include clovers that are too dominant and competitive. They will swamp the weaker grasses and other plants. But where a mixture has been prepared expressly for meadow gardening it may be taken that the clovers included will be the wild sorts and not alarmingly vigorous. If they have been excluded from a mixture this is probably because clovers (and other legumes), enrich the soil with nitrogen, whereas it is a poor nutrient status that will foster the wellbeing of the greatest number of wild flowers.

The common weeds of neglected turf will be included in most mixtures; such as buttercups, moon daises, bird's foot trefoil and dandelions (don't you dare to despise this wonderful flower). However, very considerable wastage inevitably occurs when direct sowings are made. So much seed just never makes the grade. It is really more effective to make plantings into your turf, once it has become established. John Chambers is now offering small plants for this purpose. An alternative method which will come cheapest and be the most effective in the end, is to sow selected wild flower seeds, obtainable in individual packets, and treat them initially as you would flowers or vegetables for the garden. That is, either sow them in pots or boxes and then line them out in a spare row to grown on, or sow them in a row from the outset. When established, you can move them into your meadow area. This will give them a flying start and they will soon spread by self-seeding or by their own vegetative take-over methods.

Before discussing the introduction of more precious material and the range of appropriate plants that is likely to succeed, I must say something about grass cutting. The first cut, in high summer, is the difficult one. In an orchard or similar area, you can draw a 5½ foot grass cutter-bar behind a tractor. On a smaller scale, an Allen scythe with front-mounted 3 foot cutter-bar will cope with the longest grass if there is a helper available to follow up and rake the grass out of its way when it is on its return journey. To own this kind of machine which you will only use once a year is expensive. Far better to hire one by the day from a local merchant of farm and garden machinery. You need to book well ahead. We usually ask for one in the last week of July for three days. Most gardeners will feel unable to wait that late. If you've nothing later-flowering than daffodils to worry about, and nothing (like wild daffodils themselves or fritillaries) that you are anxious should ripen and scatter their seeds, then you can cut as early as the turn of May and June or even in mid-May. But this is to admit that you're not really sold on wild gardening in grass at all.

Long grass on steep banks is very difficult to cope with, except with an old-fashioned hand-scythe or a swop – wonderful exercise, this, and it keeps you young. I'd rather be my age, however. Ideally, so as to keep the grasses fine and the turf short for the flowering of small bulbs, you should cut again on August 24 – the day when the first colchicums appear (we are very put out if they are a day early or late, but they seldom are) and again in November, after the colchicums and autumn crocuses have flowered, but before the daffodil and Dutch iris spears are far enough through to be damaged. Thus the turf is really tight against the appearance of the winter crocuses in January. These second and third cuts are no problem. All kinds of machines will cope easily. Generally speaking, it is most satisfactory to collect and remove the mowings, as in this way you further impoverish the turf and thus encourage fine grasses that thrive on poverty and plants that cannot cope with coarse neighbours. We use a mini-tractor with rotary mower and grass-sweep behind it, collecting the mowings. All this grass, whether long or short, we compost. The short cuts I also find most useful for the permanent 4 inch-deep mulch on my rose beds.

Remember that whatever you introduce to your turf it must be able to survive these routines. If it cannot abide being cut in July or November, say, or if it comes into flower just when you want to do your cutting, it is no use to you.

342

Thus I find that *Pulsatilla vulgaris*, the pasque flower, is no use to me as it needs to remain green and leafy throughout the summer. Even so, if I gardened on chalk or lime I would have another shot at it.

Now we come to the meat in our meadow and I will start with the non-bulbous ingredients. You will probably acquire the three basic buttercup species without effort, since they are everywhere but none the less essential for that. *Ranunculus bulbosus* is the first in flower, early in May, easily recognised because it lays its ears (sepals) back. *R. repens* will thrive in boggy places but *R. acris* is the handsomest because of its upright, proudly branching habit. Similar, but having larger, semi-double flowers and growing 4 feet tall is *R. acris* 'Stevenii'. I don't know where this comes from and can find it in none of my works of reference, but it is big and bold. Goldilocks, *R. auricomus*, is usually found in woodland but grows very well in an open situation if moisture is there. I love this flower, especially when it associates with lady's smock, for they flower together in April. Try and get a strain of goldilocks in which the flowers are well formed: they rather specialise in deformity and can carry this quirk too far. Lady's smock, *Cardamine pratensis*, is, at its best, the prettiest shade of mauve. Don't be content with a washed-out strain. This is a marvellous plant for really moist ground. Beth Chatto offers the double form of it, 'Flora Pleno', and this is enchanting. Start it in a border, where it will multiply rapidly and then you can transfer pieces to your turf, but don't mix it up with the single in unfair competition. *C. latifolia* can be had from the same stable. It is larger, bolder (coarser) and of a rosier shade of mauve than *C. pratensis*.

Having got our feet muddy, let us squelch around a little longer among meadow sweet, *Filipendula ulmaria*. Undeniably a thug, but it associates miraculously with that other wild flower of water-meadows, the snake's head fritillary. The latter being early in its growth and flowering, gets it all over before the meadow sweet, which flowers in July (no early cutting, please), bulks out.

Its dropwort cousin, *F. vulgaris* (better known by Bentham-and-Hookerites as *F. hexapetala*, or to those bred on Sowerby, as *Spiraea filipendula*) grows on well-drained chalky turf. The double form is an old cottage garden plant and really rather a nuisance in a border where it flops around, flowers all too briefly and is the devil to get rid of because of its innumerable, earth-coloured tubers. Get rid of it into your turf, therefore, where it will be absolutely in its element.

All your plantings, incidentally, even of tussocky items like this, should be made with a narrow-gauge bulb-planter of 2 to 2½ inch diameter. With this handy implement you can remove plugs of soil at the rate of one every two or three seconds. If the hole needs enlarging, this is easily done. I always have a trug of old potting soil by me and drop some into the bottom of the hole, then firm in the bulb or plant with a bit more potting soil and the best of the top soil from the plug. Bulb-planters of a wide diameter make for very heavy work.

A variety of legumes make beautiful turf ingredients, though I must warn against one of these, the spotted medick, *Medicago arabica*, with trifoliate leaves, heads of mingy, yellow flowers and a sprawling habit that drags to the horizontal all the plants among which it grows. After seeding, it dies and leaves the ground almost bare until its next crop of seedlings germinates in the autumn. This is the moment to catch it with a selective weedkiller – any such as you use on your lawns. One application has a knock-out effect and little else showing in October that matters will be affected by this dose.

I have already mentioned the clovers and bird's foot trefoil, *Lotus corniculatus*. Colonies of the meadow vetchling, *Lathyrus pratensis*, with yellow pea-flowers in axillary spikes, look well and spread underground to make large patches. Of the same habit but really far more impressive is the tufted vetch, *Vicia cracca*, with dense spikes of blue (very nearly blue, anyway) flowers. At the time of writing I have a potful of melilot seedlings (*Melilotus officinalis*) that I long to establish in my garden. The parent plants grow around the car park of my local railway station and they seed freely. This grows 3 feet tall into a widely branching plant with long, slender spikes of soft yellow pea-flowers. If I were on chalk or lime where it grows so abundantly, I should certainly introduce sainfoin, *Onobrychis vicifolia*, which makes such a show with its bright pink spikes.

Columbine is a plant that you usually see wild on the chalk. I did make a half-hearted attempt at introducing *Aquilegia vulgaris*. I brought it to my turf from parts of the garden where it self-sows, but must make another, more concentrated effort. And with *Salvia pratensis*, when I can locate a source. I remember seeing it growing wild in a churchyard in Norfolk when I was a boy of seven, and its mauve spikes looked so much at home among the grasses. This is another calcicole, as so many of the most attractive British wild-flowers are, but the majority take to other soils readily enough. I intend to have a go, soon, with the bright pink or carmine-flowered *Potentilla napaulensis*, which I brought home from a meadow in Kashmir, and other herbaceous potentillas like 'Gibson's Scarlet' should have a good chance of succeeding.

Hieraceum aurantiacum is to be highly recommended. You see it a great deal in turf in the north, though it was originally introduced, it seems. The orange colouring of this hawkweed stands out from all other turf plants and looks effective with moon daisies.

The meadow cranesbill, *Geranium pratense*, is a must in your grass garden (far showier than *G. sylvaticum*). It reaches its climax in early July when in Derbyshire you can see it with meadow sweet, greater willowherb (magenta) and brassy-yellow ragwort in a riotous display. This cranesbill has a number of equally robust cultivars which can all be put out to grass, including the double forms, the early flowering 'Mrs. Kendall Clarke' having pale lavender blooms with darker streaks, as well as the albino 'Album', which comes true from seed. They do not mind being cut down in full growth and will be covered in young foliage again within days. You should leave a corner in which they can ripen their seed and fling it around, for they have a most efficient seed-ejecting mechanism.

The nearly allied storkbills include a showy member in *Erodium manescavi*, of raw magenta colouring and having a long season. It grows to 18 inches, as against the cranesbill's 3 feet. This storksbill seeds itself inconveniently freely in my borders and I have recently transferred it to a grass setting where no colour is better placed than magenta. If I may look forward to my selection of bulbous plants, *Gladiolus byzantinus* is another such.

Doronicums should be naturalised in damp shade where the turf is thin. Their luminous yellow daisies show up beautifully here and do not bleach, as they can in sunshine. They look well with cow parsley but you will have to watch that the latter does not swamp them. Primroses, too, are happiest in damp shade. Include the coloured sorts if you have a mind to. Plant them so that their crowns are an inch or so below the general turf level. In this way they will escape being chewed up by your grass-cutters. The same with polyanthus. Having done their turn as spring bedding, you should plant them in grass where, we have discovered, the stronger kinds will last for fifty years and more.

Cowslips colonise well if allowed to seed and these are as happy in sun as in shade. There are seed strains which include red-flowered forms. If these all interbreed with your primroses the results are usually pleasing. Try and work in some greater stitchwort, *Stellaria holostea*, offered by Suffolk Herbs. Its fragile white flowers have that heart-touching quality that gives you a pang of pleasure on rediscovering them each year.

In the world of bulbs autumn is not the end but the beginning of the year. see plate 36 Our two great standbys in this season are *Crocus speciosus* and *Colchicum autumnale*, the one an autumn crocus, the other an 'autumn crocus'. The former makes a carpet, whereas the latter tends to be more clumpy in its habit. These two are pretty when closely associated because the colchicum makes the crocus look even bluer than it is, while the crocus makes the colchicum look almost pink, rather than mauve.

Other species of colchicum are not only too expensive to be used in this lavish style but they may be unable to cope with dense turf. So I have found, at least with *Colchicum speciosum album*. It existed in turf for forty years but flowered only when I restored it to a cultivated border. However, at Howick House in Northumberland, it flourishes under meadow conditions, so you never know your luck. The chequered *C. agrippinum* however, does cope very well with turf, even with me.

The pale mauve *Crocus kotschyanus* (syn. *C. zonatus*) is another candidate, but there are strains in commerce that are virtually non-flowering. All you see of them is clumps of their 'grass' in the spring. I have been unlucky in this respect. *C. nudiflorus*, though not widely offered, is excellent for our purpose as it spreads into extensive colonies by its peculiar rhizomatous corms. The flowers of this crocus are an intense shade of purple that shows up dramatically against grass, but it is shy-flowering in Ireland and appears to need plenty of sun, such as we of the south-east of England can provide.

As autumn crocuses and colchicums are purchased in late summer, when the ground is rock hard, you will often have to soak the area for eight hours or so with a sprinkler and then leave it for a day before you plant, so that the water can percolate. But if you are moving stock of these plants within your own garden – say, from a border into the grass – then spring, when they are leafy, is the time to choose, as also for winter- and spring-flowering crocuses, aconites, snowdrops and narcissus species, transplanting all these as soon as they have flowered.

It is always a race between *Crocus chrysanthus* (in one of its earlier cultivars like 'Snow Bunting'), *C. tommasinianus*, *C. aureus* and the common snowdrop, to see which will be the first to start flowering in early January. *C. chrysanthus*, with its neat habit and wide range of colours, is invaluable. It will increase both by clumping up and by self-sowing. In the second case, hybridization freely occurs and you will find yourself with many new colour forms. The bright orange *C. aureus* self-sows and so, most notably, does *C. tommasinianus*, with its palette of mauve and purple. These two go well together but the latter is especially telling mixed with the yellow winter aconite, *Eranthis hyemalis*, which also self-sows if it likes you. But it is temperamental; I have never made a go of it. Yet I know a Kentish garden on the chalk where it flourishes with the crocus in that most difficult of situations, under a beech tree. Certainly, it needs thin turf and the same is true of snowdrops which multiply and build up most freely in damp positions.

As we move into spring, the daffodil has, perhaps, too much pride of see plate 34 place, for many people's idea of wild gardening in grass begins and ends with daffodils. If you are out for the big effect with hybrid daffodils, my advice is to plant in drifts of one variety, leaving large gaps between drifts and alternating yellow with white. The gaps should comprise ¾ of the total area, but can themselves be planted up with crocuses, snowdrops and other small bulbous plants. If you buy cheap lots advertised as "bulbs for naturalising", they will be a mixture. Perhaps you will welcome this, opining that you will be able to enjoy a nice lot of different sorts. So you will, at close range and picked, but in the overall garden or park context, mixtures of bulbs can look muddled and ineffective.

The kinds of daffodils that were current in my parents' day, when our orchard was planted up around 1912, were ideal: large enough to splash but small enough to look graceful and unstrained. They weren't over-elaborate and strenuously man-made as are the majority of today's achievements. But where now are 'Emperor', 'Sir Watkin', 'Barrii' and 'Minnie Hume' to be found, except in old gardens? Never mind; some of the more modern cultivars that are still available are acceptable: 'Fortune', for instance (but not 'Carlton'); the jonquil 'Trevithian' is very free-flowering in sunny turf; 'Cheerfulness' is a good multiple-headed late flowerer and most of the small-cupped narcissi are appropriate. Some that you might fancy in turf turn out to be too weak to cope and increase – for instance, the old yellow trumpet, 'King Alfred' and the elegant white trumpet, 'Cantatrice'. And even though 'Thalia' is one of the largest of the Triandrus hybrids it is not really bonny enough in the rough. Of the Cyclamineus group, 'February Gold', however, is unsurpassed for early effect. It is preferable not to associate this with mid-season varieties as its fading will spoil the picture. By the same token, you should keep your pheasant's eyes, *Narcissus poeticus* 'Recurvus', separate from the others as they come so late. The even later double pheasant's eye is no use in grass or anywhere else, alas, as the majority of its buds are blind.

The moisture factor is all-important for the success of naturalised daffodils. They are far more reliable on heavy than on light soils. Pheasant's eyes are apt to be shy in some years, prolific in others; their bulbs multiply only too fast.

With these daffodils, you can grow the summer snowflake, *Leucojum aestivum*, which actually comes out in March and is usually at its peak in early April. 'Gravetye' is the boldest and most effective clone here and its leaves and stature are comparable to those of the daffodil. It flowers later than the other, commoner, strain of *L. aestivum* and will thrive in the wettest places, even partially submerged.

Round the edges and, indeed, right through your daffodil plantings you should have big and bold but earlier-flowering Dutch crocuses. The Dutch yellows are sterile but make clumps which you will divide when you wish to increase their range. The whites, purples and all intermediate colours self-sow and will make a carpet, given a start. If you are planting them (and this holds for other self-seeders) on a slope, you should concentrate your colonies at the slope's top. Gravity will help their seeds reach the bottom and cover the area much more quickly than if you go about it the other way.

Where you are planting on a more intimate scale, I strongly recommend giving all the big chaps just discussed, a miss. Here is your chance to specialise in and appreciate the wildings. Of the daffodils the most obvious candidate is our own native Lent lily, *Narcissus pseudonarcissus*, which you may find listed as *N. lobularis*. Unlike so many of this genus, its blooms open over a long period and, as it flowers mainly in the cold days of March, its season is protracted. Furthermore, it self-sows with abandon. *Narcissus minor* is like the last, a yellow trumpet daffodil, but in miniature and with notably glaucous foliage. It looks too tiny to cope with turf life, but this is not so. The best way with this one is to work up thick clumps quickly in a sunny border and then to split and replant singly, in rough grass, immediately they have flowered. Likewise with *N. bulbocodium*, the hoop-petticoat, which multiplies into dark grassy clumps in a border, whereas it gives up the clump formation altogether in grass and depends on self-sowing for getting around. As the colour and stature of this daffodil are exactly the same as the dandelion's, it tends to be 'lost' in a dandelion-rich sward. The blue of *Scilla sibirica* makes a fine contrast in this context and scillas are better able to live with turf than chionodoxas, though the sparrows set about them in some years.

Among the suitable anemones, our own windflower *Anemone nemorosa* and its cultivars are unbeatable. The common windflower makes dense pools of blossom, in time, from one original small tuber spreading outwards, vegetatively. It grows as well in sun as in shade, in thick turf as in thin. The pale lavender-blue 'Robinsoniana' is a strong clone with large flowers, but I like 'Vestal' best of the variants, with its tightly packed, pure white flowers.

Anemone appenina is pretty well as vigorous and especially desirable in its blue manifestations. Rather taller growing than our own windflower and with more segments to each bloom, *A. blanda* is not, on the whole, vigorous enough for my dense sward, but it is marvellous in its deep blue forms where the turf is thin. I intend to try 'White Splendour', as this does appear to have immense strength. It would also be worth trying *A. pavonina* (parent of the St. Bavo anemones) and the similar *A. hortensis* in thin but sunny turf on a sandy or chalk substrate. My clay produces too thick a herbage but its wetness is ideal for the snakeshead fritillary, *Fritillaria meleagris*, which queens it in April, both the chequered purples and the albinos and many self-sown intermediates. My mother used to raise batches from seed, prick them out in boxes and eventually plant them out, so we have many colonies that have subsequently increased their range of their own accord. What charmers they are. And not too expensive.

The dog's-tooth violet, *Erythronium dens-canis*, with rosy-lilac, nodding flowers and marbled foliage, has no less grace and it builds into clumps, easily divided when they have flowered but which are still green. Thin turf such as you find in partial shade, is best for these. If you have to buy dried off bulbs, life may be tricky as they shrivel quickly, so plant without delay.

As the grasses lengthen, so the plants that we can grow in turf become taller. Since the buttercups, hawkweeds and hawksbeards are all yellow, as are many of the legumes, blue flowers contrast especially well. Our native bluebell is one such, as is the Spanish bluebell, *Endymion hispanicus*, usually listed as *Scilla campanulata*. Its bells are larger and coarser than our species but it is a showy clump-former, and it does self-sow. Prettiest of this tribe, perhaps, is the bulb that you buy as *Camassia esculenta*, though this is probably incorrect. Anyway, it is the deep, rich blue camassia that you want and will probably get under this name. Of the same colouring as our bluebells, its flowers open widely into stars. Its clumps build up over the years, but they are sometimes blind or partially so.

This is even truer of the Dutch bulbous irises when you move them into grass, but they multiply so much in a border that you are sure to have bulbs to spare and the blue kinds, even if they flower only here and there, show up to great advantage. Florists' tulips, also, can become embarrassingly numerous in a picking plot, but look delightful in grass, where their flowers are much smaller and all the more appropriate for this reduction. Blindness must again be expected a good deal of the time. The deliciously scented yellow-flowered *Tulipa sylvestris* widely extends its territory in turf, thanks to a stoloniferous habit, but it is a costive flowerer unless you are able to acquire a free-flowering strain.

Turf is the very place for the white-flowered Star of Bethlehem, *Ornithogalum umbellatum*, where it can and does multiply to its heart's content. Anywhere else it quickly becomes a pest. I often wonder if the meadow saxifrage, *Saxifraga granulata*, would do for me, but I have never had the chance to try. There are still so many untried possibilities.

The bulb season closes with the so-called English iris. We planted a deep purple strain of this thickly in one sunny corner four or five years ago, and in its brief season, it was a magnificent sight at the turn of June and July, last year. But very flamboyant: nothing demure or self-effacing about *Iris xiphioides*.

Which orchids will do best in your turf depends on where you are. Our greatest successes are with those that grow wild around us anyway: the early purples, *Orchis mascula*, in April, followed by the green-winged orchis, *O. morio*, which is purple, too, but with less pink in it and shorter-spiked. Then, in June, comes the most prolific of the lot, the spotted orchis, best-known as *O. maculata*, though orchis with two-pronged tubers have now been hived off into the genus *Dactylorhiza*. This orchid grows as different subspecies in different localities all over the country but is a woodlander, around us in the Weald, with large spikes, 2 feet tall and often of a rich mauve colouring. In the woods it generally carries single spikes, but if you get it into a border it builds into clumps that are as showy as any perennial in this season. So you could, like so many another already mentioned, build up your stocks in your borders and then spread them around in the turf. We always leave a corner of this uncut till late August, so that they can seed, and they grow so

see colour plate xv

thickly here as to be the turf's dominant component. But the seeds are dust-light and blow all over the garden, turning up in the cracks of paving and in other undisturbed spots. Bressingham Gardens (Diss, Norfolk) offer their own house brand which they call *Orchis fuchsii* 'Bressingham Bonus'.

The green-winged orchis used to inhabit permanent pasture around here, when I was a boy and when such pastures existed. I imagine our colonies must be the only ones within miles, now. They, too, have self-sown, among other places, on top of our reservoir, which is covered with a layer of thin turf.

Wild orchids are immensely exciting, even the green-flowered twayblade, which is also plentiful in our grass, though you have to peer for it. In my unregenerate youth, before the word conservation had been heard of, my mother and I used to sally gleefully forth with trug and trowel into the surrounding country on orchid-collecting expeditions. Hence the origins of our good store. But there are specialist nurseries nowadays from whom you can buy tubers, at a price. I started with just one, at three guineas, of the Madeiran *Dactylorhiza foliosa*, some eight years ago. It has spectacular red-purple spikes and I have grown it in a damp, shady border all these years and have quite a stock now, so shall soon be able to try this, too, in the rough grass. Patience and sedentary habits are great assets to the gardener.

36   PORT LYMPNE, KENT. 1932

Colchicums naturalised in long grass. The wild garden acts as a link between the formal gardens and their parkland setting.

Robin Lane Fox

THE WILD GARDEN
IN THE LONG GRASS

Robin Lane Fox (1946–) draws on the experience of gardening at New College, Oxford, where he is Garden Master, and in his own Oxfordshire garden. He is author of a weekly gardening column for the Financial Times *and his books include:* Variations on a Garden *and* Better Gardening.

As the weather has been as frightful as the results of the recent elections[1], I want to stand back this week and present you with a style of gardening which has been dropped from our modern consciousness.

The mention of it goes down very well, especially among gardeners who own gardens, rather than enjoy them, and among those of you who save your efforts for Saturdays and Sunday afternoons between March and November.

Wild gardening sounds romantic, lazy, and easy on the week-end schedule. But the wild garden has been defined rather differently by our age. I will entice you with reports of its original state, after reminding you how the books and planners now advise that it ought to be done.

The wild garden, nowadays, lives in the shadow of late Victorian gardeners who bought rhododendrons like bedding plants and dropped lilies wherever their bank accounts permitted. Their wild flowers were exotic flowers, newly found in China and the Far East. They were massed in glades and in areas called clearings. They gave the impression that they had always lived in peace, without the attention of an army of labourers who had kept off the rabbits and bracken in their early years.

Azaleas were stored behind post and rail fences like animals in private zoos. They were to be visited down mown paths and tracks which were weed-killed and surfaced with grit. On an open plan, their banks could sweep down closely-mown vistas, about as wild a setting as St. James's Park on a July afternoon.

As the heirs to these great gardens, modern authorities on the wild garden cannot conceal for long that they expect you to begin by making beds. They dress them up with other names, drifts, clumps or ambiguous terms, like ground cover. They urge you on with pictures of mature plantings, where huge

---

[1] This piece appeared in the *Financial Times* on November 12th, 1980.

banks of wild geraniums have run into each other and blocked out rival weeds.

Before you swap the grass in your orchard for a sweep of perennial forget-me-not, you have to poison the grass with the marvellous new herbicide, Roundup, and fork all the soil. For two seasons you have to hoe off the intervening weeds. Only then do you have an alternative blanket, but it will look best when it is trimmed and cut free of its own dead flowers. After another three years, the blanket is better for splitting, uprooting and dressing with manure.

A seriously wild garden has to be planted as thoroughly as the lower slopes of the National Trust's Hidcote Manor, in Gloucestershire. Among its lacecap hydrangeas, the carpeting plants here are massed on such a scale that no other greenery intrudes. It is a total garden, maintainable because it has matured. I would hesitate to take on such a scheme in its youth, even in my small patch of lower orchard.

If you disbelieve me, I suggest you read that bold and optimistic set-text, *Plants for Ground-Cover*, by Graham Thomas, published back in 1970, when the Trust was covering ground by the acre. It sums up the hopes and successes of modern wild gardens, but its choice of plants for cover is at times too rarified for hard-pressed gardeners. Throughout, the aim is to cover the ground so thickly that it becomes an alternative garden, packed like a flower bed in which nothing wild and weedy can compete.

For a contrast, I am tempted to go back six centuries, and remind you that there were no motor mowers in the Middle Ages, and that lords were happy to walk through their flowery meadows, believing that a tapestry of flowers in long grass was the glory of a garden designed for pleasure. They picnicked in them, read, relaxed, and sported with females. The modern lawn has been a notable ally of traditional morals. However, you may perhaps wonder if these medieval gardens looked as charming in life as when painted behind the madonnas in Fra Angelico's pictures.

To reassure you, I will come up to date and remind you of wild gardens in the 1870s, when their warmest champion, William Robinson, described what he saw in private ownership. Then, there were no big beds or sweeps of ground cover which knitted boringly together. If you put his classic *Wild Garden* beside Graham Thomas's modern alternative you can see what we have forgotten. Robinson describes two gardens in my own Oxfordshire, one at Crowsley, the other at Tew Park. Both have returned to nature long ago. They were almost natural in his day, for he presents them as gardens in which "not to mow is almost a necessity". Perennials were grown everywhere among the meadow grass without any beds.

More than 2,000 species Robinson remarked, could compete very well with meadow grasses, just as they do in nature all over the Alpine meadows. In these gardens, there were no beds, no sweeps of cover. Instead, irises and aquilegias grew up through the unknown grasses.

The aquilegias delighted Robinson in their random groups, showing their heads of flower all among the waving plumes of grass. They were not segregated, nor were they protected in any way. Like daisies they took their chance. Foxgloves kept them company by the hundred, spread into the meadow from seed. Hardy geraniums ran through the turf wherever they could and were set off by clumps of herbaceous peonies in double red and purple forms. These peonies were presumably dug into a clear space at first, but as soon as the grass encroached, nobody came to the rescue. They are shown in a wood-cut, competing in full flower with long sprays of wild grass and cow parsley.

The style, Robinson insisted, is cheap and very simple. Lupins, sweet williams, and oriental poppies are all left to fend for themelves, like crocus and daffodils. They are followed by tall evening primrose, whose tap roots will combat any sort of turf. Fennel and climbing roses are grown loosely without support and continue to brighten the long grass in later summer. Perennial campanulas are scattered like dandelions.

CHAPTER X

The Challenging Garden

Osgood Mackenzie
GARDENING IN
THE WESTERN HIGHLANDS

In the year 1862 my mother bought for me the two adjoining estates of Inverewe and Kernsary, on the west coast of Ross-shire.

Kernsary lay inland, but Inverewe had a good many miles of coastline, and, after taking about two years to settle as to where we should make our home, we finally pitched upon the neck of a barren peninsula as the site of the house. The peninsula was a high rocky bluff, jutting out into the sea, and the rest of what are in Scotland usually called 'the policies' (i.e., the enclosed grounds round about the mansion) consisted mostly of steep braes facing south and west, with the exception of a narrow strip of land down by the shore – the only bit where the coastline was not rocky – and this strip, which was an old sea-beach, was turned into the garden. I may say the peninsula, whose Gaelic name, Am Plocard (the High Lump), so aptly describes it, consisted of a mass of

Osgood Mackenzie (1842–1924) was a great personality in Scottish gardening. The peninsular at Inverewe, whilst situated further north than Moscow, was transformed by informal planting with newly introduced plants such as the broad-leaved rhododendron.

see plate 37

Torridon red sandstone (which is, I think, a pre-Cambrian formation, and lies on the top of the Lewisian gneiss). This promontory, where the rock was not actually a bare slab, was mostly covered with short heather and still shorter crowberry, and positively the only soil on it was some black peat, varying from an inch to 2 or 3 feet in depth. There had been more peat originally in some of the hollows, but it had been dug out for fuel by the crofters who had occupied the place forty years before my time. There was nothing approaching good soil on any part of the peninsula, hardly even any gravel or sand; but in a few places the rotten rock and the peat had somehow got jumbled up together, and when we came across some of this we thought it grand stuff in comparison with the rest. There was just perhaps one redeeming point about what was otherwise so hopeless a subject for planting, viz., that the rock was not altogether solid.

We had to excavate a great deal of the rock behind the site of the house before we could begin to build, and we noticed that the deeper we blasted into it the softer it became, and that there were even running through it veins of a pink kind of clay; but, on the other hand, the exposure of the Plocard was awful, catching, as it did, nearly every gale that blew, and, with the exception of the thin low line of the north end of the Lewis, right away on the horizon, forty miles off, there was nothing between its top and Newfoundland; and it was continually being soused with salt spray.

The braes above the site of the house were somewhat better, but even they were swept by the south-westerly gales, which are so constant, and so severe, in these parts.

Now, before proceeding with my story, I think I ought to explain that, with the exception of two tiny bushes of dwarf willow about 3 feet high, there was nothing in the shape of a tree or shrub anywhere within sight; one of these little willow bushes I have carefully preserved as a curiosity, and on the site where the other was I lately planted an azalea, which will, I think, soon look down on its neighbour, the poor little willow.

I started work in the early spring of 1864 by running a fence across the neck of the peninsula from sea to sea, to keep out the sheep. I was very young then (not being of age when the place was bought), and perfectly ignorant of everything connected with forestry and gardening, having never had any permanent home, and having been brought up a great deal on the Continent, but I had all my life longed to begin gardening and planting and had, I fully believe, inherited a love for trees and flowers from my father and grandfather.

My mother undertook the whole trouble of house-building, and I set myself to the rest of the work with a determination to succeed if possible. Oh that I had only known then what I know now, and could have started with my present experience of over forty years! For example, I had never heard of the dwarf *Pinus montana*[1]; had I known its merits then, as I know them now, I would have begun by planting a thick belting of it among the rocks right round my peninsula, just above high-water mark, to break the violent squalls carrying the salt spindrift which is so inimical to all vegetation. I did not know that there was little use in planting *Pinus austriaca*[2], mountain ash, service, or even birches in the middle of a wood, as, though they look nice for some years, they eventually get smothered by the faster-growing trees, and one has the trouble of cutting most of them out. If I were beginning again I would commence, as I have already said, with a row of the Tyrolese *Pinus montana* above high-water mark, then put *Pinus austriaca* behind it, and for the third row I would plant that admirable tree *Pinus laricio*[3]; this triple row would form my fortification against the ocean blast, and, thus protected, behind these I would start putting in my ordinary forest trees, Scotch pines, silver firs, sycamores, oaks, beeches, etc.

If I were asked what tree I have the highest opinion of for hardiness and rapidity of growth on bad soil and on exposed sites, I would certainly award the first prize to the Corsican pine. I have seen them in their own island on mountains 9,000 feet above sea level, with nothing between them and Spain or Algeria, growing to an enormous size – some of those I measured there being 20 feet in circumference – and here, at the same age, they make nearly double the amount of timber compared with Scotch fir, and are proof against cattle, sheep, deer, and rabbits, which no other tree is, that I know of. They told me in the ship-building yards at Savona that old Laricio timber was as good as the best Baltic redwood.

I am ashamed to confess, but it can no longer be hidden, that, among trees, many of the foreigners are far and away hardier and better doers than our natives. The Scotch fir (as bred nowadays) is often a dreadfully delicate tree when exposed to Atlantic gales. It was not so in the good old times, as one finds the enormous remains of *Pinus sylvestris* forests right out on the tops of the most exposed headlands of our west coast. My brother, the late Sir Kenneth Mackenzie of Gairloch, gave me one hundred plants of the right breed from his old native fir wood of Glasleitir, on the shores of Loch Maree, which, like the rest of that good old stock at Coulan, in Glen Torridon, or in those grand glens

---

[1] *Pinus mugo* [2] *Pinus nigra* [3] *Pinus nigra austriaca*

of Locheil, are as different in growth and constitution from what are, alas! too often sold nowadays as Scotch firs, as Scotch kale is from cauliflower. I have seen the seedlings side by side in the seed-beds in my brother's Gairloch nursery, and in the months of March and April the seedlings from the bought seed were of a rusty red, as if scorched by fire, whereas the home-bred ones were of a glossy dark green.

For four or five years my poor peninsula looked miserable, and all who had prophesied evil of it (and they were many) said, "I told you so". But at last from the drawing-room windows we could see some bright green specks appearing above the heather. These were the Austrians and the few home-bred Scotch firs which had been dotted about in the places of honour near the house; and about the fifth or sixth year everything began to shoot ahead; even the little hardwood trees, which up till then had grown, or rather died, downwards, started upwards, many of them fresh from the root. Now came the real pleasure of watching the fruit of all our labour and anxiety.

The young trees had fewer enemies then than they would have nowadays. Grouse strutted about among them, wondering what their moor was coming to, but did no harm. Black-game highly approved of the improvements, and by carefully picking all the leading buds out of the little Scotch firs did their level best to make them like the bushy *Pinus montana*. Brown hares and blue hares cut over a few of the fat young shoots of the Austrian pines and oaks; but, on the whole, my young trees fared well in comparison with the way young plantations here would fare now from the rabbit plague, and the roe and the red deer!

I planted very few of the rarer trees to begin with. Wellingtonias were then the rage, and I felt bound to invest in four of them, and planted them in the best sites I could find near the house. I tried to make pits for them; I took out the little peat there was, but how well I remember the clicks the spades gave when we came to the bed rock; and next morning (the night having been wet) all we had produced were four small ponds, and I had to get an old man to bring me on his back creels of rather better soil for them from a distance. I have just measured my Wellingtonias, and in the forty-three years they have been planted they have made some 66 feet of growth, and are about 8 feet in circumference 6 feet from the ground, and their strong leaders show they are still going ahead. So much for the old man and his creels of soil!

Silver firs in the hollows have done well, and some of them are 60 to 70 feet high also. One thing has surprised me very much – viz., that oaks, of which I planted but few (thinking it was the very last place where oaks would do), are very nearly level with the firs, larches, and beeches.

It was only after the plantation on the peninsula had been growing fifteen or twenty years, and was making good shelter, that I began cutting out some of the commoner stuff, especially my enemies the 'shop' Scotch firs, as I call them, which continued more or less to get blasted by the gales of the ocean, and then it was I began planting all sorts of things in the cleared spaces – Douglas firs, *Abies Albertii*[1], copper beeches, sweet and horse chestnuts, *Picea nobilis*[2], *P. Pinsapo*[3], *P. lasiocarpa*[4], and *P. Nordmanniana*[5], *Cupressus macrocarpa* and *C. Lawsoniana, Thuja gigantea*[6], bird-cherries, scarlet oaks, etc. and now these trees appear almost as if they had formed part of the original plantation. I am still going on a little in this style, and have dotted about a lot of Eucalypti, tree Rhododendrons, Arbutus, Griselinias, Cordylines, and clumps of bamboos and Phormiums, which are giving a charming finish to the outskirts of my plantation.

Even the Eucalypti I find much hardier than that bad breed of Scotch fir: no wind, snow, or frost seems to hurt them here: and in case it may interest my readers I will name those I find thoroughly hardy: *Eucalyptus coccifera, Gunnii, Whittinghamii, cordata, coriacea*[7], *urnigera* and one or two others; but I warn all against trying *Eucalyptus globulus* – and yet that is the very species that most people persist in planting.

I ought perhaps to mention what does not do with me, viz., the common Norway spruce. They will grow in low-lying hollows at the rate of nearly 3 feet a year, but as soon as they get to about 30 feet in height they look (as my forester very aptly describes them) like red-brick chimneys among the other trees, and even if not directly exposed to the ocean gales they get red and blasted. I tried also a few *Pinus Strobus* in the peninsula, but they quite failed. I much regret not having experimented on either *Pinus Cembra* or *Pinus insignis*[8]. I know the first-named would succeed, and, as the Monterey cypress (*Cupressus macrocarpa*) does so very well, I should have the best of hopes of the Monterey pine also, as they both come, I am told, from the same locality of California.

My latest craze is cutting out spaces, enclosing them with 6 foot fences (deer, roe, and rabbit proof), and planting them with nearly every rare exotic tree and shrub which I hear succeeds in Devon, Cornwall, and the west of

---

[1] *Tsuga heterophylla* [2] *Abies nobilis* [3] *Abies pinsapo* [4] *Abies lasiocarpa*
[5] *Abies nordmanniana* [6] *Thuja plicata* [7] *Eucalyptus pauciflora* [8] *Pinus radiata*

Ireland; and I think I may venture to say that I have been fairly successful. I fear I must confess to feelings of exultation when I visit that charming collection in the temperate house at Kew, and assure myself that I can grow a great many of its contents better in the open air up here in the far north than they can be grown at Kew under glass.

What a proud and happy day it was for me, about two years ago, when Mr. Bean of Kew honoured me with a visit, and I had the pleasure of showing him my Tricuspidarias, Embothriums, and Eucryphias, my small trees of *Abutilon vitifolium*, my palms, Loquats, *Drimys*, Sikkim Rhododendrons, my giant Olearias, Senecios, Veronicas, Leptospermums, my Metrosideros and Mitrarias, etc. I have, too, some of the less common things. One of them is a nice specimen of the *Podocarpus totara*, from which the Maoris used to make their war canoes holding one hundred men, and I have a *Dicksonia antarctica*, raised from spores ripened in Arran, and my *Cordyline australis* are all from seed ripened at Scourie, in the north of Sutherland. The *Billardiera longifolia*, from Tasmania, with its wonderful blue berries, is a most striking climber. *Acacia dealbata*, the Antarctic beech, *Betula Maximowiczii* from Japan (with leaves as big as those of the lime), the New Zealand Rata, and *Buddleia Colvillei* from the Himalaya, are all flourishing, thanks to the Gulf Stream and lots of peat and shelter. There are (as I suppose must be the case everywhere) a very few things which are not happy here, and they are plants which I dare say most people would have thought would have revelled in this soil and climate, viz., the Wistarias, Camellias, Kalmias, *Euonymus*, Tamarix, and Cyclamens, but I hope to master even these in course of time. One thing I wonder at is, how so many of my exotics seed themselves far more freely than any natives, except perhaps birch, and gorse, and broom though I ought perhaps to mention that neither of the two latter is indigenous to this particular district. The strangers which seed so freely are Rhododendrons, *Cotoneaster Simonsii*, *Berberis Darwinii*, *Veronica salicifolia*, *Olearia macrodenta*, *Diplopappus chrysophylla*, and *Leycesteria-formosa*.

And now I will venture to say something about the garden (the kitchen garden, as my English friends always take care to call it).

As is often the case with us poor Highlanders, I only possess the one garden for fruit, flowers, and vegetables, and, as I have already stated, it was mostly made out of an old sea beach, which most people would say does not sound hopeful. Even now, in spite of a wall and a good sea bank, the Atlantic threatens occasionally to walk in at its lower doors, and the great northern divers, who float about lazily just outside, appear quite fascinated by the brilliant colours inside when the lower doors are left open for their benefit.

The soil of the old sea beach was a 4 foot mixture of about three parts pebbles and one part of rather nice blackish earth, and the millions of pebbles had to be got rid of. So in deep trenching it digging forks were mostly used, every workman having a girl or boy opposite him, and the process of hand-picking much resembled the gathering of a very heavy crop of potatoes in a field. The cost of the work was great, as thousands upon thousands of barrowloads of small stones had to be wheeled into the sea, and the place of the pebbles made up with endless cartloads of peaty stuff from old turf dykes, red soil carted from long distances, and a kind of blue clay marl from below the sea, full of decayed oyster-shells and crabs and other good things, and hauled up at very low tides! There is also a terrace formed along the whole length of the garden, cut out of the face of a steep brae, which was just above the old beach, and it had to be carved out of the solid gravel, and soil brought from afar put on it. The cutting at the top was fully 12 feet deep, and against it a retaining wall was built, which I covered with fan- and cordon-trained fruit trees.

When the cutting was first made we found a number of large holes or burrows, going deep into the hillside. These, we were convinced (by the various signs we found), must have been inhabited in prehistoric times by a colony of badgers, and no sooner was the light let into these galleries than up came a thick crop of raspberry seedlings, as far in as the light could penetrate. It appeared evident that the badgers (like bears) had been keen on fruit, and had made their dessert off wild raspberries, and that the eating and digestion of the fruit had not prevented the seeds from germinating (as is the case nowadays with the seeds of *Berberis Darwinii*, which the birds swallow, and then distribute all over the place). There were no signs of any wild raspberries about here at that time, but the sight of them encouraged me greatly, and I thought it a good omen, and that where wild rasps (as we call them) once grew, tame rasps could be made to grow, and my expectations in this respect have been fully justified. I think I may venture to say that my garden, which took me three or four years to make, has most thoroughly rewarded me for all the trouble and expense incurred.

In good years (as many of my friends can testify) I grow Bon Chrétien pears on standards as good as could be bought in Covent Garden Market, and, curiously, they were always better off the standards than off the walls; but, alas! last year (which was the very worst year I had experienced since my garden was made) they were (as my gardener expressed it) not equal to a good Swede turnip. I have had excellent Doyenné du Comice pears and Cox's Orange Pippin apples on my walls, and masses of plums of all sorts on the walls and on standards, and there is one thing I may mention, which I hardly suppose even my friends in the south can boast of – viz., that I have never yet, in over forty years, failed to have a full crop of apples, and, I might almost add, pears and plums as well, though the quality varies a good deal; but really our difficulty here is that we have not force sufficient to get them thinned, so thickly do they set: and all this must, I suppose, be credited to our good Gulf Stream.

And now I will turn to the flowers, and I think almost anything that will grow in Britain will grow with me. I was once in a garden in about the warmest corner of the Isle of Wight, in June, and walking round with my hostess, we came upon the gardener carrying big plants of Agapanthus in tubs from under glass to be placed out of doors. His remark as we passed him was, "I think, my lady, we may venture them out now"; and I could not refrain from answering the old man back, "If so, then I do not think much of your climate, for in the far North of Scotland we never house them, nor even protect them in winter". I have had great clumps of Agapanthus in the open for thirty years and more, and the white, as well as the blue, flowers magnificently every year.

Ixias are as hardy a perennial here as daffodils; *Crocosmia imperialis* runs about my shrubbery borders and comes up with its glorious orange blooms in October in all kinds of unexpected places, just like twitch grass; *Alstroemeria psittacina*[1], *Sparaxis pulcherrima*[2], *Scilla peruviana*, *Crinum capense*[3], the Antholizas, and several Watsonias (including even the lovely white *Watsonia Ardernei*) are quite hardy, and *Habranthus pratensis*[4] also blooms every year; and as to lilies, I have had *Lilium giganteum* 10 feet high and with nineteen blooms on it.

We never lift our scarlet lobelias, nor our blue *Salvia patens* (except when shifting them), and the dahlias are often quite happy left out all winter, and I have never happened to come across *Schizostylis coccinea* anywhere else equal to what I grow here in November and up to the beginning of December; one can see its masses of dazzling scarlet on my terrace from a boat sailing about in the bay.

Tigridias live out all the year, and some seasons they even seed themselves profusely, and I have seen the seedlings coming up thick in the gravel walks. In

---

[1] *Alstroemeria pulchella*   [2] *Dierama pulcherrimum*
[3] *Crinum bulbispermum*   [4] *Hippeastrum pratense*

a good July I have seen the tea-roses on my lower terrace wall almost as good as on the Riviera, but the hybrid perpetuals do decidedly less well here, I think, than they do, for instance, in Hertfordshire, and florists' anemones and ranunculuses and also the Moutan Paeony have so far nearly defied me. On some of my lower walls I grow the Correas, and C. *alba* blooms the whole winter through, and is most charming. Callistemons (the scarlet bottle-brush) flower, and *Cassia corymbosa, Habrothamnus elegans*[1], and *Romneya* seem quite happy; *Akebia quinata*, Lapagerias, and *Mandevilla suaveolens* are growing, but have not yet bloomed with me.

Just one more remark, and that is about our rainfall. This is supposed to be a very wet part of the country, but according to my gardener, who keeps his rain-gauge very carefully, we had under 55 inches in 1907, whereas there are places in Britain where the fall is 130 and even 140 inches.

[1] *Cestrum purpureum*

37   INVEREWE HOUSE, HIGHLAND. 1914

A vista from the peninsula of Loch Ewe with narcissi in the foreground. The trees are carefully planted to provide shelter without spoiling the view.

Frances Perry
THE WATER GARDEN

It is true that many arts depend to a great extent for their ultimate success on lavish outlay or costly accessories, but great expenditure need not be entailed over the construction of a water garden. Here, given the understanding and the observing eye, the gardener often obtains beauty at less pains than ugliness; for water does so heighten the charms of the loveliest landscape, and, by reflection, doubles the attractions of the lowliest streamside wildling. The chief snag seems to lie in the individual's rendering of the word 'understanding', for time and again one finds small and useless pools built in the most impossible places.

In constructing a water garden one should restrict oneself to natural fitness. The tumbling cascade, the dripping waterfall suggest mountainous or uneven country, but the sluggish stream and broad stretch of water are at one with the flat and undulating ground of the lowland. It would be wrong to imitate artificially such scenes in inappropriate surroundings. At the same time, much can be made of the island feature and an illusion of spaciousness can be created by forming bays or promontories at intervals around the margins. Drift planting with some of the coarser herbaceous bog perennials obscures the water at various points and varies the impressions as one gazes across it. In the larger garden it should never be possible to view the whole broad stretch of water at a glance; the largest prospect should be towards the house or some other point of vantage, and similarly, views of a river should be directed as much as possible up or down stream and not across it.

Avoid fringing the shore with belts of trees, for they impart to the water a gloomy appearance and cut off the light which is so essential to the welfare of aquatic plants. In autumn, too, the leaves of some sorts falling into the water set up toxic conditions fatal to fish life.

The conventional water garden should never be made in the immediate neighbourhood of fine natural water – be that river, lake or sea. Violations of this rule invariably give bad results. The formal pool should aim at simplicity: it depends less upon the quantity of its horticultural treasures than upon their quality and the suitability of site and surround. It cannot be too strongly

Frances Perry VMH (1907–) specialises in water and bog gardening, perennials and hardy bulbs. She is gardening editor of The Observer *and has often broadcast on radio and television. She was also the first woman to be elected to the Council of the Royal Horticultural Society and to become its Vice-President.*

stressed that 'that odd spot in the garden where nothing else will grow' will *not* do for the water garden.

The circular pool must be in a central position with the ways of approach broad and well defined. It is so obviously an artificial design that one does not seek to disguise the fact, and planting should be restrained and only plants of a purely aquatic nature used. I have a personal objection to fountains, but they are perhaps less out of place in the round pool than anywhere else. The ceaseless spraying of the water creates pleasing musical cadence, gives a quiet air of activity to the pool and is useful inasmuch as it serves to oxygenate the water. Care must be taken, however, to check their play at eventide (lest the temperature of the water be lowered too drastically), and it is essential that the circumference of the pool be sufficiently wide to catch all the water again. The grass or stone surround must never be allowed to become wet.

Since water gardens came into favour, pools have been made from a variety of materials. In 1731, Phillip Miller wrote in the *Gardener's Dictionary*: "In some gardens I have seen plants cultivated in large troughs of water, where they flourish very well and annually produce great quantities of flowers, but as the expense is pretty great (their insides requiring to be lined with lead to preserve them) there are few people who can be at that charge." Nowadays we swear by concrete, for it has proved reliable, inexpensive and easily obtainable by most of us[1]. Concrete pools can be made in two ways: they may be either raised or sunken. That is to say, they are either built into the earth so that the top lies flush or just below the level of the ground, or the margins are raised a foot or more above the surroundings. The latter method is employed in those formal gardens which involve the use of straight lines and geometrical patterns, or are of architectural design. They are quite commonly seen, of an oval or rounded shape, set in the midst of a rose garden, framed by an elaborate arrangement of beds or walks. They are more affected by changes in weather conditions than the other sorts and the sides must be made considerably thicker to withstand the extra strain.

The sunken pool lies snug and warm in the earth and its walls can be made thinner, for they receive some support from the ground alongside. They are usually square or oblong, but an informal outline may be readily obtained by constructing a shallow trough margin around the extremities of the pool proper.

[1] Waterproof polythene liners have now become an easy alternative
but concrete is still used, particularly for raised pools.

In selecting the site for the water garden choose the most open position possible. Water Lilies, and incidentally most aquatics, favour abundant sunshine for maximum growth and tend to bloom much better in such situations. The shelter of trees or shrubs is only permissible towards the north-east, where they serve to protect the pond in winter.

Before commencing operations it is a good plan to mark out the outline with stakes: this gives an accurate idea of the dimensions and acts as a guide during excavation. Take out the soil to a depth of 2 feet 6 inches, thus allowing for 6 inches of concrete, 4 inches of soil and 18 to 20 inches of water – ample depth for most Water Lilies. After excavation – and this is important – the ground must be consolidated to render it capable of supporting the tremendous weight shortly to be imposed upon it. Unless the ground is absolutely firm and level in all parts the chances are that part of the tank will subside in the loose portion and a leaky tank will result. Clay soils – with their propensities to drying and shrinking during the summer months – must be covered with an inch layer of ashes to prevent the transference of these cracks to the concrete. If the sides are of a loose crumbly nature they can be held in position temporarily by straight boards.

For the actual concreting operations use only the finest materials; it is poor policy to economize in this respect. Use only the best Portland cement, clean washed river sand and a good quality aggregate (of a size grading from ¾ to ³⁄₁₆ inch). Use the constituents in the proportions of 1:2:2 and mix them several times in the dry state before adding water. Make the walls and sides 4 inches thick and the bottom 6 inches thick. The trough margin need only be 10 inches deep with 4 inch sides and bottom.

Once the pond is finished it should be thoroughly tested against leakage, and then some means employed to deal with the poisonous properties which will seep out of the new concrete. There are two methods of setting about this. One consists of applying some substance which will completely seal over the surface – forming a veneer as it were – while the other goes to the root of the trouble itself and aims at counter-acting, with acid chemicals, the alkaline properties as they are emitted. For the first plan there are several proprietary preparations on the market: one of these should be painted over the exposed surfaces according to directions and will completely seal the pores, thus rendering the pool both innocuous and waterproof. For the second method fill the pool with water and stir in sufficient commercial syrupy phosphoric acid to show a slightly acid reaction to litmus paper. The process must be repeated daily until the water remains acid for two successive tests at intervals of twenty-four hours. Incidentally, when the pond is made in the autumn and kept filled with water all winter, it is possible to empty and use it right away for planting in the spring, as by then the water will have absorbed most of the impurities.

The best time for planting the coarse-rooted aquatics (Nymphaeas, Nuphars, Aponogeton, etc.) is in early spring, when the dormant tubers are just starting into growth and the water is becoming warmer. May is generally looked upon as the ideal month for moving Water Lilies, but the season may well be extended for a month either way. The lesser aquatics, submerged oxygenators, etc., can be transplanted right up to early autumn.

A good rich soil is essential for Water Lilies: they need plenty of nourishment to sustain the tremendous amount of growth expended each season. The top spit off pasture land incorporated with one-sixth of its bulk decayed cow-manure, the whole well rotted down for five or six months, makes ideal compost. Cow manure, however, is not always procurable, but coarse bonemeal makes an admirable substitute (used in the proportions of a 6 inch potful to a barrowload of loam). For planting purposes use the soil in a damper condition than is usual for potting, and plant very firmly or the roots may work loose when water is added. In a small pool, where the whole area is to be thickly planted, it is often the practice to cover the floor with 3 or 4 inches of prepared compost, topping this with 2 inches of screened loam – unadulterated with manure. This is a necessary procedure to prevent any cow manure from rising to the surface and decomposing, thus fouling the water and poisoning any fish life. The Water Lilies and other aquatics can then be planted into this and the pool *gradually* filled with water. This slow filling of the pool is a great point in the cultivation of the Water Lily. The water must be added gradually, in direct ratio to the growth of the plant, so that it becomes warmed up betweenwhiles and is never so deep as to swamp the young plant. Frequently the filling of the pool – from planting time – covers a period of six to eight weeks.

Another plan is to set the roots in baskets or aquatic pans (with holes bored here and there around the sides), afterwards placing them in the required positions in the pond. This plan finds favour when large areas of water are under consideration or in natural ponds difficult to empty. In time the baskets disintegrate and the Water Lilies root into the natural bottom of the pond. In cases where there is no soil already present the baskets must be renewed every three or four years and the roots divided.

368

When transplanting, take a good look at the root of the Water Lily before you set it in the soil. It may have a rhizomatous rootstock (like the German Iris), in which case it must be set horizontally under an inch of soil with the crown just exposed. On the other hand, it perhaps belongs to the 'Marliacea' group with a large-rounded, Celery-like tuber and fibrous roots; in this case set it vertically up to the crown and spread the roots out well. On receiving a consignment of plants, remove any dead or broken foliage and slightly trim the roots; it frequently happens that the original leaves die off, but this need not give cause for alarm. If planting has been properly done and the water added gradually, new leaves will appear in a few days.

In normal winters, Water Lily roots growing in 12 to 18 inches of water should be quite impervious to frost, but, for the sake of any fish life present, it is as well to break a hole in the ice and keep it open to allow surface absorption of air. The shallow pool, however, may freeze through more quickly, so in very severe weather lay boards across from side to side, covering these with mats or layers of straw. Branches of resinous trees – such as Pine or Fir – also afford good protection, but all covering must be removed directly a thaw sets in or the plants may start into premature growth.

For the average-sized pool (depth of water about 18 inches) an excellent white Water Lily is 'Gonnêre'; the double flowers are cup-shaped and sit squat on the water, while the plant is in bloom practically all the summer. Another good white is *N. odorata maxima*, a charming North American variety with medium-sized flowers and a delicious fragrance. *N. Marliacea chromatella* and *Moorei*, with handsome chocolate-mottled foliage and soft canary-yellow blooms, are old favourites, but their depth of colour is now surpassed by the new American variety 'Sunrise' – the finest yellow Water Lily we have – with rich butter-yellow, star-shaped blooms.

Best and darkest of the reds is 'Escarboucle'. It grows prolifically and bears enormous flowers with star-shaped petals. 'Rose Nymphe' has rich rosy flowers standing several inches out of the water, while *N. odorata* 'Wm. Shaw' is a most desirable variety with pointed rose-pink flowers and orange stamens.

Some of the orange and copper coloured forms are interesting to grow. Among the best are 'Aurora', with soft rosy-copper blossoms which change with age to orange-salmon; 'Graziella,' very free-flowering with copper-yellow blooms; and 'Paul Hariot', whose cup-shaped flowers start life canary-yellow, then gradually turn to pink as the blooms mature.

see plate 33
and colour plate XVI

No Lily pool is complete without a number of aquatic plants to clothe its banks and break the formal outline. The planting must not be overdone, however: water plants grow so rapidly as to cover half the pool in a very short time, so only the most ornamental, less robust sorts should be selected for the small pool.

The following list of plants embraces a certain number which come into this category: lack of space forbids adequate descriptions, but all are hardy and easily procurable.

Aponogeton distachyus, Water Hawthorn. Strap-shaped leaves, black-and-white forked flowers. Floating.

Aponogeton leptostachyus (*A. Kraussianus*). Sulphur-yellow flowers standing out of the water.

Butomus umbellatus, Flowering Rush. Pink umbels of flowers, sword-shaped leaves. Height 2 to 4 feet.

Calla palustris, Bog Arum. Of creeping habit, heart-shaped leaves, small, white, arum-like flowers. 9 inches.

Caltha palustris and *palustris plena*. Single and double Marsh marigolds. Height 9 to 12 inches.

Decodon verticillatus (*Nesaea verticillata*), Water Willow. Shrubby perennial grown for autumnal coloration of the Willow-like leaves.

Dracocephalum palustre. Spikes of pink 'Snapdragon-like' flowers. Height 12 to 15 inches.

Echinodorus ranunculoides. Narrow lanceolate foliage, terminal umbels of three-petalled rosy-lilac flowers. 12 inches.

Eriophorum latifolium, Cotton-grass. Broad grassy foliage, umbels of snow-white cotton-like tufts. 2 feet.

Houttuynia cordata. Spikes of white flowers, heart-shaped leaves. Height 6 to 24 inches.

Hydrocleys Commersonii, Water Poppy. Not always hardy. Thick floating leaves and light-yellow Poppy-like flowers standing out of the water.

Menyanthes trifoliata, Bog-Bean. Trifoliate leaves, clusters of pinkish-white fringed flowers. Height 6 inches; creeping habit.

Myosotis palustris. The Water Forget-me-Not, 9 to 12 inches.

Orontium aquaticum, Golden Club. Golden-yellow spadix, silvery-green foliage. 12 to 18 inches.

Peltandra alba, Arrow Arum. White Calla-like flowers succeeded by red berries, arrow-shaped foliage. 8 to 20 inches.

Pontederia cordata, Pickerel Weed. Blue spikes of flowers and heart-shaped leaves. Tidy habit. 18 inches to 2 feet.

Ranunculus Lingua grandiflora, Great Spearwort. Large buttercup-like flowers. Height 2 to 3 feet.

Sagittaria sagittifolia japonica and *japonica flore-pleno*. Single and double white-flowered Arrowheads. Sagittate leaves. Height 12 to 18 inches.

Vita Sackville-West
STARTING FROM SCRATCH

HIDCOTE MANOR

Hidcote Manor, through the generosity of that fine gardener, Major Lawrence Johnston, was the first garden to be presented to the recently formed Committee for the preservation of gardens of outstanding merit under the joint auspices of the Royal Horticultural Society and the National Trust. It lies, secluded and remote, in the leafy country on the borders of Worcestershire and Gloucestershire, far from any considerable town, but within a few miles of Broadway and Chipping Campden, along winding and hilly lanes that could be nowhere but in the very depths of England. Its own farm surrounds it, including a tiny hamlet, extremely picturesque with thatched roofs, and cottage gardens in which I suspect Major Johnston of having taken a very practical interest; and from the top of the garden you command wide views over woods and meadows, with not a house in sight, right away to Bredon Hill on the opposite side of the valley. The manor-house itself is charmingly unpretentious, in the Cotswold style, with a forecourt, and a chapel on one side.

When Major Johnston first acquired Hidcote 42 years ago, he had nothing as a basis to his garden except one fine Cedar and two groups of Beeches. The rest was just fields, and I cannot believe that to any but a most imaginative eye it can have seemed a very promising site. There was no particular shape to it;

Vita Sackville-West (1892–1962) is well known as the creator of the garden at Sissinghurst Castle, Kent, where formality of design is combined with informality of planting. She was gardening correspondent for The Observer.

standing high, it was somewhat wind-swept; there was nothing in the nature of old walls or hedges to afford protection; the soil was on the heavy side. It must have required immense energy, optimism, foresight, and courage to start transforming it into what it is to-day – a matured garden full of variety and beauty, the achievement of one man in his lifetime.

There are several points of view from which we may consider Hidcote. It appeals alike to the advanced gardener in search of rare or interesting plants, and on the aesthetic side to the mere lover of beauty, content to wander down broad grass walks flanked with colour, turning continually aside as the glimpse of little separate gardens lures him. The combination of botanical knowledge and aesthetic taste is by no means axiomatic, but Major Johnston possesses it in the highest degree. To my mind, Hidcote is a flawless example of what a garden of this type should be – but before going any further it would be as well to define what we mean by 'a garden of this type', for Hidcote amongst its other merits displays remarkable originality, and thus should perhaps not be associated with any 'type' at all.

Would it be misleading to call Hidcote a cottage garden on the most glorified scale? (It covers 10 acres, but acreage has nothing to do with it.) It resembles a cottage garden, or, rather, a series of cottage gardens, in so far as the plants grow in a jumble, flowering shrubs mingled with Roses, herbaceous plants with bulbous subjects, climbers scrambling over hedges, seedlings coming up wherever they have chosen to sow themselves. Now in a real cottage garden, where the limitations and very often the pattern – for example, the curve or the straightness of the path leading from the entrance gate to the front door – are automatically imposed upon the gardener, this charming effect is both restrained and inevitable: it could not, we feel, be otherwise. It is very largely accidental. But in a big garden like Hidcote great skill is required to secure not only the success of the actual planting, but of the proportions which can best give the illusion of enclosure; the area must, in fact, be broken up in such a way that each part shall be separate from the other, yet all shall be disposed round the main lines of the garden in such a way as to give homogeneity to the whole. At Hidcote this has been achieved by the use of hedges, with openings cut for the convenience of communication, rather than by the use of walls and gates; tall living barriers which do much to deepen the impression of luxuriance and secrecy. In one such enclosure, I recollect, no larger than a fair-sized room, where moisture dripped and the paths were mossy and the walls were made of the darkest Yew, scarlet ropes of *Tropaeolum*

see plate 7

372

speciosum trailed all over the hedges, more amazingly brilliant in that place full of shadows, than ever it had appeared on a whitewashed cottage in Scotland.

The garden falls into six main portions. First the forecourt, which is lavishly planted all round the walls with Hydrangeas, the Hidcote Hypericum, *Solanum crispum*, Magnolias, Buddleia, Choisya, Carpentaria, and *Schizophragma hydrangeoides* climbing beyond the first-floor windows. After passing through the house, you come out on to the old Cedar spreading its branches see plate 38 over a couple of steps, and look down the wide grass walk which is the principal axis, terminating in a short flight of steps flanked by two little summer houses or pavilions with a slightly Chinese up-tilt at the corners of the roof, and leading finally to a wrought-iron gate between brick piers, commanding the view away to Bredon. On the right hand side of this wide walk, and raised above it, lies a *very* large grass lawn, oval in shape, with a mound on which stand two or three big Beech trees; another group of Beech trees is at the opposite end; it is spacious, simple, and peaceful. Beyond this, concealed behind hedges, is the kitchen-garden with the glasshouses and the collection of old-fashioned Roses. On the left-hand side of the wide walk are most of the little separate gardens to which I have referred; and beyond them again, over a little stream, is the part of the garden known as the Wilderness – several acres of trees and shrubs, either for flowering in the spring or for colouring in the autumn.

I am aware that this dry tabulation can convey no idea whatsoever of the variety and beauty of the garden at Hidcote. Even now, I have omitted several features, such as the other wide grass walk between twenty foot hedges of mixed Beech and Hornbeam; and the heath garden; for in truth, there is so much to say that it is impossible to compress it into a single article. This place is a jungle of beauty; a jungle controlled by a single mind; a jungle never allowed to deteriorate into a mere jungle, but always kept in bounds by a master hand. There is a nice distinction between formality and informality. I shall attempt to describe it in words, although it is an impossible thing to reproduce the shape, colour, depth, and design of such a garden through the poor medium of prose.

What I should like to impress upon the reader is the luxuriance everywhere; a kind of haphazard luxuriance, which of course comes neither by hap nor hazard at all.

I have already remarked on the originality of Major Johnston's garden.

This originality displays itself in several ways. We must always remember that the fashion of one generation becomes the commonplace of the next; but that is no reason why we should not pay a grateful tribute to the person who had the first idea. We have all, in these difficult gardening years, turned towards the flowering shrubs and flowering trees and the Roses-grown-as-shrubs; we have become used to seeing them no longer relegated to what used to be called the shrubbery – and a dingy thing that usually was – but mixed with other plants in that now almost obsolete thing, the herbaceous border. This method is now rapidly becoming customary, but I must recall the comment made on Hidcote by someone who saw it in its early days: "This man is planting his garden as no one else has ever planted a garden." The garden at Hidcote was bare then; it is no longer bare; it is packed and crowded; not an inch of soil is visible; and that is part of its originality.

Major Johnston maintains, moreover, and how rightly, that if you cram your beds and borders with what you do want, there is less room for what you don't want – weeds.

I have heard gardeners criticise the Hidcote garden because flowers of a kind are not grown in bold masses. It is almost a precept, usually a good one, that big clumps are preferable to small clumps, and that if you have twelve plants of a kind it is better to set all twelve together than to divide them into two lots of six or three lots of four. The advantages and disadvantages of this system are obvious: while the plants are in flower you obtain a more showy effect, but when they are out of flower you are left with a blank. Major Johnston has got the best of both methods, by scattering his plants so lavishly everywhere. Thus there is never a vast blank, and never a corner without colour. This must not be taken to mean that no bold massing occurs. It does, in some instances. The 'old' Roses are massed, and many Hydrangeas; Primulas also, along the stream; *Paeonia peregrina* on either side of a path; Fuchsias in a special garden of their own; and many other things too numerous to mention. But generally speaking you are likely to find a patch of humble annuals nestling under one of the choicest shrubs, or a tall metallic *Onopordon arabicum* (or was it *O. acanthium*?), towering above a carpet of Primroses, all enhancing the cottage-garden effect to which I have already referred.

I remember in particular a narrow path running along a dry-wall; I think the gardener called it the rock garden, but it resembled nothing that I had ever seen described by that name. At the foot of the wall grew a solid mauve ribbon of some dwarf Campanula. It may have been *C. garganica* and this, of course, after the Hidcote principle, had been allowed to seed itself also in brilliant patches wherever it did not rightly belong. Out of the dry-wall poured, not the expected rock-plants, but a profusion of Lavender (the deep Hidcote variety, superior in every way to the common *Spica*) and wands of *Indigofera*; there was *Choisya ternata* also, and some Cistus; and an *Azara microphylla* on the bank at the top of the wall, which had been allowed to grow into a real tree quite 15 feet in height; and I fancy there was a creamy, fluffy apparition of *Hydrangea integerrima* looking over the top of a hedge somewhere; but it is difficult to remember details in a garden so thick with detail. I remember also a particularly brilliant picture composed of Major Johnston's own climbing Rose, originally known as 'Hidcote Yellow' but now called 'Lawrence Johnston', its rich butter-yellow holding its colour splendidly in conjunction with the flame-and-orange of *R.* 'Signora' its next-door-neighbour on the wall. I ought to have taken more notes and trusted less to memory. Above all I regretted the absence of Major Johnston, who had always been my host on previous visits to Hidcote when no thought of writing an article was in my mind. He could have told me much.

No description of Hidcote would be worth anything without mention of the hedges, and here again the originality of the planter is apparent. There is a great deal of Yew, but Major Johnston has not been content with plain Yew, beautifully as he has employed it. In one place there is a mixed hedge of Yew and Box, an attractive combination with its two shades of green: he has realized how many different shades of green there are in Nature, not forgetting the value of dark pools of water with their *chatoyant* reflections, and has made use of all these greens in a way that would have delighted Andrew Marvell. Different textures of leaf have also been made to play their part, in the 'flatness' of Yew contrasted with the inter-planted shine of Holly. Then there is one harlequin of a hedge, with five different things in it; Yew, Box, Holly, Beech, and Hornbeam. Like a green-and-black tartan.

The hedges of Copper Beech entirely redeem the Copper Beech from its suburban associations; they may not inaptly be compared to an Isfahan carpet, with their depths of rose-madder and violet, and the tips of young growth as sanguine as a garnet seen against the light.

There is just enough topiary to carry out the cottage-garden idea; just enough, and not so much as to recall the elaborate chess-men at Hever Castle or tortured shapes at Levens Hall. The topiary at Hidcote is in the country tradition of smug broody hens, bumpy doves, and coy peacocks twisting a fat

375

neck towards a fatter tail. It resembles all that our cottagers have done ever since the Romans first came to Britain and cut our native Yew and Box with their sharp shears. This is right for Hidcote, and just as it should be: Major Johnston has used the old tradition with taste and restraint, and has supplemented it with some arches of a serene architectural value.

Nor must I forget the quincunx of pleached Hornbeam, set behind the two small garden-houses. It may not be an exact quincunx in the geometrical sense but the word will serve. It gives a sudden little touch of France to this very English garden. Neat and box-like, standing on flawlessly straight little trunks, it has always been so perfectly clipped and trained that not a leaf is out of place.

I have but barely mentioned the large, thickly planted area known as the Wilderness. This is partly because in the month of June, when I was last at Hidcote, the Wilderness is not at its best; it is either a place for spring, with all its flowering trees, or for August with its massed Hydrangeas, not the wig-like *H. hortensis* but the far more elegant *H. aspera maculata*; or for autumn when it becomes a bonfire of colour. I know of its spring beauty only by repute; in August I have seen the shrubby Hydrangeas – and this, surely, is the way to grow them if you have the space, in a bosky place made secret by the overhanging trees, with a trickle of water somewhere invisibly near at hand, and the smell of damp peaty soil. A little later on, before the Wilderness had reached its autumn glory, I remember a huge colony of Colchicums as you emerged on to the grass from a woodland path. I noted also a large tree of *Cercidiphyllum*; whether it was *japonicum* or *sinense* I do not know; but there could be no doubt that with its autumn colouring it must present a most astonishing sight. The Wilderness is indeed a worthy imaginative adjunct to the general design of the garden.

But on the whole I suppose it is as a botanist and plant-hunter that Major Johnston would wish to be thought of. He himself has travelled much in search of rare plants, and many others have been sent to him from all over the world by fellow collectors. The hardier subjects resulting from these expeditions are planted out, it may be at the foot of a wall where lights may be propped over them in winter; the tenderer subjects are roofed over in two plant-houses, with open sides throughout the summer. Here, again, I wished that Major Johnston had been at hand to answer many questions. I remember the big yellow trumpets of a *Datura*, and the hanging bells of several varieties of *Abutilon*; a pale *Plumbago*; great pots of fine specimens of Fuchsia; notably a rare variety of *F. corymbiflora alba*; a *Carpentaria* with the widest white flowers I had ever seen; a striped red-and-white Gladiolus from Mount Kilimanjaro, it may have been *Watsonioides*; and a general impression of dripping luxuriance, but to speak of these exotic treasures in any detail is beyond my power.

Near the larger of the two plant-houses are the propagating frames and the greenhouse containing a collection of Pelargoniums. We are now in the kitchen-garden, but in this kitchen-garden are many things more worthy of contemplation than Cabbages. Major Johnston is no orthodox gardener: he spills his cornucopia everywhere. There is, I recollect, a raised circular bed round a Scotch Pine, foaming with rock Roses of every shade, a lovely surprise, as light as spindrift, shot with many colours the rainbow does not provide. There is a full-grown pink Acacia near by, which I took to be *Robinia pseudoacacia Decaisneana*, judging by the rich pink tassels of its flowers; but I may have been wrong in my judgment, and it may have been *R. hispida macrophylla*. By that time I had become wildly intoxicated by the spilling abundance of Hidcote that I was no longer in any mood to worry about exact nomenclature, but only in the mood to enjoy the next pleasure to be presented.

There were several pleasures in that most original of kitchen-gardens. There were nursery beds full of Rose cuttings and young Syringas. I remembered how, years ago, Major Johnston had sent me off with a huge bundle of Syringas, saying "Take your chance of these. Some of them won't be worth keeping, but you may hit on some that will do." He was right. I took my chance, and now have some fine kinds growing in my garden – children of Hidcote which I am proud to possess – a grand double-white, and a true pink one which particularly pleases me.

Down the centre path of the kitchen-garden are the old Roses, planted in wide rows three-and-four bushes deep. Major Johnston grew these enchanting varieties long years before they became the fashion, and his collection includes many which are still hard to obtain. There was the blackish-purple of the *centifolia* 'Nuits de Young' (How did it come by that name? Was it called after Young's *Night Thoughts*?) and the slaty-purple of the *gallica* 'Cardinal de Richelieu'; 'Roseraie de l'Haÿ'; L'Evêque' and 'William Lobb' tangling their long sprays of amethyst; the pink 'Buttonhole Rose', with its sharp little pointed buds, also called 'Rose d'Orsay' because that famous dandy affected it in his coat. I have never been able to find this in any nurseryman's catalogue. It would take pages to enumerate them all, so let me merely revive the memory of that June day and the loaded air, and the bushes weeping to the ground with the weight of their own bloom, a rumpus of colour, a drunkenness of scents.

It is a welcome thought that this lovely garden is now available to all. There are many lessons to be learnt from it, both for the expert gardener and the amateur. The expert will find his own interests, though I suggest that with Major Johnston's approval a more elaborate system of labelling might be devised, with special regard for the rarer plants. The amateur, after he has considered and absorbed the general beauty of Hidcote – which will take him through hours of a real treat-day – would be well advised to go back and study what he may learn for the benefit of his own garden. We cannot all aspire to gardens like Hidcote, either in extent or in particularity. But, as I have suggested, there is much in the Hidcote garden which is applicable to the more modest dwelling – the cottage, the week-end cottage, the manor-house, and such diverse habitations as are to be found in our small country towns and even in the garden city. There are many hints to be taken. Why, I thought, had I not planted the pink Acacia instead of the common white one, years ago? And out of this regret came the moral of Hidcote: choose always the *best* variety, or the *best* strain. Do not be content with the second or third best. Grow it under the conditions that suit it best, e.g. I recall a colony of *Primula* 'Garriard' under a north wall, planted in a rich moist bed of peat and sand: those plants were as big as the largest lettuces. I blushed as I looked at them, remembering my own poor starved samples which hitherto I thought were doing quite well thrust into ordinary soil. A made-up bed of peat and sand should not have been beyond my scope; it was simply that I had not taken the trouble.

SISSINGHURST CASTLE

It is easy to write an article about somebody else's garden, but it is awkward (in the country phrase) to write about one's own. One hesitates to extol the successes, yet to lay the emphasis on the mistakes and failure would be to assume an apologetic humility which might well irritate the reader into exclaiming "Then why write the article at all?"

I shall, therefore, take the line that it is possible, within twenty years, to create a reasonably presentable garden, acquiring a matured appearance and losing that look of newness which we associate with the narrow orange labels of nurserymen, fluttering from the wrist-slender stems of young trees. I hope that this may be an encouraging theme for those who now stand surveying a new site and wondering how long they must wait before they can accompany their friends without shame along the paths and can look up to, instead of over, the tops of the hedges.

True, the site at Sissinghurst was not a new one: it went back to the reign of Henry VIII. This was an advantage in many ways. It meant that some of the Tudor buildings remained as a background; it meant that some high Tudor walls of pink brick remained as the anatomy of the garden-to-be, and that two stretches of a much older moat remained to provide a black mirror of quiet water in the distance. It meant also that the soil had been cultivated for at least four hundred years, and it was not a bad soil to start with, being in the main what is geologically called Tunbridge Wells sand; a somewhat misleading name, since it was not sandy, but consisted of a top-spit of decently friable loam with a clay bottom, if we were so unwise as to turn up the sub-soil two spits deep.

These were the advantages, and I would not denigrate them. But in self-justification I must also draw attention to the disadvantages. The major nuisance was the truly appalling mess of rubbish to be cleared away before we could undertake any planting at all. The place had been on the market for several years since the death of the last owner, a farmer, who naturally had not regarded the surroundings of the old castle as a garden, but merely as a convenient dump for his rusty iron, or as allotments for his labourers, or as runs for their chickens. The amount of old bedsteads, old plough-shares, old Cabbage stalks, old broken-down earth closets, old matted wire, and mountains of sardine tins, all muddled up in a tangle of Bindweed, Nettles, and Ground-elder, should have sufficed to daunt anybody. Yet the place, when I first saw it on a summer day in 1930, caught instantly at my heart and my imagination. I fell in love; love at first sight. I saw what might be made of it. It was Sleeping Beauty's Castle; but a castle running away into sordidness and squalor; a garden crying out for rescue. It was easy to foresee, even then, what a struggle we should have to redeem it.

It took three years, with the help of one old man and his son, to clear most of the rubbish away. It is perhaps rather tiresome to grumble retrospectively over troubles long since surmounted, so I will just say that within three years we had got the place into some sort of order and could begin to plant hedges of Yew and Hornbeam where we wanted them. We planted the Yews very small, 18 inches, and they have now grown so high and thick that visitors to the garden assume them to be several centuries old. I look back, now, with amusement, on those tiny Yews when they were first planted in 1933, one by one, separate, a row of little Christmas trees; when, in impatient despair, I could not imagine that ever within my own lifetime they could cohere into a dense thick hedge 10 feet above my head. Yet so it is. I cannot see over, and I cannot push through. The Yew hedges have done well. They have been a success, and that without the help of manure, organic or inorganic.

see plate 39

The walls of course were a tremendous asset, and more or less determined the shape the garden would have to take. They conveniently broke up the site into separate enclosures but there were certain difficulties which had to be overcome if we wished to create satisfactory vistas and axes. The walls were not, however, all at right angles to one another; the courtyard was not rectangular but coffin-shaped; the Tower was not opposite the main entrance; the moat walk, with its supporting wall, ran away on so queer a bias that the statue we placed on the bank behind the moat stood opposite both to the Tower and to the seat at the upper end of the moat walk. All this was disconcerting, and there were also minor crookednesses which had somehow to be camouflaged. I do not think that you would notice them from ground level now; though if you ascended the Tower and looked down, you might still give a sympathetic thought to the worried designer, with his immense sheets of ruled paper and his measuring-tapes and his indiarubbers, pushing his fingers through his rumpled hair, trying to get the puzzle to work out.

I could never have done it myself.

Fortunately, I had acquired, through marriage, the ideal collaborator. Harold Nicolson should have been a garden-architect in another life. He has a natural taste for symmetry, and an ingenuity for forcing focal points or long distance views where everything seemed against him, a capacity I totally lacked. After weeks of paper struggle he would come home to discover that I had stuck some tree or shrub bang in the middle of his projected path or gateway. We did however agree entirely on what was to be the main principle of the garden: a combination of long axial walks, running north and south, east and west, usually with terminal points such as a statue or an archway or a pair of sentinel poplars, and the more intimate surprise of small geometrical gardens opening off them, rather as the rooms of an enormous house would open off the arterial corridors. There should be the strictest formality of design, with the maximum of informality in planting. This is what we aimed at, and is, I hope, what we have achieved.

The place lent itself happily to the informality side of the task. I had the easier job. The rosy walls might not run straight, but they cried out for a tumble of Roses and Honeysuckle, Figs and Vines. It was a romantic place, and, within the austerity of Harold Nicolson's straight lines, must be romantically treated. Very English, very Kentish with its distant prospect over woods and cornfields and hop-gardens and the North Downs, and the pointed oast-houses and the great barn, it yet had something foreign about it: a Norman manor-house perhaps; a faint echo of something slightly more southern, something that belonged to the *Contes* de Perrault. *La Belle au bois dormant* – I had been right in my first impression. That was why Figs and Vines and Roses looked so right, so inevitable. I planted them recklessly, and have never regretted it. But I think my deepest stab of pleasure came when I discovered that the country people gave the name of *Rondel* to a circular patch of turf surrounded by one of our Yew hedges. There was all poetry, all romance, in that name; it suggested Provence and the troubadours and the Courts of Love; but I think I liked it even better when I realized that they were using it as a term far more Kentishly familiar to them: the name they normally gave to the round floor for drying hops inside one of our Kentish oasts.

Similarly, they called a plantation of Nuts (Ken cobs and filberts) the *Nut-plat*. We adopted both names. They may sound affected to outsiders, but they are honestly native and natural and indigenous.

* * *

Of course, we made many mistakes. They were mostly due to ignorance. I knew very little about gardening in 1930. If only I had been better informed, I should have planted more flowering shrubs and flowering trees, which by now would have grown to their prime. As it was, I planted all the wrong things and planted them in the wrong places, too close together and unsuitably grouped and ignorantly chosen. If only one could go back twenty years and have it all over again!

It was a disappointment to inherit no plants of any value from an earlier century. We might reasonably have expected an ancient Mulberry or two; a Cedar; a Tulip tree; a group of Ilexes; some venerable Yews, possibly with some remains of topiary. There was nothing, except some deteriorating Apple trees in the orchard and the Nuts in the Nut-plat, which must have been set out in their five little avenues some seventy or eighty years ago. A few vague Daffodils and Snowdrops appeared in the spring, but that was all. No, I am being ungrateful: we found a Rose, a *gallica*, running about like a weed; my friend, Mr. Graham Thomas, to whom I gave a few roots, put it on the market as *gallica* var. 'Sissinghurst Castle', but it is now thought to be *gallica* 'Tour des Maures'. This was a pleasant thing to find, but I wish there had been something more.

We started at scratch, or worse than scratch, which I suppose means the heavy handicap of weeds. These had enjoyed themselves so exuberantly during years of abandon in a propitious soil, that the moat wall was invisible and the presence of the Nut-plat unsuspected until we began hacking our way through the jungle of brambles and briars which shrouded it. One of the ideas we had decided on from the first was that the garden with all its separate rooms and sub-sections must be a garden of seasonal features throughout the year; it was large enough to afford the space; we could have a spring garden, March to mid-May; and an early summer garden, May-July; and a late summer garden, July–August; and an autumn garden, September–October. Winter must take care of itself, with a few winter-flowering shrubs and some early bulbs.

I think it may be best if I now describe how we attempted to carry out this scheme.

The Nut-plat was the obvious place for the spring garden. Having noticed that the wild Primrose flourished particularly well in the neighbouring woods, I crammed the ground under the Nut trees with coloured Primroses and Polyanthus, on the assumption that where the wild flower will flourish, so also will the cultivated hybrids. This has been a success, not a failure; it really does look like a Persian carpet of many colours for six weeks and more, from early April till the second week in May in the broken light and shade of the Nuts. Harold Nicolson had perceived very quickly that this part of the garden should be devoted to the spring, so he ordained a double row of Limes, to make a pleached lime walk in years to come. We stuck them into what was then a rough piece of meadow, and left them to grow until we could deal with them, and could eventually make a broad paved path between them, and could under-plant them with a mass of low-growing spring-flowering things, sheets of the blue Anemones such as *blanda* and *apennina*, *Omphalodes Luciliae*, interspersed with large pools of Scillas, Chionodoxa, various Muscari, *Iris pumila*, *Tulipa dasystemon* and Erythronium, the Dog Tooth Violet. None of these might be very rare or choice, but in the aggregate they made up the effect we wanted to produce: a spring garden suggesting the foreground of Botticelli's 'Primavera'.

The orchard supplemented the spring garden. It became full of bulbs and blossom.

The May–July garden is the Rondel garden, and depends chiefly upon Roses of the old-fashioned kind, of which there is now quite a collection. One must resign oneself to their short flowering period, and eke them out with other flowering shrubs in the long border under the wall. This in former days would almost automatically have become a herbaceous border, very garish in July and August, and far more pleasing no doubt to the general public, but to my mind the shrubs available to-day (many of which were of course unknown to our grandparents) are more interesting as well as more saving of labour. We have not, however, adhered rigidly to the exclusion of anything but Roses and shrubs: there are also many Irises, and Paeonies in a shady bed; a big group of *Eremurus robustus* against a background of Yew; Figs and Clematis and Roses on the wall; some Yuccas; and as many Pansies as I can get.

The white-and-grey garden overlaps chronologically: it begins to look well in June, when the little avenue of Almond trees down the centre is draped with the lacy white festoons of *Rosa filipes* and the genuine old 'Garland' Rose, grown from cuttings taken from a very ancient climber at Knole, and when generous plantings of *Lilium regale* come up through the grey Artemisia and silvery *Cineraria maritima*; but it is perhaps at its best a little later on, when the great metallic-looking Onopordons have grown up, and clouds of *Gypsophila* 'Bristol Fairy' throw a veil round the pencils of a white Veronica, and a few belated white Delphiniums and white Eremuri persist. It is essentially a garden to sit in on a warm evening, because it looks so cool and unaffected by the long hot day. This bit of the garden is Sissinghurst's youngest child, a post-war child, and it has not yet been taught to do all that is required of it. Still, it promises well.

This brings us up to the end of August, the month which makes us most ashamed of our garden. By the middle of September it starts to recover itself a little, for a final spurt. There is a bright blue rectangular pool of *Gentiana sino-ornata*, which can give nothing but pleasure. Cyclamen come up everywhere. Some autumn trees begin to colour: *Parrotia persica*, Liquidambar, *Prunus Sargenti*, Cercidiphyllum, Disanthus and a long bank of Azaleas which I forgot to mention as a feature when in flower (and in scent) towards the end of May. The orchard takes on an autumnal beauty, comparable with its spring beauty, as the apples turn red and the leaves of the Cherries hang blood red above mauve chalices of Colchicum.

And then one says to oneself, "There is nothing to look forward to until the Witch-hazel and the Winter-sweet break into flower and the tiny species Crocuses, and the little Irises, and spring comes again."

One says also to oneself, "Have I done the best I could by this responsibility which I took on?"

38   HIDCOTE MANOR, GLOUCESTERSHIRE. 1930

Pink and grey borders framing the first section of the Great Alley. "A cottage garden on the most glorified scale."

39   SISSINGHURST CASTLE, KENT. 1942

The herbaceous border in the Walled Garden containing similar plants and
grouping to the Hidcote border. A remarkable achievement 'from scratch'.

Valerie Finnis
RAISED BEDS FOR ROCK PLANTS

Valerie Finnis VMH (1924–   ) was trained at Waterperry Horticultural School near Oxford and built up a rock plant nursery and hardy plant collection there. In 1970 she moved to Northamptonshire where she continues to garden with her husband Sir David Scott. She has taken photographs of flowers and gardens for the last twenty-five years.

Towards the end of May 1971 it became clear that I was about to embark on the largest gardening exercise of my career – moving several thousand plants from one garden to another 60 miles away. And it had to be done in June; a most unsuitable month I thought at the time.

I had been collecting plants for over 25 years at the Waterperry School of Horticulture near Oxford: the school was changing hands and I had to transfer some of my collection to a new situation in Northamptonshire in an area noted for its wonderful loam. I found, however, that the soil in my new home was unlike any loam I had ever handled, being a heavy clay, and the climate was considerably colder than in my part of Oxfordshire. The new site for my plants was an old-established vegetable garden, sloping slightly to the north, in something of a frost pocket and exposed to all points of the compass except the south! It had, however, the very considerable advantage of being surrounded by stone walls 4 feet high, an ideal background for rock plants, which are out of place in front of high walls. The garden was an oblong shape about 70 yards by 14 yards and there was a 4 foot border all along the walls. Adjoining the vegetable garden was an old stonemason's yard some 15 yards square with open sheds on one side and walls up to 10 feet high on the other three sides. Altogether I found that I had over 150 yards of wall to play with.

To survive in cultivation, rock plants must have good drainage and it should also be possible to weed them without much difficulty. There is more intricate weeding to be done among alpines than among any other plants; what is more it is while weeding that an alpine gardener keeps in touch both with the health and well being of his plants and with their whereabouts – important when there are thousands of different ones. I decided therefore to make raised beds all along the north and south walls of the vegetable garden and in the stonemason's yard. A hundred and fifty yards of raised beds may seem to be a lot to look after but these beds can be maintained with much less trouble than a similar area occupied by flowers, vegetables or even shrubs. For the edges of these beds we decided on railway sleepers set on their long narrow side to

386

make a low wall. Stone would have been nicer and bricks or concrete would have done equally well but we had not time nor the material for that. Sleepers were surprisingly difficult to find but we got hold of 80 second-grade ones. There are six grades. The top grade would have been needlessly expensive and the other grades are apt to be unsightly. To make the raised beds we placed the sleepers on edge with their outer edge along the grass path, stapled them together and, to keep them upright, nailed them to strong stakes of yew firmly driven into the ground on the inside. It is well worth while taking a lot of trouble to get the sleepers dead level and straight. The area between the sleepers and the wall was then filled in with soil until it came a few inches higher than the sleepers. As we had to plant at once, we could not, as ideally we ought to have done, allow time for the soil to settle naturally but, as it was dry, firmed it down gently before planting. The soil we used was a loam (which we got from Oxfordshire!) mixed with peat and grit – 50 per cent loam, 25 per cent peat and 25 per cent grit. The latter was flint grit $3/16$-inch, which is neutral and blends in colour with the local stone walls. Along the south wall the natural drainage was so good that no special material was required at the bottom of the bed and the bed itself needed to be no more than the depth of one sleeper on edge. We made the bed along the north wall two sleepers high as the drainage was less good, lined it with thick polythene sheeting and filled it with two parts acid loam and one part peat to accommodate my calcifuge plants.

When the beds were finished and I looked at the long, empty, bleak borders I was rather alarmed, but we filled them with plants in no time and I was really amazed at their appearance after no more than a year's growth.

My method of transplanting was as follows: I put the plants dug up at Waterperry into polythene bags, packing those in pots into trays, and loaded the lot into my car, drove over to the new garden, unpacked the plants the next morning and planted madly all day. Luckily, very luckily for me, June 1971 was wet and cool; ideal for the job! After planting, I spread a good layer of grit on the surface to act as a mulch, and I am glad to say that I have lost hardly any plants. I took care that those I lifted were not out of the ground for more than a few hours, never dried out and were firmly planted. My success inclines me to think that June can be a very good month for transplanting alpines and dwarf bulbs, provided the plants are never allowed to get dry or are over-watered after planting.

My raised beds contain a great diversity of plants and although they are almost all hardy, some of them appreciate protection from winter wet (e.g.

many grey foliaged plants) so I put a sheet of glass or a cloche over them in winter, firmly secured against the winter gales. Like most plantsmen I am an incurable magpie, and I cannot resist acquiring and trying to grow in the open a lot of plants which need alpine house conditions. My little alpine house is over full and anyhow I much prefer plants in the open ground rather than in pots. The plants themselves look better and I don't have to spend time watering pots. Accordingly certain parts of the raised beds have been set aside for species of borderline hardiness and I find that the simplest way of protecting them is by covering them with a dutch light (I was fortunately able to acquire second-hand ones locally) slanting at an angle of about 45 degrees with their lower edge resting on bricks on the top of the sleepers and their upper edge hooked, by means of pieces of bent iron screwed on to them, over a round iron rod parallel to the wall resting in supports driven into the wall at the appropriate height. The lights can be easily slid apart for ventilation and watering and lifted off with ease. Air circulates freely through the gap between the bricks at the bottom and the space at the top between the wall and the frame. This is important. The plants are covered by these lights from November to April, according to the weather, and if summer is scorching hot the lights can be used for shading.

I have also used these lights for my collection of Kabschia saxifrages which occupy about 10 yards of one raised bed and are all the better for protection from winter wet and hot summer sun.

A visitor to these raised beds will find no exciting colour schemes. I have said that I planted madly at the start and so I did. I had to! Apart from seeing that quick spreaders were not planted up against dwarfs I just put in the plants as they came to hand, so to speak. I don't believe that alpine plants can ever clash and if occasionally I produce something that looks like a carefully planned group it is entirely by accident.

The beds I have made hitherto have been up against walls, but I have just constructed another raised bed in the open with sides made of elm boards and have covered it with 2 feet high Access frames which will give me more or less alpine house conditions for the plants.

These beds have now been in existence for 18 months and I have found that, in contrast to what happened at Waterperry, few campanulas have done well – perhaps slugs are to blame for this. An exception is *Campanula raineri*, the true form too, which has been excellent. *Dryas octopetala* var. *minor*, a shy flowerer at Waterperry, has been covered with bloom and is quite enchanting. *Daphne cneorum eximia* has spread at an almost alarming rate and has given me a bonus crop of October flowers. This deep-pink, sweetly-scented daphne obviously relishes my alkaline soil and good drainage – it never does well in badly-drained soil. *Eritrichium strictum*, now *E. rupestre* var. *pectinatum*, produced its ice blue forget-me-not flowers for weeks and tiny seedlings are appearing in the grit around it. Surely *Euryops acraeus* is one of the very best silver-leaved plants, especially in winter. It is so lovely that I don't mind if its yellow daisy flowers do fail to appear and so far I have seen no sign of the rust from which it is said sometimes to suffer. Mr. Alan Bloom has introduced countless fine hardy plants and his *Geranium* 'Ballerina' must be one of the best, with its beautifully veined flowers continually appearing during the summer. I had no idea until recently that there were so many species of edelweiss and I don't know a better one than *Leontopodium discolor* from Japan with its particularly fine silver leaves. I never grew *Lithospermum* 'Grace Ward' or 'Heavenly Blue' at Waterperry owing to the alkaline soil but the lime loving *L. oleifolium* from the Pyrenees gives me immense pleasure, creeping along under the limestones with flowers as blue as you could wish. Last April I was given a plant of *Oenothera macroglottis*. It produced a huge white flower every morning or every other morning until mid-October! By mid-day it was pale pink and by evening it had faded to deep rose. To my joy the plant is starting to run and will need more space. John Watson's new introduction from Turkey of *Origanum rotundifolium* planted in various parts of the garden, with one plant in the alpine house for safety, has flourished in every position and I think well deserved its Award of Merit in 1972. At the moment I cannot praise too highly phlox 'Chattahoochee' from Northern Florida. Like the origanum I have tried it in all sorts of places and it has succeeded everywhere especially in peat. It was still in flower in November. It has a lovely blue flower with deep purple eye and good dark green shining foliage, but as yet it has not experienced a real winter with me. The form of *Potentilla nitida rubra* which I collected in the Dolomites flowered well though its silver foliage alone makes it worthwhile. *Primula marginata* 'Linda Pope' with its jagged edged leaves enjoyed the new garden with a touch of crushed tufa rock in the soil and grew robustly. I think it likes to be divided and replanted in fairly good soil every few years. The various forms of *Pulsatilla vulgaris*, especially the red, flowered well even in late summer so they are obviously content. Great praise has deservedly been given to Ken Aslet's *Verbascum* hybrid 'Letitia', a fine dwarf mullein with a long succession of yellow flowers.

Coming now to the plants which I protect in winter, I allow the blue, orange and pink pimpernels (*Anagallis*) to seed around, for they are easy to weed out when necessary; but I propagate *Anagallis* 'Sunset' vegetatively, to make sure that this fine large-flowered apricot-coloured hybrid remains true. Many people have obviously found the answer to increasing *Anchusa caespitosa*, judging by the plants which I have seen in the Valley Garden at Harrogate and in nurserymen's exhibits at the Royal Horticultural Society shows, and so far with me it is definitely doing well!

My plant of the New Zealand *Helichrysum coralloides* was so relieved to end its six years of life in a pot that when planted out it became quite luxuriant but did not lose its character. Likewise *H. virgineum*, its pink, papery buds shining in late spring, behaved equally well when released from its pot. I have what I trust to be the true *Helleborus lividus*. It was a seedling direct from Majorca and looks superb in mid winter. I am particularly fond of *Hypericum cuneatum* which comes from Syria and has enchanting tiny orange-scarlet buds; I keep some plants of it in my alpine house as a precaution. As I had several pot-bound plants of the good pink form of *Lewisia tweedyi* I planted out a few and on the whole they have done very well. *Omphalodes luciliae* with its blue-grey foliage and opalescent blue flowers is an ideal alpine house plant and seems to do just as well in this border. *Raoulia australis* and *R. lutescens* are fine little silver carpeters but, if you have not got it already, try *R. hookeri*. If the birds don't pick it to pieces you will I am sure be delighted with this New Zealander. Perhaps I should not mention verbenas when talking of alpines, but the flaming scarlet *Verbena peruviana* (*chamaedryoides*) is dazzling in late summer and the strain which I have from Japan is, I think, a little hardier than one I have grown in the past.

I must mention some of the celmisias which are really doing well in the north facing peat borders. *Celmisia coriacea* and *C. sessiliflora* remain silver all the year round, the plants never look tatty or change at all, except to get larger and at times to produce their white daisy flowers. They are all magnificent foliage plants. So vivid were the greeny blue flowers on the young plants of *Corydalis cashmeriana* that we could see them from the windows of the house 50 yards away. I, perhaps recklessly, divided the roots when the foliage died down and look forward to larger patches of blue this year. In the great hurry of planting I must have inadvertently popped in a seedling of *Mertensia maritima* and for two summers it has spread right over the edge of the sleepers down to the path. I have extolled the beauty of one phlox and have no hesitation in praising another: *Phlox adsurgens*. If it likes your garden it is quite lovely. I believe it is wise to plant out young ones in new soil occasionally, for it is not as a rule very long-lived. *Primula clarkei* is growing almost like a cabbage and early in spring is a mass of little pink primrose flowers which hide any sign of foliage. I have always thought I could never succeed with such asiatic primulas as *P. aureata* unless I were in Scotland, but with a cloche cover in winter my plant has flowered well and has lovely farinose leaves. The various colour forms of *Ramonda pyrenaica* and *R. nathaliae*, which by rights should be planted in north facing crevices in rock, do splendidly in the flat-topped peat bed. I know little about rhododendrons but the sight of *R. leucaspis* in early spring (again protected by cloche) and *R.* 'Blue Tit' make me fear that I may be becoming a dwarf rhododendron fan. I am glad to say that many of the soldanellas are flowering well but I do take precautions to keep down the slugs.

To maintain these borders in good order is not difficult. Careful and regular weeding is the main work. We try, but seldom succeed, not to pass by a weed! I plan to top dress the borders each winter with a gritty peaty mixture with possibly a little bone meal added, but only peat on the acid soil borders. I realize that in four or five years time parts of the borders will need re-planting and the soil renewing as so many of these alpine plants are not very long-lived in our gardens.

Readers will have realized that the construction of my raised beds involved a lot of really heavy labour – 40 tons of soil, 9 tons of grit, 80 sleepers and numerous bales of peat had to be transported considerable distances by barrow over uneven ground. My husband and I could never have done it on our own. But we were fortunate in having to help us Ted Barrett who works on a nearby estate and could occasionally spare a few evenings off. He is a man who can lift a railway sleeper as though it were a matchstick and who never stops or seems to get tired; we owe him a deep debt of gratitude. Apart from him we had no help and no mechanical aids.

Besides the part of the garden devoted to alpines (*and* vegetables!) we have about two acres planted over the last 25 years with trees, shrubs and hardy plants of all sorts. We find it a pleasant contrast to go from the show cases of the alpine borders which I have described, to the light and shade of these trees and shrubs and grass paths. We hesitate to call our garden a garden. There are no colour schemes or carefully designed vistas. We prefer to call it a home for plants – we trust a good home!

A well-constructed rock garden in suitable surroundings is a thing of beauty, as any visitor to Wisley will know. There are countless lovely small rock gardens, but even the smallest is not easy to construct artistically, needs the right setting and is often difficult to look after. So for the ordinary gardener wishing to grow rock plants I feel that the raised bed has many advantages. It is easily made on any level piece of ground; rocks are not essential; just a surround of sleepers or stone or brick filled in with soil – soil from your own garden if it is suitable, which mine was not – mixed with peat and grit and with a few stones judiciously placed, although this is not really necessary. With no more than four sleepers you can enclose an area which will accommodate a multitude of plants. Moreover on a raised bed the plants are brought nearer to the eye and thus better enjoyed, while maintenance and access are simplified, especially for the not so young or disabled.

Anne Scott-James
CHALK GARDENING

Anne Scott-James (1913–   ) has been a gardener all her life. She owns a cottage on the Berkshire Downs where she has made a traditional cottage garden. After Oxford, she went into journalism (Vogue, Woman's Editor of Picture Post, Editor of Harper's Bazaar and columnist on current affairs for the Daily Mail. Her books include The Cottage Garden, Sissinghurst: the making of a Garden and The Pleasure Garden.

Whenever two or three gardeners are gathered together the talk soon gets round to soil and I, who have a cottage garden on the chalky Berkshire downs, am usually patronized by those with acid acres rich in gentians and azaleas. "You garden on chalk? Poor you!", as though I had a problem family living next door.

But I do not see myself as a gardener to be pitied. I *like* chalk. I like chalk country – the freedom of the downs, the clarity of the chalk streams, the beech woods which line the roads – and I like chalk-loving plants. To me, no rhododendron thicket can match the silvery leaves of my whitebeams in spring, my clematis flourish amazingly and my pinks and peonies flower without effort. My garden has drawbacks which I do deplore, being cold and exposed to all the winds of heaven, but the chalk soil has positive merits. Chalk drains well and it is much easier to work than clay.

Chalk does, however, present two special problems. First, you are limited in your choice of plants, for though most plants will grow on acid soil, many cannot endure lime. You have to specialize, learning to sift the calcicoles from

392

the calcifuges, and I can now often tell, just by looking at an unfamiliar plant, whether I could grow it or not.

Secondly, you have to water and feed a chalk garden prodigiously. Chalk is a soft, porous form of limestone which readily absorbs rain so that the topsoil is nearly always dry. And organic matter quickly decomposes in chalk and must be constantly renewed. The chalk garden is usually short of nitrogen, and trace elements, such as iron, may become locked up in the soil and be unavailable to the plants.

THE CHOICE OF PLANTS

Anyone new to chalk gardening would be wise to do some reading before investing in the expense of plants. The classic on the subject is F. C. Stern's *A Chalk Garden*. Sir Frederick Stern, who was a gardener of top calibre, made a chalk garden before the war out of a chalk pit at Highdown, in Sussex, and see plate 40 described the making and the planting in this book. Though his resources were large, his findings are of infinite value to the most modest gardener.

It is also sensible to visit and study some of the fine chalk gardens which are open to the public, such as Highdown itself, now the property of Worthing Borough Council, and the delectable gardens at Cranborne Manor in Dorset and Charleston Manor in Sussex. I personally like those gardens best where only chalk-loving plants are grown, appropriate to the soil and site. Some chalk gardeners build special peat beds and grow lime-haters like azaleas, but I find them as unharmonious as a Venetian chandelier in a thatched cottage. Grow them as specimens, certainly, in pots and tubs, but do not blend them with the natural chalk flora in the open ground.

I think of plants for the chalk garden as being of three classes. There are whole families of ardent chalk-lovers. There are plants which will tolerate lime if the other factors are propitious. And there are mixed families of plants, like the lily family, of which some like lime while others detest it.

In my experience, all members of the following families thrive on chalk: hellebores, clematis, peonies, dianthus, anemones; doubtless there are many other genera which are equally calcicole.

I have grown a high proportion of the hellebore family, from the majestic *H. corsicus* down to the modest *H. viridis* which grows in our local woods, and all have flourished and seeded freely. (My only failure has been with *H. niger* where I think the trouble has been slugs, not lime.) All clematis seem to do well

393

LEAVES FROM THE GARDEN

with me, from the rampant species to the large-flowered hybrids. I follow the growers' instructions about planting and feeding and have not yet encountered the distressing disease of wilt.

Peonies and dianthus seem to me positively to prefer chalk to any other medium. I grow as many peonies as I have space for (their flowering period is too short and their way of dying too grotesque for them to be perfect garden plants) and many dianthus. I find that pinks and sweet williams love the sharp drainage, as do border carnations, which I have admired in neighbouring gardens, though I do not grow them myself; in our hedgerows, wild soapwort abounds. Anemones in all their varieties love chalk, and were particularly noted by F. C. Stern as calcicole plants. Glades carpeted with *Anemone blanda* are one of the features of Highdown.

Outside these genera, there are hundreds of plants which are reliable. Euphorbias in great variety, hardy geraniums, campanulas, irises, cyclamen, helianthemums, monarda, oriental poppies, borage, nearly all bulbs, most annuals, heleniums, scabious, penstemons, many saxifrages, violets and pansies, sweet rocket, foxgloves, columbines, hostas, doronicum, lysimachia, angelica and all things umbelliferous, woody herbs like sage, thyme and lavender, sunflowers, alchemilla, honeysuckle, vines, *Crambe cordifolia*, acanthus, stocks, nepeta, wall-flowers, periwinkles, iberis, valerian, achillea, antirrhinums, galega and many leguminous plants, petunias, dahlias, lily-of-the-valley, primroses, sedum and echinops have all grown contentedly in my garden, and better gardeners than I could quadruple this list. Those with sheltered gardens can grow the lovely *Romneya coulteri*, a tall ballet dancer of a flower with a *tutu* of white papery petals.

Coming to shrubs, the catalogue of lime-lovers is infinite. I believe that the majority of shrubs tolerate lime, and though one must forgo rhododendrons, azaleas, camellias, hamamelis, tree heathers, vaccinium, pieris and Japanese maples, one can stuff the garden with dogwoods, whitebeam, cistuses, buddleias, potentillas, elaeagnus, euonymus, santolina, lilac, jasmine, osmanthus, olearia, hypericums, senecio, some hebes, some prunus, berberis, kolkwitzia, weigela, spiraea, viburnums in all their variety, cotoneaster, philadelphus, daphne, box and yew, and, luckily, with all the winter-flowering shrubs except *Hamamelis mollis*. *Viburnum fragrans*[1], *Mahonia japonica* and *Chimonanthus praecox* are all happy on chalk. The deepest deprivation one

[1] *Viburnum farreri*

suffers is the camellia, and if I were ever tempted to betray my philosophy and make a peat bed, it would be to grow 'Donation'.

The gardener who, through shortage of time, space or inclination, does not want to experiment and risk failure, could have a thickly populated garden by choosing safe lime-lovers such as these.

The second category of plants for the chalk garden consists of those which will put up with a high lime content so long as the other factors are in their favour. Perhaps they need extra moisture or a sheltered corner or some special diet, such as Sequestrene to release the iron in the soil and cure any tendency to chlorosis. These mildly calcifuge plants may hit or miss. If they fail, the reason is not always obvious, for the same plant may do well in one garden and fail in the garden next door. Busy gardeners may not want to bother with chancy plants, but there is great pleasure in growing them when the risk comes off. Some of my experiences with hit-or-miss plants are as follows.

Great success with sweet peas, which are said to be subject to striation on chalk soils, though I have never found it so. Only moderate success with phlox, which dry out faster than I can water them. Total failure with *Dicentra spectabilis*, which grows well elsewhere in the village. Reasonable success with hydrangeas, which I bolster with peat and Sequestrene; the climbing *H. petiolaris*, however, needs no help and *H. villosa* is slow-growing but satisfactory. Reasonable success with lupins, notorious limehaters, but they do not last more than two or three years. Delphiniums prosper. Very little success, alas, with brooms, which I love, *Genista lydia* being the easiest. Magnolias fail with me, owing to the exposed site, though a fellow chalk gardener has fine specimens of some six varieties, including *M. stellata*, *M. × soulangiana* and *M. wilsonii*.

As a philosophy, I think it worth growing mildly calcifuge plants so long as a) their treatment is not too expensive and b) the struggle is not stubbornly prolonged. If a plant looks sickly over a long period, euthanasia is the thing.

The third category of plants for the chalk garden is perhaps the most interesting, the families which are divided in their views on lime. Roses and lilies are conspicuous here, and heathers, gentians and primulas also have mixed tastes.

Since plants are expensive today, most gardeners like to have fore-knowledge of the varieties which are likely to suit them. In my salad days, I learned the hard way, then I began to compare notes with other chalk gardeners in many parts of Britain, and would have been spared many disappointments if I had done so earlier. Roses are always a subject of controversy.

Most of us believe that hybrid teas are scarcely worth growing at all on chalk. A few vigorous varieties, like 'Madame Butterfly' or 'Ena Harkness', may do tolerably well, but will not produce a full quota of flowers, while weaker hybrid teas are sure to develop chlorosis. I also believe that miniature roses and Provence roses, particularly moss roses, will need too much cosseting, while some rugosas will give trouble. (Plants of Japanese origin should always be viewed with suspicion; Chinese plants, on the other hand, are usually calcicole).

If you cut out hybrid teas, you still have a choice of hundreds of suitable roses. Nearly all floribundas, nearly all climbing roses, and a large number of shrub roses, both old-fashioned and modern, will do extremely well, and gardens in our district are as rich in roses in June as those in Somerset or Essex clay.

One is safe with any vigorous floribunda – 'Queen Elizabeth', the incomparable 'Iceberg', 'Plentiful', 'Rosemary Rose', 'Europeana', to name a few. I always find yellow roses difficult, but 'Allgold' and 'Chinatown' are among the more reliable.

Climbing roses are highly satisfactory, and many climbing varieties of famous hybrid teas will give you a hybrid tea type of flower for cutting – 'Climbing Etoile de Hollande', 'Climbing Lady Hillingdon', 'Climbing Caroline Testout', or 'Climbing Madame Butterfly'. Other climbers and ramblers which I have seen grown on chalk with complete success are 'Albertine', 'The New Dawn', 'Dr. Van Fleet', 'Bobbie James', 'Guinée', 'Madame Alfred Carrière', 'Madame Grégoire Staechelin', 'Paul's Lemon Pillar', 'Souvenir de Claudius Denoyel', 'Gloire de Dijon', 'Sanders' White' and 'Albéric Barbier', while the Chinese species, like *Rosa filipes*, grow to the treetops. The yellow climbers may present more difficulty, particularly the pretty *Rosa foetida* 'Persiana', which hates lime. 'Mermaid' is perhaps the best yellow climber, a fine rose for any soil.

With the exception of the Provence roses, most shrub roses can be grown. The bourbons are outstandingly good, like 'La Reine Victoria', 'Madame Isaac Péreire' and particularly 'Zéphirine Drouhin'. So are the hybrid musks, like 'Prosperity' and 'Buff Beauty', the damasks, the hybrid perpetuals, and most varieties of *Rosa gallica*. Of the modern roses, one picks a few names at random: 'Frühlingsgold', 'Nevada', 'Maigold', 'Elmshorn', 'Dortmund'. Nearly all the rose species, of which so many come from China, are foolproof on chalk, and look particularly right for the chalk scene.

The choice of lilies in a chalk garden is more restricted, and lime-hating lilies must be grown in tubs. I have consulted many chalk gardeners on this point and there are only a few lilies which are agreed by all to be satisfactory. Outstanding among them is *L. regale*, wholly lime-tolerant. So is the spectacular *L. henryi*, the tall orange lily from China, and also *L. testaceum* and *L. martagon*. On the other hand, the Japanese *L. auratum* is hopeless and *L. pardalinum*, of North American origin, is difficult. Most chalk gardeners give good marks to *L. hansonii*, but surprisingly few can grow *L. candidum*. Sir Frederick Stern found it a sickly patient at Highdown.

Most of the heathers dislike lime, with the exception of *Erica carnea*, which does well enough, but to my eye looks too Scottish and peat-loving to be in tune with the chalk scene. It is only lately that I have discovered that some of the gentians will take lime, not, of course, *G. sino-ornata*, but *G. acaulis* and the graceful willow-leaved gentian, *G. asclepiadea*, which, given to me at Sissinghurst two years ago, is giving me wholly unexpected pleasure.

The primula family is also divided, though perhaps this is a matter of water rather than lime. Primroses, oxlips, polyanthus and auriculas do well in my garden, but it is too dry for what Reginald Farrer called the 'wet-bobs'; I think *P. japonica* and *P. florindae* will take to chalk if there is a pool or stream.

CULTIVATION OF THE SOIL

F. C. Stern, who created Highdown from virgin chalk, found that he had to break up the soil to a depth of two feet and improve the quality of the topsoil, and that then the plants could root.

The chalk gardener's aims must be to make the soil more retentive of moisture, to reduce the alkalinity, and to correct any particular deficiencies. To hold the moisture, as much organic matter as possible must be worked in, peat, farm manure, compost or leaf mould. The ideal thing would be to import peat in quantity and lay it as an under-blanket one or two spits deep, but the experts who recommend this, most of whom garden on acid soil, seem to have no idea of the cost. I always plant with peat and lay it as a mulch on a few favoured shrubs, but to stuff the whole garden with peat is out of the question. One must just face the fact that in dry weather one will have to water lavishly. I do, however, mulch the whole garden once a year (twice would be better) with farm manure, compost or leaf-mould, and the garden simply eats the stuff.

Organic matter, with peat again as first choice, should in theory also reduce the alkalinity, but can this be achieved in practice by the amateur?

Long ago, I sent two samples of soil from my garden to Wisley for testing. One sample was taken from the best part of the garden, where the soil has been worked for 170 years, where there is three feet of crumbly topsoil, which I in my time have nourished with lots of good food. The pH factor of this sample was found to be 7·5. The other sample, taken from a horrid rough bank, full of flints and lumps of chalk, was 7·9. All those years of cultivation had reduced the pH factor by only 0.4. So perhaps one had better settle for alkalinity and choose plants accordingly.

One can and must, however, correct special soil deficiencies, and a quick-acting organic fertilizer is essential in spring, and rose food on the roses two or three times in the season. All fertilizers chosen should be of high nitrogen content and acid-reacting. Specially recommended by experts are dried blood (for quick results) and hoof-and-horn or fish manure (for long-term results); bonemeal should be used sparingly, if at all. As has been said already, if chlorosis occurs, dose with Sequestrene. It may well be that foliar feeds, getting straight into the leaves, will prove to be the perfect meal for plants on chalk, but I am afraid I have not enough experience to pontificate.

Chalk gardeners are a close club and a brief talk with a fellow member is often more rewarding than reams of advice from the rhododendron men.

40   HIGHDOWN, WEST SUSSEX. 1937

A view across the chalk pit. Sir Frederick Stern created Highdown from virgin
chalk. He had to break up the soil to a depth of 2 feet and improve the quality of
the top soil so that the plants could root.

399

Beth Chatto
DRY GARDENING

*Beth Chatto (1923—)
inspired by her husband's
ideas about the ecology of
garden plants and her
friendship with the great
gardener Sir Cedric
Morris, became interested
in growing and
propagating unusual
plants. In 1960, she
started her unique garden
near Colchester in Essex
and in 1967 a nursery.
She exhibits most years at
Chelsea and has won a
gold medal each time since
1977. She has written*
The Dry Garden, *and*
The Damp Garden, *and*
Plant Portraits *for the*
Sunday Telegraph
Magazine.

It is not too difficult to write about plants and gardening in high summer. The problem then usually is to isolate one idea from too many, apart, of course, from making the time to sit down, pick up a pen and think coherently. But I am moved today at the end of a January that has seen continual snow and frost, to do just that, having frittered away a whole morning in my garden appreciating those plants that look well in spite of it all.

The soil on the south side of my house is exceedingly well-drained gravel, and in summer we are affected by drought for some weeks during the growing season. In winter, one of my favourite bits of the garden is this piece of bone-dry gravel which in times past has been such a problem area – in particular a long narrow bed which lies beneath a west-facing wall.

Two years ago I decided to make a raised bed here to improve the quality of the soil. The existing wall of about 5½ feet high was made of cement blocks, so I ordered more, and we built a retaining wall, three blocks high, and measured the width of the new bed by my ability to reach easily the back of it so that weeding would not be difficult. Then we filled in the space with a mixture of top soil, old rotted muck, peat and grit. Now there is scarcely a day when I do not linger along this bed for longer than I should, tempted by the wide variety of plants that flourish there.

In this bitter season the most decorative shapes there just now are two widely separated plants of *Euphorbia myrsinites*, the form I obtained from Washfield Nursery in Kent. The usual form is well worth having, but this one seems just that bit finer, with bold wedge-shaped wax-blue leaves set like scales around the lax stems which sprawl across the bed, and down the face of the low wall, in starfish fashion. When the flower rosettes have expanded you will really see the difference in this form as each little individual flower is touched with shades of orange. The flowering season for *E. myrsinites* can extend from February to the end of May, but there is no part of the year when this plant is not a pleasure to look at.

Arabis ferdinandii-coburgii (what a clumsy name!) has stood well, its delicate-looking cream and green rosettes barely flecked with brown, creeping their way among the inch-deep layer of fine grit which tops the bed. This helps to conserve moisture in summer and also helps to deter weed seedlings. In winter it helps to keep dry the foliage of those plants that will not stand alternate wetting and freezing.

I have several thymes which I value as much for their foliage effect in winter as for their flowering in summer. Quite outstanding is *Thymus* 'E. B. Anderson'. It makes raised mats, about an inch or two high which show up from afar as every leaf is totally enamelled gold, which intensifies as winter progresses. Hugging the stones nearby is *Thymus minimus* whose pressed-flat mats of tiny dark green leaves make splendid contrast.

Among the small sedums on my raised bed are some I particularly love in winter. *Sedum spathulifolium* makes succulent rosettes which turn to plum purple under their coating of powdery-wax. The pale green mounds of *Sedum acre* 'Aureum' have already begun to turn pale creamy yellow as the new young shoots start to grow. This vivid patch of colour lightens up the edge of the wall bed for weeks, well into the spring.

Several forms of *Draba* with their round bun-like dense shapes are fascinating to me, together with a minute plant, *Armeria* 'Bevan's Variety', which covers itself with large stemless flowers. *Douglasia vitaliana* has made irresistible close little tuffets of grey-green leaves, attractive in January between a few pieces of rock, but by May they will be lost beneath the tight-packed stemless flowers like vivid yellow half-opened primroses.

Less fortunate are some of the helichrysums, notorious for not standing winter wet. *Helichrysum bellidioides* which quickly makes a tangle of creeping stems clothed in tiny grey and silver leaves looks brown in the middle but all the young shoots rooted in the grit look healthy. What a pretty thing it is in June crowded with inch-high stems topped with surprisingly large papery-white daisies. *Helichrysum milfordiae* also has survived round the edges. Both of these I should have covered with panes of glass. So too with *Helichrysum virgineum* – this plant has survived here for years without protection, but this winter its handsome clumps of white-felted leaves are reduced to pulp with snow alternately melting and freezing again.

In winter I especially value the sempervivums. There are hundreds of them, all fascinating. I love to sit on the edge of my wall and study the perfect symmetry of those succulent rosettes richly tinted now in shades of red, mahogany, purple or green tipped with brown. One which has a most delightful habit is quite a small pale green rosette which in spring radiates a mass of long stems across the gritty surface to form a new plant at the end of each. If you leave them to it, the next year the whole process starts again, and you will have a maze of entangling stems trying to put down babies to root. The name, appropriately, is *Sempervivum octopodes*.

A most unlikely plant perhaps to give drama and size to the border, but which to me looks just right, is *Penstemon isophyllus*. Planted against the back wall it has made a woody frame which fans out tall stems more than head high, hung with light sealing-wax-red tubular flowers. I have fixed vine eyes to the back wall and threaded old army telephone wire through to make a grid pattern. This is an unobtrusive support for plants which I use to soften the plain cement blocks.

The loveliest thing so far that I have trained through this grid is a fine form of *Clematis macropetala*. Everything about it is good. Finely cut dark foliage sets off fat round buds which hang thickly like purple grapes. These flare open into frilled semi-double deep blue flowers. Eventually the petals drop and in a short while the wall is veiled with swags of gauzy seed heads which disintegrate in mid-winter.

Although it had for several years been a lovely feature in my Mediterranean garden, *Artemisia arborescens* is looking quite dreadful, its delicate foliage drooping like dirty dish cloths! It grows wild on the western seaboard of Portugal so we are asking a bit much for it to survive these conditions.

The poor ballotas look thoroughly browned, but this is mostly top tender growth and old flowering stems. They have always before broken fresh growth from the woody base. But *Marrubium cylleneum* nearby, which some people confuse with *Ballota pseudodictamnus*, is still showing plenty of life in its terminal rosettes which when fresh are a silky sage-green like old Victorian velvet.

The main backbones of the Mediterranean borders appear to be undamaged. The great shining green mass of *Cistus ladanifer*, and, for me the hardiest of all cistuses, *Cistus × corbariensis*, whose crinkled dark green leaves only become more russet tinted as the cold bites, are all standing well.

These shrubs are now feeling the benefit of a thin diet from the depth of gravel beneath them which produces tough leathery growth.

I shall be very pleased if my plants of *Sisyrinchium striatum* 'Variegatum' survive outside. I have strong clumps planted in very dry gravel, and so far, although the tops are browned the young basal shoots look quite fresh. It is well worth keeping a few potted up because the new growth and extending flower stems are bright cream with the minimum of grey-green stripe, the whole thing topped with a spire of creamy-yellow flowers; perfect beside a rich blue like *Veronica* 'Crater Lake Blue'.

Another important feature of my dry garden, which is reviving before my eyes as I write, is a splendid mass of *Euphorbia wulfenii* 'Lambrook Gold'. Early this morning every leaf hung huddled and wrinkled against its stem. Now, with thin sunlight, although still below freezing, it has plumped itself out like a good hen. Each stiff but curving stem is just beginning to turn over its rose-tinted top-knot of leaves as it prepares to make that spectacular cylindrical head of lime-green eyes.

*   *   *

It is now five full months since I wrote the above, and I am reviewing the situation in mid-June after the longest, coldest, wettest winter I can remember in my gardening life. Walking along my dry borders I can only marvel at the persistence and endurance of plants which carry on while we fuss and fret about the weather. My greatest loss during the tedious weeks of winter was work not done because of the conditions.

The only plants I lost completely in the garden were *Artemisia arborescens*, and *Helichrysum virgineum*. I have not yet replaced them. The *Artemisia* was a valued feature and I miss its light mass of silvery white foliage.

Some of the old plants of *Euphorbia wulfenii* were either killed outright or too badly damaged to be worth keeping, but young ones survived and flowered well. *Euphorbia biglandulosa* did not flower, I suspect it needs a hot summer previously, but the plants came through in good condition. The *Cistus* were more affected than usual, most *Cistus purpureus* were killed outright but that I always find tender. *C. ladanifer* and *C. × corbariensis* are the most hardy, and these were scarcely affected on the gravel soil; on better soil they were slightly damaged.

I did eventually, almost too late, put a few panes of glass over *Helichrysum milfordiae*, *Origanum dictamnus*, and several forms of *Raoulia*, which are all now rewarding me with rapidly increasing growth.

I was delighted that *Sisyrinchium striatum* 'Variegatum' came through. It still looked miserable in April, but is in good leaf now, sending up its spires of creamy-yellow flowers.

Convolvulus mauritanicus I hovered over anxiously, all top growth was as dead as could be. But it has come back from deep down buds, rather like the fuchsias, which have also all returned. My *Helichrysum bellidioides* survived all round the edges where the young shoots lay in pure grit.

The ballotas were badly affected, some died, but enough survived to provide new shoots for propagation. However, *Marrubium cylleneum* was not the least affected and might well be used where *Ballota* is unreliable.

The santolinas, including the lovely green-leafed form *S. virens*, all came through undamaged. As did a magnificent plant of *Veronica perfoliata*, also known as *Parahebe perfoliata*, at least a yard across and almost as high. Each stem pierces through joined pairs of waxed blue-grey leaves, reminiscent of eucalyptus (both come from Australia). Each is topped with several long drooping sprays of soft purplish blue flowers. The whole effect is most elegant and attractive.

To conclude. Most of the damage done to my plants last winter was caused by alternate soaking and freezing of foliage. Plants which survived this best were growing in very well-drained situations. The lowest temperatures recorded were about 16°F of frost, but with some snow cover the soil was not frozen to any depth, so underground shoots, roots, bulbs and tubers were generally not affected. The almost total absence of spring weather meant that many plants and shrubs were very slow to recover, especially those from more southern countries. However, a long and sometimes anxious wait has at last seen almost all my plants restored to life and vigour.

Even *Teucrium fruticans* has reappeared. I had left its lifeless cage of branches to make a support for the delicate climbing trails of *Tropaeolum tricolor* which had survived outside in the bone dry gravelly soil beneath. Both are sited against a south wall. In early June I noticed new shoots breaking from the base of the *Teucrium*, which will, you can be sure, completely replace the old wood by autumn, so that next year perhaps, those little schools of red and black fish, the flowers of *Tropaeolum tricolor*, will float again in seas of grey-blue *Teucrium*, as they have before.

Acknowledgements

CHAPTER I

THE FORMAL GARDEN

Humphry Repton: Of Pleasure-Grounds and Flower-Gardens (*Repton's Landscape Gardening* — ed. Loudon 1840); William Gilpin: Dress Ground (*Practical Hints on Landscape Gardening* — 2nd ed. 1835); Shirley Hibberd: The Parterre (*The Amateur's Flower Garden* — 1878, Groombridge and Sons); Reginald Blomfield: In Favour of the Formal Garden (*The Formal Garden in England* — 2nd ed. 1892, Macmillan, reprinted by kind permission of the author's estate); John D. Sedding: The Geometrical Garden (*Garden Craft Old and New* — 1891, Kegan Paul, Trench, Trinker & Co. Ltd.); Viscountess Wolseley: Ornamental Pots (*Gardens, their Form and Design* — 1919, Edward Arnold); Paul Edwards: The Topiary Garden (*English Garden Ornament* — 1965, reprinted by kind permission of Bell and Hyman Ltd); Russell Page: A Small Excursion into Formality (*The Education of a Gardener* — 1962, reprinted by kind permission of William Collins Sons & Co. Ltd.).

CHAPTER II

ORNAMENT

John B. Papworth: Fountains Rediscovered (*Hints on Ornamental Gardening* — 1823); George Sitwell: Statues: The Imaginative Ideal (*On the Making of Gardens* — 1909, reprinted by kind permission of Gerald Duckworth & Co. Ltd); Thomas Mawson: Statuary and Garden Seats (*The Art and Craft of Garden Making*

— 5th ed. 1926); Christopher Hussey: The Place of Ornament (*The Place of Ornament in the Garden* — 1929, RHS Journal Vol. 54); George Carter: Sculpture in the Garden (*On Sculpture in the Garden* — 1984, RHS Journal Vol. 109, reprinted by kind permission of the author).

CHAPTER III

THE TOWN GARDEN

J.C. Loudon: A Modest Villa Garden (*The Villa Gardener* — 1850); Donald Beaton: The Society's Garden at Kensington Gore (*The Cottage Gardener* — 1861, Vol. 25); Thomas Hay: Gardening in London (*Gardening in London* — 1931, RHS Journal Vol. 56, reprinted by kind permission of Roy Hay); Beverley Nichols: A Note on London Gardens (*Down the Garden Path* — 1932, Jonathan Cape, reprinted by Antique Collectors Club 1983, reprinted by kind permission of Eric Glass Ltd. and the author's Estate); Lanning Roper: Problems and Limitations (*Successful Town Gardening* — 1957, Country Life, reprinted by kind permission of the author's Estate); Xenia Field: Gardening in Boxes, Baskets and Tubs (*Gardening in Boxes, Baskets and Tubs* — 1975, RHS Journal Vol. 100, reprinted by kind permission of the author); John Brookes: Planting a Very Small Garden (*Improve your Lot* — 1977, Heinemann, reprinted by kind permission of William Heinemann Ltd).

CHAPTER IV

ROCK AND WALL GARDENING

William Cobbett: Enclosing Kitchen-Gardens (*The English Gardener* — 1829); Edward Kemp: Rock and Fern Gardens (*How to Lay Out a Garden* — 1864); Canon Ellacombe: Old Walls (*In a Gloucestershire Garden* — 1895, Edward Arnold); Herbert Maxwell: Some Plants for Walls (*Flowers: A Garden Notebook* — 1923, Edward Arnold); Gertrude Jekyll and Christopher Hussey: Overgrowth (*Garden Ornament* — 1927, Country Life/Newnes Books); Will Ingwersen: Building and Planting a Retaining Wall (*Building and Planting a Retaining Wall* — 1954, RHS Journal Vol. 79, reprinted by kind permission of the author).

CHAPTER V
BORDERS

Shirley Hibberd: Hardy Border Flowers (*The Amateur's Flower Garden* — 1878, Groombridge and Sons); Gertrude Jekyll: The Main Hardy Flower Border (*Colour in the Flower Garden* — 1908, Country Life/Newnes Books); Jason Hill: The Miniature Herbaceous Border (*The Contemplative Gardener* — 1940, reprinted by kind permission of Mrs. Jillian Leech and Faber and Faber Ltd.); Margery Fish: That Patch of Silver (*An All the Year Garden* — 1958, Collingridge, reprinted by kind permission of Henry Boyd-Carpenter); Percy Cane: Special Borders (*The Creative Art of Garden Design* — 1967, Country Life/Newnes Books, reprinted by kind permission of Dr. John Elliott); H.E. Bates: Planting for Late Summer (*A Love of Flowers* — 1971, Michael Joseph, reprinted by kind permission of Laurence Pollinger Ltd. and the author's Estate).

CHAPTER VI
ROSES

William Paul: the Formation of the Rosarium (*The Rose Garden* — 1848); S. Reynolds Hole: A Note on Manures (*A Book about Roses* — 1869, Blackwood); Reverend Joseph Pemberton: A Guide to Planting (*Roses, their History, Development and Cultivation* — 1920, Longmans); E.A. Bunyard: Old Roses (*Old Roses* — 1938, RHS Journal Vol. 63); Graham Stuart Thomas: Rose Species in Nature and in the Garden (*Shrub Roses of Today* — 1985 ed., reprinted by kind permission of the author and J M Dent & Sons Ltd Publishers.); F.C. Stern: Growing Roses on Chalk (*A Chalk Garden* — 1960, reprinted by kind permission of Faber and Faber Ltd).

CHAPTER VII
THE FRAGRANT GARDEN

Frances Jane Hope: Pleached Alleys (*Notes and Thoughts on Gardens and Woodlands* — 1881); William Robinson: Sweet-smelling Flowers (*The English Flower Garden* — 1883); Jason Hill: The Invisible Garden (*The Curious Gardener* — 1932, reprinted by kind permission of Mrs. Jillian Leech and Faber and Faber Ltd.); E.A. Bowles: Fragrance: An Appreciation (*Fragrance in the Garden* — 1953, RHS Journal Vol.

78, reprinted by kind permission of The Bodley Head); Arthur Hellyer: the Search for Summer Fragrance (*Financial Times* — 1977, reprinted by kind permission of the Financial Times).

CHAPTER VIII
WOODLAND AND SHRUBBERY

Jane Loudon: Trees and Shrubs in Pleasure-Grounds (*Gardening for Ladies* — 1841); William Robinson: The Woodland Garden (*The Garden Beautiful* — 1906); Charles Eley: Hedges (*Hedges* — 1931, RHS Journal Vol. 56, reprinted by kind permission of Sir Geoffrey Eley); M. Haworth-Booth: Planting, Feeding and Weeding (*The Flowering Shrub Garden* — 1938, Country Life/Newnes Books, reprinted by kind permission of the author); A. T. Johnson: Rhododendrons in Woodland (*Rhododendrons in Woodland* — 1951, RHS Journal Vol. 76); Patrick M. Synge: Coloured Bark in the Winter Garden (*Flowers and Colour in Winter* — 1979, Michael Joseph, reprinted by kind permission of Mrs. M.G. Synge).

CHAPTER IX
THE WILD GARDEN

William Robinson: Notes on the Wild Garden (*The English Flower Garden* — 1883); Walter P. Wright: Working with Nature (*Beautiful Gardens* — 1907, Cassell & Co. Ltd., reprinted by kind permission of Macmillan Publishing Company); Sir Arthur Hort: Wild Corners (*The Unconventional Garden* — 1928, Edward Arnold); Christopher Lloyd: Meadow Gardening (*Meadow Gardening* — 1976, RHS Journal Vol. 101, reprinted by kind permission of the author and Anthony Sheil Associates Ltd.); Robin Lane Fox: The Wild Garden in the Long Grass (*Financial Times* — 1980, reprinted by kind permission of the author).

CHAPTER X
THE CHALLENGING GARDEN

Osgood Mackenzie: Gardening in the Western Highlands (*Gardening in the Western Highlands* — 1908, RHS Journal Vol. 34); Frances Perry: The Water

Garden (*The Water Garden* — 1940, RHS Journal Vol. 65, reprinted by kind permission of the author); Vita Sackville-West: Starting from Scratch (*Hidcote Manor* — 1949, RHS Journal Vol. 74 and *The Garden at Sissinghurst Castle, Cranbrook, Kent* — 1953, RHS Journal Vol. 78, reprinted by kind permission of Curtis Brown Ltd on behalf of the author's Estate); Valerie Finnis: Raised Beds for Rock Plants (*Raised Beds for Rock Plants* — 1973, RHS Journal Vol. 98, reprinted by kind permission of the author); Anne Scott-James: Chalk Gardening (*'I'm on Chalk'* — 1975, RHS Journal Vol. 100, reprinted by kind permission of the author and of A.P. Watt Ltd); Beth Chatto: Dry Gardening (*Winter Appraisal* — 1979, RHS Journal Vol. 104, reprinted by kind permission of the author).

PHOTOGRAPHIC ACKNOWLEDGEMENTS

The publishers are grateful to the following for their kind permission to reproduce the photographs in this book:

BLACK AND WHITE

Country Life 1–5, 7–11, 15–18, 20–22, 29–31, 33–40; The Royal Commission on the Historical Monuments of England 6, 12–14, 19, 32; The Harry Smith Horticultural Photographic Collection 26–28.

COLOUR PLATES

The Royal Commission on the Historical Monuments of England I, II, IV; Marianne Majerus III; Kenneth Scowen V; The Harry Smith Horticultural Photographic Collection VI (Valerie Finnis)–IX, XI–XII, XIV, XVI; Country Life X, XIII; Impact Photographic Ltd (Pamla Toler) XV.

Index

Page numbers in *italic* refer to illustrations

Alexander Place, no 14, South Kensington, 99
Alton Towers, Staffordshire, 51
Andrews, H C, 240
Apethorpe, Northamptonshire, 30
Arley Hall, Cheshire, *266*
Arnold Arboretum, 254
Ashbrooke, Lady, *266*
Ashridge Park, Hertfordshire, 17, *29*

Bacon, Francis, 54, 73, 77, 276
Baker, John Gilbert, 280
Banks, Sir Joseph, 257
Barnsley House, Gloucestershire, 81
Barron, William, *40*
Barry, Sir Charles, *25*, 41
Barslem, 57
Bates, H E, 198–203
Battersea Festival Gardens, 45
Bean, W J, 149, 360
Beaton, Donald, 88–90
Bicton, Devonshire, 72
Bicton, Shropshire, 22
Bitton, Gloucestershire, 140, 144, 285
Blomfield, Reginald, 30–32, *50*, 65
Bloom, Alan, 389
Bodnant, Gwynedd, *295*, 321
Bowles, E A, 256, 276–285
Bressingham Gardens, 350
Bridgeman, Charles, 76
Brookes, John, 123–128

Broughton Castle, Oxfordshire, 59
Brown, Lancelot 'Capability', 18, *21*, 25, *40*
Brympton d'Evercy, Somerset, 186
Buckingham Palace, 96
Bulstrode Park, 18
Bunyard, E A, 230–243, 255
Burnett of Leys, Lady, Col plate VIII

Cambridge University Botanic Garden, 244, 324
Camera Square, Chelsea, *87*
Cane, Percy, 193–197
Carter, George, 76–82
Cassiobury, Hertfordshire, 23
Caversham, 25
Cecil, Robert, Col plate I
Chambers, John, 341
Charleston Manor, Sussex, 393
Charterhouse School, Surrey, 45
Chastleton House, Oxfordshire, *33*
Chatto, Beth, 343, 400–404, Col plate XVI
Chequers, Buckinghamshire, 30
Chestnut Nursery, 205
Christchurch College, Oxford, 73
Claremont Park, Surrey, 51, *223*
Clumber, Nottinghamshire, 22
Cobbett, William, 129–134
Cobham Hall, Kent, *319*
Compton House, Wiltshire, *179*

411

Compton Wynyates, Warwickshire, 41
Conway Castle, Caernarvonshire, 160
Cranborne Manor, Dorset, 393
Crathes Castle, Kincardineshire, Col
    plate VIII
Crowsley, Oxfordshire, 353
Crystal Palace, 88, 135, 138
Cutbush, William, 41

Danesfield, 23
Dartington Hall, Devon, 193
de Caus, Isaac, Col plate I
Denton Hall, Buckinghamshire, 142
Dyffryn, Glamorgan, 57

East Lambrook Manor, Somerset, 185
Easton Lodge, Essex, 74
Edinburgh Royal Botanic Garden, 104
Ednaston Manor, Derbyshire, 67
Edwards, Paul, 41–43
Eley, Charles, 296–303
Ellacombe, Henry, 140–142, 144
Elvaston Castle, Derbyshire, 40, 41
Elwes, Henry, 279
Embankment Gardens, No 12,
    Chelsea, 113
Encombe, Kent, 68
Enville Hall, Staffordshire, 173, 216

Falaise, Castle of, 140
Farrer, Reginald, 200, 202, 256–7, 273,
    279, 397, Col plate VII
Fetherston, John, 44
Field, Xenia, 114–123
Finlay, Ian Hamilton, 79
Finnis, Valerie, 386–392
Fish, Margery, 185–191

Folly Farm, Berkshire, 71
Forrest, George, 254
Fulcher, Raf, 77

Gilpin, William, 21, 22–25, 303
Glynde College for Lady Gardeners,
    35
Gravetye Manor, Sussex, 292, 330, 331
Great Dixter, Sussex, 339, Col plate XV

Haddington, Lady, Col plate XII
Haffield House, Herefordshire, 88
Hampton Court, 43, 78
Hanley, 57
Harrogate, Valley Garden, 390
Hascombe Court, Surrey, 193
Hatfield House, Hertfordshire, 285,
    Col plate I
Havering-atte-Bower, Essex, Col plate
    XI
Haworth-Booth, Michael, 304–311
Hay, Thomas, 91–99
Hellyer, Arthur, 286–288
Hestercombe, Somerset, 67, 69, 73,
    Col plate II
Hever Castle, Kent, 375
Hibberd, J S, 26–29, 165–172
Hidcote Manor, Gloucestershire, 41,
    50, 184, 311, 353, 371, 384, 385, Col
    plate X
Highdown, Sussex, 159, 192, 252, 253–
    260, 393, 394, 397, 399
Hill, Jason, 180–183, 267–274
Hill, The, Hampstead, 243, Col plate
    IV
Hole, Dean Samuel Reynolds, 217–222
Holkham Hall, Norfolk, 17
Hooker, Sir Joseph, 257, 328, 338

Hope, Frances Jane, 261–263
Hort, Arthur F, 336–339
Howick House, Northumberland, 346
Hungerdown House, Wiltshire, 193
Hussey, Christopher, 64–74, 153–158, *303*, Col plate II
Hyde Park, 94

Iford Manor, Wiltshire, *62, 63*
Ilmington Manor, Warwickshire, Col plate X
Ingwersen, Will, 160–164
Inverewe, Highland, 355–363, *364*
Ionides, Basil, 68

Jekyll, Gertrude, 65, 80, 153–158, *173, 174*–178, 185, 198, 203, 233, 315, 316, Col plate II
Jellicoe, Sir Geoffrey, *139*
Johnson, A T, 312–318
Johnston, Major Lawrence, *50*, 371–378

Karr, Alphonse, 141
Kemp, C E, 153
Kemp, Edward, 135–138
Kensington Gardens, 57
Kensington Gore, RHS Garden at, 88–90
Kensington Palace, 17, 39
Kernsary, Highland, 355
Kew, Royal Botanic Gardens, 88, 93, 104, 129, 142, 145, 149, 156, 250, 257, 280, 360
Kiftsgate, Gloucestershire, Col plate IX
Kingdon Ward, Frank, 256, 315

Lambeth Palace, 24, 86
Lane Fox, Robin, 352–354
Langley, Batty, 78, 79
le Grice, Edward, 287
Le Nôtre, André, 76
Leonardslee, Sussex, Col plate XIII
Levens Hall, Westmorland, 71, 375
Leverhulme, Lord, Col plate IV
Linnaeus, Carolus, 336
Liverpool Garden Festival, 76, 77, 80, 81
Lloyd, Christopher, 339–351, Col plate XV
Lloyd, Mrs, Col plate XV
Lloyd, Nathaniel, Col plate XV
Loder, Edmund, Col plate XIII
Longleat, Wiltshire, 329
Loudon, Jane, 289–292
Loudon, J C, 83–87, *87*, 289, 291, 297
Lutyens, Edwin, 46, 65, 67, 69, 70, 71, 73, 80, Col plates II & XV

Mackenzie, Osgood, 355–363
Manners, Lady Victoria, *113*
Mason, William, *21*
Mawson, Thomas, 57–61, *243*, Col plate IV
Maxwell, Sir Herbert, 143–151
Messel, Ludwig, *335*
Meyer, F N, 254
Miller, Philip, 366
Milles, Herr, 66
Moreux, Charles, 77
Morris, Sir Cedric, 400
Muir, Mrs, Col plate IX
Myddleton House, Middlesex, 276

Nashdom, Buckinghamshire, 70

National Rose Society, 114, 217, 224
National Trust, The, 64, 153, 223, 244, 319, 371
Nesfield, William Andrews, 90
Nesfield, William Eden, 41
New College, Oxford, 352
Newport, 57
Newton Ferrers, Devonshire, 69, 70
Nichols, Beverley, 100–104
Nicholson, Harold, 380, 381
Norton Conyers, Yorkshire, 55
Nuneham Courtenay, Oxfordshire, 19, 21
Nymans, Sussex, 41, 235, 241, 248, 335

Old Place, Sussex, 152, 153
Oxford University Botanic Garden, 185

Packwood House, Warwickshire, 44
Page, Russell, 45–49, 50
Painswick Rococo Garden, 41
Papworth, John, 51–53
Parc Monceau, Paris, 59
Paul, William, 205–215, 220
Paxton, Sir Joseph, 135
Pemberton, Joseph, 224–230, 240, 258, Col plate XI
Perry, Frances, 365–371
Peto, Harold, 62, 63, 65, 77
Pitmedden, Grampian, Col plate VIII
Port Lympne, Kent, 46, 67, 72, 75, 351
Powis Castle, Powys, 69, 70, 71
Pye, William, 77

Redleaf, 23
Redouté, P J, 239, 257
Regents Park, 96

Renishaw Hall, Derbyshire, 54, 56
Repton, Humphry, 17–20, 29, 46, 76, 81
Robins, Thomas, 79
Robinson, William, 25, 30, 65, 149, 264–265, 292–294, 325–330, 330, 331, 353, 354
Roper, Lanning, 104–112
Rothes, Countess, Col plate V
Rousham, Oxfordshire, 78
Royal Central Parks, 91
Royal Horticultural Society, 88, 104, 279, 286, 320, 365, 371, 390

Sackville-West, Vita, 50, 371–384
St Catherine's Court, Somerset, 69
St Catherine's Hill, Hampshire, 42
St James's Park, 96
Sassoon, Sir Philip, 46, 67, 75
Saunders, William Wilson, 141
Savill, Sir Eric, Col plate VII
Savill Garden, Windsor Great Park, 323, Col plate VII
Scotney Castle, Kent, 64, 303
Scott, Sir David, 386
Scott-James, Anne, 392–398
Sedding, J D, 34–35
Sheringham Hall, Norfolk, 17
Shrubland Park, Suffolk, 25, 89, 292
Sissinghurst Castle, Kent, 80, 371, 378–384, 385, 392, 397
Sitwell, George, 54–56, 56
Skensby, Yorkshire, 43
Somerhill, Kent, 23
Stern, F C, 159, 253–260, 393, 394, 397, 399
Stoneleigh Abbey, Warwickshire, 69
Stonypath, Lanarkshire, 79
Stourhead, Wiltshire, 78

Strawberry House, Chiswick Mall, Col plate V
Street, G E, 34
Strong, Sir Roy, 76
Sudbury, Derbyshire, 22
Suffolk Herbs, 341
Sutton Place, Surrey, *139*
Synge, Patrick M, 320–324

Talbot Manor, Norfolk, 248
Tate, Elizabeth, 81
Tew Park, Oxfordshire, 353
Theophrastus, 336
Thomas, Graham Stuart, *223*, 244–252, 353, 382, Col plate IX
Tilden, Philip, 72
Tipping, H Avray, 65
Tradescant, John (The Elder), Col plate I
Tresco, 150
Triggs, H Inigo, 46, 65
Trinity College, Cambridge, 73
Trinity College, Dublin, 142
Tyninghame, East Lothian, Col plate XII

Valley Field, 18, 19
Valmarana garden, Vicenza, 55
Veitch nursery, 254, 256
Verity, Simon, 81
Versailles, 17, 37, 51

Wakehurst Place, Sussex, 250
Warwick Castle, 41
Waterperry School of Horticulture, 386
Watson, John, 389
White Barn House, Essex, Col plate XVI
Wilkinson, Sir Gardner, 34
Willmott, Ellen, 65, 235, 236, 241
Wilson, E H, 148, 149, 256, 259, 315
Wilton House, Wiltshire, 69
Wing, Rutlandshire, 43
Wise, Henry, 43
Wisley Gardens, Surrey, 248, 323
Woburn Park, Bedfordshire, 43, 327
Wolseley, Viscountess, 35–39
Wootton Court, Warwickshire, 43
Wren, Christopher, 43
Wright, Walter Page, 332–334
Wroxton Abbey, Oxfordshire, 41